DISAFFECTED

PERVERSE MODERNITIES   A SERIES EDITED BY JACK HALBERSTAM AND LISA LOWE

DISAFFECTED   XINE YAO

THE CULTURAL POLITICS OF UNFEELING IN
NINETEENTH-CENTURY AMERICA

DUKE UNIVERSITY PRESS · DURHAM AND LONDON · 2021

© 2021 Duke University Press
All rights reserved
Designed by Aimee C. Harrison
Typeset in Portrait by Westchester Publishing Services

Library of Congress Cataloging-in-Publication Data
Names: Yao, Xine, [date] author.
Title: Disaffected : the cultural politics of unfeeling in nineteenth-century America / Xine Yao.
Other titles: Perverse modernities.
Description: Durham : Duke University Press, 2021. | Series: Perverse modernities | Includes bibliographical references and index.
Identifiers: LCCN 2021002641 (print)
LCCN 2021002642 (ebook)
ISBN 9781478013891 (hardcover)
ISBN 9781478014836 (paperback)
ISBN 9781478022107 (ebook)
Subjects: LCSH: American literature—19th century—History and criticism. | Literature and society—United States—History—19th century. | Race in literature. | Affect (Psychology) in literature. | Stereotypes (Social psychology) in literature. | Sentimentalism in literature. | Emotions in literature. | African Americans in literature. | Asians in literature. | BISAC: SOCIAL SCIENCE / Ethnic Studies / General | LITERARY CRITICISM / American / General Classification: LCC PS217.R28 Y36 2021 (print) | LCC PS217.R28 (ebook) | DDC 810.9/353—dc23
LC record available at https://lccn.loc.gov/2021002641
LC ebook record available at https://lccn.loc.gov/2021002642

Cover art: Lucia Lorenzi, *icarus*, 2020. Carbon black pigment ink, gouache, and watercolor, 10 × 14 inches. Courtesy of the artist.

Publication of this book is supported by Duke University Press's Scholars of Color First Book Fund.

CONTENTS

Acknowledgments / vii

INTRODUCTION / 1
Disaffected from the
Culture of Sentiment

1 THE BABO PROBLEM / 29
White Sentimentalism and
Unsympathetic Blackness in
Herman Melville's *Benito Cereno*

2 FEELING OTHERWISE / 70
Martin R. Delany, Black-Indigenous
Counterintimacies, and the
Possibility of a New World

3 THE QUEER FRIGIDITY
OF PROFESSIONALISM / 107
White Women Doctors, the Struggle
for Rights, and the Marriage Plot

4 OBJECTIVE
PASSIONLESSNESS / 138
Black Women Doctors
and Dispassionate Strategies
of Uplifting Love

5 ORIENTAL
INSCRUTABILITY / 171
Sui Sin Far, Chinese Faces,
and the Modern Apparatuses
of U.S. Immigration

CODA / 208
Notes toward a Disaffected
Manifesto beyond Survival

Notes / 211
Bibliography / 243
Index / 269

ACKNOWLEDGMENTS

One of the most fundamental conditions of possibility for finishing this book—a condition that too often remains unmentioned—was staying alive. So I acknowledge this as a starting point to indicate how inadequate my acknowledgments are: despite my best efforts, this citational practice will always be a partial recognition of the messy convergences of intimacies and counterintimacies that have produced, challenged, enabled, beleaguered, and nourished me. You will have to imagine for yourself the no-less-necessary detachments in apposition to these attachments and in opposition to certain intimacies.

The Yao family: Mom, Dad, Cathee, and our beloved felines. My dear aunt Teresa, as well as Uncle and Auntie Dodo. I miss my grandparents (Brian and Mamie Yu and Annie Yao) still.

My uneven personal trajectory that has gone into this book has been variously situated on the lands of the Haudensaunee, Mi'kmaq, Cayuga, and Musqueam peoples—and came to close as I am now located in the former heart of empire. Funding that made this work possible came from the Social Sciences and Humanities Research Council of Canada; an Andrew W. Mellon Foundation Fellowship with the Library Company of Philadelphia and the Historical Society of Pennsylvania; the Frances Clark Wood Institute for the History of Medicine; and many funding sources at Cornell University, including several Humanities Dissertation Writing Group grants from the Society for the Humanities, Interdisciplinary Reading Group Grants from the Institute for Comparative Modernities, the M. H. Abrams Summer Graduate Fellowship, and the American Studies Program at Cornell for archival visits to the Historical Library of the College of Physicians in Philadelphia, the Massachusetts Historical Society, and the American Antiquarian Society.

Many thanks to my committee members, Eric Cheyfitz, George Hutchinson, and Shelley Wong, and special appreciation for my supervisor Shirley Samuels, who supported me as a scholar and a person. Shirley encouraged her students to create lateral networks of support: many thanks to the Americanist Reading Group, especially Brigitte Fielder, Jonathan Senchyne, and Jesse Goldberg. Thank you to my postdoc supervisor, Mary Chapman, for continuing this feminist scholarly mentoring practice, and to Shawkat Toorawa, who treated me like a colleague as soon as I stepped on campus.

The First Book Institute provided an invaluable opportunity: thank you to Sean X. Goudie, Priscilla Wald, and the institute staff for maintaining this resource for early-career scholars. I am grateful to my fellow participants, in particular Katie Walkiewicz, Sunny Xiang, Chris Perreira, and Ben Bascom. Previous iterations of this work have benefited from my moderators, fellow panelists, and audiences at meetings of the Futures of American Studies Institute, the Modern Language Association, the American Studies Association, C19: The Society of Nineteenth-Century Americanists, the British Association of American Studies, the Max Planck Institute for Human Development, the Critical Ethnic Studies Association, the American Literature Association, the Association of Canadian College and University Teachers of English, the American Comparative Literature Association, and the Association for Asian American Studies. There have been many keen and generous eyes on my work to my benefit over the years, such as Ana Schwartz's and T. J. Tallie's.

To my PhDivas cohost, Liz Wayne, thanks for camaraderie and care across the STEM/humanities divide. There are too many people in my communities routed through Cornell for me to thank; it broke my heart to leave and to know we would never reassemble in the same configurations again. Gratitude to my Vancouver circles—particularly members of the queer, feminist, and BIPOC (Black, Indigenous, and People of Color) circles, including Kiran Sunar, Kristi Carey, Aidan Davis, Corey Liu, Kavelina Torres, Katrina Sellinger, Lucia Lorenzi, Hannah McGregor, and Fern Ramoutar. In London I was sustained by many relationships with new friends: thank you in particular to Ifeanyi Awachie, Jade Bentil, Ama Budge, Emily Floyd, Lo Marshall, and Rianna Walcott. Much gratitude to Christine Okoth, for the insights that helped me through the penultimate stage of the manuscript process during the COVID-19 lockdown. Credit to Steve Morrison for supporting me as I stumbled across the final stretch. Thanks also to certain unnamed digital spaces, for those everyday lateral minoritarian intimacies.

On April 10, 2020, during the first COVID-19 lockdown, Lucia shared on Instagram the third in her ink painting series "About Touch and Intimacy during the Pandemic." In the caption, she remarked, "Not sure how to resolve the piece yet, so I'm stepping away from it, turning it around, seeing what works so far." A continent and an ocean away, I was mesmerized by her creative rendition of the paradoxes of intimacy and distance that spoke to my work as I struggled to finish it. Thank you, friend, for generously sharing your gorgeous artwork with me. To me, this collaboration of sorts captures something of the queer of color ethos, femme survival, and Black-Asian counterintimacies that informs the feeling otherwises of *Disaffected*.

Working with Duke University Press has been a pleasure. Courtney Berger and Sandra Korn have been patient and supportive; the many other staff members have been incredibly helpful during this process—which I understand is intense at the best of times, and even more so during the pandemic. The rigorous scrutiny of the copyeditors has greatly contributed to the polish of the words you see before you.

Any failings are mine alone; in admitting my fallibility, I hope for your patience, for all I can promise is my continued commitment to try to do right by others. I humbly request your reciprocity in this mutual, uneven process of knowledge-making, meaning-making, and community-building.

In my experience it is no contradiction that the entanglements of certain defiant, weary expressions of refusals to care can be transformed into collective care. To you and to so many others: thank you for keeping me alive.

INTRODUCTION

Disaffected from the Culture of Sentiment

affectability: The condition of being subjected to both natural (in the scientific and lay sense) conditions and to others' power
affectable "I": The scientific construction of non-European minds
—Denise Ferreira da Silva, *Toward a Global Idea of Race*

By disaffection, I emphasize not only emotional distance, alienation, antipathy, and isolation but also to center this word's other connotation of disloyalty to regimes of power.—Martin F. Manalansan IV, "Servicing the World: Flexible Filipinos and the Unsecured Life"

I thus am able to conceive of the opacity of the other for me, without reproach for my opacity to him. To feel in solidarity with him or to build with him or to like what he does, it is not necessary for me to grasp him.—Édouard Glissant, *Poetics of Relation*

WHITE FEELINGS, white tears, white fragility, white women's tears, white men's tears: these phrases circulate within popular antiracist social justice discourse galvanized by the Black Lives Matter movement. These phrases articulate frustration with the ongoing manifestations of what scholars have variously called the "unfinished business of sentimentality," the legacies of the "intimacies of four continents," and "the biopolitics of feeling."[1] They name the weaponization of white feelings in everyday life.[2] Behind these uses is the implicit statement: we know—indeed, have always known—that white feelings produce and maintain structures of domination.[3] To depend upon white feelings as the catalyst for social change reinscribes the world that enables their power. No more business with white sentimentality. Withhold from those colonial intimacies. Refuse to feel according to the hierarchies of the biopolitics of feeling. Be disaffected.

There is ambivalence. There is discontent. Perhaps one of the more radical manifestations of this critical dissatisfaction can be seen in a 2017 polemic by the writer and popular social media critic Robert Jones Jr., known as Son of Baldwin, who writes from a Black queer perspective. The essay "I Don't Give a Fuck about Justine Damond" responds to the killing of an unarmed white American woman by a Black police officer by breaking down the dynamics of racialized sympathy and emotional labor tied to legacies of Black enslavement:

> Most white people rely on this idea that black people, in situations where white people are in pain, are only ever to be soothing and understanding; only ever to be Mammy or Uncle Remus; only ever to extend condolences; only ever to embody loyalty; only ever to offer the empathy and sympathy that most white people purposely and haughtily deny when the situation is reversed—almost as if most white people still see us as their property.
>
> When the situation is reversed, when we require empathy and sympathy, then suddenly we're all of the opposite things that these once-needy white people previously said we were. When the shoe is on the other foot, then they assess us as immoral, violent, criminal, subhuman, unworthy.[4]

Black and Indigenous women who are victims of police brutality, as Son of Baldwin points out, do not receive the same sympathy. So, writing several years after the emergence of the Black Lives Matter movement, he chooses to be unsympathetic about the death of Justine Damond despite the anger he knows his stance will provoke. "My disinterest is white people's fault," he declares.[5] In a follow-up post, he asserts that he is unmoved by the backlash he has received from enraged white readers withdrawing their allyship to those he calls the "black/brown domestics," insisting on the importance of white feelings.[6] "Sentimentality, the ostentatious parading of excessive and spurious emotion," accused James Baldwin in his indictment of Harriet Beecher Stowe's paradigmatic protest novel *Uncle Tom's Cabin* (1852), "is the mark of dishonesty, the inability to feel; the wet eyes of the sentimentalist betray his aversion to experience, his fear of life, his arid heart; and it is always, therefore, the signal of secret and violent inhumanity, the mask of cruelty."[7] Referring to his "heart already full to capacity for all the dead black people killed by police," Son of Baldwin develops the antisocial affective implications of his namesake's critique. "I'm very much onto something with black apathy as radical opposition to their toxic ecology. And I believe it may be a key to liberation," he concludes.[8] The violence of white tears described by James Baldwin becomes projected onto those who refuse to be moved by them and are condemned as the ones unable to feel, with arid hearts, secret and violent inhumanity. Nonetheless, Son of Baldwin rejects that unspoken social contract of sympathy—for these unfeeling vilifications are already built into the structures of the United States predicated upon Black enslavement and Indigenous dispossession.[9]

Disaffected looks to American literature of the long nineteenth century to rethink the ongoing racial and sexual politics of unfeeling not as oppression from above but as a tactic from below. This book deliberately reads against the grain of the culture of sentiment to refuse the usual move of arguing for the humanity of minoritized subjects by enlisting literature to affirm that they feel too. *Disaffected* asks what we can apprehend if we stay with the negativity of unfeeling and suspend its rehabilitation. Through this provocation, I seek to excavate unfeeling occluded by the stifling imperatives of the political stakes of sympathy. In her preface to *Incidents in the Life of a Slave Girl* (1861), Harriet Jacobs signals her ambivalence about the political necessity of writing about herself as a formerly enslaved Black woman who is keenly aware of the stakes of her reworking of the genre of the slave narrative and the conventions of sentimentalism: "I have not written my experiences in order to attract attention to myself; on the contrary, it would have been more pleasant to me to have been silent about my own history. Neither do I care to excite sympathy for my own sufferings. But I do earnestly desire to arouse the women of the North to a realizing sense of the condition of two millions of women at the South, still in bondage, suffering what I suffered, and most of them far worse."[10]

Jacobs alludes to the compromises behind the cultural equation between true feeling and right action exemplified by *Uncle Tom's Cabin* that continues to overdetermine the politics of recognition underlying cultural fantasies of justice and social change. "There is one thing that every individual can do,—they can see to it that *they feel right*. An atmosphere of sympathetic influence encircles every human being; and the man or woman who *feels* strongly, healthily and justly, on the great interests of humanity, is a constant benefactor to the human race," concludes Stowe.[11] Her call to humanity for the corrective of universal sympathy collapses naturalized, individual affective capacities with impersonal, collective affective intensities. Jacobs was spurred to publish her own abolitionist narrative after the humiliation of reaching out to Stowe with her life's story and requesting the opportunity for her daughter to travel with the famous writer to England—only to have Stowe reject the possibility of writerly collaboration; turn down her daughter; and instead express her intention to appropriate Jacobs's experiences as material for her new book, *The Key to Uncle Tom's Cabin* (1853).[12]

Obscured in Stowe's injunction to "feel right" is the structural positioning of those privileged to be hailed as "every individual," "every human being," or "man or woman" with the authority to translate that sympathetic identification into action for "the human race." For them to be unsympathetic is a choice: their moral failure is an aberration that does not compromise their presumed status as subjects. This schema conceals the grounds for the politics that determine the recognition of the subjugated, a disciplinary apparatus that governs the terms of sociality: one must be recognized *as* sympathetic to be deserving of sympathy from those with the agency to sympathize. Thus, the marginalized do not have the luxury of being unsympathetic without forfeiting the provisional acceptance of their capacity for affective expressions and, therefore, the conditional acceptance of their humanity.

Disaffection / Reframing Recursive Debates about Sympathy and Sentimentalism

The philosophers Sylvia Wynter and Denise Ferreira da Silva have argued that the category of "Man," referring to bourgeois Western whiteness, overrepresents itself as universal humanity structured upon the suppression of racialized modalities of the human as mere derivations.[13] If we follow lines of inquiry opened up for us by their insights, what operations will we find concealed and enabled by the construct of universal feeling as a symptom and signifier of that coloniality? Affectability, according to da Silva in her study of Enlightenment universality transmuted into the biopolitical apparatuses of global modernity, is "the condition of being subjected to both natural (in the scientific and lay sense) conditions and to other's power."[14] Affectability defines raciality: the "transparent I" has the agency to know and affect, while the "affectable I" is the susceptible, the "scientific construction of non-European minds." In this way da Silva recalls for us Baruch Spinoza's foundational proposition about the nature of the emotions in relation to the world. Spinoza states, "By emotion I understand the modifications of the body by which the power of the acting of the body itself is increased, diminished, helped, or hindered, together with the ideas of these modifications."[15] Although not written with affect studies in mind, da Silva's definition of affectability, as Tyrone Palmer observes, points to "the inextricability of 'affect' from power."[16] *Disaffection, then, threatens a break from affectability.*

In Stowe's *Key to Uncle Tom's Cabin*, the supplementary text documenting the "truth" of her novel's depiction of slavery in response to the outcry from proslavery apologists, she divulges the racialized hierarchy of the transparent and the affectable that produces the universal. The "Anglo-Saxon race," asserts the white abolitionist, is "cool, logical, and practical," with an obligation to sympathize given its "dominant position in the earth."[17] In contrast, she places "the negro race" under the umbrella of "Oriental nations" to articulate "a peculiarity which goes far to show how very different they are from the white race": "They are possessed of a nervous organization peculiarly susceptible and impressible. Their sensations and impressions are very vivid, and their fancy and imagination lively. In this respect the race has an Oriental character and betrays its tropical origin. Like the Hebrews of old and the Oriental nations of the present, they give vent to their emotions with the utmost vivacity of expression, and their whole bodily system sympathizes with movements of their minds."[18]

Here we can observe how da Silva's affectability maps onto what Mel Chen terms the animacy hierarchy, which encompasses the spectrum of the human and nonhuman, the organic and the inorganic, the living and the nonliving.[19] According to Stowe's enduring sentimental model of justice, racialized peoples are legible only through their affectability. Emotional expression is presumed to be the signifier of affective human interiority, what Rei Terada calls the "expressive hypothesis."[20] If they do not accept this condition of affectable vulnerability, they fail to demonstrate their emotions as evidence of their subjectivity and, therefore, status as human subjects. The coloniality of this bind means that this process is always precariously iterative, contingent upon recognition by those already overrepresented as the universal human. Sympathy is "one of the fundamental ethical questions/problems/crises for the West," Saidiya Hartman observes in conversation with Frank B. Wilderson III, "It's as though in order to come to any recognition of common humanity, the other must be assimilated, meaning in this case, utterly displaced and effaced."[21]

I ask, then, how does unfeeling operate as the constitutive outside to that totalizing system, and what challenge can disaffection pose? In this regard, I take unfeeling not simply as negative feelings or the absence of feelings, but as that which cannot be recognized as feeling—the negation of feeling itself. By foregrounding the heuristic of unfeeling as disaffection in its affective, causal, and political meanings, this book makes key interventions in our understanding of affect and politics in American literature and culture, a paradigm that has disproportionately affected the world. First, I reconsider unfeeling as an index of the underacknowledged spectrum of dissonance and dissent that critiques the demands of sympathetic recognition shaped by sentimentalism, questioning the liberal project of inclusion. Second, I explore unfeeling, in both the responsive and demonstrative senses, as a quotidian tactic of survival and a counterintuitive, and sometimes counteractive, mode of care. Finally, I propose that these antisocial affects are vilified as unfeeling because they have insurgent potential that may not be legible or instrumentalized toward resistance. If we follow Raymond Williams's definition of structures of feeling as the affective workings of ideology in lived experience, we may consider disaffection to be the unfeeling rupture that enables new structures of feeling to arise.[22] In other words, the reading of unfeeling as oppositional negation functions as a defensive denial of the quickening, flourishing, and renewal of alternative forms of sociality made possible by feeling otherwise.

In this book I trace a representative array of queer, racialized, and gendered modes of disaffected unfeeling that emerges within dominating structures of feeling from a range of precarious positions within the axes of oppression that constitute the biopolitical hierarchy. These groupings—unsympathetic Blackness, queer frigidity, Black objective passionlessness, and Oriental inscrutability—are not meant to be taxonomic or exclusionary, but to articulate a few key coded categories in the cultural imagination deployed to flatten out and invalidate individual and collective subtleties.[23] These nascent, fleeting, and sometimes failed modes of affective disobedience capture transgressive desires, ambivalences about relationality, and complicated investments that cannot be readily redeemed into the trajectory of liberal politics—and may even be damaging and countereffective.

In this contrarian manner, I read Herman Melville's *Benito Cereno* (1855), Martin R. Delany's *Blake; or the Huts of America* (1861), Elizabeth Stuart Phelps's *Doctor Zay* (1882), Frances Ellen Watkins Harper's *Iola Leroy* (1892), and *Mrs. Spring Fragrance* (1912) by Sui Sin Far (the pen name of Edith Maude Eaton). These narratives published after Stowe's novel engage the major sociopolitical issues of their day in ways that question the coercive relationship between Stowe's paradigmatic model of right feeling and political progress. I discuss these literary works in the explicit and implicit contexts of the struggles toward fantasies of justice linked to the Fugitive Slave Act of 1850; the Fourteenth and Fifteenth Amendments to the Constitution on Black citizenship and Black men's suffrage, respectively; Black and white women's rights activism toward suffrage that would be addressed by the Nineteenth Amendment; and the Chinese Exclusion Act of 1882.[24] I explain how these texts register ambivalence toward the very demand for sympathetic recognition—which, as Glen Coulthard (Yellowknives Dene) argues in his indictment of the processes of reconciliation for Indigenous peoples in Canada, is colonial and coercive.[25] These writers strategically employ the conventions of sentimentalism but then portray disaffected characters whose obdurate composure and divisive actions defy the expectations of right feeling that structure the politics of recognition. Rather than simply refuting negative portrayals of unfeeling contoured by racial and sexual politics, they reappropriate this apparent emotional lack as the affective symptom of dissatisfaction in ways mindful of the uneven political stakes and punishments risked by different subjects. I show how literature disrupts reading practices that crave affective access, legibility, and affectability. I thus bring into relief the complex and dynamic ways that minoritized subjects shaped the cultural, political, and even professional discursive arenas where these struggles took place, including the developing field of gynecology and the conflict between monogenesis and polygenesis theories of human development in race science.

I am not so much interested in fine-tuning the distinctions between agentic volition and instinctual physiology that attend the generally held taxonomization of the strata of affect, feeling, and emotional expression—ordered along the polarization of the axes of interiority to externalization and unconscious to conscious—as I am in stressing the flexible operations of how these differentiations naturalize scales of the human, nonhuman, living, and nonliving that Chen groups under the rubric of the animacy hierarchy.[26] Of greater concern to me are the operations of unfeeling as a form of antisocial discontent about, if not outright defiance of, the compulsory norms for expressing feeling along with susceptibility to the feelings of others. Unfeeling can signal skepticism and reluctance to signify the appropriate expressions of affect that are socially legible as human, which can rise to the refusal to care and sympathize as part of the expected cues of deference that maintain and structure biopolitical hierarchies of oppression. Lauren Berlant points out that withholding can operate as a sign of civility for the privileged and is "often deemed good manners in the servant class," and for those so-called "problem populations," such disaffection signals the threat of the ungovernable.[27] The popular understanding of emotional labor, a term originally coined by the sociologist Arlie Hochschild, is a useful way to address the uneven expectations about who does this labor and for whom according to the overlapping but irreducible processes of

Introduction

racialization, class differentiation, and their modulations of sexual difference that persist despite the promise of socioeconomic mobility.[28] In this light, the literary works I discuss explore pathologized models of affective disobedience and agency that defy and rework scientific and legal discourses naturalized by the culture of sentiment. Through tactical shifts in mood, voice, and perspective, they offer glimpses into how accusations of unfeeling mask the transgressive validity, lived necessity, and emerging possibilities of antisocial affects and gestures that may be counterproductive to the conventional demands of advocacy. These writings demonstrate the inextricable relationship between the everyday and formal, institutional scales of the politics of sympathetic recognition that make up the governmentality of sentimentalism.

I linger with unfeeling, rather than dismissing or exonerating it. By focusing on unfeeling as disruptive negation, I aim to introduce a way of reframing the perennial Americanist fixation with oscillating between the structural complicity of sentimentalism or the feminist recuperation of its political and cultural work that goes back to Ann Douglas's and Jane Tompkins's generative disagreements about *Uncle Tom's Cabin* decades ago.[29] Sentimentalism remains an enduring—though often disavowed—rhetoric, genre, cultural mode, set of material relations, ideology, and episteme. Our understanding of sentimentalism has expanded to take seriously its essential part in the coercive American national project of citizenship and belonging, as shown through the work of Berlant and Pier Gabrielle Foreman.[30] It plays this part as an ethically fraught political tool for abolitionist and feminist agendas.[31] It is gendered not only as feminine and domestic, but also as important to the redefinition of consolidated masculinity in the private and public spheres.[32] In addition, its materiality informs embodiment and even the development of consumer materialism.[33] And most importantly, its constitutive racialized and colonial violences are complex.[34] It infiltrates even institutional bastions considered the obverse of sentimental: Kyla Schuller insightfully draws attention to its operation as a technology of scientific biopower, which she calls the biopolitics of feeling.[35] But if, as Shirley Samuels writes, sentiment is at the heart of nineteenth-century American culture, what does it mean to withdraw from that totalizing embrace, to be heartless?[36] Given that Schuller claims the biopolitical hierarchies of feeling are based upon the impressibility of bodies and minds, what if the failure of intractability were understood as, well, being unimpressed? Unfeeling dissents from the biopolitics of feeling, hinting at other ways of organizing life that might be suppressed, overlooked, adjacent, incipient, insurgent, resurgent, or still to be imagined. Bearing these questions in mind as I join conversations that rethink prevalent models of action and feeling, I analyze these literary works written in the wake of Stowe's influence for the ambivalences, refusals, and failures of true feeling that frustrate the conditions underlying the politics of recognition.[37]

"Tender violence," as Laura Wexler calls it, undergirds American imperialism and its assimilationist, settler colonial enterprise wielded against Black people, Indigenous peoples, and immigrant populations.[38] Sentimentalism is part of the logic of the transnational intimacies of empire that, as Lisa Lowe notes, draw together Black enslavement, Indigenous dispossession, and Asian indentured servitude across seemingly disparate geographies as the material conditions for the usual affective, personal senses of intimacies that produce the Western liberal subject.[39] My daunting task, then, is to approach literature designated as American without reifying the United States or taking the nation as a limit. Instead, I hope to use American literature as a way to address the continued production and exportation of a sentimental nationalism and its imperialist corollary exemplified by the likes of Herman Melville's good-hearted American captain who intervenes on behalf of enslavers in the Southern hemisphere, but simultaneously disputed or redefined by disaffected dissenters as imagined by Martin Delany, Elizabeth Stuart Phelps, Frances Ellen Watkins Harper, and Sui Sin Far.

Affect Studies Has a Race Problem

We can recall that W. E. B. Du Bois begins *The Souls of Black Folk* with the question, "How does it feel to be a problem?"[40] Muñoz views Du Bois's famous question as an "opening," not an "impasse": "Thus feeling like a problem is a mode of minoritarian recognition."[41] In my first chapter I begin my discussion of unfeeling with the example of Herman Melville's fugitive Senegalese Babo, not his white New Yorker Bartleby, to emphasize that affect studies has a race problem. By centering Babo in his Blackness, I question why it has been easier for critics to become attached to white Bartleby's enigmatic inexpression as the universal figure of transgression, his popularity reiterating the inexhaustible extension of sympathy for him by the narrating white lawyer.[42]

Affect's deracinated universality is part of its appeal as a critical turn, surmises Clare Hemmings, making it a productive way out of the impasse of deconstruction and hegemony by attending to embodied experience, aleatory attachments, and the quirky textures of everyday life as potentially transformative. Hemmings traces two major approaches to affect: one that follows Eve Sedgwick, drawing upon the work of the psychologist Silvan Tomkins (wherein the appeal is how the "affective freedom of attachment becomes a mark of the critic's freedom"), and another that can be traced to Brian Massumi, who draws inspiration from Gilles Deleuze (wherein "the affective's autonomy places it outside the reach of critical interpretation").[43] Affect, Hemmings concludes, is useful, but it is naïve to believe that it is beyond the social realm: critics draw attention to the whiteness of affect studies, indicting the overlap between the inadequate discussions of race and the racial citational politics of its intellectual tradition.[44] Despite Sara Ahmed's oeuvre on how affective economies shape the significations and relations of individual and collective bodies and Sianne Ngai's work on racialized animatedness—and, to some extent, her discussion of irritation—these authors too often remain exceptions regardless of their influence.[45] Work by David Eng and Jasbir Puar has enabled us to better understand how affect operates on geopolitical and transnational scales through diaspora, kinship, debility, and capacity, yet these authors' insights highlight the insidious convenience of the epistemic erasures and colonial portability of more abstracted, universalist frameworks of feeling.[46] In this vein, postcolonial and feminist writers of color like Audre Lorde, Frantz Fanon, Gloria Anzaldúa, Cherríe Moraga, and Claudia Rankine have been ignored as theorists of affect despite the centrality of feeling to their work.[47] Indeed, as Naomi Greyser beautifully illuminates for us, nineteenth-century Indigenous women writers like Sarah Winnemucca Hopkins (Northern Paiute) had to negotiate between settler colonial understandings of sympathy and their distinct tribal languages and traditions to assert the importance of the deep reciprocity of affective geographies as part of their practices of survivance and sovereignty.[48]

On the level of scholarship, then, we must confront the fact that the systemic refusal to take these conceptualizations of feeling as valid mirrors the historical and cultural denials of the feelings of peoples of color and other disaffected and marginalized populations: in this sense, they are subordinated as unfeeling within the academic episteme, too.[49] Demands for change in the academy have been made, and there have been calls for decolonizing or racializing affect studies by recognizing how affect operates for peoples of color and adopting non-Western taxonomies and paradigms of affect.[50] In this regard, my final chapter on Oriental inscrutability takes up the Chinese concept of face to challenge the presumption of universal feeling. Thus, this book deliberately looks to thinkers like the Caribbean philosopher Wynter not to decontextualize them, but for how they provoke us to rethink context and scope, to disturb the streamlined sense of Western intellectual tradition.[51]

Through what I view as an ongoing antisocial turn in affect theory, I suggest that unfeeling constitutes a break from dominant models of feeling. Affect aliens like the feminist killjoy and the angry Black woman, according to Ahmed, disrupt normative conventions of happiness.[52] What, then, are the implications of alienation from affect itself? For critics like Berlant and Wendy Lee, the phenomenon of unfeeling entails both frustration and promise. "By disaffection, I emphasize not only emotional distance, alienation, antipathy, and isolation but also to center this word's other connotation of disloyalty to regimes of power and authority," writes Martin F. Manalansan IV in his discussion of Filipinx domestic workers navigating the global economy.[53] A counterpoint to demands for Third World feelings and labor, this model of disaffection acts as a quotidian performance that enables the execution of labor as well as the potential for activism, with the appearance of being unmoved concealing its potential for the choice to move and be moved in other ways.[54] The matrix of power that overrepresents the universal human through the abjection of those positioned as other is the condition that determines the intelligibility of feelings as signifiers of human interiority, producing the subjection of unfeeling and its exile beyond the horizon of the social.[55] Put another way, marginalized unfeeling is the unrecognized underside of universalized feelings of the dominant.

I use "unfeeling" as a broad term for a range of affective modes, performances, moments, patterns, and practices that fall outside of or are not legible using dominant regimes of expression. The range includes withholding, disregard, growing a thick skin, refusing to care, opacity, numbness, dissociation, inscrutability, frigidity, insensibility, obduracy, flatness, insensitivity, disinterest, coldness, heartlessness, fatigue, desensitization, and emotional unavailability. In short, people who are disaffected break from affectability and present themselves as unaffected. Inexpressive expressions stubbornly contradict the supposed universality of affects' encompassing intensities, tracking the edges of their influences and suggesting a beyond to their limits.

Unfeeling signals a break from the emotional respectability required by the politics of recognition.[56] Although the appearance of lack signifying an absence of interiority is the primary association, unfeeling also stands in for embryonic, fleeting, or inarticulate expressions that are so minor or deliberately diminished that they are unacknowledged.[57] The pejorative connotations of the words and phrases associated with unfeeling attempt to delegitimize how these tactics articulate dissent or—below that coherent threshold of political instrumentalization—index dissatisfaction with and ambivalence (however futile) about existing structures of feeling. I stress that the denigrated figurations of unfeeling cannot be understood without addressing the dimensions of how they are racialized, queered, and gendered as part of legacies of survival and resistance intertwined with traumatic genealogies of hegemonic oppression. These antisocial affects may be perceived as such only because their insurgent potential offers a way out of dominant ways of being and enabling new structures of feeling to arise.

Theories of queer annihilation and refusal offer a vocabulary for considering transgression as legitimate in itself, regardless of whether or not it appears to be viable or useful.[58] Disaffection has its immediate roots in the meeting between the antisocial turn in queer theory and queer of color critique—a meeting represented by the provocative tensions between Lee Edelman's and José Esteban Muñoz's approaches. The spirit of this book owes much to Edelman's embrace of queer negativity and transgression regardless of instrumentalization alongside Muñoz's gestures toward the ways that queer of color critique in particular can seek generative possibilities beyond the normative through attending to the horizon of queerness as an opening, rather than only a shattering.[59] However, paying attention to these intellectual traditions alone is insufficient for addressing the rhizomatic aspects of how unfeeling works for the disaffected who are positioned throughout the biopolitical hierarchies of differentiation.[60] My approach to the antisociality of unfeeling as epistemological and ontological refutation seeks to honor and bring together conversations about disobedience, negativity, and the limits of the social running through queer theory, Black studies, Indigenous studies, and Asian North American studies to better grapple with the interlocking dimensions of its biopolitical implications.

Provincializing Sympathy / The Coloniality of Universal Feeling

I propose to examine unfeeling through provincializing the concept of sympathy that forms the basis of sentimentalism. The principle of sympathy has been held by Americanist scholars as key to the development of the United States as a nation-state: identification across difference shapes belonging, ideas of citizenship, and the construction of the body politic. Sympathy emerges from the colonial imposition of the Enlightenment episteme, whose universality is a function of the overrepresented status of whiteness and which is both product and producer of the intimate transnational violences of imperialism that made Western modernity possible. According to the paradigmatic definition that opens Adam Smith's *Theory of Moral Sentiments* (1759), "by the imagination we place ourselves in his situation, we conceive ourselves enduring all the same torments, we enter as it were into his body, and become in some measure the same person with him, and thence form some idea of his sensations, and even feel something which, though weaker in degree, is not altogether unlike them."[61] Sympathy enables the recognition of feelings: "Whatever is the passion which arises from any object in the person principally concerned, an analogous emotion springs up, at the thought of his situation, in the breast of every attentive spectator" (10). In this regard, I want to emphasize the foundational nature of sympathy as more than a historical antecedent: sympathy is the fundamental mode of apprehending affects, feelings, and emotions—and deeming them legitimate.

This "fellow-feeling" works both ways in the world: one is pleased to receive sympathy and "hurt by the want of it," and we are also pleased to sympathize and "hurt when we are unable to do so" (15). The person who does not sympathize or accept the sympathy of others recurs throughout Smith's treatise as an object of affront. On the one hand, to not have sympathy for another provokes a breakdown of sociality more profound than differences of opinion: "We become intolerable to one another. I cannot support your company, nor you mine. You are confounded at my violence and passion, and I am enraged at your cold insensibility and want of feeling" (21). On the other hand, when "we cannot enter into his indifference and insensibility," as in the case of people who do not react to insult or injury, such people are seen as "contemptible" and just as bad as their aggressor (35 and 34). The consequence of not sympathizing is to forfeit receiving sympathy. Wendy Lee, in her reading of Bartleby, notes that for Smith, insensibility can rise to "a public offense instead of just a personal insult," escalating "to unite others in their resentment, even and perhaps especially in those who have no apparent stake in the conflict."[62] This specter of the unfeeling subject acts as the antisocial corollary to sympathy as the "fellow-feeling" basis of civilized sociality.

I find it telling that later Smith abandons the guise of universal abstraction to reveal how the schematics of sympathy reproduce the material relations of colonialism. Shifting to the global stage, he divides humanity along the line of sympathy: while the "civilized nations" are said to be "founded upon humanity," the "rude and barbarous nations" are focused on "self-denial."[63] This anthropological differentiation gives context to his earlier discussion of virtuous control versus unfeeling lack: the first is "the very principle upon which that manhood is founded," while the second "deserves no applause" for those "altogether insensible to bodily pain" (152 and 156). Want of feeling is not neutral but linked to depravity, for it is possible to grow "callous by the habits of crimes." According to Smith, "the vilest and most abject of all states" is the "complete insensibility to honour and infamy, to vice and virtue" (118). The figure of "the savage" is the ultimate figure of unfeeling: he "expects no sympathy from those around him, and disdains, on that account, to expose himself, by allowing the least weakness to escape him" (205). The savage is inexpressive and unreactive, refusing to change "the serenity of his countenance or the composure of his conduct and behaviour." The criminal is racialized, while all the racialized are criminal: the former has the privilege of agentic individuation, and the latter is the indistinguishable stand-in for the entire race.

Unlike the civilized nations, these barbaric peoples of color are prone to "falsehood and dissimulation": "It is observed by all those who have been conversant with savage nations, whether in Asia, Africa, or America, that they are equally impenetrable, and that, when they have a mind to conceal the truth, no examination is capable of drawing it from them" (208). These Asian, Black, and Indigenous peoples deny affectability, caring not whether they are sympathetic to Western scrutiny—and Smith is unsympathetic in turn, unable to recognize these racialized feelings. He complains that "they never express themselves by any outward emotion," conveniently eliding the colonial dynamics of the epistemological imperative (208). Consequently, he views the violent actions of the inexpressive savage as a moral lack, whereas similar deeds by the "civilized" white Westerner are within the bounds of sociality, "convincing the spectator, that they are in the right to be so much moved, and of procuring his sympathy and approbation" (208).[64] Smith is unable to comprehend the possibility of the emotional complexity of peoples of color or the validity of their affective interiority as fully human subjects. For Smith, they are inexpressive and therefore unsympathetic; for Stowe, they are expressive and therefore sympathetic. Rather than a conflict within what da Silva would call affectability, they illustrate its bind. Eighteenth-century Enlightenment racism locked the coloniality of sympathy into national projects and the understanding of the global; the nineteenth-century sentimental project consolidated that formulation of sympathy into the liberal logics of belonging and political action. To acknowledge sympathy only as feeling across difference erases its violent origins in the matrices of domination that produce the system of racial difference. We should instead apprehend the hierarchies built into sympathy, a concept that has been foundational to the geopolitical configurations of modernity—including the construction of the United States.

Sympathy, much like the present workings of affect studies in the academy, has operated as a strategy of engulfment to subordinate non-Western taxonomies and paradigms of affect, emotion, and feeling as mere variations if not to outright invalidate them beyond the threshold of recognition as feeling. In this sense, sympathy functions as the fundamental condition of affective intelligibility for the spectrum of feelings in all degrees of expressiveness and intensities. To understand the erasures of the unfeeling, we must read the archive in oppositional ways. In Smith, for instance, we can discern the anticolonial disaffection of those "equally impenetrable" peoples of "Asia, Africa, or America" that prefigures twentieth-century articulations of Third World solidarities. Indeed, it is relevant to note that although Charles Darwin's *The Expression of Emotions in Man and Animals* (1872), which argues for the universality of readable affects across races and species, is considered part of the paradigm shift to emotions as external and physiological, Darwin vents a frustration similar to Smith's. Darwin footnotes the challenge of extracting ethnographic knowledge about emotions from Indians through the network of the British colonial apparatus due to their "habitual concealment of all emotions in the presence of Europeans."[65] I speculate that nonequivalent convergences between these forms of disaffection from colonial intimacies can give rise to what I elsewhere designate "counterintimacies." Counterintimacies produce the conditions for insurgent solidarities, as I explore in chapter 2—which views the Caribbean as a site that brings together those disaffected peoples from Asia, Africa, and the Americas that so frustrate Smith.

Unfeeling as Theory in the Flesh

Taking up the ethical charge to decolonize affect studies, I turn to queer and feminist of color theorists whose underappreciated contributions to the intellectual histories of feeling—lack of recognition erasing their theorizations about the unrepresentable status of unfeeling in the dominant episteme—paradoxically positions them as thinkers who uniquely pay attention to this disaffected sense of unfeeling. Unlike the affront of unfeeling to Smith's "fellow-feeling," in this tradition I suggest that we can track unfeeling as a theory in the flesh, not as opposition to feeling but as its complement in lived experience within the affective hierarchies of biopolitics. In her original preface to *This Bridge Called My Back*, Moraga speaks to the lived experiences of the women of color collected in the volume: "Our strategy is how we cope—how we measure and weigh what is to be said and when, what is to be done and how, and to whom and to whom and to whom, daily deciding/risking who it is we can call an ally, call a friend."[66]

There is a necessary calculus of refusals: the apparent lack or dulling of affect can be a defensive tactic of everyday psychic survival in a world predicated upon racial and sexual violences. "To cope with hurt and control my fears, I grew a thick skin," states Anzaldúa, and Lorde writes, "In order to withstand the weather, we had to become stone."[67] Their images of thick skin and stone indicate that the callousness of insensitivity may be a development of an affective callus, a protective hardening of the sensitive psyche against the wear and tear of everyday life and the repetitive tasks of racialized and gendered emotional labor. However, uncritical valorization of unfeeling as triumphant resistance ignores its risks. As Anzaldúa acknowledges, the tactic runs the risk of being misread and vilified: "I am not the frozen snow queen but a flesh and blood woman with perhaps too loving a heart, one easily hurt."[68] This antisocial armor can be turned against those it is meant to protect, for Lorde notes that the cultivation of a stony exterior can lead to Black women hurting other Black women: "we bruise ourselves upon the other who is closest."[69] Unfeeling can be a dangerous gambit, but the pathologization of its manifestations obscures how cultivating unresponsiveness and inexpressiveness is an effect of the structural alienations in the culture of sentiment—and symptoms of dissatisfaction.

Making space to reclaim the legitimacy of the feelings of queer women of color requires decentering dominant sympathies to the point of being unfeeling toward them. In her letter to Mary Daly, Lorde makes explicit the uneven emotional labor placed upon women of color and raises the possibility of disengaging: "I had decided never again to speak to white women about racism. I felt it was wasted energy because of destructive guilt and defensiveness, and because whatever I had to say might better be said by white women to one another at far less emotional cost to the speaker."[70] Lorde reserves the right to refuse the demands of emotional labor that would center hurt white feelings to attend to her own emotional well-being. Likewise, Anzaldúa resists the pressures to pay disproportionate attention to the feelings of others: "She has to learn to push their eyes away. She has to still her eyes from looking at their feelings—feelings that can catch her in their gaze, bind her to them."[71] The demand to sympathize can be coercive, making the rejection of identification a political decision that may be the first step toward shifting existing structures of feeling. To choose not to care, not to be moved, pushes against the expectations of affectability.

Nonetheless, these writings by queer women of color testify that these feelings can be recovered even though they had to be suspended for the sake of survival. Rather than absence or negation, unfeeling may enable dormant, incipient, and insurgent affects. Unfeeling used strategically can be put in the service of the eventual flourishing of feeling, as with Anzaldúa's figure of the *india*-Mestiza: "She hid her feelings; she hid her truths; she concealed her fire; but she kept stoking the inner flame."[72] Their feelings qua feelings do not require expression or recognition for legitimacy, and unfeeling in another sense names the outsiders' frustration with these dissenting modes of emotional life that may seem ineffable to them. For her own creative growth, Anzaldúa works to consciously reshape her structure of feeling, or what she calls her "belief system," through not just affirmation but also destruction: "Those I don't want, I starve; I feed them no words, no images, no feeling."[73] I suspect that there is a congruence, then, between these processes of disaffection and Muñoz's disidentifications: the suspension of relationality allows for creative remakings in the struggle to reach the horizon of queerness, with its potentialities and possibilities. Unfeeling is the detachment from attachments to hegemonic structures of feeling and the potential for striving toward a radical politics of liberation.

Antisocial Affects and the Suppression of Insurgent Sociality in Colonial America

Drawing upon these nuanced theorizations of psychic survival and taking a brief look at foundational scientific and medical American texts, we can begin to discern the suppressed workings of affective complexity among Black and Indigenous peoples demonized as unfeeling. Thomas Jefferson, Stanley Stanhope Smith, and Benjamin Rush take up Adam Smith's concept to articulate the biopolitical frameworks of the new settler colonial nation regulated and naturalized through feeling, suggesting that affective agency may intervene not only on the personal level but also on a biopolitical scale. Across these writings are accounts of the dulled, diminished, and absent affective expression and pain attributed in particular to Black and Indigenous peoples. These attributions appear in inconsistent ways that ultimately serve the settler colonial nation-state by positioning Blackness and Indigeneity as exclusionary and antagonistic. In *Notes on the State of Virginia* (1785), the inaugural text of American race science, Thomas Jefferson understood the symbiotic relationship between scientific knowledge and legal authority: his discussion of scientific racial difference is placed in Query XIV, titled "Laws," with the subtitled question "The Administration of Justice and Description of the Laws?"[74] "To our reproach it must be said, that though for a century and a half we have had under our eyes the races of black and of red men, they have never yet been viewed by us as subjects of natural history," observes Jefferson, bringing the brutalities of his American iteration of the Enlightenment episteme to bear upon Black people to justify chattel slavery. He makes claims about the affective and physical excesses of Black people—"more ardent," "more an eager desire than a tender mixture of sentiment and sensation," "more of sensation than reflection"—reinforcing their racialization as what da Silva terms affectable and Ngai calls animated.[75]

Allegations of unfeeling come out of Jefferson's frustrations with any obstacles to his prerogative to epistemological mastery, blurring the porous distinction between physical and psychological as well as collapsing the difference between exterior expression and affective interiority. During his degrading assessment of Black people's bodies, he judges the richness of their melanin as inferiority because it blocks his expectations of affectability: "that eternal monotony which reigns in the countenances, that immovable veil of black which covers all the emotions of the other race."[76] Is the veil immovable or refusing to be moved? Jefferson accuses Black people of inherent insensibility: "Their griefs are transient. Those numberless afflictions, which render it doubtful whether Heaven has given life to us in mercy or in wrath, are less felt, and sooner forgotten with them" (146). Of course, Jefferson does not acknowledge that he numbers among those afflictions that bring such grief: the enslaved have reason to guard their feelings against enslavers, resisting the emotional dimension of the labors of chattel slavery that would make even their affects fungible. Refusal to recognize the fullness of Black feelings feeds into Jefferson's contempt for Phillis Wheatley's poetry as an expression of those feelings: "The compositions published under her name are below the dignity of criticism" (147). These factors contribute to his conclusions about Black inferiority: frustrated by Black opacity, he infamously cannot decide upon polygenesis or monogenesis as the appropriate scientific rationalization to estrange Black people from the category of the human (150). Jefferson's claims about Black lack of emotional depth are his complaints about the limits to his total domination over Black bodies and psyches. To grow thick skins and become stone like Anzaldúa and Lorde, then, is part of a long tradition of disaffected defiance.

Stanley Stanhope Smith's rebuttal to Jefferson argues for monogenesis but further transmutes universal sympathy into the field of scientific knowledge, developing racial differentiation as racialized affects. *An Essay on the Causes of the Variety of Complexion and Figure in the Human Species* (1787) argues that humanity is "united together by a common system of feelings and ideas," but the titular "varieties" reflect hierarchies of the human—demonstrated in part through physiognomy as the "index of our feelings," with the face as physical evidence of affective, moral, and cognitive faculties.[77] Inexpression becomes an embodied signifier of the uncivilized: "In proportion to their improvement in the arts, and to the progress of science among them there is a characteristic and common *expression*, which results from the similarity of the operations of the mind, and of the subjects about which these operations are employed. But savages in every region are usually distinguished by a countenance so dull and stupid, when not excited into ferocity by hostile and revengeful passions, as to induce many writers to regard them as an inferior grade in the descent from the human to the brute creation."[78] There are echoes of Adam Smith's observations about the withholding of unsympathetic peoples of color around the world, with Stanley Stanhope Smith affirming the hierarchy of humanity through science.

While Jefferson focuses on the abject state of Black people, he briefly valorizes the "Indians," who have "their reason and sentiment strong," in comparison.[79] In deliberate contrast, Stanley Stanhope Smith dedicates his text to the inferiority of Indigenous peoples and critiques Jefferson's assertions about Black people, defending Wheatley and ascribing "the apparent dullness of the negro principally to the wretched state of his existence," under the conditions first of Africa and then of chattel slavery.[80] This disagreement between Jefferson and Smith perversely puts Blackness and Indigeneity in competition for the constitutive singular nadir of human ontology, reifying their comparative racial positions as antagonistic when enslavement and settler colonialism are intertwined as the multiple, nonequivalent conditions of possibility for the United States. Throughout his treatise Smith speaks of the "American savage" as "vacant and unexpressive—the whole composition of his countenance, is fixed and stupid, with little variety of movement in the features" (192). Smith continually reaffirms his contempt for Indigenous peoples: "Destitute of that variety of ideas and emotions which give variety to the human countenance, the same vacancy of aspect is spread over all; the same set and composition, nearly is given to the features" (230-31). These "savages of America" are beyond the bounds of sympathy: they "know nothing of the finer feelings of the heart, and that soft interchange of affections which give [sic] birth to the sentiments of compassion and sympathy" (402-3). These "aboriginal tribes of North-America" are known for their "uncommon power of supporting pain" (411). In this inversion of Jefferson's treatment of Black versus Indigenous peoples, Smith does not recognize the nuances of Indigenous affective survivance in the face of settler colonial's genocidal violence, what Dian Million (Tanana Athabascan) might later have considered to be connected to Indigenous feminist "felt theory," which she expresses as Native women's "sixth sense about the moral affective heart of capitalism and colonialism."[81] Indigenous kinships and cosmologies are incomprehensible to Smith's colonizing gaze.

Another link in this intellectual history of articulating racial difference through feeling and unfeeling can be found in Benjamin Rush's notorious medical treatise on Black people and leprosy (1799), which opens by positioning itself as an explicit contribution to the discourse created by Smith's essay, taking whiteness as the standard measure of humanity and feeling. Leprosy, according to Rush, causes all the physical signifiers of Blackness; therefore, Blackness itself is a disease that can be cured. "The leprosy induces a morbid insensibility in the nerves," states Rush in his litany of evidence for this hypothesis. "This insensibility belongs in a peculiar manner to the negroes."[82] Black unfeeling becomes a literal symptom of pathologization, read as a physical property of the diseased body. Rush quotes a medical study by Benjamin Moseley, who claims that Black people "are void of sensibility to a surprising degree," citing his surgeries upon Black bodies compared to white patients as his major proof (quoted on 297). (Moseley's claims continue to influence the unequal treatment of Black people in the medical profession today.) Black people are characterized as having "morbid insensibility," "indifference," and "apathy" (297). Here we may recall Son of Baldwin's "black apathy" as a tactic to explain the consternation presented by that racialized unfeeling. To "cure" Blackness would enfold Black people back into the category of the universal human, Rush argues, and his Christian-inflected monogenesis subsumes racial particularities into whiteness originated by Adam and Eve as that "one pair, easy, and universal" under the coercive auspices of "universal benevolence" (297). Even though Rush attempts to discredit the institution of slavery, the reliance upon this framework of universalist humanity and sympathy reinscribes the same structural violences that slavery does. Across these key early American texts we can read how unfeeling registers epistemic failures of recognition that signal the stubborn trace of dissent, the abjection of the resilient practices of quotidian survival that gesture to the subversive politics of minoritarian ways of being and knowing.

Unfeeling as Interlocking Traditions of Minoritarian Critique

The novels and short stories I analyze in this book respond in complex ways to how modernizing American scientific and legal structures regulate, produce, and naturalize feeling. Each chapter responds to the influences of Adam Smith and Harriet Beecher Stowe on prevailing cultural norms in the American culture of sentiment by focusing on texts that allow us to track a spectrum of queer, racialized, and gendered genealogies of unfeeling in relation to the historical context of these scientific and legal discourses. To trace the interrelated differentiations that constitute the global biopolitical apparatus of feeling through the lens of the American context as a point of entry, I follow unsympathetic Blackness, queer female frigidity, Black objective passionlessness, and Oriental inscrutability as illustrative, but hardly exhaustive, modes of unfeeling that are attributed to different populations and that flatten out the textures within these categories of difference or otherwise elide the changing negotiations between a subject and the collective. Through reading literature, I seek to recover the nuances and ambivalences that emerge from the contours of a range of situated lived experiences that are collapsed into denigrating tropes that discipline representation and behavior and thereby foreclose social and political possibilities. The writers of the works I discuss use the space of fiction to question the politics of sympathetic identification in the cultural imagination informed by sentimentalism.

There are two organizing logics to this book's trajectory: one historicist and the other comparative. First, I track how writers respond to the sentimentalist paradigm in relation to major developments in science and law as modernizing disciplines from the mid-nineteenth century after the publication of *Uncle Tom's Cabin* through the turn to the twentieth century. Beginning with a consideration of Melville's and Delany's engagement with race science and the Fugitive Slave Act of 1850; moving to Phelps's and Watkins Harper's responses to sexology, gynecology, and the entrance of women into medicine in relation to constitutional amendments expanding and delimiting citizenship depending on race and gender; and ending with Far's considerations of anthropology and the enduring effects of the Chinese Exclusion Act of 1882, I articulate the ways in which American novels reflect on sympathy and action in the public and private spheres. This arc through the antebellum and postbellum periods and the turn of the century allows us to follow how the sentimental politics of recognition both transforms and endures in the cultural imagination. Second, this book shows its debts to Ahmed and Ngai not only in its intellectual influences but also in its organizational strategy: each chapter is structured upon attention to a different mode of unfeeling. For each mode, I examine how writers imagined affective agency in relation to the shifting contours of interlocking axes of oppression by paying attention to the distinct but interrelated embodied situatedness of Black, Indigenous, white, and Asian characters. Dedication to taking apart the liberal political project and the discourse of humanism in their systemic entanglements demands interdisciplinary considerations of the forms of insurgent critique arising from the different fields of critical race and ethnic studies inflected by feminist and queer theories. In this regard, I follow the methodologies of scholars like Jodi Byrd (Chickasaw), Lisa Lowe, and others in defying the false divisions between archives and fields of study.[83] The divisions of these chapters attempt to be less identarian—not so much invested in stable categories of race and gender as if they were parallel—than an approach for sketching out the hierarchical, comparatively constituted articulations of biopolitical racial difference that produce the spectrum of normative and deviant gender and sexuality.

If the enslaved, as Saidiya Hartman declares, is the unthought of being, how can we understand the role of unfeeling?[84] Thanks to the coloniality of sympathy, any expression of Black affect can be considered unfeeling in terms of its validity as feeling qua feeling. To put it another way, Black feelings, like Black lives, don't matter—and to say that all feelings matter, like all lives matter, is no mere distraction. Confronting the structural abjection of Blackness has meant a refusal to compromise with the systems of power and the promise of inclusion into category of the human, as articulated by the intellectual genealogy of Black feminists like Wynter, da Silva, and Hortense Spillers.[85] Understanding the foreclosure of Blackness can be a catalyst for abolition, however, rather than an impasse to liberation.[86] My first two chapters take up the schema of Man, sympathy, and unsympathetic Blackness to interrogate the national and transnational enmeshments of white American sentimentalism, and chapter 4 turns to Black feminism to address the gendered dynamics of Man as inextricable from that hegemony. Chapter 1 argues that Melville's *Benito Cereno* critiques the racial dynamics of sympathy in both Stowe and Adam Smith. The novella ironically frames the naïve Captain Delano as the exemplary white feeling American subject in contrast to Babo, as the treacherous Black unfeeling object. By attending to the construction of Delano's sentimental sense of self through his sympathies for Benito Cereno, triangulated through Babo, I trace how Delano's benevolent racism echoes ongoing scientific and legal discourses: first, the rhetoric of physiognomy, phrenology, and craniology in their promotion of the polygenetic theory of evolution; and second, the judicial decisions of Melville's father-in-law, Chief Justice Lemuel Shaw of the Massachusetts Supreme Judicial Court, about fugitives, which expose Northern complicity with the Fugitive Slave Act of 1850. *Benito Cereno* demonstrates how scientific racism and unjust laws influence the white racist American mind, cohering through the optics of paternalistic sentimentality. Seen through this frame, Babo illustrates the dangers for the unsympathetic Black subject who demonstrate what Fred Moten calls the evidence "that objects can and do resist" in the history of Blackness: to be unsympathetically unresponsive to the emotional demands of whiteness means foreclosing recognition as worthy of sympathy.[87] In his rewriting of the historical account of the mutiny, Melville erases Babo's social ties at his execution. The novella resonates with Afropessimism: Melville depicts a world built upon the obliteration of Black feelings that overdetermines the inevitability of Black death, both social and literal.[88]

Although Delany has a structural understanding of anti-Blackness similar to that of Melville, where Melville presents Black negation as the consequence of taking white hegemony as the only world, Delany fights for hope because he believes that there are other possible worlds repressed by white supremacist coloniality. "Black texts and narratives require reading practices that reckon with black life as scientifically creative," writes Katherine McKittrick, a practice inspiring complementary chapters 2 and 4 on Delany and Watkins Harper.[89] As chapter 2 explores, Delany's *Blake, or the Huts of America* (1861) imagines how dissenting unsympathetic Blackness can reclaim science and law as part of an assemblage of counterintimacies that can unite Black and Indigenous subjects in rebellion. The early Black nationalist thinker's only novel demonstrates the necessity of being disaffected from white sympathies as a starting point for new structures of feeling. In an earlier series of pivotal letters arguing with Frederick Douglass about *Uncle Tom's Cabin*, Delany turns to fiction to weave a story of white injustice against an Indigenous man, declaring—in a reformulation of Smith's definition of sympathy—"I feel somewhat like that Indian."[90] I track what Britt Rusert has called "fugitive science"—the reclaiming of science for Black emancipation—in the ways that Delany unfolds affective, biological, and political kinships with Indigenous peoples in his novel as well as his political and scientific writings.[91] Unsympathetic to whiteness, the eponymous Blake finds other allies—starting with members of the Choctaw Nation—which culminates in a political discussion of Black-Indigenous entanglements made suggestively physical through his masculinist and homosocial erotics with the younger Choctaw chief. Blake catalyzes an affective network of counterintimacies among peoples of color across the United States, Canada, West Africa, and the Caribbean, thereby redrawing the coloniality of sympathy to unmake the structural conditions of Black enslavement and Indigenous dispossession that produce the modern world. To this end, Blake attacks race science and the Fugitive Slave Act as divisive perversions of an original cosmology. In *Blake*, manipulations of science and law by the dispossessed, as well as the revolt itself, attempt to return these disciplines to the natural order: through a decolonial physics, disaffected Indigenous and other peoples of color are pulled into orbit around a Black revolution that impacts the world even on the scales of the living and the nonliving environment. The novel's experiments with Black-Indigenous counterintimacies point to key convergences between Black studies' emancipatory aims and Indigenous studies' call for literal, rather than metaphorical, decolonization. Overturning instead of accepting the bounded limits of the world that coloniality produces does not mean destruction but resurgence. Following the thinking of Jodi Byrd, Tiffany King, Justin Leroy, Robin D. G. Kelley, and others across Black and Indigenous studies, my analysis shows Delany's work as an early iteration in a genealogy that works through the difficult inextricability of Black liberation and Indigenous decolonization.[92] Delany responds to racialized affective hierarchies—such as those proposed by Jefferson and Stanley Stanhope Smith—that continue to pit Black and Indigenous histories against one another. Delany's strategic use of unfeeling seeks to find compatibility between Black and Indigenous political projects for their radical possibilities by rejecting the sentimental colonial politics of recognition critiqued by Fanon and Coulthard.[93] Blackness and Indigeneity need not be exclusionary categories, and for Delany, blurring the distinction between them offers the hope of reclaiming African Indigeneity. Nonetheless, Delany's struggle to reconcile the tensions between these two groups' overlapping frameworks underlines how they have been structured as the foundational antagonisms of the United States. Cuba is the novel's site of Black, Indigenous, and Asian anticolonial convergences; indeed, it is worth turning to queer Cuban theorist Muñoz's unfinished work, which imagines the sense of brown and the brown commons: "Brownness is coexistent, affiliates, and intermeshes with blackness, Asianness, indigenousness, and other terms that manifest descriptive force to render the particularities of various modes of striving in the world."[94]

Chapters 3 and 4 turn away from work by and about men to considerations of women's histories of and writings on the sexual and racial politics of unfeeling for white and Black women entering medical science during fights for women's rights. The fear of frigidity, a queer unwomanliness, haunts the women doctors (both historical figures and literary characters) who must negotiate heteronormative affective expectations in their shift from the private to the public sphere while pathologized by gynecology. In chapter 3 I complicate feminist epistemologies of science to reframe this history of white women in medicine by tracking the homology between the invention of anesthesia as a technology of controlled unfeeling and the pathology of queer female frigidity that the sexologist Havelock Ellis diagnosed as "sexual anesthesia."[95] I investigate how white women physicians manipulated the unfeeling professionalism of medicine as a subversive tactic to anesthetize the coercive affective imperatives of marriage and family. I discuss queer female frigidity through a focus on Elizabeth Stuart Phelps's *Doctor Zay*, along with readings of essays and memoirs by early women doctors like Elizabeth Blackwell and Mary Putnam Jacobi, in context with the coeval publication of other women doctor novels such as William Dean Howells's *Dr. Breen's Practice* (1881), Sarah Orne Jewett's *A Country Doctor* (1884), and Annie Nathan Meyer's *Helen Brent, M.D.* (1892). These novels structure their marriage plots with the woman doctor, who is focused on her career and wary of relationships, being in tension with the male lawyer who woos her and serves as both antagonist and love interest. This clash between institutional authorities that both claim to reflect the natural order reveals the still-extant gender inequality that mirrors the struggles for suffrage leading to the Nineteenth Amendment: although the woman doctor has professional authority, the male lawyer's love represents the affective force of heteronormativity. These novels about white women doctors raise questions about the dangers of desire for inclusion without radical change to structures of power.

The suffrage activist Frances Ellen Watkins Harper indicts the compromises made by white feminist activists in their pursuit of suffrage and the limited vision of political belonging that sacrificed Black women's enfranchisement for the Fourteenth and Fifteenth Amendments. In chapter 4, I center Black women, whose occlusions haunt the earlier discussions. Taking Black women seriously as medical practitioners alongside the coeval development of detached scientific objectivity pushes back against the well-documented history of Black women's exploitation by medical science, particularly gynecology. By reading Watkins Harper's novel *Iola Leroy* in conjunction with medical texts by Rebecca Lee Crumpler and Rebecca J. Cole, the first Black women doctors to receive medical degrees in the United States, I revisit Ann duCille's "passionlessness," a tactic developed by Black women to assert their sexual and affective agency, in relation to the supposedly dispassionate objectivity of medical science—that ruse of professional and epistemic authority.[96] These seemingly counterpoised phenomena of unfeeling that develop coevally during this century converge for Black women doctors who crafted an objective passionlessness for the sake of both concealing and tending to their passions. Crumpler's *Book of Medical Discourses* (1883) and Cole's MD thesis "The Eye and Its Appendages" (1867) adapt scientific objectivity to create their own authority to work toward Black emancipatory ends, anticipating the Black feminist health studies of Moya Bailey and Whitney Peoples.[97] In particular, Cole's underread thesis is an exemplar of negotiating the tensions between one's situated standpoint and professional discourse. Decades before Du Bois's double consciousness as second sight, Cole presented her meditation on the eye or I and embodied sight informed by the nondialectical tensions of objective passionlessness to meet the final requirements of her medical degree. As many Black feminist scholars have argued, *Iola Leroy* is a striking example of how Black women writers played with sentimentalism's conventions about white womanhood and the marriage plot. Mixed-race Black Iola Leroy chooses her Blackness and Black kin, a demonstration of what Foreman describes as the "anti-passing narrative."[98] By foregrounding Black feminist thought, I propose to read *Iola Leroy* as a novel about the suppressed possibility of the Black woman doctor who affirms her Black mother to cure the pathology of the sentimental tragic mulatta trope and chattel slavery's congenital stigma of *partus sequitur ventrum*, in which a child's status as enslaved follows the enslavement of the mother. I consider the eponymous character as a potential doctor herself, whose refusal to love the white Dr. Gresham and her choice of the Black Dr. Latimer demonstrate that strategic unfeeling toward whiteness makes possible the healing work of transformative Black love. Through a tactful calculus of detachments and attachments, *Iola Leroy* engenders other forms of belonging in defiance of the failures of the Fourteenth and Fifteen Amendments in terms of citizenship and suffrage for Black men, as well as the deficiencies of the eventual Nineteenth Amendment for women's suffrage that was in practice limited to white women.

My final chapter turns to the establishment of the apparatuses of modern American immigration that transposed the model of sympathetic identification into governmental and cultural evaluations of literal acceptance and rejection into the nation. The diasporic tensions of Asian American studies (what David Palumbo-Liu has called the dynamic of Asian/America) and Kandice Chuh's assertion that the field is a subjectless discourse illustrate the disciplinary skepticism of national belonging and the naturalized coherence of subjects.[99] The work of Sui Sin Far is perhaps least accurately categorized as American literature solely, since she also lived and worked in England, Canada, and the Caribbean. I reassess the well-worn Yellow Peril stereotype of Oriental inscrutability attributed to the Chinese in the late nineteenth and early twentieth centuries through Sui Sin Far's journalism and short-story collection *Mrs. Spring Fragrance*. By tracing the genealogy of the Yellow Peril through evolutionary and anthropological race science and the Chinese Exclusion Act of 1882, I articulate how anti-Chinese anxieties clustered around the inexpressive racialized alien—the twin Oriental specters of the coolie and the sex worker as identified by Nayan Shah—associated with a dangerously different taxonomy of feeling.[100] The Chinese concept of face functions as both an embodied symbol and a cultural concept that threatens to decenter the universalist assumptions about faces and feeling discussed in my first chapter. I propose a radical reconsideration of Sui Sin Far's work: ambivalent about humanizing the Chinese to a white gaze through sentimentality, Far uses Oriental inscrutability to deny invasive anthropological access into Chinese affective interiority, since the condition of sympathy is intermeshed with the regulatory demands of immigration that insist on transparent, affectable subjects. For Far's characters, detachment and distancing are alienating though they function as coping mechanisms against alienation; their reserved composure reallocates affective reserves. This chapter joins conversations about Asian American antisociality articulated by scholars like Summer Kim Lee and Vivian L. Huang, taking Sui Sin Far as a queer and disabled mixed-race Chinese woman who theorizes a queer feminist disabled Asian diasporic sensibility.[101] Oriental inscrutability names an everyday means of surviving Far's chronic condition of affectability, manifested as painful hypersensitivity. Through her writings, we can track the affirmation of inscrutability as dissatisfaction that rejects the demands of citizenship; the antisocial moments in her oeuvre betray uncertainties about the political instrumentality of disaffected feeling for the Chinese and herself. Oriental inscrutability's legibility as a trope readily identifiable by that phrase allows us to ponder the shifting comparative privilege of diasporic Asianness positioned against Blackness and Indigeneity that enables the relative recognition of Asian affective opacity. This final chapter gestures toward the ongoing integration of the sentimental politics of recognition into the apparatuses of immigration and citizenship. In both this chapter and chapter 4, my method is to approach these works by Black and Asian diasporic writers as early woman-of-color feminist theorizations.

I draw inspiration from disciplinary imperatives across the different fields of critical race and ethnic studies to critique and dismantle frameworks that pose as universal and to dissent from the cooptation of justice. The stigmatization of queerness, Blackness, Indigeneity, and Asianness can inspire disruptive potential for other ways of being that shatter norms rather than acceding to the ceaseless duties of refutation for the sake of inclusion. The organization of these chapters aims to present a framework that is dynamic rather than rigid, and comparative rather than exclusionary, wherein focuses on contextualized threads of unfeeling help provincialize sympathy by splintering its hegemonic universality. These articulations of disaffected insubordination emerge from the specificities of their imbricated fields and reflect the incommensurable textures of lived and historical positionalities. I view this as a methodological strength: their unruly and difficult convergences resist the homogenizing discourse of universalist feeling, which both differentiates hierarchically and collapses that very difference in ways that overrepresent the white Western subject.

In our historical moment, the concept of sympathy has been updated as empathy in the continued hope for a better politics of feeling bound up with morality and justice.[102] I gesture toward the legacies of these expressive requirements for political recognition in the fantasies of justice in the present-day American culture of sentiment for racialized immigrants performing citizenship and the defiance of movements like Black Lives Matter. Through the strong presentation of a weak theory, I hope to offer a way out of the bind between the poles of critique and defense that have dominated our understanding of sympathy, while also eschewing a primarily descriptive approach of tracing the workings and effects of feeling and unfeeling. Lingering with, rather than debunking, the specter of unfeeling in its function as an antisocial rebuttal to discourses of universal feeling provides greater nuance in our understandings of politics and literature for the marginalized. In contradistinction to the insistence on affect in relation to attachments and porousness, we need to acknowledge the affective importance of detachments and boundaries. What possibilities open up when we explore the implications of Édouard Glissant's "right to opacity" in terms of feeling?[103] Can a calculus of uncaring allow for us to better care for ourselves and others?

The trajectory of this project concludes with Far, situating an Asian diasporic sensibility in relation to the previous chapters' charting of the entanglements of emancipatory, decolonial, feminist struggles routed through the United States as construct. A confession: interwoven with the other structuring logics of *Disaffected*, it is no coincidence that I finish with Far because of our parallels. Through the book's organization I have worked through my own positionality in relation to histories, nations, structures, disciplines, communities, and loved ones—deferred until the end according to the usual scholarly suspension, if not denial, of any affective attachments to our work. In my coda, I write from my own experiences of alienation and solidarity to suggest some ways that unfeeling can be taken up in everyday life, particularly by marginalized scholars struggling to survive in the academy. Through this project I hope to articulate something that, if not useful to others, may resonate with their experiences. Ultimately, this book proposes that feeling otherwise is the precondition for thinking and imagining otherwise. This opening is an invitation to you, too, my reader, to speculate about the possibilities of feeling otherwise.

1

THE BABO PROBLEM /

White Sentimentalism and Unsympathetic Blackness
in Herman Melville's *Benito Cereno*

I HAVE A PROPOSAL: what if we considered Babo instead of Bartleby in our discussions of Melville's explorations of refusal? I seek to shift attention from the scrivener to the enslaved. There is a popular tendency to uphold Bartleby as Melville's universal figure of noncompliance: he is imprisoned and eventually dies for his adherence to his signature phrase "I would prefer not to," with no further explanation of his enigmatic resistance. This "Bartleby problem," Wendy Lee concludes of the insensible and unfeeling scrivener, "recapitulates both the philosophical question of how a person lives if he does not move as well as the ethical challenges of recognizing or tolerating such a being."[1] Yet while Bartleby frustrates, he is still intelligible as a subject with affective interiority, however inaccessible. At the beginning, the narrating lawyer laments that there cannot be "a full and satisfactory biography of this man. It is an irreparable loss to literature," a testimony to his faith in the validity of Bartleby's unavailable life.[2] Despite the scrivener's recalcitrance, the lawyer attempts to extend every possible generosity to this fellow white man whom he cannot understand—echoing the American Captain Amasa Delano's sympathies toward the withholding Spanish enslaver Benito Cereno in Melville's 1855 novella. These are not sympathies ever offered to Babo and the other enslaved Africans, who face death if they rebel against chattel slavery's system of social death. Philosopher Adam Smith's "fellow-feeling" can recognize people like Bartleby as unfeeling but still human foils.[3] After all, Melville's story closes with the universalizing exclamation, "Ah Bartleby! Ah humanity!"[4] Reevaluating unfeeling through the scope of what Kyla Schuller terms the biopolitics of feeling allows us to attend to its queer, racialized, and gendered modes and genealogies that carry different risks and rewards in their challenging of the sentimental politics of recognition.[5] "How does it feel to be a problem?," according to W. E. B. Du Bois, is the unspoken question asked of him as a Black person in the United States.[6] What might the Babo problem teach us about the racial mapping of feeling and unfeeling?

"'Faithful fellow!' cried Capt. Delano. 'Don Benito, I envy you such a friend; slave I cannot call him.'"[7] Delano, a captain from Duxbury, Massachusetts, believes his heart is in the right place when he praises Babo to Cereno on the basis of the enslaved Senegalese man's loving care for the white enslaver. Set off the coast of Chile, *Benito Cereno* is based on an episode from the real Delano's memoir *Narrative of Voyages and Travels* (1817).[8] The novella follows the white captain of the American *Bachelor's Delight*, who believes he is helping the *San Dominick*, a Spanish slave ship in distress. During the transfer of supplies, the captain is disquieted by the enslaved Black men, women, and children who outnumber the white crew and by the absence of white authority figures like the enslaver Alexandro Aranda, who is said to have been struck down by illness. Nonetheless, his sympathies are with Cereno, the *San Dominick*'s captain, who behaves strangely despite the close ministrations from the enslaved Babo. Whenever Delano becomes suspicious, he is reassured by Babo's performances of tender devotion. When the baffled American finally takes his leave, the tale of the *San Dominick*'s weather woes and illness turns out to have concealed the ship's true history: Cereno leaps after Delano, with Babo close behind, dagger in hand—a shocking revelation for the American that overturns his assumptions about who was the captive and who was the master. While the Americans fight alongside the Spanish to recapture the ship and reenslave the Black fugitives, the canvas hiding the bow of the *San Dominick* falls aside to reveal that the mutiny substituted the enslaver Aranda's skeleton for the original figurehead of Christopher Columbus. After the victory of enslavers and colonizers, the reader is presented with selections from the legal deposition of the events. Order appears to be restored: the narrative's focus returns to the two captains, now true friends, while the surviving African men, women, and children are remanded into chattel slavery and Babo is publicly executed. The traumatized Cereno's death soon follows.

Throughout most of the novella, the third-person narration stays close to Delano's perspective, attentive to the shifts in his inner life during these events—but this intimacy is inflected by an undertone of ironic detachment. After Delano's introduction, he is said to be "a person of singularly undistrustful good nature, not liable, except on extraordinary and repeated incentives, and hardly then, to indulge in personal alarms, any way involving the imputation of malign evil in man."[9] His point of view captures something quintessentially American about his emotional understanding of the world and his own goodness.

The sentimental Delano embodies Harriet Beecher Stowe's famous affective injunction from the end of *Uncle Tom's Cabin*, published in 1852, three years before *Benito Cereno*'s serialization: "There is one thing that every individual can do,—they can see to it that *they feel right*. An atmosphere of sympathetic influence encircles every human being; and the man or woman who *feels* strongly, healthily and justly, on the great interests of humanity, is a constant benefactor to the human race."[10] Despite not sharing Stowe's abolitionist beliefs, Delano does not mistake the contradiction between Babo as enslaved by Cereno and Babo as friend to Cereno: Melville captures what Saidiya Hartman has identified as the structuring paradox of the legibility of Black humanity to whiteness being predicated upon Black subjugation.[11] Although ostensibly acknowledging Babo's humanity, Delano recognizes the enslaved man only through his affective performances of labor for his enslaver, the true recipient of the American's sympathies. Through this triangulation, Delano affirms himself as sympathetic. However, the rebellion of Babo and his fellow Africans violates the terms of this affective recognition across difference: to play off Denise Ferreira da Silva's terminology, the fugitives show themselves to be disaffected rather than affectable.[12] Following his right feelings, the good American leads the violent suppression of the African uprising on the Spanish slave ship and restores the enslavers' authority over the fugitives, leading to Babo's beheading. While for Stowe the universality of right feeling leads to the right kind of politics (which benefits the whole of humanity), Melville disrupts this instrumentalist assumption: the captain's "benevolent heart" is inextricable from the racialized and gendered system of American governmentality over hierarchies of feeling and humanity.[13]

Delano's initial perception of Babo as a sympathetic enslaved "friend" is inextricably related to his later view of the Black man as an unsympathetic villain. "Unsympathetic" is a word that cuts both ways in its negation: to not have sympathy for others means forfeiting the recognition that they are deserving of sympathy. Here I am interested in how *Benito Cereno* offers us ways to understand the white sentimental politics of recognition that in turn demands the affective labor of Black peoples and other minoritized peoples as the condition and the limit of their humanity that structures the white fantasy of universality.[14] For many critics the narrative's careful attention to Delano's misunderstanding of the racial dynamics on the *San Dominick* have made the novella an examination of the hermeneutics of racism.[15] If, as Shirley Samuels writes, "sentimentality is literally at the heart of nineteenth-century American culture," racism is literally and figuratively at the heart of the narrative.[16] *Benito Cereno* critiques Stowe's sentimentalism and its legacies, as Peter Coviello notes: "for Melville Delano is first and foremost a sentimental reader, whose racism and incompetence in fact follow from his sentimentality."[17] I take Delano's psychic life as a case study in how structures of feeling reveal the constitutive scalar relationship between the individual and public politics of recognition: his perspective lays bare his affective investments in existing hegemonies.[18] Feeling is never simply the private affective capacity of the individual but is also constitutive of public national sentiments and their political projects of belonging, interlocked with colonial and imperialist transnational intimacies of labor and domination.[19] The narrator challenges the reader to question whether the American's "benevolent heart" might influence his "quickness and accuracy of intellectual perception"—slyly phrased so that any answer "may be left to the wise to determine."[20] Indeed, the reader is implicitly challenged as to whether they will be affected by Delano or disaffected from his structure of feeling.

If feeling is a fundamental technology of biopolitical domination, then we need to historicize and theorize unfeeling as an affective index of dissatisfaction and dissent toward survival and resistance. In reading Babo through Delano, I am concerned less with the limits of white sentimentalism toward the ideal of a truer universal than I am with how white sentimentalism suppresses and renders illegible the emergence of alternative structures of feeling that would threaten its posturing as universal. Recognition, as argued by Frantz Fanon in the colonial context and Glen Coulthard in the settler colonial context, operates as an apparatus for the production and maintenance of power.[21] Following the work of da Silva and Sylvia Wynter, my discussion questions the ideal of the universal human race that I argue is intertwined with the sentimental discourse of universal feeling that in turn produces the politics of recognition: the Africans' uprising signals the insurgent potential of the assumed failures of action and expression by disaffected peoples of color.[22] Trace references to Indigenous and Asian resistance hint at the global and comparative dimensions of anticolonial struggles. Attending to the structural centrality of anti-Blackness, I open this first chapter with my analysis of Babo's disaffection as a consequence of the formational demands for Black people's affectability, given what Sianne Ngai calls animatedness—the expectations for their excessive affects and demonstrative physicality.[23] Babo's refusal to comply with the terms of this social contract renders him in Delano's eyes its antisocial negation: the unfeeling specter of unsympathetic Blackness that seeks not inclusion into but liberation from the American's structures of feeling that are founded upon the violent subsuming of racialized affects. No expression of Black affect is deemed truly legitimate.

Within the biopolitics of feeling, the perception of inappropriate, diminished, or even absent affects by the marginalized are vilified because these affective modes of turning away challenge the engulfing dynamics of agency, causation, and circulation that are braided into the discourse of universal affect as the expressive marker of the human. *Benito Cereno* explores the scientific and legal discourses of white sentimentalism that regulate the legibility of racialized affects under the coercive auspices of universal feeling during the long nineteenth century in the United States. Rather than acting as correctives to unjust science and law, sympathy and sentimentality were constitutive of anti-Black scientific and legal discourses, turning their authoritative claims into moralized structures of oppression.

In this chapter I consider the novella's two most striking images—the Spanish enslaver Aranda's skeleton and the Senegalese rebel leader Babo's severed head—in terms of the overturning and restoration of expected visions of power, material artifacts of the scientific racism and unjust laws that undergird Delano's sentimental worldview. These visual displays stand out as significant deviations from the real Delano's memoir. The asymmetrical treatment of Aranda's and Babo's remains is linked to the treatment of racialized bodies as scientific specimens and as demonstrations of legal authority, illustrating the performances of scientific and legal discursive power in visual and material culture. Through its ironic distance from Delano's affective certainty of what feels like the natural order, Melville's text makes visible the messy biopolitical violences of sentimentalism that the rise of scientific objectivity and legal formalism cannot fully occlude. I argue that through its attention to Delano's affective interiority in relation to the public spectacles of the skeleton and the severed head, *Benito Cereno* articulates the sentimental processes behind the politics of recognition in the America of the long nineteenth century that continue to influence fantasies of justice in the cultural imagination.[24] Delano imposes this cultural imperialism as his benevolent international intervention, a forceful translation into his

American paradigm not simply from the Spanish language but also from the Spanish colonial, Latin American, and African contexts.[25]

This chapter has two main divisions that trace different institutional apparatuses that make up the American biopolitics of feeling: the first traces the influence of scientific discourse, and the second traces the authority of legal discourse. Delano's way of seeing, his literal point of view, draws upon popular scientific discourse that justifies his sympathies toward those he observes through obsessive attention to faces and heads as signifiers of affective interiority and, therefore, humanity. These optics of recognition are informed by the influences of physiognomy, phrenology, and craniology on visual culture—fields of scientific study whose legitimacy would wax and wane over the century and that were founded upon the violation of predominantly Black and Indigenous peoples' bodies.[26] Race science is the overt manifestation of the sciences writ large as the biopolitics of feeling: hierarchies of being and agency based on the capacities to feel and be affected within a scientific episteme itself founded upon sentiment and sympathy in its thought, methodology, practice, and rhetoric. On the level of the individual, these disciplinary knowledges are in turn naturalized as structures of feeling. Delano's gaze is directed by his heart: his view of the backwardness of the Africans is informed by his nostalgia for his childhood, framed by an imagined cultural past of undisturbed Black primitivism and white nobility. His sense of self as a sympathetic subject within this hegemonic structure of feeling depends upon the emotional labor of Babo and the other Africans as affectable, tractable affirmations of his own humanity. However, Babo's orchestration of the *San Dominick* subverts these demands for racialized affectability: he manipulates anxieties about the display of emotional expression as signifiers of subordinated affective interiority. Rather than a break from white epistemological mastery, however, this revelation demonstrates the ways in which the demand for sympathetic Blackness is positioned in contrast to the fear of unsympathetic Black resistance—whose illegibility to white sentiments gestures beyond the horizons of dominant structures of feeling and their limited politics. During the ensuing conflict, the sight of the enslaver Aranda's skeleton rallies the Spanish and Americans in defense of their shared affective investments in defending whiteness against the possibility of Black liberation.

After the battle, the narrative shifts from Delano's everyday individual politics of recognition to its imperialist, institutional counterpart, with the Spanish legal deposition recounting the African revolt and the legal restoration of order that validates Delano's American sense of the world in a transnational context. The rationale undergirding the illusion of objective distance provided by the legal documents is the same sentimental rhetoric shared by race science: a call for universal justice predicated upon that same natural order and structured upon racialized abjection. In his depiction of Delano and his crew helping the Spanish return the Africans to slavery, Melville addresses the ongoing turmoil around the Fugitive Slave Act of 1850 during his writing: the narrative condemns both proslavery lawyers who euphemize chattel slavery through sentimentalism and those complicit liberal moderates like his own father-in-law, Massachusetts Supreme Judicial Court chief justice Lemuel Shaw, who—in *Roberts v. The City of Boston*—infamously upheld the act to deny the fugitive Thomas Sims a writ of habeas corpus. The sight of Babo's head on a pole contrasts with the display of Aranda's skeleton: the law renders one justice, while the other is obscene. The subversive display of Aranda's skeleton is overthrown by the closing spectacle of Babo's head as a symbol of order restored in the world: the fugitive leader dismembered into a craniological specimen suitable for race science's appropriation as evidence, tautologically reaffirming that what the American felt was right all along. In closing the chapter, I speculate on the place of racialized affects in Melville's portrayal of a world invested in white feelings, a conclusion that is inflected by Afropessimism: founded upon the erasure of any index of Black dissent and self-determination as unfeeling, the world of the novella cannot represent any possibility of the alternative structures of feeling that could be galvanized by Babo's gaze, which is defiant even in death.

The Seeing Mania / Science, Sentiment, and the Structuring of Recognition

If we follow Adam Smith's figuration of sympathy as "fellow-feeling," we can say that Delano understands himself as a feeling fellow. From the beginning of *Benito Cereno* his sight is emphasized in conjunction with his signature "good nature."[27] The *San Dominick* "viewed through the glass" is an object of intrigue as the captain "continued to watch her," and "the longer the stranger was watched the more singular appeared her maneuvers." But despite suspicions that might have arisen from these observations, Delano does not fear evil from the Spanish ship. The narrative continues to focus on the American's unfolding perception of events: he is obsessed with faces and heads as signifiers of meaning, showing how his eye—and, therefore, his literal point of view—is informed by the expectations of race science. By shifting the original account of Delano's encounter with the Spanish slave ship *Tryal* from 1805 to the fictionalized encounter in 1799, the 1855 novella's temporal scope captures the visual developments of the various race sciences, from the field of physiognomy in the late eighteenth century to the sciences of phrenology and craniology popular in American culture by the mid-nineteenth century. Through *Benito Cereno* we can trace the historical contours of the politics of recognition on the individual level of how one sees and is seen in everyday life.

In the *American Phrenological Journal* (1846), Orson Squire Fowler announces the visual impact of the popular science: "Its observations so thoroughly interest as to create a *seeing mania* which scrutinizes everybody and every thing. And the more you learn of it, the more it will promote still further observation."[28] The phrenologist's phrase "seeing mania" articulates what Jonathan Crary has more broadly argued is the rise of the modern techniques of the observer.[29] Through the influence of science on nineteenth-century American visual culture, faces, heads, and skulls acted as the visible material signifiers not just of character and ability but also of differences within the hierarchy of the human. The overlapping disciplines of physiognomy, phrenology, and craniology affirmed vision as a technology of scientific judgment. Although they are now viewed as racist pseudosciences, these once respectable fields enjoyed varying degrees of institutional credibility, and their research and paradigms laid the ground for the development of the disciplines of anatomy, psychology, and neuroscience.[30] These interlocking discourses helped train the average American eye in the techniques of scientific visual evaluation, combining the expertise of the Foucauldian clinical gaze with a culture of everyday panoptic scrutiny and thereby providing widespread justification for racial prejudices to be naturalized and as evident as sight itself.

The scientific dependence on the visual as a primary tool of analysis meant the proliferation of images of faces, heads, and skulls to illustrate theory.[31] One edition of Johann Lavater's *Essays on Physiognomy* boasts 360 engravings, and practitioners of popular phrenology used these iconic diagrams of the head's faculties and organs to advertise their services.[32] In contrast to the physiognomic and phrenological manuals printed in a small and lightweight format to maximize their distribution and affordability, the expensive folio format of Samuel George Morton's *Crania Americana* imbued the author's ethnological findings with gravitas and delivered the full impact of John Collins's striking seventy-eight lithographs that depicted Morton's extensive skull collection.[33] The scholarly *Types of Mankind* by Josiah Clark Nott and George R. Gliddon, which boasted contributions from scientific authorities like Morton and Louis Agassiz, includes several foldout color prints that display schematic renditions of the faces, skulls, and characteristic fauna associated with each race's place of origin. The "types" are meant to be instantly recognizable by the displays of distinctive anatomy: "how indelible is the image of a type impressed on a mind's eye!" proclaims the tome.[34] In contradiction to modern standards of evidence, the title page of *Types* declares that its research is drawn from "ancient monuments, sculptures, and paintings" as well as the expected crania, but the dependence upon art, under the presumption of mimetic representation, recurs throughout the head sciences.[35] Phrenologists regularly used busts and paintings at their demonstrations to affirm the timelessness of their principles and use the visages of deceased famous individuals as examples.[36]

However, art in this period was shifting in response to phrenological principles. Hiram Powers was inspired by phrenology in his sculpting and even distributed the movement's pamphlets, while the popularity of the science meant that artists were pressured (in the case of Augustus Saint-Gaudens) to give their sitters flattering phrenological portrayals, or (like Henry Inman) were savvy about altering their busts and paintings to do so.[37] These aspirational representations indicate the bias of science's reliance on the visual: the faces of white, moneyed subjects have the privilege of signifying an idealized individuality, while racialized faces are reducible to types. In his approach to ethics, Emmanuel Levinas unintentionally channels the head sciences' fixation with their preferred object of study: according to the philosopher, "the face is meaning all by itself," and the epiphanic alterity of the face-to-face encounter demands ethical responsibility between those subjects.[38] But this assumption about the irreducible alterity runs into the unexamined problem of universality that Gilles Deleuze and Félix Guattari critique in their discussion of faciality. Although the face acts as a way of tying meaning to a subject, the assumed face is that of "your average ordinary White Man": "Racism operates by the determination of degrees of deviance in relation to the White-Man face."[39] In one exemplary comparative diagram, *Types of Mankind* presents the contrast between racial norms and deviations by placing the caricatured faces of Black men beside those of primates, while the representative face of whiteness is the classical bust of Apollo Belvedere.[40] The chosen faces and heads of physiognomic and phrenological texts and demonstrations are of idealized white men, which are reaffirmed as normative ideals by science.

This hypocrisy reflects what da Silva calls the analytics of raciality that produced the modern configurations of global power and ethics: nineteenth-century Western science transposed the Enlightenment ideals of universality and self-determination into the biopolitical systems of knowledge that recast social and bodily differences and processes into exterior manifestations of inherent differentiation that still took whiteness as the human universal.[41] The specific genealogies of racism in American science from the shift from eighteenth-century theories of environmentalism and difference to the codified biological racism of the nineteenth century have been well documented.[42] The role of scientists' individual sentiments, disavowed as corrupting biases according to modern standards of scientific objectivity, tend to be at the forefront of these histories of scientific racism. However, sentiment and science both reinforced discursive justifications for racism.[43] Rather than the antithesis to the assumed cold rationality of science, sentimentalism was fundamental to scientific thought, practice, and methodology in ways we are still understanding. In her groundbreaking work, Jessica Riskin draws attention to the key role of affect in the development of scientific empiricism in the eighteenth and nineteenth centuries. According to Riskin, "ideas, emotions, and moral sentiments alike were expressions of sensibility," leading to what she calls "sentimental empiricism": "by tracing emotions to sensory experience, [sentimental empiricism] implied that moral sentiments might be subjected to empirical scrutiny and manipulation, which was the foundation assumption of the moral sciences. However, by the same logic applied in reverse, sentimental empiricism also infused empirical experience, and therefore natural science, with sentiment and moral import."[44] While focused on French scientific developments, Riskin gestures toward their influence in the American context: Benjamin Franklin's popularity in France, she suggests, was in no small part due to his use of sensibility in science.[45] Following these insights into the place of sentimentalism as a scientific concept, Kyla Schuller argues that we need to pay attention to the overarching biopolitics of feeling. "Sentimentalism," she states, "in the midst of its feminized ethic of emotional identification, operates as a fundamental mechanism of biopower."[46] Sentimentalism was then and is now more than a moral, aesthetic, or rhetorical mode: feeling is a technology of domination, molding bodies and populations as part of political projects. Revising da Silva's terms and drawing upon the multivalent meanings bound up in the term "affect," I focus on affectability as the principle and process of this differentiation between the affective (people who have agency over feeling and can act upon others) and the affectable (those whose feelings are reactive and are susceptible to the affective). According to this system, to feel improperly or not feel at all as a marginalized individual thus implies inferiority if not outright failure in the terms of affectability and ultimately exposes their conditional legitimacy as human subjects. At the same time, these demonized transgressions against the biopolitics of feeling suggest a space outside of the recognition of this sentimental governmentality: a space for people who are disaffected, rather than affectable, in all its affective, causal, and political senses.

If we look to the writings of the scientists, we can see how they understood their racism through sentimentalism about the ideal of universal humanity that produced, even as it purported to erase, human difference and the abjection of the racialized based on affectability. Returning to Lavater, his take on national physiognomy sowed the seeds of race science with his assertion that "each must be ennobled according to its primitive nature," reassuring those lower on the racial hierarchy that they "yet ought not the lowest of the human race be discouraged" for they were equally beloved by God.[47] After all, Lavater's work proclaims on its title page to be "designed to promote the knowledge and the love of mankind."[48] Phrenology helped systematize the connection between science and emotion: the major classes of the phrenological organs include those called the "sentiments" by George Combe and the "affective faculties, or feelings" by Fowler—which, in echoes of affect theory, according to Combe, "every faculty stands in relation to certain external objects."[49] Morton solicited an essay from Combe for *Crania Americana*, in which Combe's comments on sympathy as the principle behind the phrenological organs appear alongside the lithographs of the skulls of Indigenous people who had been murdered in the recent Seminole War. Combe writes without irony: "Sympathy is not a faculty, nor is it synonymous with moral approbation. The same notes sounded by ten instruments of the same kind, harmonise, blend softly together, and form one peal of melody."[50] Under the same benevolent auspices, Orson Squire Fowler and his family published lectures and pamphlets on the manipulation of the domestic feelings for better marriages and the improvement of the (white) race. Of course, these works on hereditary descent include statements on racial difference according to phrenological principles. Fowler could state both that "the avenues to the human heart are the same in all ... all yield to the power of love; all love their children" and that the "colored race is characterized quite as much by the tone of their feelings, the peculiarities of their intellects and expressions, as by the color of their skin."[51] In *Types of Mankind*, race science and slavery justify one another through a compassionate appeal to the greater good: "the Negro thrives under the shadow of his white master, falls readily into the position assigned him, and exists and multiplies in increased physical well-being."[52] Dedicated to Morton, *Types of Mankind* opens with a memoir of the founding skull collector as a sensitive soul: we are told that he had a "nervous temperament, delicate fibre, acute feelings, and ardent sympathies."⁵³ Much like Delano, whose racism is guided by his benevolent heart, these proponents of race science fashioned themselves and their scientific theories as sympathetic through the sentimental subordination of racialized others.

AMASA DELANO'S SENTIMENTAL PERSPECTIVE /
NARRATIVE FOCALIZATION AND RACE SCIENCE'S SEEING MANIA

The 1855 publication of *Benito Cereno* situates Melville's writing at the fraught intersection of visual culture and race science that was framed by the cultural impact of Stowe's sentimentalism in the period leading up to the Civil War. Melville can be counted among those interested in both science and art: he read many works on art history by luminaries such as John Ruskin and Giorgio Vasari, as well as scientific texts like Charles Darwin's journal and a volume of Georges Cuvier's *The Animal Kingdom*.⁵⁴ Melville owned about four hundred individual prints, and his final published work, *Timoleon*, explores his love of art.⁵⁵ As for Melville's knowledge of physiognomic sciences in particular, during his trip to England in 1849 he purchased a copy of Lavater's *Essays on Physiognomy* for ten shillings, and in an 1854 letter to Richard Lathers he refers to his returning of Lathers's copy of Combe's best-selling *Constitution of Man*.⁵⁶ In an August 16, 1850, letter to the publisher and editor Evert A. Duyckinck, Melville jokes to his friend about the pandering of phrenologists: "A horrible something in me tells me that you are about dipping your head in plaster at Fowler's for your bust."⁵⁷ Lynn Horth speculates that Melville may have learned about the phrenological Fowlers as early as 1835, due to the practices of the brothers and their students in Albany and Lansingburgh, New York. For instance John C. Hoadley, Melville's brother-in-law, had his head examined by Lorenzo Fowler.⁵⁸ Both science and art are woven into the foreground and background of Melville's life and work.

Benito Cereno was first published as a serial in a literary periodical dedicated to both subjects: *Putnam's Monthly Magazine of American Literature, Science, and Art*, which included regular updates on the fine arts, politics, and discussions of science. Melville debuted numerous other works in the periodical, such as "Bartleby the Scrivener" and *Israel Potter*. When *Types of Mankind* appeared in 1854 as a salvo by polygenesis's proponents, the July edition of *Putnam's* included an extensive discussion of the book that ended up agreeing with its claims. The review, "Is Man One or Many?," accepts polygenesis's use of art as evidence for the unchanging and separate nature of the races based on "different physiognomies" that "enable us, for the most part, to distinguish them at a glance."[59] In the January 1855 issue, however, the essay "Are All Men Descended from Adam?" argues for monogenesis in part on the basis of the "mysterious sympathy which inspires whole nations with the emotions of a single man," while still maintaining that physiognomy is the distinctive characteristic of racial difference.[60] *Benito Cereno* was published in the last three issues of that year for readers who were informed about contemporary visual culture as well as antebellum debates about scientific racism.

Delano would have been readily identifiable as a participant in the popular race science's "seeing mania," that biopolitical technology of sentimental recognition.[61] Once aboard the *San Dominick*, Delano's "one eager glance took in all faces, with every other object about him," and when he first looks specifically at the people who are the ship's cargo, the old Africans picking oakum are described as having "heads like black, doddered willow tops."[62] Throughout his guided tour of the ship, the captain's gaze is drawn to faces and heads as organized receptacles of legible meaning and personhood, but he parses them unevenly according to race: white faces are continually recognized and privileged with gazes that can be returned, while Black faces are continually erased, ignored, or downplayed and often rendered simply as heads with the status of objects. While the physiognomic face expresses the holistic representation of individual human interiority, the head in phrenology—if one is not in the position to be pandered to by its practitioners as a subject of admiration—quantifies one's capacities into an object of study. During one of many times when Delano is on the verge of revelation about the ingenious racial masquerade, he is "standing with eye directed forward" and believes that the Spanish sailors "returned the glance and with a sort of meaning. He rubbed his eyes and looked again; but again seemed to see the same thing" (83–84). When he then enters the scene, he looks only to white faces for answers, with "his eye curiously surveying the white faces, here and there sparsely mixed in with the blacks," and after failing to get answers from a Spanish sailor, he looks "round for a more promising countenance but seeing none, spoke pleasantly to the blacks to make way for him" (84 and 85). Because he affectively prioritizes white faces, Black faces barely register for him as subjects.

The visual evidence of race science gives reassuring authority to Delano's racist sympathies and directs his interactions, while sentiment simultaneously acts as the tool that naturalizes science by allowing its ideological influence almost invisibly to shape "the blunt-thinking American's eyes" (68). His recognition of Black people is contingent upon their being affectable and animated projections of his own feelings. After noting the oakum pickers, with "that first comprehensive glance" that "rested but an instant upon them," he also notices the hatchet polishers, who have "the raw aspect of unsophisticated Africans," and he frames their labors as "the peculiar love in negroes of uniting industry with pastime" (60). The same snap judgment of Delano's first glance on the *San Dominick* combines race science's evaluation of Black inferiority with sentimentality's euphemizing of enslaved labor as a particularly insidious approach to anti-Blackness. Rather than viewing Blackness as evil, Delano's condescending stance reduces Blackness to a benign childlikeness: "There is something in the negro which, in a peculiar way, fits him for avocations about one's person" in subservient roles—something stemming from "the great gift of good-humor" (98). Delano takes as proof the phrenological and craniological "evidences" of racial differentiation and ability, reproducing their sentimental logics. According to the division of the affective and the affectable, these people are suited for servitude due to "the docility arising from the unaspiring contentment of a limited mind, and that susceptibility of bland attachment sometimes inhering in indisputable inferiors," and accordingly sympathetic whites "took to their hearts, almost to the exclusion of the entire white race, their serving men, the negroes" (98). If even depressive types like Samuel Johnson and Cereno can benefit from having their very own enslaved African, Delano muses to himself, how would such an enslaved person "appear to a benevolent one?" (98). For Delano, Babo's attentions to the Spanish captain spring forth from "that affectionate zeal which transmutes into something filial or fraternal acts in themselves but menial; and which has gained for the negro the repute of making the most pleasing body servant in the world" (62). Slavery becomes a mutually beneficial relationship in this mind-set. Despite his origin in free Massachusetts, the northerner Delano's sentiments are akin to those of the southerner George Fitzhugh—who, in his infamous defense of chattel slavery titled *Sociology of the South*, argues: "Slavery opens many sources of happiness and occasions and encourages the exercise of many virtues and affections which would be unknown without it. It begets friendly, kind and affectionate relations."[63] Inasmuch as expressions of feeling are seen as evidence of humanity, recognition for Black people depends upon their emotional labor oriented toward the sustaining of whiteness.

For the American, his fond attachment to the flat visual signification of Black bodies acts as a reminder of nature's racial hierarchies, which constitute the structuring principle of the world he believes in: just seeing a Black person quells his suspicions whenever anything threatens to disrupt his sense of order. In one such moment of anxiety, Delano's observation of an unnamed Black woman and her child cheer him by playing to his sympathies about the proper roles allotted by gender and race. Viewing the two people as "a pleasant sort of sunny sight," he at once dehumanizes and sentimentalizes both bodies through the language of nature in what Coviello calls "a kind of sentimental apotheosis":[64] the woman is "like a doe in the shade of a woodland rock," a "dam," while her child is a "wide-awake fawn" and "its hands, like two paws" while it tries to nurse like a piglet, "its mouth and nose ineffectually rooting to get at the mark; and meantime giving a vexatious half-grunt."[65] Even though a strange man is gawking at her breasts, the woman "started up, at a distance facing Captain Delano," and pretends not to see him, "as if not at all concerned at the attitude in which she had been caught," reinforcing his sense of confident voyeurism as the observer rather than the observed. By showering her child "with maternal transports, covering it with kisses," she elicits a smug sentimental response from the captain who converts Black motherhood into the mammy trope: "There's naked nature, now; pure tenderness and love, thought Captain Delano, well pleased." The scene recalls for us Hartman's insight into the paradox of recognizing the humanity of the enslaved: "This incident prompted him to remark the other negresses more particularly than before. He was gratified with their manners: like most uncivilized women, they seemed at once tender of heart and tough of constitution; equally ready to die for their infants or fight for them. Unsophisticated as leopardesses; loving as doves. Ah! Thought Captain Delano, these, perhaps, are some of the very women whom Mungo Park saw in Africa, and gave such a noble account of. These natural sights somehow insensibly deepened his confidence and ease."[66] This moment is pure embellishment on Melville's part: there is no equivalent encounter with African women or children in the historical Delano's account. While there are hints of the woman's agency in her performance to distract the interloper, Delano views Black maternal love as existing only for his spectatorship and emotional gratification. Respect for Black families goes only so far: during the tale about the fever and lack of water that has devastated those on board, the narrator makes the sly comparison that while "whole families of the Africans" have perished, by contrast "yet a larger number, proportionately, of the Spaniards" have died.[67] When compared to white injury, Black mortality will never be enough to draw white sympathy. Here Melville's addition indicts the overlap between the sentimentalization of slavery and the heteronormative family in such texts as Fitzhugh's, which used the oppressive construction of the domestic sphere to argue for the validation of slavery through the naturalness of familial affection. Fitzhugh claims that slaves "are part of the family, and self-interest and domestic affection combine to shelter, shield and foster them." He later clarifies his opposition to women's rights through recourse to the same truth that "the family government, from its nature, has ever been despotic."[68] The final touch in the passage is Delano's mention of white explorers of Africa like the Scottish Mungo Park and the American John Ledyard, which brings together sentimentalism and ethnographic knowledge through reminders of the transnational scope of systemic anti-Blackness.[69]

THE ANTI-BLACKNESS OF WHITE NOSTALGIA

The subversive performances of the rebel Africans mirrors Delano's expectations of the natural order of those who affect and those who are affectable, in which white people's feelings are coddled by Black emotional labor. The relationship between Babo and Cereno is the exemplar of this sentimental dynamic for Delano: in his sustained reading of the interactions between the two men, the American triangulates his own desire for Black subservience to whiteness through nostalgia for both his personal past and an inherited cultural past, tying together his idyllic New England childhood with the brutality of the Atlantic slave trade. Ann Douglas's influential critique identifies nostalgia as a key component of sentimental discourse: sentimentalism "attempts to deal with the phenomenon of cultural bifurcation by the manipulation of nostalgia," as exemplified by the death of little Eva in *Uncle Tom's Cabin*.[70] The pathologized emotion of nostalgia has been theorized a longing less for a place than for a time: such a desire, according to critics such as Linda Hutcheon and Fredric Jameson, acts as a temporal projection that is always political in its manipulation of history.[71] Bluntly, "nostalgia is history without guilt," according to Michael Kammen.[72]

Delano recognizes Babo's Black face only in relation to Cereno's white one, as a nostalgic reflection of the American's own sense of self in the world. This contrast in perceived physiognomic worthiness reproduces the biopolitical hierarchy of differences in emotional expression and affective agency: Babo's feelings are taken to be of a lower instinctual order, merely reactive and responsive to the governing influence of Cereno's expressions. In Delano's initial encounter with Babo, the latter's visage is rendered as a "rude face, as occasionally, like a shepherd's dog, he mutely turned it up into the Spaniard's," and later, when Delano questions the relationship between Spaniard and African, "Babo, changing his previous grin of mere animal humor into an intelligent smile, not ungratefully eyed his master"—who affirms the man's value to him.[73] The American repeatedly notices Babo's preoccupation with Cereno's face, reading this attention as a slavish attentiveness to Cereno like that of a dog to his owner. This sentimental canine metaphor for the Black man's performance of emotional labor later resurfaces in different reformulations that precipitate the captain's nostalgia for his own childhood. The American associates the incoming boat *Rover* from his ship with recollections of his younger self as "Jack of the Beach" and describes the boat "as a Newfoundland dog" docked by his Duxbury, Massachusetts, home, with its loving loyalty like that of "a good dog; a white bone in her mouth" (91). Only good things happen to good people, Delano reassures himself: "Who would murder Amasa Delano? His conscience is clean." And soon after, he views Babo's emotional performance as external confirmation of his internal affirmation of the moral order. He is "met by Don Benito's servant, who, with a pleasing expression, [was] responsive to his own present feelings," in a physiognomic validation that recalls his earlier reading of Babo's canine devotion to Cereno. But now Delano is acknowledged to have the power of affectability, with the capacity to be an "owner" of both dogs and enslaved peoples.

Childhood memories based upon disavowed Northern anti-Black racism return to more explicitly reinforce Delano's nostalgic associations with Black servitude when he watches Babo shave Cereno: "At home, he had often taken rare satisfaction in sitting in his door, watching some free man of color at his work or play. If on a voyage he chanced to have a black sailor, invariably he was on chatty and half-gamesome terms with him. In fact, like most men of a good, blithe heart, Captain Delano took to negroes, not philanthropically, but genially, just as other men to Newfoundland dogs" (99). Fitzhugh, in his sociological defense of slavery as "healthy, beautiful, and natural," declares: "A man loves not only his horses and his cattle, which are useful to him, but he loves his dog, which is of no use. He loves them because they are his."[74] To the nostalgic American, Babo's solicitous care of Cereno can only be a reflection of loving loyalty like that of a dog's. During dinner, Delano continues to repeatedly view Babo's attention to Cereno in canine terms: "The black was still true to his master, since by facing him he could the more readily anticipate his slightest want," and "he only rested his eye on his master's."[75] The degraded place of Blackness in race science is validated in Delano's structure of feeling as fond nostalgia for his bucolic New England past, a vehicle for his feelings about the natural order that reinforces his own identity in that system. It is little wonder that at one point, despite his upbringing in the free North, Delano tries to purchase Babo for fifty doubloons, to fulfill this fantasy of being pandered to by Black emotional labor for epistemological and ontological affirmation. In this fixation with seeing Babo's face first in orientation to Cereno's and then in relation to his own emotional needs, we can see these readings as iterative reassurances that the expression of Black feelings can exist only for whiteness, warding off the unthinkable possibility of Black self-determination even on the scale of Babo's affective interiority. The Senegalese man is required to be effacing and is himself effaced.

By contrast, Delano continually scrutinizes the subtleties of Cereno's face for deeper meaning and agency because he does not question the validity of the man's affective interiority. During their interactions, Delano is attuned to numerous tics of Cereno's physiognomy such as when his "face lighted up; eager and hectic, he met the honest glance of his visitor" or when "his pale face [appeared] twitching and overcast" (69 and 77). Although many people on the ship desperately clamor for the visitor's attention when he first boards, Delano gravitates to the captain to "[assure] him of his sympathies" (60). As fond as Delano may be of Babo, he never addresses him directly or offers him the same care he repeatedly proffers Cereno, who appears to scorn it. When Delano thinks that Cereno might be treating Babo cruelly, he has a rare negative view of slavery: "Ah, this slavery breeds ugly passions in man.—Poor fellow!" he laments, and he "was about to speak in sympathy to the negro"—only to stop himself and return to his sentimental understanding of the institution, framing it as "a sort of love-quarrel, after all" (103). Unlike the limited affects that Delano can recognize in Babo, Cereno is allowed to display a rich range of emotional expressions that even include the negative—alienating "reserve," "inkept and unknown emotion," "cold constraint"—and still retain the American's sympathies (63, 73, and 79). For instance, after skepticism about the explanation for the sad state of the *San Dominick*, Delano "drown[s] criticism in compassion, after a fresh repetition of his sympathies" to Cereno (69). When the enslaver Aranda is mentioned as a casualty of the supposed fever that took its toll on the ship's populations, Cereno's "heart-broken" air causes Delano to believe that "he divined the cause of such unusual emotion," and he quickly reaffirms his identification with Cereno. The American shares his own loss of a friend at sea: "I think that, by a sympathetic experience, I conjecture, Don Benito, what it is that gives the keener edge to your grief" (71 and 72). Indeed, such "fresh repetition of his sympathies" is repeatedly extended by Delano, regardless of the other man's indifferent expressions or suspicious behavior.

Even when contemplating the possibility of Cereno's mendacity, following the perversity of sentimental race science, Delano views Cereno as superior in all facets to Babo and the other Africans and still finds the former sympathetic. Worried that something undefined is wrong on the *San Domi-*

nick, Delano cannot attribute agency to the Africans: "the whites, too, by nature, were the shrewder race," while the Black people "were too stupid" (88 and 89). Reluctant to concede the possibility of superior Black intellect, Delano prefers to imagine whiteness as villainous rather than viewing it as imperiled. After entertaining the elaborate speculation that Cereno might be an imposter, Delano turns to a physiognomic reading of his fellow captain for reassurance: "Glancing over once more towards his host—whose side-face, revealed above the skylight, was now turned towards him—he was struck by the profile, whose clearness of cut was refined by the thinness incident to ill-health, as well as ennobled about the chin by the beard. Away with suspicion. He was a true offshoot of a true hidalgo Cereno" (76). For Delano, Cereno's face is testimony of his superior breeding as a hidalgo, a member of the Spanish nobility: racial notions of inheritance come into play as phenotype becomes synonymous with character, ability, and morality. More than the supporting evidence supplied by others on the ship, Delano trusts his fellow captain's "very expression and play of every human feature, which Captain Delano saw" and that, to his mind, "seemed impossible to counterfeit" (81). Ultimately, he concludes, "who ever heard of a white so far a renegade as to apostatize from his very species almost, by leaguing in against it with negroes?" (89). Delano's anxieties about the dangerously uncanny sights of the slave ship are relieved by visual reminders of white supremacy.

While Babo's enslavement evokes a personal nostalgia for Delano, the hidalgo Cereno's nobility exemplifies another dimension of nostalgia's idealization that ties the American's experience with domestic chattel slavery to its transnational colonial networks. Cereno's wan refinement speaks to both nostalgia's romanticizing powers and its original medical definition as a wasting disease.[76] Delano sees him as "the Spanish captain, a gentlemanly, reserved-looking, and rather young man to a stranger's eye, dressed with singular richness."[77] Later, he returns to Cereno's attire as a sartorial emphasis of the innate gap between the Spanish captain and the meagerly attired Babo: "The Spaniard wore a loose Chili jacket of dark velvet; white small-clothes and stockings, with silver buckles at the knee and instep; a high-crowned sombrero, of fine grass; a slender sword, silver mounted, hung from a knot in his sash—the last being an almost invariable adjunct, more for utility than ornament, of a South American gentlemen's dress to this hour" (89). The incongruity of his decadent dress complements his aristocratic fragility, making him deserving of Babo's obsequious care: the costume reminds Delano of "the image of an invalid courtier tottering about London in the time of the plague" (68). Delano is able to grasp that the Spanish captain is under some form of duress, an "involuntary victim of a mental disorder," but translates his ailments into a walking diagnosis of the original medical meaning of nostalgia—which also represents the nostalgic past that Delano yearns for: "This distempered spirit was lodged, as before hinted, in as distempered a frame" (63 and 62). The American's attraction to the inequalities of Old World aristocracy is depicted not as hypocrisy, but as the standard exception built into New World democracy: when giving out water, Delano "complied, with republican impartiality as to this republican element, which always seeks one level, serving the oldest white no better than the youngest black; excepting, indeed, poor Don Benito, whose condition, if not rank, demanded an extra allowance" (94). The ironic phrase "republican impartiality as to this republican element" indicts this false egalitarianism: Delano's nostalgic fantasies highlight how American democratic ideals are bound up with transnational histories of the slave trade that cannot be disavowed as the sole responsibility of European nations. His racism is given authoritative weight by visual scientific evidence and is filtered through his desires for both a personal and a cultural past—the romanticized racial hierarchy of genteel servitude and noblesse oblige embodied by the humble Babo and hidalgo Cereno.

The fluid resilience of Delano's racist structure of feeling allows for the creative flexibility of his interpretations of race science even when literally facing the faces that challenge the logics of the systems that justify his bigotry. In addition to Babo in his canine deference, Delano notices only a few named Black characters—including Atufal, who is represented in a way that emphasizes only brute physicality: "the moving figure of a gigantic black" (72). The only Black face Delano lingers on is that of the steward, Francesco, because he is of mixed race: "Captain Delano observed with interest that while the complexion of the mulatto was hybrid, his physiognomy was European—classically so" (104). The disjuncture momentarily throws off Delano's certainty about the visual distinctiveness of racial hierarchy. He struggles to adapt the precepts of his understanding of race science, despite his misgivings about miscegenation: "'Don Benito,' whispered he, 'I'm glad to see this usher-of-the-golden-rod of yours; the sight refutes an ugly remark once made to me by a Barbadoes planter; that when a mulatto has a regular European face, look out for him; he is a devil. But see, your steward here has features more regular than King George's of England; and yet there he nods, and bows, and smiles; a king, indeed—the king of kind hearts and polite fellows.'" He must affirm the inherent superiority of whiteness through the royal association, but when "a regular European face" is cast in darker skin, he must justify Francesco's lowly social position. The result is a compromise:

Delano asserts Francesco's comparative nobility among the enslaved but frames it with the same obligations for racialized emotional labor as "the king of kind hearts and polite fellows." When he asks if Francesco "always proved a good, worthy fellow," Cereno's affirmative answer helps reestablish the physiognomic connection between face and character. Miscegenation, then, for Delano has to be reformulated to fit his preexisting views about race: of course the "mulatto" steward has to be good, "for it were strange, indeed, and not very creditable to us white-skins, if a little of our blood mixed with the African's, should, far from improving the latter's quality, have the strange sad effect of pouring vitriolic acid into black broth; improving the hue, perhaps, but not the wholesomeness." Even though Delano does not want to completely condone miscegenation, to deny Francesco's heritage would mean to surrender a belief in the righteous goodness of the natural order. Thus, he ends up imagining a white version of the one-drop rule that does not allow Francesco to ascend in the racial hierarchy but maintains the American's uninterrupted faith in the white racial superiority's beneficial effect on all aspects of the lower races.

UNSYMPATHETIC BLACKNESS AS REVOLT

The narrative takes a turn when it is revealed that the Africans are no longer cargo, but actually the masters of the slave ship. The revelation of Aranda's skeleton ends this section much as Babo's execution closes the novella. Yet Delano's sentimental dependence on race science is not so easily overcome: the battle does not break his ideology so much as display its persistence. Before returning to his ship, he casts a glance over the slave ship and smiles: he "saw the benign aspect of nature" in the aesthetic charm of the setting sun framing the tableaux of enslavement anchored by "the chained figure of the black" (113). Pleased by this sight, Delano reacts to Cereno's farewell with "instinctive good feeling" (114). He leaves with his affirmed sense of self as sympathetic because of his right feelings toward his fellow captain, even his goodness has not been fully recognized: "a sort of saddened satisfaction stole over Captain Delano, at thinking of the kindly office he had that day discharged for a stranger. Ah, thought he, after good actions one's conscience is never ungrateful, however much so the benefited party may be" (113). This resentment resurfaces in the initial chaos when Cereno makes his frantic escape into the American boat: Delano reverts to his earlier suspicions about the agency of white villainy and Black unthinking subservience. He exclaims that Cereno is a "plotting pirate" and sees Babo's pursuit of his enslaver as "apparent verification" of his perception of the events before him: "the servant, a dagger in his hand, was seen on the rail overhead, poised in the act of leaping, as if with desperate fidelity to befriend his master to the last; while, seemingly to aid the black, the three white sailors were trying to clamber onto the hampered bow. Meantime, the whole host of negroes, as if inflamed at the sight of their jeopardized captain, impended in one sooty avalanche over the bulwarks" (115). Even at this moment, he cannot acknowledge the possibility of Black agency and resistance. The Spanish captain is still understood as the primary agent of the action, while Babo must be responding out of his love for his enslaver. Likewise, the Africans' reaction must be in sympathy with Cereno, and it is framed as an instinct built into their racialized bodies as part of nature's hierarchies of the affective and the affectable.

When "the scales dropped from his eyes" at the last possible moment, Delano finally recognizes Babo as the leader of the revolt rather than a loyal slave, but this revelation does not constitute a break from the American's way of seeing (116). Babo attacks not only the two captains but the literal and figurative heart of this sentimental order: "dagger presented at Captain Delano's heart, the Black seemed of purpose to have leaped there as to his mark" (115). Disarmed by Delano, Babo then switches to a second dagger that he aims "at the heart of his master, his countenance lividly vindictive, expressing the centered purpose of his soul," and here the Senegalese man's face is finally acknowledged but is still read as a transparently legible sign of his limited interiority according to the standards of race science (116). In retaliation, Delano "smote Babo's hand down, but his own heart smote him harder" (116). This successful defense symbolizes Delano's reaffirmation of the sentimental order: "his own heart" is still centered as the valid locus of feeling and action. Delano's sympathies resume unchanged: he acts with "infinite pity" for Cereno's safety (116). The sentimental politics of recognition remains intact, with Black faces still not fully acknowledged: during the ensuing battle the Black rebels' "red tongues lolled, wolf-like from their black mouths" (120). In comparison, similar facial contortions by the white sailors within the same paragraph are described thusly: "the pale sailors' teeth were set" (120). The recognition of agentic and moral capacity is still subjected to the terms of legibility according to race science.

The potency of visual signifiers informed by scientific racism endures with the public presentation of the dead: the skeleton of the white Aranda acts as a rallying spectacle for the Spanish and the Americans alike on the basis of their shared affective identification with whiteness in defense of Black enslavement and the world order it produces. When the conflict between the Africans and the combined forces of the Americans and Spanish begins, Aranda's remains are discovered lashed onto the *San Dominick*: "Suddenly revealing, as the bleached hull swung round towards the open ocean, death for the figurehead, in a human skeleton; chalky comment on the chalked words below, FOLLOW YOUR LEADER" (117). Despite acting as "death for the figurehead," Aranda's bones are not a mere death's head or a skull but an entire skeleton: even in death, the former enslaver has the privilege of not being dismembered down to the singular scientific object of Melville's day. When Cereno cries out at the sight, "'Tis he, Aranda! My murdered, unburied friend!,'" he both identifies and identifies with the man's bones. The skeleton both retains Aranda's individuality and is a memento mori—characterized by the unacknowledged racialized universality that privileges whiteness, even white bones.[78] After the victory of whiteness, the enslaver's remains are given the dignity of burial in the vaults of St. Bartholomew, reflecting the status of their owner when he was alive. For all of Babo's clever control of American racist expectations, the hierarchy according to race science has been reaffirmed by the Africans' defeat by the combined forces of white American and Spanish sailors.

The uprising confirms that the suppression of the specter of racialized disaffection is the condition that sustains white sentimentalism and the biopolitics of feeling. If feeling is the marker of humanity, unfeeling is the abject opposition to that false universalism. Smith's colonial theorization of sympathy expands the moral sentiment from personal virtue to the principle of sociality on a global scale. Unlike the true feelings of white Western peoples, "barbarians, on the contrary, being obliged to smother and conceal the appearance of every passion, necessarily acquire the habits of falsehood and dissimulation. It is observed by all those who have been conversant with savage nations, whether in Asia, Africa, or America, that they are all equally impenetrable, and that, when they have a mind to conceal the truth, no examination is capable of drawing it from them."[79] Frustrated by this recalcitrance, Smith attributes the failings of sympathy and expressiveness to the disaffected peoples of Asia, Africa, and America who are impacted by the violences of colonial projects rather than reconsidering whiteness as the affective universal with the power of recognition over the rest—indeed, the majority—of the world. When Delano first surveys "all the faces" of the *San Dominick*, the narrator relates that upon boarding a ship, "especially a foreign one, with a nondescript crew such as Lascars or Manilla men," the effect of those "strange costumes, gestures, and faces" is enigmatically "unreal."[80] Before the American rests his gaze upon the heads of the elderly Africans, this homogenized history of exploited nonwhite labor—"Lascars or Manilla men" referring to sailors predominantly from India and the Philippines but also including members of other Asian, Arabic, and East African peoples—is an important reference: they are "nondescript," the individuality of character wiped from their faces. Reminders of the global dimensions of dissent against empire and whiteness by Indigenous peoples and peoples of color recur, framing Delano's fear of Black resistance. During his early concerns about deception, he recalls that "Malay pirates" have a reputation for luring foreign ships into their harbors or creating a false display on their decks to entice boarders, "beneath which prowled a hundred spears with yellow arms" (80). Amid the battle of the *San Dominick*, the Ashanti warriors are described as "delirious black dervishes" (116). The fugitives' concerted attack with their hatchets is said to be "Indian-like," perhaps recalling the Indigeneity stripped from these Africans by enslavement (118). Positioned in contrast to the sympathetic Delano—who, as a feeling fellow, sympathizes with Cereno—Babo betrays his obligations to feel for his enslaver and therefore transgresses the terms of recognition: he is unsympathetic. This is a risk that he and the other Africans accept as they take their chance for liberation. The corollary to the uncivilized reactive feelings attributed to racialized and colonized peoples is the paradoxical fear of their affective agency: the fear that, like Babo and his people, underneath the appearance of affectability they might be unfeelingly disaffected from the biopolitics of feeling.

The Legal Politics of Recognition and the Fantasies of Justice

The absence of law seems to typify the encounter between Delano and those onboard the *San Dominick*: the southern coast of Chile is said to be notable for "the lawlessness and loneliness of the spot."[81] The purported "true history of the *San Dominick*'s voyage" claims to emerge through the legal documents compiled, certified, and declared "as much as is requisite in law" by Don José de Abos and Padilla, "His Majesty's Notary for the Royal Revenue, and Register of this Province, and Notary Public of the Holy Crusade of this Bishopric, etc."[82] Melville sets up a sharp contrast between the novella's beginning and ending: opening with a state of nature and closing with the state of law underscored by Babo's execution. However, if we view sentimentalism as a form of governmentality, we can understand this shift as indicating the harmony between the everyday individual politics of recognition, as seen through the sentimental Delano's scientifically informed gaze, and the formal state politics of recognition, which wields juridical authority and violence.

The shadow of the law haunts the entirety of the narrative: critics such as Jean Yellin and Carolyn Karcher have noted how the histories of Black resistance like the Haitian Revolution, the *Amistad* case, and Nat Turner's rebellion inform Melville's writing about Babo's attempted mutiny.[83] The specifics of this legal and political context are inextricable from the novella's serial publication: thanks to Frederick Law Olmsted's editorship, *Putnam's* was the first major national publication to take a stand against slavery. The effects, debates, and activism surrounding the Fugitive Slave Act of 1850 frame the novella: the three parts of *Benito Cereno* published in 1855 appeared alongside several articles about race and slavery, such as pieces on the Kansas-Nebraska Act of 1854 and a review of Frederick Douglass's autobiography.[84] Even Melville himself is implicated since, as aforementioned, his father-in-law, Chief Justice Shaw, upheld the Fugitive Slave Act. The narrative depicts the regulatory formalized violences of the biopolitics of feeling: the legal deposition and ensuing execution of Babo acts as a continuation of, rather than a rupture from, white epistemological mastery that is naturalized and produced through the culture of sentiment. In this light, *Benito Cereno* dramatizes the inherent limitations of the politics of recognition as a tool for social change from the perspective of people like Delano, who through their right feelings enforce the conditions of the institutions that maintain and depend upon Black enslavement and other forms of injustice.

Analyses of the debates about slave law often tend to take as fact the abolitionists' characterization of themselves as right feeling, in contrast to the unfeeling apologists for slavery. The sentimentality of abolitionist novels and rhetoric exemplified by Stowe were seen to combat the coldhearted cruelties of slave law through the appeal to the affective politics of recognition. In his discussion of Stowe and slave law, the legal scholar Alfred Brophy claims that "abolitionists sought a jurisprudence based on love, while the proslavery responders emphasized the role of law in maintaining order."[85] He alludes to the clash between natural and formalist approaches to the law, in which legal formalism's emphasis on the mechanical application of principles in the making of deductive judgments is held to be complicit in the maintenance of the legality of slavery. In his history of American law, Morton J. Horwitz maps the shift from thinking about law in general as the cultural expression of the universal principles of natural law to thinking about legislation as policy that regulates society and governs moral behavior. Legal formalism framed the law through "the appearance of being self-contained, apolitical, and inexorable"—in other words, granting the illusion of objectivity to the legal protection and production of existing social inequalities.[86] Echoes of the construction of scientific objectivity as an apparatus of authority are no mere coincidence: as Horwitz declares, "the attempt to place law under the banner of 'science' was designed to separate politics from law, subjectivity from objectivity, and laymen's reasoning from professional reasoning."[87] Brophy asserts that legal formalism developed from what he condemns as the "cool legal inhumanity" of proslavery discourse: "Where abolitionists believed that emotion might lead one to the correct path, proslavery writers believed that rigorous logic and application of practical morals were necessary. In their opinion, it was logical, dispassionate thought that ensured that best results for society."[88] Likewise, Robert Cover argues that the 1840s and 1850s saw the revanche of formalism in regard to slavery, according to which "the more mechanical the judge's view of the process, the more he externalized responsibility for the result."[89] Sentimentality and sympathy would seem to be the antithesis of proslavery arguments in terms of their connection to the dispassion of legal formalism's prominence.

In its critique of Stowe's call for right feeling, *Benito Cereno* unpacks the congruences between Delano's sentimental belief in the goodness of the natural world as justified by race science and the underacknowledged role of sentimentalism in the defense of the legal institution of slavery exemplified by the Fugitive Slave Act of 1850. Delano's way of seeing, according to Susan Weiner, reflects American legal reasoning insofar as both posit "a realm of knowledge that is objective, clear, and readily accessible."[90] However, this legal knowledge and practice grew out of the culture of sentiment, as Melville was well aware. Merton Sealts lists the 1849 edition of Samuel Warren's *Moral, Social, and Professional Duties of Attorneys and Solicitors* among the books owned and read by Melville.[91] Far from a dispassionate system of rules, in the first lecture collected in his book, Warren positions the legal profession as part of the greater sentimental project of social management. The public's relationship to lawyers is an intimate one: speaking on behalf of the public to the legal profession, Warren says they "open to you the most secret recesses of our hearts," and "to your eyes are exposed hearts bleeding and quivering in every fiber."[92] In response to the needs of the public, lawyers must give "sympathizing words of counsel and guidance" (18). The feelings that animate the law are not cold, but sentiments that refined for the benefit of the sympathetic body of civilized society: "The law is the power by which civil society is constituted, and sustained in existence; overpowering the unruly elements of our fallen nature; with heaven-born energy converting the savage into the citizen" (24). Lawyers are motivated by this higher, inborn emotion: "The love of society, gentlemen, is an original instinct of tendency of our nature," negotiating between private emotion and public sentiments for the greater good (24). Balancing liberty and authority is at the heart of the legal professional's duty. Driven by the "spirit of affection and reverence for our free institutions," lawyers have the authority to negotiate feelings: "Our hearts are trained into a patriotism and loyalty which warm, which enlighten, which strengthen the character, and discipline the will" (28). The modern professional lawyer must discipline his emotions to become an integral part of sentimental society. Moreover, this superior feeling does not obviate law's kinship with science: "the law necessarily and gradually assumes the aspect and acquires the character of a complicated science," and Warren speaks approvingly of the "scientific lawyer" (118 and 33). Much like the scientist's professionalization, that of the American lawyer meant the importance of the sympathetic: the civilized governing of one's own feelings and those of others to regulate the greater society, which affirmed one's biopolitical position as affective rather than affectable.

Although legal formalism was wielded in slavery's favor, apologists for slavery depended just as much as their abolitionist opponents on appealing to the moral and social force of natural law. Recall that in Fitzhugh's sociological study in support of slavery, he uses the law as a metaphor for his sentimental principle: "Love for others is the organic law of our society."[93] The lawyer Thomas R. R. Cobb justifies slave law as the natural law befitting that state of nature proposed by race science. Cobb's *An Inquiry into the Law of Negro Slavery in the United States of America* extensively engages *Types of Mankind* along with the other research done by Morton and his colleagues. Cobb, a future Confederate officer and founder of the University of Georgia School of Law, frames the enslavement of Black people as natural and good through claims that combine concerns for the enslaveds' physical and emotional well-being: "that a state of bondage, so far from doing violence to the law of his nature, develops and perfects it; and that, in that state, he enjoys the greatest amount of happiness, and arrives at the greatest degree of perfection of which his nature is capable. And, consequently, that negro slavery, as it exists in the United States, is not contrary to the law of nature."[94] *Southern Institutes*, by George S. Sawyer, another lawyer, also defends the institution of slavery through the same references to Morton, Nott, and Agassiz, illustrating the marriage of the sentiments of natural law with the justification of legal formalism. Sawyer posits the need of a "philosophy of both the natural and civil law" for organic harmony and order.[95] In a curious approach to precedent and legal formalism, he argues that the place of slavery in the U.S. Constitution and the existence of laws about slavery prove "that the negro race, by universal consent of the civilized, are [sic] considered a separate and distinct race of beings, suited only to their own peculiar state and condition" (201). According to this circular logic, "inferiority is the position in which nature has placed them; and so long as they are in the same community with the whites, laws and institutions necessarily have been, and must be adapted to them in that condition. It is not the statute law that creates slavery, but it is rather an adaptation of itself to the precious condition in which it finds the slave" (233). Support for slavery comes from right feeling—specifically, love for the Union and the nation. Sawyer begins by stating, "It is the duty of every friend of the Union as well as of every true lover of his country, to cast his mite of oil upon the troubled waters" (iv). However, love for the slave is most important: "If there is one spark of true philanthropy, if there is one sincere emotion of friendship and kind regard for the welfare of the slave, known to the Anglo-Saxon race, that exists in its greatest purity and most unalloyed state in the benevolent heart of the Southern master" (224). After relating an anecdote about the tender care given to a dying old slave by his owner, which echoes Delano's desire for the overlap between dogs and Black people, Sawyer compares this "kindred sentiment" to feelings toward "some faithful old dog or horse, that has long since passed his days of usefulness" (226). In contrast to the sympathetic enslavers, Sawyer alleges that the hypocritical North has an "entire want of social sympathy": there is only "cold, distant, and repulsive feeling for the negro race in the free States" (230). References to *Uncle Tom's Cabin* abound in Sawyer's book: after recounting the death of a free Black family by cholera in the North, he asks rhetorically, "But where was [sic] Senator Bird, Honest Old John Van Trompe, Simeon Halliday, Phineas Fletcher, Giddings, and Senator Chase?" (229). Apparently the abolitionists are too busy "transporting Eliza and her little Harry, by underground railroad, to Canada." Insofar as sentimentalism is a technology of biopower, in the struggle over slavery both sides claimed that affective weapon as their own: with the authority of universal feeling at stake, accusations of unfeeling served to invalidate the opponent by denying the recognition of the other's purported right feelings.

However, Delano is from the land of the abolitionists so scorned by Sawyer and Cobb. Melville is attuned to Delano's hypocrisy as a northerner who both fondly reminisces about how in Massachusetts he took "rare satisfaction in sitting in his door, watching some free man of color at his work or play," while earlier having asked to buy Babo for fifty doubloons.[96] Delano complicates any moral righteousness the North might have about slavery and the treatment of Black people. A year before the first installment of *Benito Cereno* appeared in print, the Boston minister Nehemiah Adams published *A South-Side View of Slavery*, a defense of the institution by a northerner that would go through multiple editions. Adams claims to write sympathetically "as a lover and friend of the colored race," structuring the book on his own unfolding experience of staying in the South and based on the question, "How am I to feel and act?"[97] Adams continually emphasizes how the enslavement of Black people inspires sympathy in their enslavers, who "love them greatly and feel an intense desire to protect them" (43). In fact, "Southern hearts and consciences, I felt reassured, were no more insensible than mine. The system had not steeled the feelings of these gentlemen" (69). Chattel slavery is not viewed as an anti-Black system of abuse and degradation, but a sympathetic institution: "good and kind treatment of the slaves is the common law," Adams claims (36). Like many who wrote in favor of slavery, he devotes an entire chapter to criticizing the falseness of *Uncle Tom's Cabin*, and—in a curious affinity with modern antiracist critiques—accuses Stowe of racism in her portrayal of Topsy: "I was angry with myself to find how I had suffered poor Topsy to form my notions of childhood and youth among the slaves" (161). Ironically, *A South-Side View of Slavery* was republished by Ticknor and Fields, the same Boston company that would later reissue *Uncle Tom's Cabin* in 1862. Delano embodies the sentimental hypocrisy of northerners like Adams, a real Massachusetts citizen.

Melville's novella demonstrates this lack of paradox as the constitutive relationship between the everyday legality of the institution of slavery and sentimentalism as articulated by Hartman. After the *San Dominick* is first sighted by Delano, the ship is said to be "a Spanish merchantman of the first class, carrying negro slaves, among other valuable freight"—a description that neatly categorizes the Africans as animate commodities.[98] When Delano rationalizes the apparent unruly state of the ship's passengers, he observes that the *San Dominick* is like "a transatlantic emigrant ship, among whose multitude of living freight are some individuals, doubtless, as little troublesome as crates and bales," while others are more recalcitrant (64). Delano can recognize Babo as a piece of such "living freight," according to the system in which Black bodies are made into fungible property, even while he praises Babo wholeheartedly, telling Cereno, "I envy you such a friend; slave I cannot call him" (67). Thus Adams can declare without a hint of irony that selling human beings is "not a reckless, unfeeling thing" and scorn the phrase "chattel slavery," complaining "it is obvious that this unfeeling law term has no counterpart in [Southern] minds, nor in the feelings of the community in general."[99] Likewise, Sawyer echoes Melville's "crates and bales" comparison: "The idea of a person becoming property, a mere chattel or thing, as a brute, a bale of merchandize [sic] and the like, subject to be bought and sold, is but a fiction of law, for mere form of convenience, that has no counterpart in reality."[100] The body of the slave, Sawyer declares, is "a sacred trust placed in the master's hands by law for their mutual good."[101] Objectification perversely produces humanization: as the novella indicates, it is precisely through the legal degradations of slavery that people such as Adams, Sawyer, and Cobb can view Black people with limited sympathy and even affection.

FUGITIVE FEELINGS / ACTS OF DISAFFECTION AND THE FUGITIVE SLAVE LAW OF 1850

For an enslaved person to escape became not just a matter of the owner's loss of property but a deeply felt personal offense and a threat to the entire biopolitical order validated by race science and slave laws. Once Delano realizes Babo's masquerade, there is no question that the Americans will help the Spanish quell the revolt that threatens them on an existential level. A new term emerges that is inflected by the contemporary legal frame of thinking: fugitivity, a concept that Fred Moten and Stefano Harney associate with Blackness and that defies governmentality.[102] The *San Dominick* becomes the "fugitive ship," while the Africans are parsed as "the fugitives."[103] This framing of the revolt in terms of fugitivity, with even the once-slave ship turned traitor to its original cause, speaks to the compulsion to remand escaped slaves exemplified by the Fugitive Slave Act of 1850. As part of the Compromise of 1850, an attempt to reduce growing antebellum tensions, the act was approved by the House of Representatives in a vote of 109 to 76 and was signed into law by President Millard Fillmore on September 18.[104] The act drew its validation from Article 4, Section 2, Clause 3 of the Constitution, which gave enslavers the right to pursue escaped slaves, as well as the Fugitive Slave Act of 1793, which mandated the surrender and rendition of fugitive slaves to their enslavers.[105] The Fugitive Slave Act of 1850 expanded the previous laws and made them more efficient: Now the law was to be executed by commissioners appointed by U.S. Circuit Courts. Moreover, U.S. marshals were tasked with aiding the commissioners and could be fined a thousand dollars if fugitives were to escape while in their care, and commissioners were incentivized to remand fugitives to owners since they would earn $10 for each fugitive if they did, but only $5 if they did not.[106] As Stephen Middleton puts it, "Federal marshals were thereby made into de facto slave catchers, strategically stationed across the North to act on behalf of slave owners in hunting down runaways."[107] Enslavers were allowed to pursue fugitives with a warrant or even to recapture them without due process. Moreover, marshals and their deputies were authorized "to summon and to call to aid the bystanders, or *posse comitatus* of the county" aid in the recapture of fugitives, and "all good citizens are hereby commanded to aid and assist in the prompt and efficient execution of this law, whenever their services may be required."[108] Both neutrality and resistance are criminalized, for Section 7 of the Fugitive Slave Act of 1850 addresses the possibility that any action would be taken to aid a fugitive or hinder slave catchers: anyone doing so would be punished by a fine of up to a thousand dollars and imprisonment for up to six months.[109] Thus, slave recapture was nationalized as a social duty to maintain peace and cohesion in the Union and, symbolically, in the state of affairs presented as the natural order by the slave laws. Delano does not hesitate in his responsibility to Cereno to recapture people as living property. He even incentivizes his own sailors on this mission as potential commissioners with both money and the economic value of the Africans as freight: the ship "and her cargo, including some gold and silver, were worth more than a thousand doubloons. Take her, and no small part should be theirs."[110]

Seeing the effect of the Fugitive Slave Law of 1850 in *Benito Cereno* further ironizes not just Melville's exploration of the racist complicity of *Uncle Tom's Cabin*'s sentimentality but also his own uncomfortable proximity with what Brook Thomas describes, in his discussion of Melville and the law, as "a way of thinking shared by many people in power during the antebellum period."[111] As noted above, Melville's father-in-law, Lemuel Shaw, upheld the institution of slavery. The links between Melville and Shaw were familial as well as financial: Shaw became Melville's father's friend in 1820 and was engaged to Melville's aunt before her untimely death; Melville married Shaw's daughter in 1847; Shaw gave Melville loans and financial advice for travel as well as a New York City residence in 1847 and a farm in Pittsfield, Massachusetts, in 1850; Melville borrowed books from the Boston Athenaeum through Shaw's library membership there; and Shaw helped Melville find work and supplied him with introductions to people abroad in 1849.[112] Critics such as Steven Winter read Melville's writings like *Billy Budd* as an indictment of his father-in-law's profession: according to Winter, Melville "well understood what kind of man his father-in-law, the revered judge, really was. He was an exceedingly ugly man."[113] Cover also assesses Shaw in light of *Billy Budd*, but he may overstate Shaw's abolitionist leanings when discussing his decision to uphold the Fugitive Slave Law: "The effort cost Shaw untold personal agony" in this "horrible conflict between duty and conscience."[114] By way of contrast, the constitutional legal historian Leonard Levy claims that "there is nothing in the cast of the man's [Shaw's] mind, temperament, or associations suggesting that his judicial obligation to enforce Congressional law necessarily conflicted with his personal opinions."[115] Nonetheless, whatever reservations Melville had about his generous father-in-law, the dedication of *Typee*, his first novel, reads: "To Lemuel Shaw, Chief Justice of the Commonwealth of Massachusetts, this little work is affectionately inscribed by the author."[116] The complicities of the biopolitics of feeling are intimate.

Shaw's moderate antislavery writings demonstrate the negotiation of the right kind of feelings for the right kind of people that ultimately would not challenge the system of chattel slavery.[117] I view two of Shaw's public writings cited by Levy as the primary examples of Shaw's antislavery thought, which emphasized moderation, national security, and gradualism. In his June 11, 1811, address to the powerful Humane Society of Massachusetts—a body of distinguished doctors, lawyers, and ministers founded in 1791—Shaw praises the members' philanthropic efforts, which are "interwoven with the best and strongest feelings of [their] hearts."[118] He admires their "proudest triumphs to [sic] science," but his speech focuses on "the moral views, to the benign influences on the heart" (6). Shaw appeals to the shared mission of universal sympathy that draws these men esteemed by society together for the sake of humanity: "How beneficial an exercise of the heart, to cherish and invigorate that powerful principle of universal sympathy, which, originating in the tenderest affections of domestic life, embraces at length in the arms of its charity, every individual of the human race?" (7). The human race is differentiated according to degrees of "moral excellence" that raise the civilized man "in the scale of being, little lower than the angels," as opposed to "in the dust with the brutes" (9). The "brutes" are not explicitly identified, but the divide between affective and affectable is clear. Shaw turns to the abolition of the British slave trade as his first example of the moral development of mankind: he frames the fight for abolition as a battle against "the power of interest, of prejudice, of corruption, to darken the mind, and paralize [sic] the feelings, of an enlightened, liberal, and benevolent community," but now "better principles have been diffused, and better feelings impressed" (11). Fighting for the "righteous cause of the injured African" reflects "infinite honor, not only to its advocates but to human nature"—with no recognition of the particulars of Black experiences, well-being, or self-determination (11). Shaw asserts that the names of William

Wilberforce and Thomas Clarkson will be "remembered and repeated, in the peaceful villages of Africa, until her native sons shall learn to emulate the virtues, whilst they aspire to the attainments of such illustrious men"—but, of course, these iconic abolitionists were white Englishmen, and Shaw makes nary a mention of the ongoing efforts by Black and white abolitionists in his own country (12). In fact, the speech avoids any mention of slavery and abolition in the United States. Abolition was not about Black emancipation: Black suffering is seen as an occasion for the exercise of white virtues to affirm that those civilized white men are sympathetic. Following the biopolitics of feeling, there was a distinct limit to the Humane Society's universal sympathy: abolition was not a cause they supported.

In his 1820 "Slavery and the Missouri Question," published in the *North-American Review*, Shaw claims to deplore the American slave trade while simultaneously complaining that critiques of the domestic institution of anti-Blackness by outsiders "wound our feelings."[119] He calls for a moderate, gradualist approach to accommodate the sensitivity of white feelings that must be centered at the expense of Black suffering: "Slavery, though a great and acknowledged evil, must be regarded, to a certain extent, as a necessary one, too deeply interwoven in the texture of society to be wholly or speedily eradicated" (138). According to Shaw, there is a correct emotional stance for approaching the topic: "It should be approached with great calmness and good temper, with great firmness of purpose, with pure, enlightened, and benevolent feelings; but at the same time with that sober and discriminating benevolence, which regards not merely absolute right, but attainable good, and which in the eager pursuit of a desirable end, will not blindly overlook the only practicable means of arriving at it" (138). He calls upon the members of his audience to affirm themselves as those affective, civilized individuals on the top of the human hierarchy, adopting a milquetoast ethical orientation toward chattel slavery that would not disrupt the system they benefit from. Despite inveighing against the Atlantic slave trade as a "continued series of crimes," this man of allegedly superior sympathies claims that domestic chattel slavery is a separate issue and subject to states' rights (141). As for addressing the circumstances of free Black people, he basically shrugs his shoulders. Segregation arises due to policy and history, but also to "impassable barriers, by mutual and long cherished feelings of contempt, detestation, and revenge"—as if Black dissatisfaction and anger were equally responsible for upholding systemic racism (158). In fact, Shaw's 1849 decision in *Roberts v. The City of Boston* would be cited as precedent in no less a decision than the landmark *Plessy v. Ferguson* ruling that legitimized racial segregation.[120] For a model for Delano, Melville had to look no further than to his father-in-law, who provided an example of the sentimental hypocrisies of Northern racism.

Legal formalism's illusion of self-contained inevitability washes Shaw's hands of personal culpability in his decision to uphold the Fugitive Slave Law of 1850—a decision that validated sentimentalism's biopolitics and propagated it as objective reality. Likewise, the purported truths of the legal deposition in *Benito Cereno* retroactively authenticate the ideological foundation of Delano's conviction in "good nature": the legal documents are said by the narrator to be "the key to fit into the lock of the complications which precede it."[121] The deposition takes over the narrative, with Melville reproducing the dry style of the excerpts in the original Delano's memoir, with their performance of distanced objectivity. The document reconstructs the events for the historical record: the deposition recounts and authenticates the slave revolt from the white perspective, revealing Babo's agency and leadership in the mutiny only to vilify both him and his people. Even though Delano's perception of the *San Dominick* was wrong, his authority remains and his worldview is confirmed through the document's affirmation. As Dennis Pahl comments, the deposition "epitomizes the entire history in the way it tries to totalize events while at the same time revealing its own particular violences."[122] This official history mimics the role of precedent in legal decisions: both affirm a particular take on the present through the citation of an authoritative past and thereby structure the future. The conclusions drawn and the resulting verdict only confirm what was already known about the place of white mastery and Black subservience. Melville's use of these documents, as Weiner observes, reflect how his contemporary society "used the law to reinforce the already established fact of slavery."[123] The dry deposition dominates the end of the novella with its importance and length, reflecting the overbearing role of the juridical that has such necropolitical power over the enslaved. Chattel slavery's ongoing violent histories are sanitized as the legal status quo.

Through the deposition we can track the workings of the state apparatuses behind the official politics of recognition, whereas we have to read against the grain to understand Black agency. Here, the law and science serve as twin authorities: the documents open with Cereno's account as deponent—paired with the certification of the royal notary "as much as is requisite in law"—and they close with the authenticating signature not of the Spanish captain but of Doctor Rozas, who has Cereno under his care at the Hospital de Sacerdotes.[124] The conversion of Aranda's skeleton into the substitute figurehead of the ship becomes evidence of the depravity of the Black fugitives' attempted subversion of the moral and natural order. Secure in his beliefs about that order of affectability, Aranda had assured his friend Cereno that the 160 African men, women, and children did not need to be locked up in the hold or fettered because "they were all tractable" (122). Seven days later he learned that the Black people he had enslaved did possess agency. While in the original text the enslaver Aranda is thrown overboard by the people he tried to own as property, Melville's story takes a different approach: "the Negro Babo stopped them, bidding the murder be completed on the deck before him, which was done, when by his orders, the body was carried below, forward" (125). Cereno begs to know the fate of the corpse but remains ignorant until the fourth day, when "the Negro Babo showed him a skeleton, which has been substituted for the ship's proper figurehead" of Christopher Columbus (126). The fictional Babo's ingenious revision of colonial history and its violences challenges the order of white supremacy. In his influential postcolonial reading, Eric Sundquist describes this display as "the entire story of New World history told from the European American point of view—that is stripped down to the rudiments of its own carnage: the master becomes the sacrificial emblem of his own vicious system of power."[125] Babo's treatment of Aranda's bones plays with race science's relationship to visual culture and affective racial identification: starting with Cereno, Babo asks each member of the crew "whose skeleton that was, and whether, from its whiteness, he should think it a white's."[126] His query reverses race science's logic, with essential interiority embodied by the bones that now reflect the absent externalization of face and dermis as differentiated signifier of racial identity and humanity. Babo's threat hinges on using these sentimental logics of recognition: unless the Spaniards help the Africans, they "shall in spirit, as now in body, follow [their] leader" (126). In response, "each Spaniard covered his face," a gesture confirming racial physiognomic recognition (126).[127] Babo's subversive parody as portrayed the legal deposition, however, serves as part of the official case for his death sentence because he defied the basis of Western civilization. During the subsequent battle, Aranda's skeleton becomes resignified as a positive locus for right feeling to inspire right action: his white skeleton is viewed as "beckoning the whites to avenge it."[128] The victory of the whites on the high seas and in court acts as moral and legal recognition that the natural order that privileges whiteness was justly maintained, while Black agency is recognized only through condemnation.

SYMPATHETIC BENITO CERENO, UNSYMPATHETIC BABO, AND THE QUESTION OF JUSTICE

Thanks to the juridical apparatus of the biopolitics of feeling, justice is served and Delano feels justified. Through the lens of the law, the story of the *San Dominick* and its passengers becomes disciplined into linearity and legibility: "Hitherto the nature of his narrative, besides rendering the intricacies in the beginning unavoidable, has more or less required that many things, instead of being set down in the order of occurrence, should be retrospectively, or irregularly given; this last is the case with the following passages which will conclude the account."[129] Like the order of the story, Delano's sense of order is also restored. In the original Delano's account, Cereno is ungrateful to the American and avoids him after the *San Dominick* incident: part of the historical legal proceedings address the Spanish captain's refusal to pay for services rendered by the Americans and Delano's need to prove his good character in court. Although in pursuit of what he views as his rightful monetary reward, the real Delano records in his *Narrative* that he intervened in the affairs of the slave ship *Tryal* "from pure motives of humanity."[130] Melville's retelling changes these events to maintain his focus on the transnational solidarity of sentimental white supremacy. In the novella, the triangulation of white sympathetic recognition has been renewed and completed: Delano and Cereno are united in friendship as fellow white men—"their fraternal unreserve in singular contrast with former withdrawments"—thanks to their shared fight against the antagonist Babo, the specter of unsympathetic Blackness (352). Perversely, the reinstitution of Black social death and the assurance of Babo's death provide the basis for their shared social life. When Cereno lauds him for his bravery, Delano replies, "Yes, all is owing to Providence, I know; but the temper of my mind that morning was more than commonly pleasant, while the sight of so much suffering, more apparent than real, added to my good-nature, compassion, and charity, happily interweaving the three" (136). The self-righteous Delano dubs himself a philanthropist to his fellow white man and finally receives the full recognition he felt he deserved for his right feelings. He has not given up on his sentimental frame of mind, but he finds another way to justify his perspective on the world as truth: "Besides, those feelings I spoke of enabled me to get the better of momentary distrust, at times when acuteness might have cost me my life, without saving another's" (57). Although his perceptions of the *San Dominick* were false, this is no epistemological break for him: he embraces his ignorance as his innocence, for justice according to the law of nature has been served.

Cereno's excessive sense of having been wronged by Babo follows from this triumph of sentimentalism: he has been marked by his experience of a brief reversal of the expectations of affectability and must affirm himself as affective. He fixates on his persecution, consolidating Delano's sympathy: "Again and again, it was repeated, how hard it had been to enact the part forced on the Spaniard by Babo" (135). He notes that his "heart was frozen" when he was worried about Delano's safety and his own, thanks to Babo's undermining of the sentimental conventions inscribed by anti-Blackness (136). After Babo's failed murder attempt with the dagger, Cereno "refused to move, or be moved, until the negro should have been first put out of view" (117). Once freed from the Black man's influence, Cereno exercises his affective authority to erase Babo from his vision without even having to take direct action. Nonetheless he has been affected to the point of ill-health, simply naming "The negro" as the cause of his affliction (117). Despite having all his structural privileges restored, he languishes like the wan aristocrat he is: at the tribunal he is unable to look at Babo and faints. Cereno indulges his sense of victimization to the point of his own demise: he dies a wasting death, which, according to sentimental genre conventions, was the fate of those poor souls too good for this world. Thus, he characterizes himself as a sympathetic victim and Babo as an unsympathetic villain, despite the actual power dynamics of enslavement and Cereno's role in condemning the Black man to death.

Babo's postmortem beheading (the result of a lawful execution) functions as the abject racial reversal of Aranda's death (an obscene murder). While both remains are publicly displayed to terrorize their respective racial communities with the consequences of following their leader, one can compare the divergences between white and racialized bodies in their postmortem treatment and attendant visual signification: Babo's "body was burned to ashes," leaving only his head, while Aranda's intact "recovered bones" rest in peace (137). Placing Babo's head on a pole, "that hive of subtlety," in part reflects the phrenological fetishization of the head as the material object of visual analysis. As the narrative emphasizes, the African's "brain, not body, had schemed and led the revolt."

Babo's severed head leads the reader back to the multivalent violences of race science: one can trace the shift from living face to mute head to eventual skull specimen. In her study of race science's obsession with heads, Ann Fabian points out the contemporaneous correlation between Nat Turner's rebellion, during which "slaveholders executed suspected plotters and stuck their heads on stakes" as warnings, and Morton's skull collection for *Crania Americana*, which included "heads of African tribal leaders who led a bloody resistance to settlement on their lands by former American slaves" plucked from their stakes in Liberia for scientific research.[131] The authoritative science that informs Delano's gaze and confirms his racial prejudices is based on empirical data wrested from exhumed bodies of peoples of color and is a product of national and colonial projects. Among Morton's careful descriptions of each skull's origins, we find one "remarkably characteristic Indian head" that belonged to a Seminole warrior killed during the Second Seminole War, which was ongoing during and after the publication of *Crania Americana*.[132] Like Shaw's decision to remand Sims to slavery through a retreat to legal formalism, the purported objectivity of science attempts to sanitize the means of its own production and its resulting effects. Melville's novella returns context to the effects of race science on the American way of looking, reminding us that representative violence is inevitably linked to other national and transnational forms of brutality.

In contrast to abolitionist arguments for feeling as a weapon against unfeeling scientific and legal institutional oppressions, Melville's *Benito Cereno* reveals to us how both disciplines were imbricated in the nineteenth-century culture of sentiment as part of the biopolitics of feeling. The ironic narrative focus on Delano illustrates how the American's racism is justified by contemporary science and law but naturalized by love, not hate. Despite Delano's failings, the order of his world is restored: he has been affirmed in his sense of self as sympathetic in a world that is sympathetic to his whiteness.

The Babo Problem / Unthought, Unfeeling

"Babo is the most heroic character in Melville's fiction," writes C. L. R. James. "He is a man of unbending will."[133] Babo is "unbending" in defiance of the demands of his affectability. In contrast to his show of tractable deference on the *San Dominick*, Babo becomes a figure of complete withholding: "Seeing all was over, he uttered no sound, and could not be forced to. His aspect seemed to say, since I cannot do deeds, I will not speak words."[134] To the question of "How it feels to be a problem?," Du Bois responds much like Babo, "I answer seldom a word."[135] The narrative cannot comprehend that his choice to be unmoving is his defiant noncompliance with the system of affectability that would recognize him only through animatedness for the benefit of whiteness: after failing to kill the captains, Babo's action is represented as having "at once yielded to the superior muscular strength of his captor."[136] Until the end, he will not submit to the sentimental demands of the politics of recognition because he knows that under this system any expression, no matter how heartfelt, cannot earn him sympathy: he remains "voiceless" and has to be "dragged to the gibbet" as a final gesture of physical noncompliance.[137] It is only as an object that he, as a decapitated head, can be finally recognized as returning the white gaze: "The body was burned to ashes; but for many days, the head, that hive of subtlety, fixed on a pole in the Plaza, met, unabashed, the gazes of the whites; and across the Plaza looked towards St. Bartholomew's church, in whose vaults slept then, as now, the recovered bones of Aranda; and across the Rimac bridge looked towards the monastery, on Mount Agonia without; where three months after being dismissed by the court, Benito Cereno, borne on the bier, did, indeed, fellow his leader."[138] "The history of blackness is testament to the fact that objects can and do resist," Moten famously declares.[139] In the final long sentence of the novella, with its multiple clauses, the narrator tracks Babo's gaze across space and time to show that it is directed at his former enslaver Cereno—whose death three months later closes the narrative. Babo's "unabashed" expression signals the rebel's final fugitive performance of unfeeling as refusal to accept the criminalization of Blackness—which I suggest is part of what Koritha Mitchell calls a critical demeanor of shamelessness produced by Jim Crow lynching and modern mass incarceration.[140] The ambiguity of the last noun combined with the ordering structure of the clauses implies the Senegalese man's deadly power to affect, even when he is demoted in death to an unmoving object in the biopolitical hierarchy of feeling and animacy. If Aranda's bones were able to rally Spanish and Americans across national difference through a shared sympathy for whiteness, who might be inspired by Babo's unsympathetic Blackness and, perhaps, be sympathetic? We are told only about the whites who bear witness to the spectacle of the execution and its morbid aftermath.

The novella leaves us with this unanswered question and the marked absence of any potentially sympathetic people, Black or otherwise. Yet the city of Lima had a robust Afro-Peruvian population, and Babo's gaze over the Rimac looks toward the San Lázaro district, the majority of whose population historically consisted of Indigenous and Black peoples.[141] According to Saidiya Hartman and Frank B. Wilderson III, "On the one hand, the slave is the foundation of the national order, and, on the other, the slave occupies the position of the unthought."[142] Unfeeling may be considered kin to the unthought. In his adaptation of the original Delano's account, Melville writes a narrative that can be considered as aligned with an Afropessimist take on the totalizing negation of Black affects and, in turn, Black sociality: the novella downplays or omits the Black women, men, and children who could feel otherwise about Babo's final defiance. According to the historical account of the revolt, Babo was not the one executed: the real Babo died during the battle, and it was his son, Mure, who was hanged and beheaded, along with four others, for acting "as captain and commander of them."[143] This Babo was indeed "the ring leader," but he shared this role with his son, who took on "the appearance of the submission of the humble slave" to monitor Cereno during Delano's visit (335 and 338). Melville's Babo is severed from his familial ties and collaborators. The story also erases the enslaved Black women and children who were forced to be present at the execution: the sentence passed on March 2, 1805, stated that "the negresses and young negroes of the same gang shall be present at the execution, if they should be in that city at the same time thereof" (quoted on 347). The centrality of Black women's contributions to resistance to the Atlantic slave trade on ships has been elided. As the historian Jane Landers argues, the archive shows that revolts were more likely to occur the greater the number of women were aboard.[144] Both the real and fictional legal documents hint that these women played a greater role in the uprising than explicitly acknowledged: they are said to be "knowing to the revolt" and to have influenced the deaths of their enslavers, including Aranda, and during the battle they "sang melancholy songs" to motivate their men.[145] These events do not enter the narrative proper because they were not witnessed by the white characters: Melville adds in the deposition that "all this is believed, because the negroes have said it." These women remain unnamed in both the historical and literary accounts, falling below the threshold of recognition given to their male counterparts as disaffected insurgents. Black social death is inexorable: Melville's Babo dies alone, denied any vestige of sympathy and sociality.

In adapting the historical record, *Benito Cereno* enacts the erasure of alternative racialized structures of feeling, banished as "unfeeling" and outside the category of the universal human that, as Wynter and da Silva have shown, is founded upon the abjection of Blackness. This is a world governed by white feelings that will not and cannot recognize or tolerate racialized affects that fall outside dominant structures of feeling. Liberation for Babo and the other Africans, however, meant their disaffected defiance of these structures of feeling and therefore their risking illegibility as feeling. Here we must acknowledge the unsettling dynamic of such a narrative, which anticipates something akin Afropessimism in its reading of the world as it is: Melville critiques the conditional sympathy granted Black people and the deadly consequences to unsympathetic Blackness as the negation on which the "figure of the human" depends, but he accepts that foreclosure. He does not speculate about what affects, actions, and imaginings could emerge from the radical choice to feel otherwise in such a world. In the following chapter I read Martin Delany's *Blake; or the Huts of America* for an exploration of those possibilities—an exploration that refuses to accept that world as the only world—and the alternative structures of feeling that could lead toward a new world for Black, Indigenous, and other peoples of color.

FEELING OTHERWISE /

Martin R. Delany, Black-Indigenous
Counterintimacies, and the Possibility of a New World

UNSYMPATHETIC BLACKNESS CHALLENGES the sentimental biopower of the global order. Like Herman Melville, Martin Robinson Delany indicts the legacy of Harriet Beecher Stowe's sentimentalism and the world it sustains. "He wrote, that is to say, from Babo's point of view," says Eric Sundquist of the early Black nationalist thinker's only novel.[1] Where Melville's Babo dies alone, however, Delany's Blake triumphs through community. I shift from Melville's retelling of a failed slave revolt to Delany's speculations about revolution, treating the two works as counterpoised explorations of unsympathetic Blackness. While for Melville Black feelings are unrecognizable and unrepresentable as the consequence of the Africans' rebellion against affectability, in *Blake; or the Huts of America* Delany imagines the ways in which turning away from white feelings makes possible a Black-led transnational insurgency of disaffected peoples of color.[2] Whereas Melville hinted at broader global anticolonial sentiments, Delany brings together Blackness and Indigeneity to think about emancipation and decolonization together as a way to transform the world.

Uncle Tom's Cabin is "the *master book* of the nineteenth century," declares Frederick Douglass to the readers of his namesake newspaper in the March 4,

1853, article "A Day and a Night in *Uncle Tom's Cabin*."[3] Douglass praises Stowe's sentimental novel for its successful appeal to universal feeling: "The word of Mrs. Stowe is addressed to the soul of universal humanity. That word, bounded by no national lines, despises the limits of Sectarian sympathy, and thrills the universal heart."[4] Martin R. Delany, his former collaborator, was less sympathetic to Stowe: Delany's response was a scathing letter printed in *Frederick Douglass' Paper* that lambasted *Uncle Tom's Cabin* as representative of the failures of white sentimental politics.

Delany's and Douglass's ensuing epistolary debate, published over a few months in *Frederick Douglass' Paper*, is considered by scholars like Richard Yarborough and Robert Levine to be representative of persistent disagreements among Black thinkers about literary and political tactics.[5] Citing Douglass's piece and an anonymous article published in the same month that Delany saw as deferring to Stowe's authority, Delany's letter makes clear his view of the authors' approach: "Now I simply wish to say, that we have always fallen into great errors in efforts of this kind, going to others than the *intelligent* and *experienced* among *ourselves*; and in all due respect and deference to Mrs. Stowe, I beg leave to say, that *she knows nothing about us*, 'the Free Colored people of the United States,' neither does any other white person—and, consequently, can contrive no successful scheme for our elevation; it must be done by ourselves."[6] Who might be "the intelligent and experienced" individual from the Black community who could contrive a successful scheme for elevation and yet who has been otherwise ignored by their people? The implication is that it is Delany himself. His political tract *The Condition, Elevation, Emigration, and Destiny of the Colored People of the United States* (hereafter, *Condition*) was published in the same year as *Uncle Tom's Cabin* (1852) but received a fraction of the attention, accolades, and sales garnered by Stowe's novel.[7] Perhaps particularly galling for Delany was that *Condition*—unlike *Uncle Tom's Cabin*—did not even earn a review in *Frederick Douglass' Paper*. Douglass's subsequent letter defends Stowe and resurrects that slight: Delany's book, writes Douglass, "leaves us just where it finds us, without chart or compass, and in more doubt and perplexity than before we read it."[8] In a racialized clash of literary genres, a white woman's sentimental novel that invokes white sympathy trumped a Black man's political tract about Black self-determination. In an April 15 letter titled "Uncle Tom," Delany accuses Stowe of profiteering from the real experiences of the enslaved by borrowing from slave narratives, including Douglass's. Delany cites Stowe's *Key to Uncle Tom's Cabin* to mention her inspiration for the titular Tom, Reverend Josiah Henson, and proposes that the original publisher of Stowe's novel, Jewett and Company, should pay Henson royalties because of the profits extracted from "this good old man, whose *living testimony* has to be brought to sustain this great book."[9] Much like his fungibility under chattel slavery, Henson is a fungible literary resource. To Delany, white sentimentalism acts as another apparatus for the extraction of value from Black people.

Overlooked in this iconic debate is the moment when Delany shifts from a discussion of sympathy across a Black-white binary of racial difference to discussing a comparative framework that includes Blackness alongside Indigeneity. In his following April 18 letter, "Mrs. Stowe's Position," he elaborates upon his original assertion of Stowe's ignorance of Black people, admitting that his comment was "ironical" but maintaining that white people "know nothing, comparatively, about us."[10] After listing other initiatives by Stowe in the name of Black elevation that would only reaffirm white supremacy, he recounts this tale:

> There is an old American story about an Indian and a white man, hunting game together; when they shot wild turkeys and buzzards, agreeing to divide, taking bird about; the white huntsman being the *teller*. In counting, the white man would say, alternately taking up either bird, "turkey for *me*, and buzzard for *you*—buzzard for *you*, and turkey for *me*." He growing tired of that method of counting the game, soon accosted his friend: "Uh! how's dis? All *buzzard* for me; but you never say, *turkey* for me, once." I feel somewhat as this Indian did; I am growing weary of receiving the *buzzard* as our share, while our tellers get all the *turkeys*. That "is not the way to 'tell' it" to me.[11]

The dualities of Indigenous-settler and Black-white are distinct but overlap. Delany identifies himself and, by association, other discontented Black Americans, with the frustrated unnamed Indian who is relegated to an abstract past: hunting game analogizes the problems of American nation building, in which cooperative ventures with white friends reproduce structural inequality. His decolonial critique of the "old American story" is Delany's only turn to narrative as a rhetorical strategy in his arguments. He rejects what the white "teller" has to say, strongly implying that he will be the one to "tell it" as "it" should be told. I see this instance as a transitional moment between his political and scientific writings and his only turn to fiction—his novel *Blake; or, the Huts of America*, which constitutes his "telling" response to Stowe's story of Black experience and white sympathy in *Uncle Tom's Cabin*.

What I want to highlight is the crucial role of Delany's unnamed Indian in this neglected anecdote that lays the groundwork for his later novel: "I feel somewhat as this Indian did," he writes. With this phrase he retheorizes Adam Smith's Enlightenment formulation of the "fellow-feeling" of sympathetic identification as the affective basis for societies, thereby defining the difference between civilized nations and those "savage nations, whether in Asia, Africa, or America."[12] Through the distancing of Delany's simile, there is no attempt to lay claim to experience or "situation" and "same torments," whereas Smith imagines that "we enter as it were into his body, and become in some measure the same person with him."[13] Rather, Delany's "feel somewhat" conveys a dynamically ambivalent negotiation between the mutuality and incommensurability of *feeling through and with* the relations of situatedness.[14] To build upon Lisa Lowe's insights about the nonequivalent structural violences that constitute modernity, the abjection of Black and Indigenous feelings as unfeeling produced the affective intimacies of the Western liberal subject universalized as Smith's "fellow-feeling."[15] The function of the phrase in Delany's narrative is to center the racial dynamics of feeling between disaffected Black and Indigenous peoples, dissociating the dynamics from the right feelings of white people that are held up as the universal basis of sociality and citizenship. This sentiment bears an anticipatory resemblance to the scholar Tiffany King's description of her affective responses when she witnessed the toll of dispossession on Indigenous feminists while also feeling the legacies of Black enslavement: convergence without conflation.[16] These cross-racial counterintimacies between Black people and Indigenous peoples present an alternative, untold narrative to the story told by white America: if associations with whiteness reinscribe the hegemonic biopolitics of feeling, what could emerge from affirming a Black-Indigenous coalition? Unlike in his allegory, in the novel *Blake*, Delany does not leave "this Indian" to vanish in the abstract past: he confronts the contemporary dimensions of the ongoing dispossession of Indigenous peoples with specific reference to the Choctaw to expand upon the subversive potential within the affective, political attachments of "feeling somewhat as this Indian."

However, this exemplar of anticolonial counterintimacies features only men. Delany pleads, "Believe me when I tell you, that I speak it as a son, a brother, a husband and a father; I speak it from the consciousness of oppressed humanity, outraged manhood, of a degraded husband and disabled father; I speak it from the recesses of a wounded bleeding heart—in the name of my wife and children, who look to me for protection, as the joint partner of our humble fireside."[17] In this passage Delany reworks the terms of white domestic sentimentalism into Black patriarchal sentimentalism. He claims not to have read Stowe's novel: "I am not competent to judge, not having as yet *read Uncle Tom's Cabin, my wife* having *told* me the most I know about it."[18] (Levine, for one, is skeptical of this assertion, pointing out Delany's extensive knowledge of the book during this exchange.)[19] Here Delany's wife, Catherine, acts as a symbolic buffer between his "outraged manhood" and *Uncle Tom's Cabin*'s sentimentality. Delany's performance of his ignorance, whether real or symbolic, suggests that his wife is more affectable and more vulnerable to possible corruption by the novel he so disdains. Although Delany proclaims that Catherine is his "joint partner" and calls elsewhere for Black women's education, scholarly evaluations suggest a different reality. Levine accuses Delany of burdening Catherine with all domestic responsibilities while he traveled for his career and points to gendered correlations between masculinity and freedom throughout Delany's writings that implicitly devalue women.[20] Black women are politically suspect: in his epistolary exchange with Douglass, Delany uses the free Black singer Eliza Greenfield, who was under the control of a racist white manager, as his example of Black susceptibility to internalizing self-hatred.[21] In short, according to Paul Gilroy, Delany holds the dubious distinction of being "the progenitor of black Atlantic patriarchy."[22] In wresting the power of feeling away from Stowe's abolitionism, Delany replaces a white feminized sentimentalism with a Black masculinized model that leaves little space for Black women.

Delany's reworking of sentimental discourses has been understood as central to his Black political enterprise, which was based upon science. He affirms Black self-love and science together as fundamental to racial uplift, cohering communities, and reconfiguring ideals of belonging for Black people. Along with other Black practitioners of science, the charismatic thinker knew that, like the sentimental race scientists implicated by Melville, science's biopolitical power came not so much from the ideal of cold impersonal objectivity but from the social relationalities of affect. Reading Delany in conjunction with the Negro Convention movement, Glenn Hendler notes that Delany's concept of citizenship rearticulates the conditions of public sentiment and scientific ideas of race for a new counterpublic.[23] His work is part of what Britt Rusert has identified as the tradition of "fugitive science," the Black praxis of "minor" science, in the sense of Gilles Deleuze and Félix Guattari's minor literatures that can challenge racism and its institutions.[24] Delany was among the first three Black students to be accepted to Harvard Medical College, after having previously been refused admission to several other medical schools.[25] However, Harvard's liberal progressiveness reached its limit in the midst of the furor around the Fugitive Slave Act: Delany's fellow students successfully petitioned to have him and his fellow Black students dismissed from the school. Dean Oliver Wendell Holmes complied, forcing Delany, Daniel Laing Jr., and Isaac H. Snowden to withdraw without earning their degrees.[26] The fall of 1850 saw the passage of the Fugitive Slave Act combined with Delany's ignoble dismissal from Harvard, a moment that Levine identifies as triggering Delany's "large-scale disillusionment with white abolitionists."[27] Yet while this precipitated Delany's disgust with the law as symbolic of the flawed status quo, his connection to science only deepened with his growing sense of its relationship to race and power. Indeed, his writings demonstrate that the political stance of unsympathetic Blackness means not the repudiation of feelings, but the recalibration of the racial politics of affect.

With a focus on Black-Indigenous counterintimacies, this chapter proposes to take seriously that feeling otherwise enables the conditions for imagining otherwise. By repudiating the expressive and responsive demands of affectability that undergird white sympathies, Delany calls for unfeeling toward whiteness as the emancipatory affective precondition necessary for insurgent racialized structures of feeling, which in turn are needed to structure a new world for collective liberation. I take "I feel somewhat as this Indian did" as an entry point into the underexamined role of Indigeneity's importance to Delany's vision of transnational Blackness throughout his writings, and I focus on his novel, *Blake*. The novel was partly serialized in the *Anglo-African Magazine* in 1859 and then republished in its entirety in the *Weekly Anglo-African* from 1861 to 1862. Delany's protagonist, Henry Holland (eventually revealed to be the eponymous Blake), is roused into action against the institution of slavery when his wife and child are sold. His quest for justice takes him across the United States, Canada, West Africa, and Cuba, exploring the global tentacles of the slave trade and subverting them by establishing a transnational network of revolutionaries of color that foregrounded Black participants. With the novel's final chapters no longer extant, the revolt it portrays remains suspended: its potential is untested but also unrestrained. Like *Uncle Tom's Cabin*, *Blake* takes the Fugitive Slave Act of 1850 as a rallying moment for organized resistance against American legal injustice against Black people. The parallels are confrontational: while for Stowe white sympathy can reform flawed institutions exemplified by the law, for Delany both white sympathy and the law are symptomatic of the irredeemable disconnect between the world as it is and how it should be. Starting with Delany's understanding of Black-Indigenous histories in his nonfiction writings, this chapter considers his hero Blake's radical methodology of unsympathetic Blackness in the context of the novel's staging of the failures of white sentimental tropes. The argument then moves to the Black-Indigenous insurgent counterintimacies in his chapters on the Choctaw and the maroons of the Dismal Swamp, which build into a transnational revolution. Delany's fantasy of a cross-racial coalition as a subversive force is both political and scientific in its rewriting of the divisive hierarchies of race science that undergird biopolitics and its normative sentiments. *Blake* calls for the abolition of the supremacy of white feelings, envisioning the possibility of a new world through cross-racial, transnational feelings that reappropriate the interlocking colonial intimacies of Black enslavement and Indigenous dispossession that produced Smith's overrepresentation of sympathy as universal feeling. In Delany's project of radical world building, cross-racial feelings are scaled up as the model for a new science and, a new biopolitics predicated upon the complex relationships between peoples, all being part of a greater ecology of interrelated animate and inanimate beings and thereby creating an alternative cosmology to remedy an unjust world.

Through Delany's work we can trace the difficulty of overcoming the persistent tensions between Black and Indigenous peoples in history as well as the divides between them in the cultural imagination, and the fields of Black and Indigenous studies themselves that endure—despite the work of Tiya Miles, Sharon Holland, and others on excavating ongoing historical and theoretical considerations of the intersections between Black emancipation and Indigenous sovereignty, especially the overlooked experiences of Afro-Native people.[28] It is useful to recall that Frank B. Wilderson III characterizes the essential subject positions of Black, Red, and White as the structural antagonisms that make up the United States[29]—thus, solidarity is difficult by design. Fraught questions about the status of Black people as settlers on dispossessed Indigenous lands, Indigenous enslavement of Black people, complicities with institutional and historical oppressions, and different conceptual horizons of liberation and decolonization all complicate any easy move to political solidarity. Blake's visit to the Choctaw Nation is often glossed in passing as a comparative gesture to shared Black and Indigenous experiences of violences and forms of resistance, as in Timothy Powell's postcolonial reading.[30] In his extensive study of Delany's life and writings, Levine warns that the Black nationalist's transnational vision is less coalitional than settler colonial: "his project threatens to duplicate the European 'founding' of America, with all that it portended for natives and other subjugated groups."[31] I map how Delany attempts to address the comparative and even antagonistic structural positioning of Black and Indigenous peoples that is integral to American civil society and, moreover, the geopolitics of modernity—and his understanding that disrupting those structural apparatuses through the dynamisms of Black-

Indigenous counterintimacies is key to destroying that world so that it can be remade. His desire for Indigeneity is manifested in the implied masculinist homoerotics of entanglement between Blake and the younger Choctaw chief. In addition, Blake's journey to West Africa and then the Caribbean suggests a recovered Black Indigeneity whose slippage with Turtle Island Indigeneity authorizes a claim to the lands of the Americas. To paraphrase Patrick Wolfe, however, patriarchal settler colonialism is a structure Delany struggles to escape from and not an event he can readily move beyond[32]—which is most blatantly apparent in his troubled treatment of Black and Indigenous women as necessary sacrifices in the novel's grand scheme.

Rather than accepting the conditions of a world based upon the subordination of Black affects as unfeeling, with "I feel somewhat as this Indian did," Delany mobilizes the productive convergences of genealogies of racialized disaffection to overthrow and remake that world. While in *Benito Cereno* that world is the only world, banishing Black and other dissenting peoples of color from sociality as its constitutive ground, Delany refuses to accept the ruse of whiteness that overrepresents itself and its affects as universal. *Blake* is a fantasy of Blackness that is not beholden to the right feelings and actions of whiteness, and it explores unfeeling dissent as strategic detachment from the demands of white sentimental biopolitics as a way to imagine a biopolitics of "feeling somewhat as" other peoples of color. My use of "people of color" reflects Delany's use of "color" and "colored people": while he often uses "colored" as synonymous with "Black," he also strategically uses the capaciousness of "color" to refer to other racialized, colonized peoples. The Chickasaw scholar Jodi Byrd clarifies racialization and colonization as distinct although "concomitant global systems that secure white dominance."[33] As we will see, this messiness for Delany becomes a tactic to bring Black and Indigenous peoples (and even other racialized populations) together in solidarity, which sometimes strategically conflates them to strengthen anticolonial critiques and political claims. In this sense I use "people of color" when writing about these broader collectives, and when discussing Black and/or Indigenous peoples, I will identify them as specifically such.

Delany seeks to disrupt the colonial dichotomization of Blackness and Indigeneity as antagonistic to each other. Contrary to the reductive exclusionary logic of Blackness as diasporic dispossession versus Indigeneity as autochthonic rootedness, he shows how the Black diaspora can simultaneously enact deep relationships to land, respect the survivance of the dispossessed Indigenous diaspora, and hope to recuperate African Indigeneity. This project shows its flaws as it struggles with the slippages between coalition and conflation, alliances and appropriation. At his best, by creating a model of feeling by centering the importance of solidarity between peoples of color, Delany can envision the speculative project of radical world making. The project becomes a way of establishing a more inclusive, embodied, and experiential version of science as opposed to the increasing institutionalization of science as an elite professional discipline in the nineteenth century; it makes possible a more just system of laws that benefits everyone as part of the natural consequence of responsibilities to others and the world in spite of the Fugitive Slave Law of 1850; it affirms the importance of communities in a greater web of relationships by reimagining colonial intimacies beyond the limits of nationhood and their constitutive violences; and it builds legitimacy for dispossessed peoples through affective connections to the land. Perhaps most importantly, in its rejection of the false comforts of white sentimentality, *Blake*'s flawed explorations make it possible to begin an alternative discourse of feeling that would allow the disaffected to imagine the possibility of a better way of being together.

"The Old American Story" /
Black, Red, and White Historical Dichotomies

Delany condemns the coercive terms of the white sentimental politics of recognition by attacking the inconsistency of white sympathies for Black people. He accuses Stowe of hypocrisy in her support for the colony of Liberia while looking down on self-emancipated Haiti.[34] Delany states, "I must be permitted to draw my own conclusions, when I say that I can see no other cause for this secular discrepancy in Mrs. Stowe's interest in the colored race, than that one is independent of, and the other subservient to, white men's power." He understands that white sympathy is not merely contingent inconsistency but also—as we have seen in chapter 1—a colonial regulatory violence that naturalizes white supremacy. Delany exposes the racialized power dynamics undergirding the pose of universal sympathy that Douglass lauds in Stowe's work, concluding that she has "no sympathy whatever with the tortured feelings, crushed spirits and outraged homes of the Free Colored people." This critique combined, with his rhetoric of self-respect and self-governance, draws attention to the need for modes of feeling centered on Blackness and independent of whiteness.

Through declaring "I feel somewhat as this Indian did," Delany acknowledges kinship but also difference, reworking the deracinated universalist equivalence of Smith's articulation of sympathy. Delany's earlier political writings demonstrate his understanding of the enmeshed histories of Black people and Native Americans that informs his portrayal of "the old American story." *Condition* opens by establishing a general framework of oppression: "In all ages, in almost every nation, existed a nation within a nation" defined "by the deprivation of political equality with others."[35] He de-essentializes race and other forms of difference as mere signifiers, noting that "the objects of oppression are the most easily distinguished by any peculiar or general characteristics."[36] Despite his investments in Black nationalism, Delany does not seek to exceptionalize the ontology of Blackness through enslavement as the source of Black primacy. Rather, he views "the old American story" as the intertwined histories of Black and Indigenous peoples. "The projects of slavery and colonialism have never been concerned with which came first, or which is more elemental," observes Justin Leroy. "They have in fact thrived on the slippages and ambiguities of their relationship to one another."[37] Delany's history of the Americas begins with the understanding that "colored people and Indians" were grouped into the same class, with the abuse of Indigenous peoples of the region providing a template for the later treatment of Black people.[38] Thus, racial slavery originates in Indigenous dispossession through settler colonialism. According to Delany, "the Indians . . . in the early settlement of the continent, before an African captive had ever been introduced thereon, were reduced to the most abject slavery," and he acknowledges that "two millions and a half [Indigenous people had] fallen victim to the cruelty of oppression and toil."[39] The prejudice behind this exploitation and the shift to African enslaved labor had to do with perceived alienness to whiteness: "The Indians, who being the most foreign to the sympathies of the Europeans on this continent," were first selected, followed by Africans, "consequently being as foreign to the sympathies of the invaders of the continent as the Indians."[40] The use of the phrase "foreign to the sympathies" as the structural rationale for the oppressions that were the conditions of possibility for the United States brings Black and Indigenous peoples together as simultaneously unsympathetic to whiteness and resistant to its demands for their affectability.

Delany discusses the often-erased existence of Afro-Natives as the embodied symbol of the potential for cross-racial solidarity despite the history of how Black and Indigenous peoples were often reclassified vis-à-vis each other or collapsed into a single category depending on the needs of different national projects.[41] He points out the familial connection that emerged from the intimacies of colonialism: "The aborigine of the continent, is more closely allied to us by consanguinity, than to the European."[42] Indeed, William Katz estimates that one third of present-day Black people in the United States have a Native ancestor, and Jack Forbes states that "*Native-American-Black African intermixture was very common*" and provided "*the major source of the 'free' population of part-African descent everywhere prior to c.1650.*"[43] Claiming kinship between Native Americans and Black Americans is therefore both political and biological. Delany weaponizes these counterintimacies, calling on Black people to "unite and make common cause in elevation, with our similarly oppressed brother, the Indian."[44] The groups have a shared disaffection. As a result, Delany's retelling of history takes the structural differences between Black and Indigenous peoples as relational, not schematic, and he develops an argument for political convergence between Black liberation and Indigenous sovereignty.

Despite Delany's acknowledgment of kinship and desire for solidarity, his efforts show the influences of settler colonialism. For him, Black-Indigenous coalition means entitlement to land as part of his project for Black elevation, although he does not discuss what decolonization would mean for Indigenous people: "We have even greater claims to this continent," he argues.[45] Rather than pushing a truly decolonial agenda, according to Rochelle Zuck, his language mirrors white justifications of the seizure of Powhatan lands through the marriage of Pocahontas and John Rolfe.[46] Delany invokes the myth of the vanishing Indian: "This noble race of Aborigines. . . . They sunk by scores under the heavy weight of oppression, and were fast passing from the shores of time."[47] Although he acknowledges the shared experience of enslavement by Europeans, he claims that when faced by the same adversity, "the Indian sunk, and the African stood" (57). Anticipating criticism, he claims that this is not an insult, while pointing out anti-Blackness among Native peoples as a product of whiteness: "We adduce not these historical extracts to disparage our brother the Indian—far be it: whatever he may think of our race, according to the manner in which he has been instructed to look upon it, by our mutual oppressor the American nation; we admire his, for the many deeds of noble daring, for which the short history of his liberty-loving people are replete: we sympathise with them, because our brethren are the successors of their fathers in the degradation of American bondage" (62). Still, echoes of racial hierarchy reassert themselves amid the overturning of the white supremacist order. To repudiate Black inferiority, Delany argues for the superiority of his people at the expense of Indigenous peoples: "their superiority, and not inferiority, alone was the cause which first suggested to Europeans the substitution of Africans for that of aboriginal or Indian laborers in the mines" (62). His fondness for this comparison was such that he repeated it in nearly identical language in his 1854 speech titled "Report on the Political Destiny of the Colored Race on the American Continent," delivered at the National Emigration Convention of Colored People. His vision of solidarity veers from coalition to colonialism: "That the continent of America was designed by Providence as a reserved asylum for the various oppressed people of the earth, of all races, to us seems very apparent."[48] On the one hand, his musing recalls Byrd's contentious concept of the "arrivant," borrowed from the Caribbean poet Kamau Braithwaite, to designate people who are dispossessed by the violences of colonialism and imperialism as a disruption to the settler-Indigenous binary.[49] On the other hand, Delany inadvertently reveals the difficulties of coalition, for his silence about Indigenous sovereignty suggests how this project might still reproduce a version of what Byrd has critiqued as the role of "Indianness" as a "transit of empire."[50] Delany's vision of cross-racial alliance seems to promise revolution through counterintimacies against whiteness, stating that "the West Indians, Central and South Americans, are a noble race of people; generous, sociable, and tractable—just the people with whom we desire to unite."[51] Yet his frame for progress as a people and a civilization relies upon North America as an exemplar: these Indigenous peoples and the residents of the Global South "who are susceptible to progress, improvement and reform of every kind ... now desire all the improvements of North America," although "they have no confidence in the whites of the United States."[52] He assures his readers that those in the rest of the Americas place "every confidence in the black and colored people of North America," making it clear who the leaders of this new regime should be while also using the term "colored," which had a shifting taxonomy that could include Indigenous peoples.[53]

Antiracist Race Science?

Delany's understanding of political history is inextricable from his passion for natural history: justice is the natural order. Inasmuch as the race sciences, both polygenetic and monogenetic, were weaponized as rationales for the subjugation of peoples of color, *Condition* is a political manifesto that retells the development of the races to rebut claims of Black and Indigenous racial inferiority. Histories of enslavement and oppression disciplined the bodies and psyches of peoples of color, and any resulting weaknesses should be viewed as symptoms rather than confirmations of essential difference. In 1879, Delany intervened more directly in race science with *Principia of Ethnology: The Origin of Races and Color,* an often contradictory treatise that combines both monogenetic and polygenetic arguments and promotes both a common human origin and a static system of the so-called pure races of Black, White, and Yellow or Red.[54] Delany argues against both what he calls Darwinian "development theory" and the work of ethnologists like Josiah Nott and George Gliddon.[55] As Frank Rollin (the pen name of Frances Anne Rollin) comments in her 1883 biography of Delany—written while he was still alive and possibly composed with his help—Delany's arguments use "acknowledged scientific principles" but are derived from his "peculiar and original theories."[56] Throughout his career he used his medical skills to aid his community and lectured on the scientific basis for racial equality by reinterpreting "the comparative anatomical and physical conformation of the cranium of the Caucasian and negro races"—hijacking the standards of scientific evidence beloved of Samuel George Morton and others for the use of fugitive science.

Ethnological considerations of what she calls Afro-Native "speculative kinship" constitute a crucial aspect of Rusert's study of fugitive science that reevaluates Black people as practitioners and participants in nineteenth-century science, not just as its victims and objects.[57] Prior to the publication of Delany's *Condition*, Robert Benjamin Lewis, himself Afro-Native, authored the popular *Light and Truth* (1836),[58] a subversive ethnology of Black and Indigenous peoples that went through many reprintings and prompted the author to give book tours. Rusert notes that in *Condition* Delany calls Lewis's text derivative; even more scathingly, he suggests that due to its inaccuracies in overcorrecting race science to make all noteworthy historical personages Black, *Light and Truth* should be paired with a white supremacist race science text by Gliddon.[59] Although Delany also insults Lewis as "wholly unqualified for the important work" of combating the dominant paradigm of race science, he may disavow the influence of what Rusert calls Black and Indigenous "speculative kinship" articulated by *Light and Truth* on *Condition* and his later ethnological writings.[60] After all, Delany's insistence on biological and political kinships between Black and Indigenous peoples challenges the hierarchies of race science—particularly the separation of races espoused by the American school of polygenesis. Together, such cross-racial counterintimacies might be able to reverse the logics of the scientific analytics of race behind the global systems of domination: the once-affectable, now-disaffected peoples seeking the power to effect change.[61]

In his exchange with Douglass, Delany transmutes his knowledge of colonial history and comparative racialization into narrative: the "old American story about an Indian and a white man." Given his emphasis on the literal and material in his analyses of *Uncle Tom's Cabin*, this allegory of white American exploitation is striking as a sudden turn to the realm of the figurative in the same moment as his assertion of his own conception of "fellow-feeling" between Black and Indigenous peoples. This "old American story" is the occasion for both critique and creation: "That 'is not the way to "tell" it' to me," says Delany, who would engage in his own "telling" a few years later in *Blake*. If, as Douglass alleged in his initial response, Delany could not effect a plan for Black elevation through his political writings, this story signals his shift to the realm of fiction to realize his hopes. By writing a novel like *Blake*, he could devise a rebuttal to Stowe's literary juggernaut: he would radically reconfigure the terms of sentimentalism to engender the possibility of justice for Black and Indigenous peoples.

Blake / Black-Indigenous Counterintimacies and the Science of Solidarity

To Delany the world is out of balance. Like its primary intertext, *Uncle Tom's Cabin*, his *Blake* responds to the injustices of the Fugitive Slave Act of 1850, but Delany's response tells a different story. Rather than viewing white sympathies as a corrective to the act, *Blake* views both as a reflection of the failures of moral law in the United States, which can be traced to the heart of whiteness. Delany's once underappreciated novel has received a resurgence of scholarly attention because of his explorations of the legal, transnational, scientific, and economic dimensions of Blackness and enslavement. Following the reference to *Blake* by the iconic Black science fiction writer Samuel Delany as an early work of Black speculative fiction, Rusert expounds upon Martin Delany's radical interweaving of the scientific and the fantastical as integral to imagining "new worlds of freedom."[62] To create such a new world, I argue, the novel is a literary experiment in the transformative power of unsympathetic Blackness: alternative structures of feeling disaffected from white sympathies toward a transnational biopolitics of justice replace the global configurations of power produced by American and European colonial and imperial projects that in turn are undergirded by the sentimental biopolitics of hierarchized affectability. Black and Indigenous peoples, as we have seen in Delany's writings, are both "foreign to the sympathies" of white colonizers. Other modes and economies of feeling exist that are underrecognized by the white sentimental politics of recognition: "I feel somewhat as this Indian did" expresses that unfeeling disaffection from whiteness, whose discontent generates insurgent sympathies between oppressed peoples of color. Through literature Delany can transform his histories and political tracts into potential futures. Given the entanglements of Black enslavement and Indigenous dispossession in this unjust world's conditions of possibility, for Delany, imagining Black-Indigenous counterintimacies undoes these divisive structural antagonisms and opens the way for the abolition of that world.

The precise mechanics of the protagonist's plans for effecting such a total revolution are not revealed, just hinted at, and the loss of the novel's final chapters perpetually suspend the plans' potential at the cusp of narrative realization just after the Pan-African meeting of leaders in Cuba among other peoples of color. This indeterminacy acts as a strength, rather than a weakness, evocatively amplifying the narrative's speculative possibilities. The protagonist's travels within and beyond the borders of the United States, Canada, West Africa, and Cuba trace the geographies of a new nation based upon the displacements of the Black diaspora. The fostering of alternative communities for people of color who resist whiteness threatens to overturn the exclusionary conditions of belonging that constitute modern citizenship. Blake's national and transnational journey exploits the paranoia of white supremacy that, as Rebecca Biggio argues, responds to the abstract threat of Black community.[63] Blake repeats the same pattern of behavior at every new place to build counterintimacies among disaffected Black and Indigenous peoples: he bonds with these people of color, learning their names and the texture of their struggles, and orients them to the possibility of a new world to come through the expansion of his revolutionary community. Through his actions, Blake functions as a catalyst whose movements both enact and make visible the transnational web of insurgent feelings that redraws the global intimacies of enslavement and settler colonialism, replacing relationships of exploitation with organic responsibilities to one another. When the novel abruptly ends on the eve of the revolt, Blake has brought together leaders who include formerly enslaved Black Americans, free Black Cubans, and allies from Sudan. He has successfully assembled a multicultural collective that reflects the breadth of his transnational journey, with "the free Negros and mixed free people being in unison and sympathy with each other," and "masses of the Negroes, mulattoes and quadroons, Indians, and even Chinamen, could be seen together."[64] Over half a century before the publication of W. E. B. Du Bois's *Dark Princess* (1928), a Black patriarchal romance of Afro-Asian solidarity, Delany imagined a radically inclusive and decolonial order that could overthrow global colonial hegemony.[65]

Delany understood affective, political, and material changes to be governed by the same natural order, and his own scientifically informed theorizations were akin to the system that Kyla Schuller terms the biopolitics of feeling.[66] In *Condition*, Delany posits three realms of natural law—spiritual, moral, and physical—each of which can be affected only by action within its respective realm.[67] There is a natural justice in the world: he asserts that people have "natural rights, which may, by virtue of unjust laws, be obstructed, but never can be annulled" (49). The mistake of white domestic sentimentality espoused by Stowe and so popular among those still enslaved, he claims, is the turn to religion, when "there are no people more religious in this Country, than the colored people, and none so poor and miserable as they" (39). To change moral law, people must not pray but "exercise their sense and feeling of *right* and *justice*, in order to effect it," and altering "things of earth," one must look to physical law and "go to *work* with muscles, hands, limbs, might, and strength." Thus, reaching out to other oppressed peoples enacts real change in the affective and moral scales that can reverberate to bring each strata of the world's laws back into balance with what Delany views as the underlying natural order of racial justice.

DISAFFECTED FROM WHITE SYMPATHY AND ITS FAILURES

These transformations cannot rely upon white sympathies: the novel refers to legal injustices like the Fugitive Slave Act to underline the contradiction involved in appealing to the white sentimental politics of recognition when those politics produced systemic oppressions. The narrator bluntly condemns legal institutions: "Law is but a fable, its ministration a farce, and the pillars of justice but as stubble before the approach of these legal invaders."[68] In the tradition of Black, Indigenous, and other minoritized peoples not content to be subjugated as subjects of the law, Delany demonstrates his facility with legal rhetoric and history to dismiss the legal system as symptomatic of the failures of civil society.[69] *Blake* restages one of the scenes in *Uncle Tom's Cabin* that is most illustrative of the power of white domestic sentimentality confronting the Fugitive Slave Act: the fugitive Eliza's appeal to the sympathies of Senator Bird and his wife through the shared experience of losing a child. The Northern senator becomes convinced of the law's cruelty, so the Birds illegally aid the fugitives. "We have reason to know, in Kentucky, as in Mississippi, are noble and generous hearts, to whom never was a tale of suffering told in vain!," proclaims the narrator triumphantly.[70] In contrast,

Blake presents an analogous Northern politician and his wife, Judge Ballard and Mrs. Arabella, who open the novel by affirming their commitment to the institution of slavery. Like Senator Bird, this judge had previously upheld the act in a fugitive slave case, but without a pang of conscience. His wife assures the slaveholding Franks that she and her husband "seek every opportunity to give the fullest assurance that the judiciary are sound on that question."[71] Later the judge laments that "it was the incident of my life to be born in a nonslaveholding state" and affirms the Fugitive Slave Act as "a just construction of the law."[72] Ballard quotes Chief Justice Roger B. Taney's infamous *Dred Scott* decision: "persons of African descent have no rights that white men are bound to respect!"[73] What has been overlooked is how the portrayal undermines Stowe's championing of wives as the domestic voice of sentimental conscience: the wife in Delany's novel is proudly complicit in chattel slavery. The judge boasts that "my lady is the daughter of a clergyman, brought up amidst the sand of New England," but despite this prime abolitionist pedigree, "I think I'll not have to go from the present company to prove her a good slaveholder."[74] Delany challenges Stowe's belief that good white people may support bad laws but can be converted through sympathy. Rather, Delany shares Melville's cynicism that the act reveals heartfelt anti-Black racism on both sides of the Mason-Dixon line.

White characters push back against anti-Black legal injustices only when Delany's protagonist persuades them to do so, not through sentimental moral appeals but with cold, hard cash. Blake tells his fugitive companions that "money is your passport through that White Gap to freedom" and that it will carry them "across the White river to liberty" (84). The "White Gap" that Blake identifies between white people's consciences and their material self-interest anticipates the concept of the empathy gap, the rift between the efficacy of white feelings and the possibility of social change. The novel presents scenes in which abolitionist sympathies are voiced by white ferrymen who help the fugitives cross only after money changes hands. Blake knows that the most effective "free papers" are cash (140).

Displays of white feelings are ineffective distractions from the pursuit of emancipation: the novel overturns common tropes of white sentimentalism, suggesting that projects of transformative freedom must be unsympathetic to the recognitions of white feelings. Outpourings of white tears do not lead to institutional or even individual change: the whipping of Reuben, an enslaved child, has parallels to the iconic beating of Douglass's aunt Hester (or Esther), that fetishistic scene of Black suffering meant to galvanize abolitionist sympathies that has been critiqued by Saidiya Hartman.[75] The enslavers and Judge Ballard witness the spectacle of violence, with even the proslavery judge "wiping away [his] tears" at the sight—but the boy dies, forgotten, while the men retire for brandy and water.[76] In echoes of Eliza's relationship to Mrs. Shelby, when Blake's wife Maggie is sold, the enslaver's wife offers help: "'You have been kind and faithful to me and the Colonel, and I'll do anything I can for you!' *sympathetically* said Mrs. Franks" (21; emphasis added). Her schemes fail: even though Maggie was recognized as worthy of sympathy through Mrs. Franks's affective labors, white feelings do not translate into action. Blake learns not to trust well-intentioned white people: when he makes his successful escape from the plantation, Colonel Franks assumes that he was helped by Mrs. Van Winter, an abolitionist. Mrs. Franks assures her husband that despite "her strange notions that black people have as much freedom as white," the abolitionist "heartily *sympathizes* with us" (58; emphasis added). As happened with Melville's Delano, Babo, and Cereno, the racialized hierarchy of sympathetic worthiness reasserts itself.

Blake boards the slave ship *Vulture* to subvert the Middle Passage from within its workings. In echoes of Melville's *San Dominick*, the *Vulture* alternates between flying the Spanish flag and the American to reflect the makeup of its white crew. On board Captain Paul and his midshipman have an epiphany about the error of their ways—unrelated to any effort at genuine interaction with the Black people around them. A beautiful ocean sunset stirs the consciences of the two white Americans, as "the human heart manifested its most delicate sympathies" in response to nature (205). The captain vows to cease his involvement in the slave trade. In a footnote, Delany explains that he based Paul on a former "old slave-trading master of a vessel" he had encountered who "seemed sorely to repent his great sins" (206). Nonetheless, these white Americans do not change their plans to pick up enslaved Africans to sell in Cuba, nor do they stop their crew from throwing sick Black men, women, and children overboard in the echoes of the *Zong* massacre, and they play no role in the revolution in the extant text. They do not reach out to the Black people on board or try to alleviate the circumstances of the enslaved, nor does Blake attempt to collaborate with these supposedly reformed enslavers. Rather than angling for sympathy on the slave ship, Blake adopts the posture of unfeeling to focus on his mission: "With lips pressed together, Blake looked on without an evidence of emotion" (230). For Delany, white feelings are not one of the master's tools that can dismantle the master's house.

"BOTH LAY DOWN IN SHADE TOGETHER" / HOMOSOCIAL AND HOPEFUL FANTASIES OF BLACK-INDIGENOUS COUNTERINTIMACIES

While Blake avoids recruiting white characters for his rebel plot, he takes care to honor Black and Indigenous traditions of resistance, linking them to his growing community of decolonial counterintimacies. He visits the Choctaw Nation in Fort Towson, Arkansas, and the maroons of the Dismal Swamp, two rebel *imperia in imperium* that Blake needs to recruit as allies for the future nation he wants to found. Through these two episodes, Delany stages encounters with earlier alternative models of military, cultural, and epistemological resistance that can be converted into seeds of future rebellion. This narrative assemblage of histories participates in what John Ernest calls the Black tradition of "liberation historiography": "a mode of reading history in a way that respects the authority of the fragmented communities of experience," creating "agency in a self-determined understanding of history."[77] If, as Jean Fagan Yellin claims, the novel is a "revolutionary handbook outlining the organization of a guerrilla army of black liberationists,"[78] it is not insignificant that Blake must meet with Native Americans before the maroons of the Dismal Swamp. In these encounters, the novel develops Delany's allegory of the "old American story" into a more sustained and nuanced engagement that suggests Black emancipatory projects cannot be extricated from the historical precedents and coeval struggles of Indigenous resistance to settler colonialism. To escape from white sentimentalism as the dominant means of inciting political action and social change, Delany needs a new affective foundation for the revolutionary community of a better world to come, and he looks to Indigenous histories in the Americas for alternative templates of relationality.

Delany delves into the messy historical entanglements between Black and Indigenous peoples through Blake's visit to the Choctaw Nation near Fort Towson. Unlike his use of the generalized and often figurative Indian of his earlier work, Delany engages in the specifics of Choctaw and Seminole relationships with Black Americans. Mr. Culver and his nephew, Josephus Braser, both chiefs among the Choctaws, welcome Blake and his mission with open arms. Despite this hospitality, I argue that this episode is more complicated than Zuck's characterization of it as "a fantasy of political collectivity and shared ethnic solidarity" that erases "any cultural differences that exist."[79] Blake responds to this invitation from the Choctaw chiefs with the challenge, "You are slaveholders, I see, Mr. Culver!"[80] He does not hesitate to initiate a fraught discussion about the exploitation of Black people by Native Americans that complicates any naïve dream of a cross-racial alliance. The Choctaw were part of what were called the "Five Civilized Tribes" by white European colonists because the Choctaw had adopted Western culture, including the uneven assumption of plantation slavery and the attendant development of slave codes and the use of Western ideas of race—particularly among the Choctaw and Chickasaw.[81] At the time of this encounter, the Choctaw were settled in Arkansas, having been relocated there from Mississippi as part of the Indian Removal Act of 1830. According to the historian Wyatt Jeltz, chattel slavery became an institution when the Choctaw and Chickasaw decided to use enslaved Black labor to create and tend plantations.[82] Culver responds to Blake by straightforwardly admitting that he has about two hundred enslaved Black people on two plantations, but he adds that the Choctaw are "not like the white men" in their use of slavery.[83] The abolitionist Blake cannot help but retort, "I can't well understand how a man like you can reconcile your principles with the holding of slaves and—" (85). It is here that this frank dialogue is cut off by a white man.

"We have had enough of that!" interrupts Dr. Donald, "a white man, [who] married among the Indians a sister of the old Chief and aunt to the young, for the sake of her wealth and a home" (85 and 86). This disingenuous ending of an honest confrontation about Black-Indigenous antagonisms initiated and aggravated by whiteness recalls King's critique of white settler colonialism's disruptions even in academic fields.[84] Donald is related to the two chiefs through marriage, and his presence is enabled by the erasure of an unseen Choctaw woman. Her link to Indigenous collectivity is used against her, and she is framed only in relation to the men in her life: she represents a gendered resource desirable to whiteness that dilutes Indigenous sovereignty under the settler colonial logics of slow genocide. She is guilty of bringing Donald into the Choctaw Nation as a corrupting influence of white settler colonialism, a common trope that scapegoats southeastern Indigenous women: in fact, it was through white traders that the institution of Black enslavement was brought into Choctaw society. The treatment of the enslaved by their Indigenous enslavers varied depending on their familial intimacies with whiteness. According to Jeltz, "The Choctaws of mixed blood opened up extensive plantations and grew wealthy from the cultivation of cotton with their large numbers of slaves. The full blood Choctaws depended upon their livestock for a livelihood and found slave labor of little value to them."[85] In comparison to Black doctors, who will be among the leaders of the revolt later in Cuba, this white doctor demonstrates the complicity of the medical sciences in racialized oppressions. As a healer who does not heal but instead sows discord, Donald represents a false science: "A physician without talents, he was unable to make a business and unwilling to work."[86] When the younger Braser shouts Donald down and Culver sternly admonishes him to be civil, the white doctor claims, "He'll make the Indians slaves just now, then Negroes will have no friends" (86). Donald mutters "n[——]!" as he leaves, ejected by his Choctaw relatives (86).[87] His actions reflect the kind of divide-and-conquer tactics that white supremacy fosters between marginalized groups by playing into anti-Blackness. By expelling him, the chiefs engage in a variant of what the Mohawk scholar Audra Simpson terms ethnographic refusal, controlling access in a calculus based on the needs of Indigenous sovereignty.[88] Although the doctor is a nominal relative, the Choctaw choose "family first," in the words of the Beecher Bay Band member Pakki Chipps, recalling how Indigenous practices of kinship and identity operate according to different paradigms from settler colonialism.[89] Whiteness must be decentered, and in Delany's imagined scenario, the Choctaw choose to make space for dialogue with Blake, setting the conditions for possible political collaboration between peoples of color.

Once Donald—representing the specter of white influence—is banished, the difficult conversation can resume, allowing a common cause to emerge from the intersection of Native American sovereignty and Black emancipation. Before that moment of mutual respect and epiphany can arrive, however, both sides spar over ongoing injustices and stereotypes: to "feel somewhat" cannot refer to a simple equivalence of histories and embodied experiences. Culver contends that there are differences between white enslavers and Native American ones, but he also slips in a dig against Black people who are not actively resisting white supremacist institutions and thus are complicit in settler colonialism: "Indian work side by side with black man, eat with him, drink with him, rest with him and both lay down in shade together; white man won't even let you talk! In our Nation Indian and black all marry together. Indian like black man very much, ony [sic] he don't fight 'nough. Black man in Florida fight much, and Indian like 'im heap!"[90]

This excuse, articulated through Delany's questionable use of dialect, relies on a comparison that attempts to mitigate Native American practices of enslavement in comparison to the horrors of Southern chattel slavery. Historical accounts indicate that those enslaved by Indigenous people were seen as "badly spoiled" by the white enslavers of Missouri and Arkansas, who saw those particular enslaved as "difficult to control."[91] Despite the homoerotics of Black-Indigenous counterintimacies, Black and Indigenous women in intimate relation to Indigenous and Black men respectively were referred to as the suturing of a cross-racial coalition, the basis of a transformative sociality.

This portrayal of Black-Indigenous relations has a homosocial element that echoes Delany's emphasis elsewhere on ties between masculinity and freedom: "Indian like black man very much" is a statement of political and affective desire that decenters whiteness. Indeed, here we can see an intensification of Black-Indigenous intimacies, moving from shared labor to communion and the physical act in which "both lay down in shade together"—that leads to "all marry together." Entangled histories suggest intertwined bodies—the chief ousts his white relative to prioritize the erotics of Black-Indigenous counterintimacies.

In response to the Choctaws' critique of Black passivity, the conversation shifts to the dynamics of anticolonial struggle in Africa versus the Americas: Blake's vision of Black emancipation reckons with the global networks of colonialism, which includes settler colonialism in Africa and the survivance of African Indigenous peoples. Blake defends Africa as not completely colonized, while the Black diaspora struggles to unite as arrivants "scattered thousands of miles apart."[92] "America, the home of the Indian—who is fast passing away—is now possessed and ruled by foreigners," Blake retorts (86). Although Delany appears to be returning to his earlier use of the vanishing Indian myth, the chief responds by modifying Blake's phrase to point out the genocide waged against his people: Indigenous peoples are "passing away before the gun of the white man!" (87). With the reference to white violence, the debate ends. Rather than using the false equivalence of sympathy, both sides trade misunderstandings and wrongs. The frustration and anger on both sides is allowed expression; these deeply felt wrongs must be confronted, not excused, to create more just relationships and to recognize the enemy the two groups share. Nonetheless, Culver's stereotypical broken English contrasts with Blake's eloquence, giving a rhetorical advantage to Delany's hero.

Impressed by Indigenous survivance, Blake views Native Americans as potentially worthy allies or dangerous foes, asking "whether in case the blacks should rise, they may have hope or fear from the Indian?" (87). In his answer the Choctaw chief invokes the Seminoles, who earned their name—meaning "runaways"—by splitting from the Creek. These Indigenous runaways settled near communities of runaway slaves, where—according to more idealistic takes on this controversial history—this "association originally limited to mutual material advantage became cemented by reciprocal respect and affection."[93] Indigenous fugitivity meets Black fugitivity: with the history of the Seminoles and the acknowledgment of Afro-Native peoples, political history grows out of unlikely counterintimacies. The recent Seminole war is viewed as evidence that the unity between the Black Seminoles and their Native enslavers in both battle and blood are their great strength: "The squaws of the great men among the Indians in Florida were black women, and the squaws of the black men were Indian women. You see the vine that winds around and holds us together. Don't cut it, but let it grow till bimeby, it git so stout and strong, with many, very little branches attached, that you can't separate them."[94] The organic metaphor of Black and Native American intertwinement anticipates Sharon Holland's discussion of the "crossblood," people who "consistently cross the borders of ideological containment" in their identification and embrace of both heritages.[95] The existence of the crossblood, according to Holland, illustrates that "it is possible to move into the space of Afro-Native literatures with both emancipation and sovereignty in mind." After Blake confides his plans to the elder Choctaw, Culver exclaims "Ah hah! Indian have something like that long-go. I wonder your people ain't got it before! That what make Indian strong; that what make Indian and black man in Florida hold together."[96] Black and Indigenous women finally make an appearance in this exchange not as actual characters but as symbols of the triangulated conduit between Black and Indigenous men that bridges the comparative structural antagonisms of racial formation. This homosociality recalls the masculinist thinking that endures in certain forms of allegedly radical political organizing.

Historically, tensions between Black emancipation and Indigenous sovereignty were exploited by the United States throughout the nineteenth century to play both peoples off against each other. Conceptually, there are disagreements about the logics and praxes of Black emancipation and Indigenous sovereignty, exemplified by exceptionalist arguments on both sides by scholars like Jared Sexton and Patrick Wolfe.[97] Still, Delany does not view these projects as completely incommensurable, seeing them instead entangled like the crossblood vine. The Choctaw chief bequeaths an aspect of Indigenous resistance to Blake for his campaign's success, proclaiming "may the Great Spirit make you brave!" Delany draws attention to this pun with a reminder in the next sentence that Culver is "the venerable old brave."[98] This coalition is cemented by homosocial cross-racial bonding: they "retired for the evening, Henry rooming with the young warrior Braser," which is suggestive of their entwinement of political and physical desires. With the affirmation of past affiliations and the promise of future alliances, Blake continues on his journey, taking the "brave" blessing with him.

Despite the flaws in this chapter's limited portrayal of Indigenous peoples as legitimate actors and not stock literary tropes, it is a striking choice for

Delany to write the chapter "Advent with the Indians" using the Choctaw Nation, not the Seminoles, as his Indigenous interlocutors. He avoids an easy recourse to coalitional histories at the disavowal of exploitative pasts, presenting his project as aspirational speculative fiction. Of the Five Tribes, the Choctaw were second only to the Chickasaw in their near adoption of chattel slavery, with its restrictive ideas about racial purity and the exploitation of labor. On the other end of the spectrum were the Seminoles, who integrated enslaved Black people into their households in positions of equality and even gave them precedence and authority to negotiate with whites.[99] Despite Culver's assertion that "Indian and black all marry together," while there were Afro-Native people in the Choctaw Nation, intermarriage and cohabitation had been officially prohibited by the Choctaw National Council only a few decades earlier.[100] This chapter is a subtle example of the novel as speculative fiction, what Katy Chiles has recognized more broadly as the temporal manipulations of the narrative considered in the context of its serial publication, remaking and exceeding history to unite Black communities.[101] When the entirety of Delany's novel was reserialized and published in *The Weekly Anglo-African*—including this chapter—the Choctaw and Chickasaw had entered into an alliance with the Confederacy in July 1861, in part to keep their sovereignty and their investments in the institution of chattel slavery.[102] Even after Emancipation, both nations enacted laws similar to the notorious Black codes in the South.[103] Nonetheless, the Black and crossblood freedmen still identified more strongly with their former enslavers than with white Americans, causing them to push for formal inclusion into the nations—and the Choctaw Nation finally extended citizenship to them in 1885, as did the Chickasaw in the following century.[104] They would rather "feel somewhat" alongside Indigenous peoples as members of colonized dependent nations than appeal to the feelings of the white settlers for inclusion in citizenship.[105] Delany's decision to have the Choctaw cite the Seminoles, who treated the enslaved as equals and fought alongside them, comes across as hope that collaboration could exist in Black-Indigenous relations if the groups united against whiteness. In the final line of the chapter, Blake has not forgotten the Native American practice of enslavement: this was "the only instance in which his seclusions [conspiratorial meetings] were held with the master instead of the slave."[106] Through these omissions and rewritings, Delany presents a wishful fantasy of an alternative universe of Indigenous peoples who are allies instead of adversaries, without eliding transgressions.

LAND, DISPOSSESSION, AND DIASPORA / THE DISMAL SWAMP AND INDIGENOUS DISPLACEMENT

Glimpses of Indigenous sacred practices and cosmologies close the Choctaw chapter. With Blake's visit to the maroon community in the Dismal Swamp, the novel continues to explore epistemological challenges to Western ideologies by highlighting African diasporic cosmologies as decolonial resistance. This chapter has attracted critical attention for Delany's deliberate yoking of his fictional revolution to existing legacies of Black resistance in America.[107] The Dismal Swamp, the notorious wetlands of Virginia and North Carolina, is a place whose residents defy white America: it has been the "fearful abode for years of some of Virginia and North Carolina's boldest black rebels."[108] These men claim to have been involved in the American Revolution as well as every famous Black uprising, referring to Nat Turner, Denmark Vesey, and Gabriel Prosser in "sacred reverence" (112 and 113). Amid the rituals of welcoming and protection, Blake—reflecting Delany's scientific interest in the natural world—notices that the conjuring paraphernalia of the leader Gamby Gholar includes "scales which he declared to be from very dangerous serpents, but which closely resembled, and were believed to be those of innocent and harmless fish" (112). The High Conjurors, also known as Heads, anoint Blake "conjuror of the highest degree known to their art," rendering him "licensed with unlimited power—a power before given no one—to go forth and do wonders" (115). Delany's protagonist moves from skepticism about their methodology to recognition of its efficacy. As Monique Allewaert writes, "Delany moves from a concept of the fetish as evidence of a mode of (misguided) belief to a recognition of the fetish as an artifact that enables a mode of practice that produces certain effects that are positive, even politically transformative."[109] Whether or not the magic is real is not the point: the rituals demonstrate the Black community's sustained commitment to resistance through the creation of a hybrid, alternative culture that includes deception and other psychological manipulations as a source of power. Despite criticizing some of the Heads' methods upon his return to the plantation, Blake still paid homage to them and remarked that "we must take the slaves, not as we wish them to be, but as we really find them to be."[110] These men represent the revolutionary roots of Blackness in America and the adaptive creativity of Black diasporic spiritual practices.

What has been neglected in discussions of the Dismal Swamp episode is how it represents an American history of Black rebellion intertwined with Indigeneity. Delany contrasts what Levine views as the "'revolutionary pure-blood' blacks" of the Dismal Swamp with the "self-loathing mulattoes" of Charleston.[111] However, although the swamp is most famous for harboring communities of Black fugitives, that does not erase the presence there of Indigenous peoples like the Chesapeakes and the Tuscaroras.[112] Black fugitives joined the population of the region as early the late seventeenth century, with the first extant documentation of the Black presence in the Dismal Swamp showing that both Black and Native peoples had joined forces to raid nearby farms.[113] The one explicit mention of race in this chapter in *Blake* is of the men as "black rebels," yet the rituals at the end of Blake's visit include "blessings, wishes, hopes, fears, *pow-wows* and promises of a never failing conjuration" (emphasis added), signifying the inclusion of Native practices in the cultural assemblage that is hoodoo.[114] The Dismal Swamp is the site of this shared history of resistance. Moreover, the conversation about the Black fighters of the Revolutionary War gestures toward, but does not outright name, Crispus Attucks. Attucks, considered the first American martyr of the Revolution, was of mixed Black and Natick Indian heritage, and Delany lauds him in *Condition* as "a patriot of the purest character."[115] To trace a genealogy of Black resistance requires acknowledging Black peoples' intersections with Native Americans. Thus, the episode with the Choctaw comes before the chapter on the Dismal Swamp to acknowledge that the struggle began with the defiance of Indigenous peoples.

Considering the Choctaw and the Dismal Swamp as complementary aspects of the same framework of counterintimacies, I suggest that these chapters attempt to trouble the structural distinctions of Indigenous-Black antagonisms based on relationships to land. In a chiasmatic reversal, the Black diaspora's uprootedness and Indigeneity's situatedness are portrayed in these chapters as the uprootedness of Indigeneity and the Black diaspora's locatedness. While Blake, who is always on the move as he traces the dispersals of the Black diaspora, is the very figure of fugitivity, the Choctaw are an example of a people displaced for the sake of white interests—albeit for the fungibility of their lands, not their beings. They were the first Indigenous people to be formally dispossessed by the Indian Removal Act in 1830. In the space referred to by the narrator as the "nation," there is no description of the land other than the plantations, the disciplinary environment of Black enslavement.[116] Set only a few decades after the forcible uprooting of the Choctaw from their traditional lands, the chapter takes place in an abstracted space that suggests the estrangement of the Choctaw characters from their surroundings. Blake describes settler colonialism as having "dr[iven] the Indians from their own soil," suggesting echoes between the violent dispersions of the Black diaspora and the losses on the Trail of Tears. These Indigenous people have been so profoundly severed from their land that they face a loss of their Indigeneity in relation to this new space—which the narrator calls the "settlement."[117] These displaced Choctaw are staving off the fate of the Choctaw who stayed in Mississippi, taking the allotment provisions in the removal treaty to give up Indigenous collectivity and become American citizens. The others make "assimilation's Faustian bargain," as Wolfe puts it: they gain "our settler world, but lose your Indigenous soul. Beyond any doubt, this a kind of death."[118]

However, the Dismal Swamp is depicted as a site dense with environmental animatedness, where Blackness has taken root as part of the region's ecology. Entering the region is like entering a new country: "Here Henry [Blake under his old name] found himself surrounded by a different atmosphere, an entirely new element. Finding ample scope for undisturbed action through the entire region of the Swamp, he continued to go scattering to the winds and sowing the seeds of a future crop, only to take root in the thick black waters which cover it, to be grown in devastation and reaped in a whirlwind of ruin."[119] The swamp is literally fecund ground for his conspiracy, with potentially volatile consequences. These vegetal metaphors indicate that the swamp's potency in fomenting anticolonial action comes from its status as a living place of great power: it is the "mystical, antiquated, and almost fabulous Dismal Swamp," the "fearful abode," the "much-dreaded morass" (112, 113, and 114). The swamp's associations with both Blackness and Indigeneity go back to the colonial period: Susan Scott Parrish describes how the white settlers "linked the warring Indian with the dark meanders of the swamp" and associated "the runaway slave with the tangled botanical skein, unstable ground, and mysterious impenetrability of the *pocoson*, or swamp."[120] The centrality of the natural world in both spiritual traditions, Parrish suggests, indicates literal common ground between Black and Indigenous practices and epistemologies.[121] The hoodoo practices of the High Conjurors draw upon the swamp's natural powers: one of Gholar's charms is a blue stone used in the ceremony to protect Blake, which Gholar "got at a peculiar and unknown spot in the Swamp, whither by a special faith he was led—and ever after unable to find the same spot."[122] The Heads' magical paraphernalia includes organic and inorganic materials from the swamp like "onionskins, oystershells . . . eggshells, and scales," with "a forked breastbone of a small bird" used as a charm (112 and 113). The maroons have been accepted into the swamp ecology: they live with "a large sluggish, lazily-moving serpent" as their pet (114). Their gathering spaces are deep in the swamp—in "the forest, a gully, secluded hut, an underground room, or a cave"—and it is in the cave, immersed in swamp geographies, where Blake is anointed by the Conjurors. Delany attempts to show how Blackness and Indigeneity are not exclusive. In an act of political appropriation, he argues for a Black connection to space that "feels somewhat" like Indigenous locatedness, while Indigenous dispossession "feels somewhat" like the alienations of the Black diaspora.

"The Revolution of the Great Planetary System" / The Physics of Decolonial Revolution

If the white Dr. Donald represents the ways in which the sciences not only oppress but also strategically divide peoples of color, Blake seeks to establish a biopolitics of "feeling somewhat" between Black and Indigenous peoples as part of what he views as the true expression of the natural order. Delany published essays on science alongside chapters of *Blake* in the *Anglo-African Magazine*, and his short articles on comets and planets constitute part of the paratext of his novel, being integral to its project of racial uplift. "The Attraction of Planets" and "Comets," published in January and February 1859, respectively, express theories on energy and physics that Rusert views as akin to Delany's political writings, suggesting how fugitive bodies "become vectors of force and affect change in the world" as portrayed in the novel.[123] Through these essays Delany brings astrophysics together with his theories about the life sciences: in contradiction to the divisiveness of race science, he argues for the fundamental interconnectedness of all things in the affective web of life. "Comets" speculates through the lens of vitalism: "The purpose of comets would seem to be to distribute electricity throughout universal space, re-supplying the continual loss that must be sustained to systems and planets by various causes, and thereby giving life, action, health and vigor to both animate and inanimate creation, to this and distant worlds, worlds to us unknown."[124] To borrow the language of the theorists Jane Bennett and Mel Chen, Delany recognizes the vibrancy or animacy of all matter.[125] However, Delany makes no move to universalist affect: in "The Attraction of Planets" he analyzes particles and the solar system, arguing that all scales of reality governed by "a law essential to matter, of mutual attraction and repulsion."[126] These twin principles of attraction and repulsion contribute to what he praises as "the beautiful economy of their revolutionary arrangement."[127] Reflecting these cosmic laws of reality that invalidate the flawed laws of humanity, the novel experiments with a revolutionary arrangement of Black, Indigenous, and other peoples of color cohering through both mutual attraction and disaffected repulsion from white sentimentalism and its apparatuses. Rather than Smith's "fellow-feeling" born of suffering, the novel centers the galvanizing feelings of revolution to change the world on the level of physics and matter itself.

After Blake makes connections with the Choctaw and the rebels of the Dismal Swamp, his consciousness of the world grows from affirming his individual affective experience with worldly phenomena to discerning a greater schema of kinship between humans and the world that can bring justice if they remain true to its principles. Blake gazes up at the night sky from the deck of a ship on the Mississippi: "Now shoots a meteor, then seemingly shot a comet, again glistened a brilliant planet which almost startled the gazer; and while he yet stood motionless in wonder looking into the heavens, a blazing star whose scintillations dazzled the sight, and for the moment bewildered the mind, was seen apparently to vibrate in a manner never before observed by him."[128] Blake is first inclined to "attach more than ordinary importance to them, as having especial bearing in his case; but the mystery finds interpretation in the fact that the emotions were located in his own brain, and not exhibited with the orbs of Heaven."[129] Rusert views Blake's response as a shift from a supernatural outlook to "a didactic lesson in rationalism" that would later be unraveled as he discovers the "speculative roots of black metaphysics" hidden within Western science.[130] More specifically, I suggest, this event indicates Delany's philosophy about a more expansive view of sympathy initiated by his alliances with other oppressed peoples: rather than a science of detached objectivity, he centers the sympathetic human body—feeling and cognition together, with "the emotions ... located in his own brain"—as the way to participate with the energies of the universe. While the brilliance of the stars has no "especial bearing in his case," that is because he recognizes that his ability to process the phenomena is shared with other peoples. Delany uses storytelling to make his theoretical ruminations about astrophysics come alive through the eyes of his protagonist, who recognizes himself as a part of the cosmos. Nonetheless, rather than feeling comforted, Blake is still a "heartstricken fugitive, without a companion or friend with whom to share his grief and sorrows."[131] He still needs to fully connect this experience of the natural world to his project of building a revolutionary community.

A few chapters later, Blake shifts from solitary stargazing to the communal practice of knowledge by teaching his fellow fugitives how to use the stars to find their way. In what Rusert says "reads like an elementary science lesson,"[132] Blake explains how to find North to get to Canada: he sketches a picture of the Big Dipper, numbering each of the stars to explain how linking them together into the constellation helps indicate the way North.[133] The pragmatic still contains wonder: Delany inserts a verse from John Pierpont's poem "Slaveholder's Address to the North Star" in which the ignorant slaveholder has no sense of the star's importance or grandeur, comparing its remote size to a diamond in his ring: "Yet every black star-gazing n[——], / Looks up to thee as some great thing!" (quoted on 135).[134] Implementing Delany's explanation of magnetism in "The Attraction of Planets," Blake transitions to an explanation of how a compass works by delineating its properties in terms of a set of relations: its needle in relation to the cardinal directions, which are in relation to the safe spaces of the free states and Canada and, finally, to the position of his listeners' own bodies (133). Orienting oneself requires attention to one's body and senses, with even the haptic playing a role in the affective process of phenomenological grounding: "'When the North star cannot be seen,' continued Henry, 'you must depend alone upon nature for your guide. Feel, in the dark, around the trunks or bodies of trees, especially oak, and whenever you feel moss on the bark, that side on which the moss grows is always to the north.'" In contrast to Blake's solitary stargazing, these lessons are part of an extensive dialogue with the other fugitives that contributes to their affective cohesion as a community. The older generation relates the practices of hoodoo to Blake's fugitive science: Delany's hero is hailed by Daddy Joe as great as Maudy Ghamus of the swamp. With science as a catalyst, the fugitives are galvanized to become a rebel community.

THE ECOLOGIES OF AN ANTIRACIST SCIENCE OF SOLIDARITY

Delany pushes the limits of conventional science through a praxis inflected by his model of sympathy centered on peoples of color. The novel's engagement with science builds from Blake's individual, affective moment with the cosmos to a communal practice of embodied knowledge and, finally, to a way of reimagining the world by turning to cross-racial counterintimacies. The setting for this reimagining is the Caribbean, the site of the originary rupture that led to global modernity and thus the site that philosopher Sylvia Wynter might say was only appropriate for generating a new view of 1492.[135] If Blake was akin to the comet in his fugitivity and inhuman presence, as Rusert argues, with the rebel congress in Cuba his vibrant, attractive energies have drawn together Black and other bodies of color in revolution, with the goal of assembling a new system.[136] Delany writes: "Never before had the African race been so united as on that occassion [sic], the free Negros and mixed free people being in unison and sympathy with each other," in a reunion of those violently dispossessed from their communities by enslavement.[137]

Like the celestial bodies Delany discussed, Blackness exerts the powers of attraction through its magnitude, drawing in oppressed non-Black peoples of color. One could say that following the fear of a Black planet, there is the corollary anxiety about how such a world could exert its forces to pull other disaffected peoples into its orbit to reconfigure an entire system. These forces of attraction and repulsion are at work in the social configurations: "There was a greater tendency to segregation instead of a seeming desire to mingle as formerly among the whites, masses of the Negroes, mulattoes and quadroons, Indians, and even Chinamen, could be seen together."[138] In this intriguing line we can note a number of key points: foremost, the deliberate exclusion of white people to emphasize the convergence of peoples of color assembling around Blackness; a listing of these peoples that suggests a spectrum of radical involvement according to race; this catalog perhaps indicating degrees of biological and structural proximity from Blackness to whiteness; and the dubious inclusion of "even Chinamen," acknowledging the history of coolies in the West Indies.[139] Delany adds a footnote about his inclusion of the Indians, commenting that "for many years the Yucatan Indians taken in war by the Mexicans were sold into Cuba as slaves"—a fact that authenticates the Indigenous presence at this gathering and a reminder of shared histories of racial enslavement.[140] Like the order of the planets, the order of these peoples of color are joined in revolutionary movements without the dissolution of difference.

The novel theorizes the decolonial potential of what Jane Bennett calls "vibrant matter"[141] as a new global sociality that requires co-optative solidarity with Indigeneity on the level of matter to change what matters. Emotions run high at the rebel gathering and catalyze personal attachments and political affiliations through mutual feeling. The music that opens the great meeting generates an effect on the crowd that, like the energies described in "Comets," was "electrical—every kind of demonstration indicating the soul's deep sympathy and heartfelt hatred to oppression," putting physics in tandem with affect to create a just universe.[142] Throughout the speeches and discussions, both plans and feelings are shared: "The greatest emotions were frequently demonstrated, with weeping and other evidences of deep impressions made" and evocations of "deep emotions of sympathy" (259 and 284). These events filled with clustered bodies—that in turn are filled with revolutionary desire—are physically demonstrative and erotically charged. Here we can hear resonances with Delany's writing about the planets: "This excitement in small bodies is produced by friction or rubbing," and this haptic celestial harmony generates "a state of sensible electricity necessary for impelling the revolution of the great Planetary System."[143] These displays of affective solidarity between peoples of color suggest that they are drawn into orbit around Blackness thanks to its attraction and to the repulsion of whiteness, creating a different sort of revolution of the great planetary system.

The Cuban revolutionary summit subverts the hierarchies of race science: on the one hand, it rebuts the principles of polygenesis, which posited the separate nature of the different human races based on environmental context; on the other hand, Delany does not advocate for the traditions of monogenetic evolution, shunning the latest theories presented by Charles Darwin's *On the Origin of Species*—which was published in 1859, during the first half of *Blake*'s serialization. This assemblage of peoples of color reveals nature's true ecology of things: a holistic relationship to the land and all other peoples of color on the planet. The rationale for the revolution is presented as scientific, thereby naturalizing the revolutionaries' vision as lawful and righteous: "Their justification of the issue was made on the fundamental basis of original priority, claiming that the western world had been originally peopled and possessed by the Indians—a colored race—and a part of the continent in Central America by a pure black race. This they urged gave them an indisputable right with every admixture of blood, to an equal, if not superior, claim to an inheritance of the Western Hemisphere."[144] In this worldview, the separate developments of the races theorized by polygenesis usurped the organic web of relationships between people and place, without the conflation of racial distinctiveness under the guise of a false move to universal humanity implied by monogenesis. With "every admixture of blood," the phrase gestures to the existence of Afro-Native and Afro-Latinx peoples as the symbolic grounding of the diasporic Black presence in the Americas as natural and not an alien imposition. By positioning this meeting in Cuba, Delany draws attention to the site as the meeting of the peoples and geographies of the Americas.

These assertions are not voiced by any specific character. Indeed, the ambiguous third-person pronoun used throughout suggests that this overthrowing of Western science arises naturally out of the collectivity of rebel peoples of color, an expression of the world they want to bring into being: "The colored races, they averred, were by nature adapted to the tropical regions of this part of the world as to all other similar climates, it being a scientific fact that they increased and progressed whilst the whites decreased and continually retrograded, their offspring becoming enervated and imbecile. These were facts worthy of consideration, which three hundred years had indisputably tested. The whites in these regions were there by intrusion, idle consumers subsisting by imposition; whilst the blacks, the legitimate inhabitants, were the industrious laborers and producers of the staple commodities and real wealth of these places" (287). Although earlier the narrator clarifies that "a colored race" refers to "Indians," here the phrase "colored races" conveniently acts as a slippery term that encompasses all racialized and colonized peoples before a shift back to the specificity of Blackness. In this passage Delany uses the language and evidence of race science to justify the subordination of peoples of color as laborers; he manipulates that science's logic to affirm their place as the rightful citizens and even leaders of the Americas. In contrast to Delany's pragmatic negotiations and compromises with existing structures of power, his hero Blake does not need to pander to racist institutions: the performative iteration of "fact" works to replace American race science with a new science that has always already been. Whiteness becomes decentered and denaturalized: critiques of settler colonialism and chattel slavery come together with the parodying of scientific justifications of racial inferiority turned against whiteness. Adopting unsympathetic Blackness is a risk Delany takes in his fictional experiment not to reform but to abolish white sentimental biopolitics.

The Master's Tools Cannot Dismantle the Master's Structure of Feeling / The Persistence of Settler Colonial Thinking and the Erasure of Black and Indigenous Women

The ambivalence of "feeling somewhat as this Indian" allows for a radical reformulation of the concept of sympathy in defiance of the cultural politics of social change that privileges white feelings. Delany envisions bonds between peoples of color and claims to the land as part of his revolutionary schema, but nonetheless, these relationships are not entirely lateral. Delany envisions Blackness as the catalyst for counterintimacies of peoples of color bonding together over interlocking circumstances of oppression across antagonistic racial formations. His leaders are Black men, while the members of the intimate "Grand Council" are said to be "Henry Blake, Placido, Montego, the Blacuses, Carolus and Antonio, Castina, Ricardo, Rivera, Camina, the Captive Chief, Madame Cordora, Maggie Blake, Madame Barbosa, Madame Blacus, Madame Sebastina, Abyssa Soudan, and Madame Camina" (255). For all its boldness, Delany's revolutionary imagination struggles to reckon with Black, Indigenous, and other women of color in this process of elevation. Although Black women are present at this gathering, the narrator follows the litany of their names with the qualifier "the misses being admitted by courtesy, they having the confidence of the seclusion" through their relationships to the men (255). Despite Toalgabe Ogunleye's argument that Delany was an early womanist,[145] the latter's questionable treatment of Black women has troubled both his contemporaries and scholars. Anna Julia Cooper, one of the most prominent Black women activists in the latter half of the nineteenth century, singles Delany out as a representative of Black masculinist bias: "The late Martin R. Delany, who was an unadulterated black man, used to say when honors of the state fell upon him, that when he entered the council of kings, the black race entered with him."[146] In an early intersectional Black feminist intervention Cooper challenges Delany: "Only the BLACK WOMAN can say 'when and where I enter, in the quiet, undisputed dignity of my womanhood, without violence and without suing or special patronage, then and there the whole *Negro race enters with me*.'"[147] Scholars take Delany to task: Biggio calls out his "system of closed fraternity" with limited roles for women, while Jeffory Clymer accuses Delany of seeing "women of color almost entirely as symbols of purity and its potential violation."[148]

Earlier Indigenous presences are absent from the council; however, we see the inclusion of African Indigeneity. The "Captive Chief" refers to the previously enslaved Congolese Mendi, described earlier as a "native chief" of the Africans and signaling Delany's recognition of African Indigeneity that goes back to his discussion with the Choctaw about extractive colonialism and settler colonialism.[149] Despite the citation of Indigenous bodies and histories authorizing the new order's legitimacy, Delany's speculative kinship exploits the resemblance to Indigenous kinship, described by the Sisseton Wahpeton Oyate theorist Kim TallBear as "a networked set of social and cultural relations based on biological relatedness."[150] Indeed, Delany's expansive ecological vision echoes Indigenous cosmologies of ethical relationality but does not explicitly acknowledge an indebtedness, reproducing an omission that the Métis scholar Zoe Todd criticizes as the colonial suppression of Indigenous knowledge systems.[151] There are productive congruences between the projects of Black liberation and Indigenous decolonization: the Yellowknives Dene thinker Glen Coulthard draws upon Frantz Fanon's foundational *The Wretched of the Earth*, which calls for the decolonization of African nations, to articulate the Indigenous rejection of the liberal politics of recognition that would reiterate the domination of the settler-colonial apparatus. However, Coulthard's adoption of Fanon's theoretical framework has limits. Coulthard points out that "Indigenous peoples tend to view their resurgent practices of cultural self-recognition and empowerment as permanent features of our decolonial political projects, not transitional ones," and he does not take up Blackness in his adaptation of Fanon.[152] The lack of Indigenous voices from Turtle Island (an Indigenous name for North America) who could speak to the specifics of Indigenous sovereignty and decolonization is a conspicuous "somewhat" concession that taints the novel's radical vision of collective emancipation.

While *Blake* is a reimagining of Stowe's sentimental portrayal of Black masculinity, there is no such development of Black or Indigenous womanhood in Delany's novel. Although he decenters whiteness in his model of sympathy, his engagement with the gender politics of sentimentalism reinscribes heteropatriarchy, placing Black women in a compromised if not an outright subordinate position within his vision of Black elevation. The influences of Black misogynoir stand out most clearly when Delany draws parallels to *Uncle Tom's Cabin* to depart from Stowe's values and remake the power relations of sympathy. Blake takes the place of George Harris, and Maggie occupies the position of Eliza Harris. However, in contrast to the novel's focus on the heroic Blake's achieving what George might only dream of accomplishing, Maggie fades out of the narrative after she is sold—only to be rediscovered in Cuba as the amnesiac Lotty who has been tortured by her owners. Maggie has no action equivalent to Eliza's daring escape over the icy river with her child: while Maggie's memory is restored after Blake rescues her, her story remains erased, never told by Maggie herself and recounted only through the narrator's accounts of her ordeal. While Maggie's plight does not evoke the condescensions of white sympathy as Eliza's did, the former's suffering is flattened into an outrage to her husband's pride: "She had been almost daily beaten, frequently knocked down, kicked and stamped on, once struck and left for dead; and even smoked and burnt to subdue her."[153] Delany uncritically reproduces what Hortense Spillers denounces in her critique of violence against Black women in the American historical imaginary, the "materialized scene of unprotected female flesh—of female flesh 'ungendered.'"[154] In *Condition*, Delany declares: "No people are ever elevated above the condition of their *females*; hence, the condition of the *mother* determines the condition of the child. To know the position of a people, it is only necessary to know the *condition* of their *females*; and despite themselves, they cannot rise above their level."[155] To this end it is necessary to save Maggie, but to develop her as a character on equal footing with her husband is beyond the scope of the novel: tellingly, she regains her memory by calling Blake "Henry Hol—" instead of his true name, and soon after she pleads with him not to engage in politics "but be satisfied as we are among the whites, and God, in His appointed time, will do what is required."[156] Later, she is guilty of attempting to hold her husband back from his rightful role as leader, exclaiming, "I suppose then I may give up all hope of ever having you with me at all!" (242). Placido admonishes her for her selfish concerns: "The position of a man carries his wife with him; so when he is degraded, she is also, because she cannot rise above his level; but when he is elevated, so is she also." For Blake, Delany adapts the more radical language of his attempt at gender equality from his earlier writings, making it into a reminder of heteropatriarchy in racial uplift that is used to discipline Maggie into accepting her subordinate place as a Black woman.

While Indigeneity, Indigenous womanhood, and Black womanhood are essential conditions of possibility for Delany's transnational project of uplift, they indicate the limits of his imagination. Women and Indigenous people must be content to be represented by Black men such as Blake and to have their stories "told" by him. In his novel, Delany can reimagine the biopolitics of feeling, but this brave new world still feels too much like the old. No evidence exists that Delany did engage with Indigenous communities or that he imagined them as potential readers. Moreover, it is debatable whether he represents Indigenous peoples in their actuality any better than the existing American literary tradition of their depiction made famous by the likes of James Fenimore Cooper.[157] Although Delany critiques aspects of settler colonialism, his political vision of decolonization threatens to treat Indigenous peoples as just a metaphor. His struggle to fully divest from settler colonial tropes demonstrates the resilience—within even revolutionary thinking—of those intertwined structural conditions of antagonism designed to foreclose coalition. Indigeneity cannot be recruited for a Black liberatory project that does not accommodate the complex agency of Indigenous and Black women, whose subjugation constitutes the ground of hegemony.

Nonetheless, the novel refuses to surrender to the limits of the world as it is but seeks to change the structural inevitability of division into the revolutionary collective promise of what can be. Before Blake can "lay down in shade together" with the Choctaw chief Braser as a gesture of their political union, they must remove the disruptive presence of whiteness. Revolution requires a strategic calculus of detachments and attachments that encompass "even" an acknowledgment of Asian peoples: "There was a greater tendency to segregation instead of a seeming desire to mingle as formerly among the whites, masses of the Negroes, mulattoes and quadroons,

Indians, and even Chinamen, could be seen together." To imagine otherwise requires the possibility of feeling otherwise: being unsympathetic toward the demands of whiteness at the very least allows for the space needed for painful dialogues about the desire for Black-Indigenous counterintimacies in bed colluding against empire. The aspirational horizon of *Blake*'s ambition expresses the necessity and potential, however fugitive, of the collective praxis of solidarity.

THE QUEER FRIGIDITY
OF PROFESSIONALISM /

White Women Doctors, the Struggle
for Rights, and the Marriage Plot

IN 1847—a few years before Harvard Medical College ejected its first Black students, Martin R. Delany among them—Harriot Hunt became the first woman to apply to the medical school. Dean Oliver Wendell Holmes asked her to withdraw her application. The practicing healer made another attempt in 1849 that would also fail. This convergence did not go unnoticed. Mary Putnam Jacobi, herself a leader among the first generation of women doctors, writes,

> But, on the eve of success, Miss Hunt's cause was shipwrecked, by collision and entanglement with that of another [group] of the unenfranchised to privileges. At the beginning of the session, two, and later a third, colored man, had appeared among the students, and created by their appearance intense dissatisfaction. When, as if to crown this outrage to gentlemanly feeling, it was announced that a woman was also about to be admitted, the students felt their cup of humiliation was full, and popular indignation boiled over in a general meeting. Here resolutions were adopted, remonstrating against the "amalgamation of the sexes and races."[1]

Jacobi frames the affront presented by Hunt and the unnamed "colored" men as a combined insult to the "gentlemanly feeling" of Harvard's white male medical students, referring to what the scholar Dana Nelson recognizes as the consolidation of white fraternity as national civic identity in the United States.[2] Discussions of race are marginal in Jacobi's essay on the history of women in medicine, but they are part of the widespread analogy between chattel slavery and women's rights—which in turn made exploitative equivalences between axes of race and gender that ultimately subordinated one over the other, erasing Black and other women of color.[3] Women occupy "a truly colonial position," Jacobi concludes, using race as a vehicle for the comparison that universalizes the white woman as womanhood writ large.[4] The logic of the separate spheres governed white middle-class American gender roles: men could freely participate in the public sphere, while women were confined to the private sphere of domesticity. Efforts to bar women from medicine have "always been purely sentimental," she argues: "There has always been a sentimental and powerful opposition to every social change that tended to increase the development and complexity of the social organism, by increasing the capacities and multiplying the relations of its members."[5] Her rationale for (white) women's rights presents a striking minority counterpoint to the reworking of the separate spheres typified by "The Declaration of Sentiments" from the 1848 event held at Seneca Falls, New York, that is considered the first women's rights convention. In Jacobi's framing, the people against social progress are the sentimental ones. Jacobi implies that her rejection of sentimentality—which might be demonized as frigidity—is in fact her own mastery of the coolly detached analysis of the medical profession required to diagnose the "social organism" for eugenic ends.

This chapter begins the shift in this book from writings by men to writings by women responding to the nineteenth-century American culture of sentiment through critique, ambivalence, repudiation. In the first volume of Elizabeth Cady Stanton, Susan B. Anthony, Matilda Joslyn Gage, and Ida Husted Harper's *History of Woman Suffrage* (1881), their narrative that canonizes their take on the movement,[6] the iconic activists turn to sentimental race science for the naturalized justification of an implicitly white feminist agenda for suffrage: "Combe and Spurzheim, proving by their Phrenological discoveries that the feelings, sentiments, and affections of the soul mould and shape the skull, gave new importance to woman's thought as mother of the race."[7] Science signified the modernity of the movement: Lydia Folger Fowler, one of the first women to get a medical degree in the United States, is listed alongside luminaries like Mary Wollstonecraft, Lydia Maria Child, and Margaret Fuller on the dedication page of *History of Woman Suffrage*. Fowler, a suffrage activist who was the first woman to be a professor at a U.S. medical college, was married to the famous phrenologist Lorenzo Fowler and won her reputation as a practitioner of that popular race science. White women's entrance into the political sphere as they strove to achieve what would become the Nineteenth Amendment to the U.S. Constitution came with an embrace of the affective biopolitical hegemony that produced the nation-state.[8] As Kyla Schuller illuminates for us, the work of the much-praised vanguard of white feminist suffrage activists and physicians was based on a normative model of biological essentialist sex differentiation that empowered bourgeois white women who could claim their own stake in colonial biopolitics.[9] Whatever abolitionist leanings white female suffrage activists like Stanton and Anthony once espoused mutated into anti-Black racism with the passage of the Fifteenth Amendment, which granted voting rights to Black men. Bitter, Stanton and Anthony turned upon their ally Frederick Douglass and suppressed the work of Black women leaders like Sojourner Truth, Ida B. Wells, and Frances Ellen Watkins Harper—the last of whom I will discuss at length in chapter 4.[10]

In 1849 Elizabeth Blackwell graduated from Geneva Medical College and became the first American woman to earn a degree in medicine.[11] Early women doctors understood that their careers placed them symbolically at the fore of what would be called the New Woman movement.[12] Indeed, in the cultural imagination of the period the woman doctor character recurs as a voice for women's rights. Examples include Harriet Beecher Stowe's aspiring doctor Ida Van Arsdel in *My Wife and I; or, Harry Henderson's Story* (1871), Rebecca Harding Davis's eponymous physician in "A Day with Doctor Sarah" (1878), and Henry James's Mary Prance in *The Bostonians* (1885-86).[13] The white middle-class woman doctor emerges as the main character in a cluster of late nineteenth-century American novels: William Dean Howells's *Dr. Breen's Practice* (1881), Elizabeth Stuart Phelps's *Doctor Zay* (first published as a book in 1882, after being serialized in Howells's *Atlantic*), Sarah Orne Jewett's *A Country Doctor* (1884), and Annie Nathan Meyer's *Helen Brent, M.D.* (1892).[14] In these novels the woman doctor grapples with the persistent gendered issue of balancing the public and private aspects of her life, and her confrontation with the question of marriage signals the climax of these texts—each of which presents an allegory of personal and political sentiments. The zero-sum cultural paradigm of marriage versus career reflects the strict separation between the spheres of men's and women's lives in American culture chronicled earlier in the century by Alexis de Tocqueville in *Democracy in America* (1835). "In America the independence of woman is irrecoverably lost in the bonds of matrimony," he famously observes.[15]

Tensions between the marriage plot and the quest plot run throughout Anglo-American fiction about and by women in the nineteenth and early twentieth centuries, allowing for the exploration of changing gender roles through negotiations between personal agency and social structures. According to Rachel Blau DuPlessis, the most radical of these narrative strategies enable a critique of the heterosexual romance that opens space for a range of queer desires and kinships.[16] The convention of double proposals highlighted by the critic Karen Tracey, for instance, provide moments of interdeterminancy in which characters could navigate different trajectories of courtship that complicate the conservative inevitability of romantic resolutions.[17] Leslie Petty points out that many of these late nineteenth-century novels specifically dramatize debates about women's activism like suffrage work, wherein romance is the metaphorical playing field for the dynamics of the political arena.[18]

Statements in support of women's suffrage by Jacobi, Phelps, and Jewett appeared together in "Would Women Vote?," an 1888 newspaper piece that presented the opinions of over thirty famous white women of the era.[19] The professional medical authority of the woman doctor posed new challenges to the gender politics of the marriage plot during the age of the New Woman's demand for suffrage rights. In Howells's *Dr. Breen's Practice*, the eponymous Grace Breen struggles with her vocation as a physician and finally marries the factory owner Walter Libby after rejecting the misogynistic Dr. Rufus Mulbridge.[20] While she gives up formal medical practice, Breen cares for the families of the workers in her husband's factory. Phelps's exemplary Dr. Zaidee Atalanta Lloyd, known as "Doctor Zay," coolly rebuffs the advances of her patient, the unemployed lawyer Waldo Yorke. In the disquieting final scenes of the novel, Zay, weakened by illness, returns the now-practicing Yorke's affections when he promises she can keep practicing her profession.[21] Jewett's bildungsroman, *A Country Doctor*, follows the headstrong orphan Anna "Nan" Prince, who shows a natural aptitude for medicine under the tutelage of Dr. John Leslie. The novel concludes with Prince turning down the marriage proposal of the conservative lawyer George Gerry to pursue her vocation. Meyer's Dr. Helen Brent is showered with professional accolades, which makes her lawyer fiancé feel emasculated—so he marries someone else. While Brent continues her acclaimed work, her former lover finally pleads for her affections on her terms after his frivolous bride runs off with a notorious rake. Of these four works, which are often discussed as a cluster by scholars, Jewett's *A Country Doctor* has garnered the most critical attention, followed by Howell's and Phelps's novels, while Meyer's *Helen*

Brent, M.D. largely remains only a footnote to the other three.²² The didacticism of each novel's political commentary about gender roles can be correlated to the narrative's value of marriage as an index of the woman doctor's personal and professional success or failure. Will the woman doctor, in the vanguard of the New Woman movement, be domesticated? Or will she be consigned to the queer state of spinsterhood, opening new avenues of self-actualization for women of a certain race and class?²³

In light of Jacobi's scorn for "purely sentimental" opposition to women's social progress, the woman doctor character offers insight into the specter of frigidity, a queer unwomanliness that haunts both the marriage plot and the rise of the New Woman. This feminized coldness relates to the cultural ideology of women's sexual restraint that the historian Nancy Cott argues developed early in the long nineteenth century to grant white women a degree of moral and spiritual authority.²⁴ Frigidity was medicalized as a pathological condition often associated with hysteria and viewed as endemic to modernity. Often broadly used in both medical practice and the popular imagination, this queerly gendered mode of unfeeling functioned as a means of control, diagnosing the deviance of women who did not conform to their expected roles in society as affectively, somatically, and psychologically susceptible subjects to the demands of heteronormative hegemony.²⁵ I read these women doctor novels as encounters with that oppressive "gentlemanly feeling," in Jacobi's words—encounters that flirt with the possibility of queer failure through the reclamation of frigidity. In an attempt to disentangle the sexological conflations between gender identity, expression, and sexuality, this argument centers on the waxing and waning intensities of sexual and romantic desire.²⁶ I devote particular attention to Phelps's deeply ambivalent *Doctor Zay* because of the author's choice to have the primary narrative focalization through the male character's desiring perspective of his doctor. Given the cultural correlation between love and political desire, queer female frigidity registers dissatisfaction with the pressures to court the approval of men in both the private and the public spheres. I position this reconsideration of frigidity through writings by Jacobi and Blackwell, members of the first generation of white women physicians who seek to redefine sympathy and sentiment in their field while confronting expectations about their personal lives. I suggest that the operations of this professional frigidity should be considered alongside the coeval invention of anesthesia, a technology of affective and somatic management developed from the evolving repertoire of modern medical practices. To invoke Sara Ahmed's feminist killjoy tool kit, perhaps it is unsurprising there would be overlaps between painkillers and killing joy.²⁷

These woman doctor characters consider whether to numb the imperatives of marriage and family by prioritizing their medical careers, modelling a white feminist reappropriation of the masculinized authority of medical science's disciplinary detachment as a justificatory framework for their management of feelings. In all these novels save Howells's, the woman doctor is pitted against a male lawyer who is both her love interest and antagonist—a recurring convention in the majority of these texts not yet addressed by scholars. In this chapter I argue that the novels respond to anxieties about the New Woman channeled through gendered struggles over everyday emotional labor. Following Petty's work, I find that through the marriage plot the novels stage debates about the tactics involved in the fight for legal recognition of suffrage and other rights.[28] By attending to the symptom of unfeeling known as frigidity, I trace a contradictory thread running through the historical narrative of women's entrance into medicine that is usually understood as the exploitation of naturalized, gendered feelings to argue for the suitability of women as professional healers. Through this professionalized frigidity, white women doctors work through the possibility of reconceiving its pathologization as a technology of disaffection. Nonetheless, the extent of this transformation reveals its limits: even the subversion of the white bourgeois marriage plot becomes the reconsolidation of hegemony through white homonationalism.

The First Generation of Women Doctors / Frigidity as Etiology or Technology?

In "What Is an Emotion?" (1884), an argument for physiological changes as the origin of feelings rather than their effects, the philosopher William James remarks, "it seems to me that if I were to become corporeally anaesthetic, I should be excluded from the life of the affections, harsh and tender alike, and drag out an existence of merely cognitive or intellectual form."[29] This state of unfeeling, he concludes, would not appeal to "those born after the revival of the worship of sensibility." Anesthesia, the paradigmatic medical technology of somatic unfeeling, was first revealed to the public on October 16, 1846, when the Boston dentist William T. G. Morton used the vapor of sulphuric or diethyl ether as an anesthetic in a demonstration at Massachusetts General Hospital. By 1848 nitrous oxide and chloroform were also accepted anesthetic compounds for medical procedures. Anesthesia was adopted more readily into medical practice than vaccination was, becoming common within seven years of Morton's demonstration.[30] With this development, insensitivity became an expedient device of strategic numbing rather than simply a callous state of nonreactivity for both the patient's experience and the practitioner's procedure. No longer did surgeons have to choose between preserving life and inflicting pain. According to Martin Pernick's study of the cultural impact of anesthesia, due to increased rates of surgical success and a lower death rate, "the surgeon no longer needed quite so thick a self-protective emotional armor."[31]

Before the advent of this technology, the doctor's control over his affects to properly affect others was a signature trait of the profession, which was defined by its masculinity thanks to the influence of Benjamin Rush—whose practice of "heroic" medicine emphasized the manliness of treatments and the macho endurance of pain.[32] Melville caricatures heroic medicine's excesses in his novelized memoir *White-Jacket* (1850) through the character of a surgeon, Dr. Cadwallader Cuticle: "Indeed, long habituation to the dissecting-room and the amputation-table had made him seemingly impervious to the ordinary emotions of humanity. Yet you could not say that Cuticle was essentially a cruel-hearted man. His apparent heartlessness must have been of a purely scientific origin."[33] Although Cuticle represents an extreme example, this ongoing connection between masculine professionalism and disciplined emotions can be seen in Daniel Webster Cathell's manual *Book on the Physician Himself and Things That Concern His Reputation and Success*, first published in 1881 and with eleven editions by 1902.[34] Noting that business sagacity is necessary for a successful medical practice, Cathell also comments, "If you have the self-command to control your emotions, temper, and passions, and to maintain a cool, philosophic equipoise under the thousand irritative provocations given to you by foolish patients and their friends ... it will give you great advantage over nervous and excitable physicians who cannot."[35] Masculine self-discipline was key to the development of professionalism: the doctor's command over his expertise and clients is matched by his command over himself.[36] Such self-governance affirmed his right to govern, reinforcing the colonial divide of affectability. In that regard, the skilled physician not only masters detachment but weaponizes sentiment so that he can manipulate female patients: "[The doctor must] appeal to the weak side of woman—*her emotions*."[37] The validation of a precursor to emotional intelligence is but another tool of domination. However, the invention of anesthesia altered patient-doctor relationships, refining sympathy into a more complex, individual negotiation of power. As Pernick puts it, "anesthesia made possible a greater range of medical sentiments toward patients—both more routine callousness and more benevolent sensitivity."[38] Thus, as an innovation anesthesia externalized the tactical use of feeling and unfeeling associated with masculine professionalism: no longer could the naturalized gendering of feelings according to the ideology of separate spheres easily justify the exclusion of women from the practice of medicine.

Sexual Anesthesia and the Cutting Edge of Medicine

Anesthesia has been identified as a significant factor for the entrance of women into medical science by Regina Morantz-Sanchez, Pernick, and others.[39] Anesthetics were a material tool that gave women symbolic access to the affective requirements of medical practice when assumptions about feminine feelings were seen as a reason to bar them from the discipline. The technology disrupted the conventions of masculinity and femininity in the profession.[40] As Morantz-Sanchez notes, "the use of ether and chloroform weakened this argument and 'feminized' medicine by undermining more generally the heroic image of the physician."[41] Through her profession, the woman practitioner could suspend—or have an excuse for avoiding—the affective obligations imposed upon her. If the invention of anesthetics can be said to have feminized medicine, it also masculinized women doctors.

The implications of anesthesia offer a way to see the nuances in the medicalized queerness of female frigidity, anxieties about women doctors, and fixation on the romantic choices of the woman doctor character in the marriage plot. In his landmark *Studies in the Psychology of Sex* (1900), the sexologist Havelock Ellis includes in his catalog of "sexual perversions" associated with women the phenomenon known as "frigidity or hyphedonia, and (in more complete form) sexual anesthesia or anaphrodism, or erotic blindness, or anhedonia."[42] His definition of anesthesia follows Richard von Krafft-Ebing's designation for the absence of sexual instinct in his foundational *Psychopathia Sexualis* (1886).[43] Ellis uses "frigidity" interchangeably with "sexual anesthesia" as his two most common terms for discussing what he views as a medical condition prevalent among women. He concludes that frigidity, the lack of appropriate affective and somatic responsiveness to the imperatives of heterosexual desire and reproduction, must be viewed as an aberration:

> It seems to me that a state of sexual anesthesia, relative or absolute, cannot be considered as anything but abnormal. To take even the lowest ground, the satisfaction of the reproductive function ought to be at least as gratifying as the evacuation of the bowels or bladder; while, if we take, as we certainly must, higher ground than this, an act which is at once

the supreme fact and symbol of love and the supreme creative act cannot under normal conditions be other than the most pleasurable of all acts, or it would stand in violent opposition to all that we find in nature.[44]

The parallels between anesthesia as technology and the alleged abnormality of frigidity revolve around the threatening agency of women to be queerly detached. Significantly, in this volume Ellis presents his analysis of female sexual deviance in the section "Love and Pain." Consequently, the woman doctor has the prerogative to wield anesthesia, sexual or otherwise, in her professional management of her feelings and her influence over the bodies of her patients. For her purposes, then, frigidity is not a pathologized state but a professional choice.

In their gender nonconformity, there seemed to be something queer about women who demanded work and rights in the masculinized public sphere that was amplified for women doctors, who simultaneously trespassed upon disciplinary norms and had the authority to reshape them.[45] When Jacobi wrote that women physicians were charged with "unsexing themselves" in her essay "Shall Women Practice Medicine?" (1882), one of the unnamed accusers she likely had in mind was the esteemed Harvard medical professor Edward H. Clarke.[46] In his infamous *Sex in Education: Or, a Fair Chance for the Girls* (1873), Clarke decries higher education for women from his objective scientific standpoint. Women cannot engage in the work of the mind because of the limits of their bodies: the intellectual stimulation of education redirects the energy required for a woman's reproductive health. Therefore, Clarke argues, to educate a woman is to render her queer: the benighted female becomes afflicted by "the hermaphroditic condition that sometimes accompanies spinsterism" and leads to "neuralgia, uterine disease, hysteria, and other derangements of the nervous system."[47] Modernity is the etiological source of female ailments: it inflicts the tragic fate of frigidity upon the women who succumb to the lure of education.

In defiance of the likes of Clarke, by the end of the nineteenth century more women had entered the medical field than any other profession except teaching: women accounted for 4–5 percent of physicians.[48] The rush to professionalize medical science in the nineteenth century to demarcate mainstream American medicine from Indigenous, folk, and alternative forms of healing like homeopathy led to the rise of medical societies and certifications, culminating with the founding of the American Medical Association in 1847. Although the association did not admit people of color or white women for decades, these marginalized groups took advantage of the turmoil surrounding the standards of the changing profession so they could redefine what it means to be a doctor.[49] In her comprehensive history of American women in medicine, Morantz-Sanchez highlights feeling as intrinsic to the argument that the practice of medicine was a logical extension of the feminine sphere of domesticity. This "domestic feminism" approach leveraged the tradition of Rush and other intellectuals on the use of sympathy and sentimentalism as scientific framework and praxis.[50] Exemplified by Blackwell, this strategy—whether conservative in its acceptance of the two spheres or revolutionary in its subversion of that ideology of gender—extended the logic of cultural assumptions about women's affective sensibilities that naturalized the woman's place in the home: as Morantz-Sanchez remarks, "Medicine appeared especially suited for women because it combined the alleged authority of science with a dedication to alleviating suffering that seemed inherently female."[51] This practice can be seen as a precursor to feminist science studies by thinkers like Sandra Harding, Alison Jagger, and Londa Schiebinger: critiques of detached scientific objectivity and affirmations of the role of feelings towards a more feminist scientific epistemology.[52] In contrast to this feminizing of the profession, however, Jacobi eschewed the use of sentimentalism: she was committed to the set of cultural values bound up with the ideal of objective science that was implicitly associated with masculine authority—which was at the time a minoritarian approach characterized by Morantz-Sanchez as "fundamentally universalistic and assimilationist."[53] Of course, these ideologies were not dichotomous in practice: Jacobi and Blackwell were colleagues, even working together at one point in a hospital founded by Blackwell; Jacobi praised Blackwell in her history of women in medicine; and their generation of women doctors simultaneously changed the discipline and internalized its operations. By viewing these differing strategies in relation to the anxieties about the queer woman doctor, however, places pressure upon the antisentimental thread and draws attention to how the pathologization of frigidity polices and erases the validity of the woman doctor's appropriation of anesthesia as a physical and metaphorical instrument deployed for professional, personal, and political ends.

In her inaugural address at the opening of the Women's Medical College of the New York Infirmary on October 1, 1880, Jacobi reworks the masculine professionalism of medical tradition to make room for more expansive gender expressions for women without making recourse to essentialist arguments about women's affects or abilities. She declares that human minds are "living organisms which can only use what they have assimilated and digested, and wrought into the texture of their inmost fibers."[54] Jacobi articulates a position for women doctors between what the theorist Denise Ferreira da Silva calls the affectable I and the transparent I: acknowledging the permeability of being, these trained female professionals lay claim to control over that biopolitical malleability, according to the scientific ideology of impressibility identified by Schuller.[55] What is striking in Jacobi's speech is her insistence on the gendered experiences of women physicians, though she often uses a masculine pronoun to refer to them. Jacobi emphasizes sympathy as trained composure for doctors who cannot indulge in sentimental excesses. "He must be capable of sympathy with physical suffering, at once delicate and profound. To be efficacious, this sympathy must be fine, and not blubbering," she states. "Notwithstanding this personal sympathy, the physician is studying his case as coolly, impartially, abstractly as if it were a problem in algebra."[56] To compensate for sexist bias in a world where she admits that "the mass of knowledge, power, and force is still overwhelmingly on the masculine side," women must develop an intensified version of the traits coded as masculine: "To produce upon the mind of the average public the same impression as may be made by a masculine physician, the woman must exhibit comparatively more force of mind and character" (351). Jacobi shrugs off concerns about Clarke's warnings about the "hermaphroditic state" associated with spinsterism: "The question of marriage again, which complicates everything else in the life of women, cannot fail to complicate their professional life. It does so, whether the marriage exist or does not exist, that is, as much for unmarried as for unmarried women. In my opinion the increased vigor and vitality accruing to healthy women from the bearing and possession of children, a good deal more than compensates for the difficulties involved in caring for them, when professional duties replace the more usual ones, of sewing, cooking, etc." (353). Correlation is not causation in a society that relegates women to the inferior position. Rather than focusing on compensating for alleged unwomanliness, Jacobi expands the range of acceptable life choices for women by downplaying the centrality of marriage to the definition of womanhood: "Whatever is done, either with or without marriage, can evidently be well done only in proportion as more complete intellectual development and more perfect training enables the woman to cope with the peculiar difficulties inherent in her destiny." She even calls on female medical students to seek careers beyond gynecology, obstetrics, and other fields focused on women's health and find their vocations in surgery and general medicine. It is not that she does not care: rather, she refuses to care in the ways demanded by Clarke and his ilk.

For her finale, Jacobi compares women doctors to the early American colonizers, urging them to consolidate their stake in the field and, implicitly, the destiny of the nation.[57] Here we can hear resonances with the particular form of settler colonialism identified by Scott Morgensen as settler homonationalism; early white women doctors, according to Schuller, actively participated in eugenic homonationalism.[58] Comparing male medical students to "howling savages," Jacobi tells her audience, "you should learn to look at yourself as a colony just landed in a new country; compelled to found a state in spite of hardship and peril, and danger, and isolation, by means of the vigorous and intelligent co-operation of each of its members."[59] She emasculates those reactionary men who protest the inclusion of women, comparing them to failed settlers without the manly spirit required to dominate Indigenous lands. Jacobi calls upon her listeners to become like colonizers with their "self-denying, intelligent heroism, which is needed for our enterprise—for this also still deserves to be called heroic" (356). Through the invocation of "heroism" she reappropriates the strict masculinity of Rush's philosophy of heroic medicine and places herself and the female medical students in the direct line of descent from the founding father of American medicine. If there is something queer about the white woman doctor, this rhetoric of settler colonial homonationalism contextualizes her audacity as continuous with the historical arc of the national project.

The Fear of the Queer Woman Doctor / Medical Careers and the Marriage Plot

Jacobi directly rebuts Clarke's claims about the incompatibility between women's physiology and intellectual development in "The Question of Rest for Women during Menstruation" (1876).[60] Her research paper combined the results of surveys, other statistics, case studies, and the findings of experiments with variables like oxygen and urea, and it won Harvard's Boylston Prize. Nonetheless, *Sex in Education* went through at least twenty printings before the end of the nineteenth century, testimony that the specter of the queer educated woman could not be so easily dispelled.[61] The subgenre of woman doctor novels emerges from this inexhaustible cultural appetite for information about the supposed dichotomy of marriage and medicine, despite the range of apologetics from women doctors under pressure to disavow their potential queerness.[62]

In her memoir, *Pioneer Work in Opening the Medical Profession to Women* (1895), Blackwell discusses her achievement as the first American woman doctor to graduate from a recognized medical college. She turns to a journal from her youth to express the conviction she still holds: "I felt more determined than ever to become a physician, and thus place a strong barrier between me and all ordinary marriage. I must have something to engross my thoughts, some object in life which will fill this vacuum and prevent this sad wearing away of the heart."[63] Blackwell expresses the reverse of de Tocqueville's observation about the American woman and matrimony: the woman physician loses herself in her profession and bends herself to that yoke rather than to the marital one. Blackwell portrays her chosen profession as the organic outgrowth of redirecting heterosexual drives into one's vocation. Through sentimental discourse, she naturalizes her supposed frigidity as the queer spinster physician. Despite the affective differences between this and Jacobi's approach, Blackwell too figures herself as a pioneer who is proudly perpetuating the settler colonial project.

The demands of the profession provide women doctors with an excuse to numb themselves to the emotional demands of domesticity and to freeze the encroachment of impositions. The journalist Gertrude Stuart Baillie's 1894 essay for the *Woman's Medical Journal* addresses the allegations of queerness—that the woman doctor has "become more or less womanly and lose[s] those charms of person and sentimentality which are supposed to be the birthright of every woman."[64] "Should Professional Woman Marry?" takes as a given that there are indeed a higher number of spinsters in medicine compared to other professions (294). Instead, the implicit argument is that frigidity is the vilified exercise of professional affective control. These women possess those "same natural instincts as their mothers before them," Baillie claims, but "their liberal education has stored their minds with the fundamental truths of nature. They are not stunted ascetics by any means, but they have learned to make their bodies subservient to their wills" (293). Spinsterhood is a form of trained strength: women physicians "could not conscientiously give their hand where their heart was not, for their heart was given to their work . . . [they] cannot work well under the yoke of matrimony. She [the woman doctor] lives by and for the people and hence must ever be in readiness to answer their summons, which, should she be married, it might not always be propitious to do so" (294). Like women who follow the traditional cult of domesticity, women doctors view their work as a moral calling that springs from an innate femininity, but "they are no longer compelled to sacrifice themselves to their own emotions." What was once everyday emotional labor expected of women becomes formal work for which women receive money and greater social recognition.

Historical reality belies the presumed ubiquity of the spinster women doctor: in fact, such women found success in various forms of romantic relationships. Contrary to popular assumptions, Morantz-Sanchez remarks that the number of married women physicians was disproportionately high compared to women in other professions.[65] Although the sentimental Blackwell was a spinster, Jacobi the rational scientist was married to the famed pediatrician Abraham Jacobi (138). Some early women doctors even openly embraced the queer implications of their lives. Morantz-Sanchez finds multiple examples in the archive of women doctors who were collaborators in medicine and coupled in life, such as Lillian Welsh and Mary Sherwood in Baltimore and Elizabeth Cushier and Elizabeth Blackwell's sister Emily in New York City (133). Perhaps as a rebellious gesture, the lifelong spinsters of the first cohort of women physicians viewed their relationships to the profession as their preferred form of life commitment (130). These accomplished women doctors created alternatives to the constraints of the separate spheres, embracing or otherwise flouting the queer spinsterly state to which Clarke condemns intellectual women and rerouting their emotional energies to their professions and other women. As Schuller notes, "civilized sexuality made room for generative desires between white women of means" through the institution of medical science.[66]

Thus, cultural anxieties about the challenges posed by the New Woman and her struggles for agency coalesced around the figure of the woman doctor, with the marriage plot acting as the literary litmus test for the women's politics and desires. On the surface, a consideration of the four novels by Howells, Phelps, Jewett, and Meyer in their order of publication roughly suggests a triumphant evolution of the woman doctor's struggle to achieve work-life balance according to her own terms. The texts both then and now tend to be read with an eye to their veracity and politics. The British doctor Sophia Jex-Blake reviews Howells's and Phelps's novels in an 1893 essay titled "Medical Women in Fiction," in which she chooses to put aside questions of literary merit to address accuracy.[67] Jex-Blake eviscerates *Dr. Breen's Practice*, calling the eponymous character "the kind of woman who never ought to have undertaken a medical career," and views the novel's greatest insult to actual women doctors the fact that Breen's impetus for going into medicine stems from "the inevitable 'disappointment'"—a euphemism for the stereotyped failure in love.[68] Claiming that Breen is typical of the misogyny in Howells's writing, Stanton voices the need to prioritize exceptional female characters over the genre conventions of Howells's realism in light of the fight for women's rights: "They [the characters] may be true to nature, but as it is nature under false conditions, I should rather have some pen portray the ideal woman, and paint a type worthy of our imitation."[69] While Jex-Blake concedes that Howells had reasons to choose Breen as a character, she laments that "those who know even a few of the hundreds of hard-headed, cool, and capable medical women of America can hardly avoid regret that it was not one of these that was taken as the type to be portrayed on Mr. Howells's picturesque canvas."[70] She notes the stark comparison between the novels of Howells and Phelps: "I do not know whether *Dr. Zay* was written as a practical protest against *Dr. Breen's Practice*, but it would be difficult to conceive a greater contrast than is presented by the heroines in the two books. If Dr. Breen was exceptionally weak and morbid, Dr. Zay is almost preternaturally robust and healthy, in mind and body; and the amount of work she gets through without perceptible effort, and without loss of physical beauty and bloom, is enough to excite envy in the minds of most practitioners of either sex."[71] Jex-Blake is disconcerted by what she refers to as the "shadowless perfection of the heroine" in Phelps's novel, but she appreciates "that we are in this case spared the traditional 'disappointment.'"[72] Notably, however, she avoids discussing how the narrative ends. The relationship between these first works in the subgenre is complicated.[73] On the one hand, Howells encouraged Phelps's work and began the serialization of *Doctor Zay* after his *Dr. Breen's Practice* had been serialized. On the other hand, Phelps did not hesitate to comment on the flaws in her editor's writing. Drawing from their epistolary archive, the critic Jean Masteller notes that Phelps wrote to Howells, "I don't feel that Dr. Breen is a fair example of professional women; indeed, I know she is not for I know the class thoroughly from long personal observation under unusual opportunities."[74] A few years later, a review of Jewett's *A Country Doctor* in the *Nation* commented that the trend of three acclaimed popular authors writing about women doctors "makes it worthwhile to compare their stories closely."[75] After Howells's weak Breen and Phelps's initially independent Zay, Jewett's proudly single Prince has been widely viewed by scholars such as Masteller and Marjorie Pryse as a paragon of feminist modernity.[76] As for the triumphant Brent, the righteous force of whose professionalism bends her former lover to meet her terms, the character comes out of the context of Meyer's women's rights activism that included editing the collection *Woman's Work in America* in which Jacobi's essay on women doctors appeared. Meyer's preface defends her editorial choice not to have an essay on women and marriage. She writes dismissively, "So far as I knew women had never been denied that privilege, and so it could have no legitimate place in my book."[77]

Unlike the women doctor characters that were to follow, Howells's Breen is a far cry from the ideal New Woman. Undeniably, the narrator is biased against Breen: she is described as having "a child's severe morality" and acting like an "inexperienced girl" and a "shame-smitten child."[78] In a novel whose title highlights the eponymous character's practice, she is presented as strikingly unpracticed in her work and life in general: the financial means that allow her to pay for her degree also make it possible for her to avoid developing a real practice. A generous reading of Breen, however, might note how Howells's protagonist copes with the burden of representation compounded by the continual undermining of her authority by everyone around her. Breen admits that her reason for studying medicine was thwarted love, combined with pressures to emulate unnamed female medical luminaries for the sake of womankind: "I wished to be a physician because I was a woman, and because—because—I had failed where—other women's hopes are" (43). Her plans to practice after graduation under the guidance of an experienced physician are derailed by her friend and only patient, Louise, who does not respect her expertise. Louise calls for a "*man* doctor," allowing for the introduction of the macho Dr. Rufus Mulbridge, who continually dismisses Breen's abilities even when he declares his romantic interest in her (64). Breen's only supporter is Miss Gleason, who acts as a continual reminder of the pressures to live up to the ideal of the New Woman and whose idolization of Breen has lesbian overtones. "If you yield, you make it harder for other women to help themselves hereafter, and you confirm such people as these in their distrust of female physicians," Gleason warns (79). Unfortunately, Breen internalizes the misogyny in her environment, and she doubts not only herself but the abilities of other women. She is repelled by the queer associations with her profession: Gleason and her dangerously New Woman ways discomfit her. Breen is determined to cling to normative ideas of womanhood, eschewing any associations with frigidity implied by her profession: she cannot "coldly bear the confusion to which her being a doctor put men" (11). In medical school Breen once prized "masculine simplicity," but she quickly disavows this Jacobi-esque approach for its queer connotations: "the over-success of some young women, her fellows at the school, in this direction had disgusted her with it, and she had perceived that after all there is nothing better for a girl even a girl who is a doctor of medicine, than a ladylike manner" (96). In the end, she chooses to marry and abandon formal medical practice, banishing her worries about her queerness as a spinster woman doctor.

The Law of Nature versus the Science of Nature

In contrast to *Dr. Breen's Practice*, the novels by Phelps, Jewett, and Meyer all feature a male lawyer as a foil for an exemplary woman doctor, drawing out the cultural stakes for the New Woman physician in the marriage plot. Like medicine, the modern discipline of law was one of the original gentlemanly professions that, according to Burton Bledstein, lays claim to "esoteric knowledge about the universe" and thereby holds "moral authority."[79] Law did not open to nineteenth-century women to the same degree that medicine did, despite a similar upheaval in the two fields in terms of organizational licensing, the growth of specialized schools, and shifting definitions of professionalism: by the end of the century, there were only about 1,000 female lawyers to 113,500 male lawyers, while there were 7,400 female doctors to 124,600 male doctors.[80] Morantz-Sanchez contrasts the entrance of women into the two professions: "Though women lawyers justified their legal work in a similar fashion, it was harder for them to prove that law was an extension of women's natural sphere; indeed, few women preferred law to medicine in the nineteenth and early twentieth centuries."[81] The trope of pairing a woman doctor and a male lawyer in the marriage plot resonates with the gender dynamics of the two professions upheld as culturally symbolic authorities. The feminist and queer of color theorist Sara Ahmed notes about the reactionary power of love: "Love becomes a sign of respectable femininity, and of maternal qualities narrated as the capacity to be touched by others. The reproduction of femininity is tied up with the reproduction of the national ideal through the work of love."[82] These novels present the gendered clash between medicine and law as authoritative regimes of truth: the woman doctor represents a feminist view of the natural order, while the male lawyer who woos her stands in for what Jacobi describes in her history as the "sentimental and powerful opposition to every social change."[83] Masculine anxiety about the New Woman could swathe its chauvinism in well-meaning affection, thereby domesticating the professional woman. Her professional composure, maligned as frigidity, marks her resistance to that prerogative of patriarchal desire and its apparatuses.[84]

Jewett's *A Country Doctor* naturalizes Prince's childhood affinity for medical science in ways that view queerness as potential, not pathology, culminating in Prince's rejection of Gerry's marriage proposal as her initiation into adulthood. Prince's professional aspirations repurpose sentimentalism: as she gets older, "her inward sympathy with a doctor's and surgeon's work grew stronger and stronger," and when she is on the cusp of applying for medical school, "her whole heart went out to this work."[85] Jewett, herself a doctor's child, gives her character both biological and symbolic fathers who are exemplary physicians.[86] When as a child Prince puts a turkey's broken leg into a splint after observing the work of Leslie, her mentor, Marilla, her caregiver, remarks: "Her father studied medicine, you know. It is the most amazing thing how people inherit."[87] While this lineage of male doctors operates as validation, the novel decouples the profession from gender.[88] Leslie defends Prince's professional aspirations to a colleague, Dr. Ferris: "I don't care whether it's a man's work or a woman's work; if it is hers I'm going to help her the very best way I can."[89] Ferris retorts, "don't be disappointed when she's ten years older if she picks out a handsome young man and thinks there is nothing like housekeeping."[90] Leslie inverts that logic into an acceptance of Prince's potential spinsterhood: "I believe it is a mistake for such a woman to marry," for "the law of her nature is that she must live alone and work alone."[91] Leslie is echoing Elizabeth Blackwell: if Prince gives her heart to medicine, she cannot give her heart in marriage. Or, rather, this affective equation acts as an excuse for Prince to be strategically frigid: unfeelingly indifferent to the idea of matrimony and the limitations it poses to her professional ambitions.

Defying gender stereotypes and untrammeled by heterosexual norms, there is something a bit queer about Prince that has been celebrated by scholars who have raised the question of Jewett's own possible queerness, following biographical evidence that she may have been in a so-called Boston marriage— an intimate long-term relationship with another woman.[92] Jewett describes Prince's deviant sexuality in ways that resemble the asexuality of sexual anesthesia or what Krafft-Ebing and Ellis might have diagnosed as symptoms of inversion—that is, what would become known as homosexuality because it was the inverse of the normative collapse between gender expression and sexual orientation. Leslie observes that "Nan's feeling toward her boy-playmates is exactly the same as toward the girls she knows."[93] Given her indifference to heteronormative desire, the grown-up Prince develops a closer relationship with Gerry because she believes he possesses "none of the manner which constantly insisted upon her remembering that he was a man and she was a girl" (244). Her assessment is incorrect: Gerry views the encroachment of women's rights as an insult to manhood and the "usurpation of men's duties," especially "their tinkering at the laws" (294 and 295). To such a man, a prospective woman doctor like Prince is an emasculating specter: when she fixes a man's dislocated shoulder, Gerry "felt weak and womanish, and somehow wished it had been he who could play the doctor" (266). In his love for Prince, he embodies that "gentlemanly feeling" described by Jacobi that resents social progress. As Prince acknowledges, "I know that all the world's sympathy and all tradition fight on his side" (321). The narrator makes it clear that Gerry's proposal should be seen as much agonistic as it is affectionate: "All his manliness was at stake, and his natural rights would be degraded and lost, if he could not show his power to be greater than her own" (295). Even though Gerry may blame Prince for being insensitive to his feelings, her alleged frigidity responds to a greater imperative than the institution of marriage. "The law of right and wrong must rule even love," she states. "Most girls have an instinct toward marrying, but mine is all against it" (317 and 320). Her understanding of natural law trumps his. Despite the coercions of the structure of feeling associated with the domestic sphere presented by Gerry's entreaties, Prince's affects attach her to the vocation of medicine, allowing her to detach herself from the demands of heterosexual love. Marriage and medicine cannot coexist for women. "The two cannot be taken together in a woman's life as in a man's," proclaims Leslie (335). Prince chooses her profession over marriage, a confident embrace of the queer possibilities implied by the role of the woman doctor that does not heed legal barriers.

In contrast to the overt queerness of Jewett's Prince, Meyer's *Helen Brent, M.D.* imagines a transformation of the institution of marriage that can accommodate the professional New Woman. Much like Gerry, Brent's lawyer fiancé Harold Skidmore feels emasculated by his love's profession. "A woman who can deliberately give up a man's love, a wife's sphere, the only true and real life for a woman, is not capable of suffering. If you really loved me, you would have given up all this, your ambition, your profession—everything. That is love," he cries.[94] Unmoved, Brent addresses the "sphere of the husband" as a corollary to his argument about separate spheres, asking him, "Have we not both devoted our lives, our hopes, and thoughts to our professions?" (31). "I dare not link my life to yours unless you will give up your law," she stipulates, turning the tables on him (31). The reunion of Brent and Skidmore is predicted by the dialogue between the doctor and her sister about the importance of marriage to the women's movement, referring to an editorial in "a prominent woman's journal" that bears echoes of Baillie's essay and that "seemed to think the problem would be solved if professional women would not marry" (128). "Is it wise for women simply to give up the struggle, and to turn their backs on marriage, saying 'Such is not for us?'" asks Brent (129). Nonetheless, she detaches herself from the inevitability of marriage and refuses to be the one who surrenders ground in the war of love. Instead, Skidmore writes contritely to his former love at the novel's end that "some day there will come at your gates a broken Harold, as a supplicant he will come, hat off, eyes lowered, kneeling in the dust" (195-96). What is curious is that Meyer—whose manifold feminist activities included the founding of Barnard College and allying herself with women of color like Zora Neale Hurston—did not fully support suffrage: she was skeptical of arguments about female moral superiority and believed that access to the public sphere would not advance other women's rights issues, like labor reform.[95] Where Jewett has Prince discard her lawyer lover as an outdated ideological impediment to her progressive modernity, Meyer imagines a progressive shift in gender roles that would prompt changes in the heart of the law without explicitly seeking to appeal to legal recognition of women's right to enfranchisement.

"Your Heart Is as Hard as Your Lancet" / *Doctor Zay* and the Fallacy of Reverse Sexism

"In our times and to our women such a problem is practical, indeed. One need not possess genius to understand it now. A career is enough," declares Phelps of the presumed dilemma of marriage for the New Woman in her memoir *Chapters from a Life* (1897).[96] She concludes, "I believe in women; and in their right to their own best possibilities in every department of life."[97] True to this personal creed—whose development was sparked by Phelps's witnessing the toll that domesticity took upon her accomplished writer mother—themes in Phelps's oeuvre involve the importance of women's work in tandem with the validation of spinsters.[98] In *Sex in Education*, Clarke makes a poor choice when he cites Phelps, the "gifted authoress of *The Gates Ajar*," as a source of corroborating evidence about feminine weaknesses.[99] Phelps is among the luminaries rallied to dismantle his arguments in Julia Ward Howe's edited *Sex and Education: A Reply to Dr. E. H. Clarke's "Sex in Education"* (1874).[100] In her scathing riposte to Clarke, Phelps valorizes women doctors as the corrective to his medical misogyny: "Every healthy woman physician knows better; and it is only the woman physician, after all, whose judgment can ever approach the ultimate uses of the physician's testimony to these questions."[101] Her piece shows the influences of her dear friend Dr. Mary Briggs Harris, with whom she shared a work space in the 1870s. Given that *Doctor Zay* was written by such a champion of women doctors and a critic of marriage, it is strange that the resolution of the novel flattens out the eponymous character's potential queer spinsterhood. Although most of the novel derives its comedy from Zay's exceptional professionalism in contrast to the lovelorn incompetence of her patient, Yorke, the final chapters abruptly reverse this satirical dynamic as a weakened Zay's coldness melts into acquiescence when confronted by the force of the now-hale Yorke's love.

Zay is the exemplar of professional frigidity, fending off Yorke's advances with the clinical detachment and controlled sympathy that makes her an excellent physician. Unlike the other novels about women doctors and, indeed, Phelps's other works about women and their careers, *Doctor Zay* focalizes exclusively through the perspective of a male character who imposes his love on a woman who appears to believe her career is enough. In his reading of the novel, Timothy Morris claims that Yorke eroticizes Zay precisely as a result of her cool professional ethics, creating "a romantic, erotic fantasy in order to teach [the novel's] readers how to value a professional woman."[102] However, the fact that—according to Morris—the narrative in Yorke's perspective is one of "erotic suspense" has disquieting implications for the validity of professional women when seen through the sentimental lens that reproduces the prerogative of heterosexual male desire. This work holds a strange place in Phelps's oeuvre: the text falls into the transitional period in the arc of her writing charted by the biographers Lori Duin Kelly and Carol Farley Kessler: shifting the focus from single and otherwise independent women characters to weakened, dependent ones was correlated to Phelps's increasingly poor health in the late 1870s, the loss of Briggs, and her eventual unhappy marriage in 1888 to a younger man who took advantage of her wealth even when she was on her deathbed. While Kelly calls Zay an "exception rather than the rule" during this pessimistic turn, Kessler suggests that Zay's marriage represents not so much enthusiastic consent as sad compromise, as the doctor is "finally ground down"—and these different readings are indicative of the general split among scholars about the novel's ending.[103] Critics remark upon the comical feminization of Yorke: he is portrayed as a hysterical mess in contrast to her authoritative coolness, in what Kristine Swenson argues is Phelps's revision of Silas Weir Mitchell's early neurological work on female hysteria.[104] Despite the seeming reversal of the gendered power dynamic, I suggest that *Doctor Zay* questions the limits of structural transformation through its inclusion of women in the field of medicine. Significantly, Frederick Wegener argues that the blurring of the women doctor's care and romantic interest was a common trope of the time used to discredit their professionalism.[105] Yorke the lawyer forcibly reads Zay into the marriage plot: he uses his feelings to express the imperative of the natural law of his desire in order to overcome the queer unnaturalness of her trained composure and her lack of interest in marriage. Even though her medical certification conveys expert authority, he possesses control over the cultural discourse of pathologized frigidity, which he wields against her. Although he allows her to keep her medical practice, the novel's extensive attention to her reluctance to accept his proposal foreshadows the eventual union as an allegory for the New Woman's disquieting acceptance of the requirements of the state apparatus in which she seeks inclusion. The exaggerated disparity between Zay and Yorke emphasizes the inescapable power of the patriarchal social order. What in her eyes are the routine labors of care as a medical professional are, from his perspective, the suggestive porousness of emotional labor—which can be translated into a nascent love plot.

From the opening scenes, the novel refigures the myth of Atalanta and Hippomenes—about the accomplished woman who does not wish to marry and so challenges suitors to a race for her hand, which is only won when a man cheats by using the goddess of love's golden apples to distract Atalanta. Yorke, an unemployed lawyer, is headed from Boston to the small town of Sherman, Maine, to obtain his inheritance from his uncle when he becomes lost and asks directions from a young woman riding alone in a phaeton. Although she assists him in a manner described by the narrator as "simply as one gentleman might have spoken to another," he misreads her directions as flirtation.[106] In this iteration of the story, Atalanta defeats Hippomenes in the race: the mysterious woman's buggy easily outpaces his horse, leaving a disoriented Yorke to trail far behind. At a crossroad he finds an apple blossom as an indicator of the direction to Sherman and what he views as a romantic signifier. The woman's name, as he will eventually discover, is Zaidee Atalanta Lloyd, affectionately named Doctor Zay by her community. Despite his loss to her superior abilities, throughout the novel he returns to that apple blossom as the hopeful symbol of a budding romance. When he makes his final successful proposal, he triumphantly refers to the myth and even highlights the dubious nature of his victory: "I have overtaken Atalanta this time. She stopped for a leaden apple" (254). The New Woman loses the race for her independence over apples that are not golden but dross.

Yorke becomes Zay's patient after an accident, and the revelation that he is under the care of a woman doctor illustrates the upheaval of sensations, sentiments, emotions, and other feelings attached to questions of gender, embodiment, and professional authority that run throughout the plot. Before his physician's identity is revealed, Yorke willingly submits himself to medical authority: "He understood perfectly that he was a subject for science" (38). With the help of the hotel's co-owner, Mrs. Butterwell, Zay obscures her status so as to perform a humorous reveal of herself as a medical professional. When Yorke awakens, he sees a woman and demands to see the doctor instead: "'The doctor has been here,' said the woman who was serving as nurse, 'nearly all night'" (40). She reassures him that the doctor will be changing his bandages: unable to turn to see the procedure, he feels "a practiced touch," but then "color slowly struck and traversed the young man's ghastly face": "But this is a woman's hand!" he repeatedly exclaims in disbelief (42 and 44). "It is not a rough hand, I hope. It will not inflict more pain than it must . . . it will inflict all that it ought. It is not afraid," the doctor states, referring to her trained control over pain and other feelings (43). It is striking that Yorke's epiphany is haptic: questions of touching and feeling are what will frustrate him throughout the novel about the conundrum presented by the woman physician. His agitation disturbs his bandage, exposing a severed artery, and Zay reacts with "a motion remarkable for its union of swiftness with great composure. Her face had a stern but perfectly steady light" (46). She uses artery forceps to ligate the artery with "a firm and fearless touch" (46–47). Her actions and emotions demonstrate that disciplined balance between sympathetic responsiveness and cool detachment that were the ideal of the medical professional. Given the need for a rapid response, she does not use anesthesia or any other painkiller: she completes the surgery with a skillful minimization of pain, but Yorke faints. This scene sets up the novel's central dilemma of the feelings between doctor and patient, the loved and the lovelorn: professionally frigid, she appears to feel nothing, while he, the sensitive chauvinist, overwhelmingly feels everything she inflicts on him. Significantly, during their later conversation about medicine and differing worldviews, the narrator mentions in passing that they speak of "anaesthetics" among her other tools of the trade (135).

The nature of homeopathic therapeutics feeds into Yorke's desperate desire to see Zay's professional dedication as affection. In a 1909 *Harper's Bazaar* essay titled "Sympathy as a Remedy," Phelps explicates her beliefs about the role of feelings in medicine. "It may require a certain element of apparent indifference to take care of the continually and painfully sick. It is said behind the scenes that our nurses are taught by the medical staff in their training schools not to cultivate sympathy with patients, lest it wear out the nerves of the nurse," she admits, referring to the necessity of controlled unfeeling in that labor. But she argues that "every school of medicine should give a series of lectures upon the nature and value of human sympathy."[107] Homeopathy is the preferred approach to medicine for Phelps, who writes in her memoir: "I believe in the homeopathic system of therapeutics. I am often told by skeptical friends that I hold this belief on a par with the Christian religion; and am not altogether inclined to deny that sardonic impeachment!"[108] Founded by Samuel Hanhemann, who preached treatment by diluting medicine, homeopathy was a school of medicine that relied on holistic understandings of health, thereby requiring sympathy as part of its professional makeup.[109] This alternative medicine was gendered as a feminized discipline in nineteenth-century America: sectarian medical colleges were more likely than others to accept women, as shown in an 1884 survey of Chicago that found 40 percent of women practitioners were regular and 60 percent sectarian, compared to 70 percent of regular male practitioners versus 25 percent sectarian.[110] The cultural backlash against the harshness of regular medicine contributed to the success of homeopathy, whose gentler therapies led to better health outcomes.[111] Since physical symptoms were not considered enough for a diagnosis, homeopathic doctors listened carefully to their patients, producing a more individualized and, sensitive form of care in ways that the historian Paul Starr views as a precursor to some modern schools of psychiatry.[112] Female patients appreciated this approach to healing and recommended homeopathy to other women: for example, in 1869 the American Institute of Homeopathy claimed that two-thirds of its patients were women.[113] The novel's characters uphold these aspects of homeopathy. Yorke's mother, who champions New Woman causes, prefers homeopathic care, and Mrs. Butterwell makes a point of calling it "better, kinder" than regular medicine.[114] Zay is the consummate homeopathic doctor, but Yorke does not understand that her attention is professional, thinking that "many of her questions were more personal than he expected" (50). She speaks of the emotional labor of her profession that compounds the difficulties of being a woman physician in a world that already demands such ordinary affective work from women: a woman doctor must have "force" and "fineness," a requirement that "will be demanded of women, because they are women, such as has never been expected of men, or perhaps been possible to them" (165). Mrs. Butterwell tries to point out these aspects to Yorke, saying that "I wouldn't waste your feelings sir. . . . Doctor would have done her duty by you, anyhow" (57).

While this dyad of female doctor and male patient has been read by some critics as a reversal of traditional gender roles, I emphasize that the novel explores how Yorke's sense of emasculation functions as a self-pitying strategy that obfuscates structural gender inequalities.[115] It is true that his sense of abandonment when Zay is too busy to tend to him gives him some perspective: "'How *dare* men ridicule or neglect sick women?' thought Waldo Yorke."[116] His illness could be interpreted as feminizing him, and indeed he follows that line of analysis. For example, he imagines that in his role as a passive patient the "beautiful submission to the inevitable which he flattered himself he was cultivating to an extent . . . might almost be called feminine" (69). However, he finishes the thought by telling himself that his composure "assuredly was super-masculine" (69). He continually feminizes himself to indulge himself in a sense of masculine victimhood—which reaffirms the subordination of women (97). For instance, he muses: "If he could have arisen like a man, and bridged it [the challenge of his convalescence], or like a hero, and leaped into it, she would never, he said to himself doggedly, have this exquisite advantage over him. He lay there like a woman, reduced from activity to endurance, from resolve to patience" (119). In such instances Yorke dwells on these reversals to heighten his sense of the unnatural unfairness of the situation. Zay's cool competence, unhindered by his infatuation, is sometimes read as queerly masculine, but the narrator draws attention to how Yorke swiftly reaffirms her femininity to himself. In the scene in which he thinks he has been relegated to the minor role occupied by women, he observes Zay's body through his desiring male gaze: "He liked to see that she had not lost the grace of movement due to her eminently womanly form. She had preserved the curves of femineity [sic]" (97). Although as a woman doctor she embodies contradiction to him, his underlying worldview remains untroubled. These moments of his feminization and her masculinization highlight the false equivalency behind the inversion of gender conventions that does not overturn the existing order.

When Yorke attempts to profess his love, Zay uses her professional frigidity to dismiss his proposals. "How was a man going to approach this new and confusing type of woman? The old codes were all astray. Were the old impulses ruled out of order, too?" he wonders (186). But his persistence indicates his belief that the New Woman may eventually succumb to the old ways. However, Zay is unmoved by his initial proposal and interprets his affections as hysteria:

> "Do you presume to tell a man he doesn't know when he loves a woman?" cried Yorke, quivering, stung beyond endurance.
> "You are not in love," she said calmly, "you are only nervous." (191)

She diagnoses him with "a case of aphonia and aphasia" when he criticizes the limits of the scientific episteme to protest what he perceives as her unfeeling attitude toward him: "The physiological basis is not the only [valid perspective] on which life [is] to be taken, Doctor Zay. I have told you before, that I am a man as well as a patient" (206). When he invokes the separate spheres by demanding, "Are you a woman?" she counters by answering, "I am a doctor" (193). He follows the other side of this logic, complaining: "It is insufferable that any woman should treat any man as you treat me. Because I am a patient, am I not a man?" (197). No skillful argument or medical treatment will dissuade him from declaring his love, so he invokes the blunt force of his emotions: "I will love you. You cannot help it. I will tell you so. You cannot help it. You must accept it. You must endure it. You must remember it. I shall not allow you to forget it" (197). Regardless of the comedy derived from her repeated deflations of his amorous sentiments through her medical authority, there is something unsettling about his refusal to accept her steadfast rejections as a valid response.[117]

Despite Zay's loving care for her community, according to Yorke's logic, if she is unfeeling to his feelings she must be frigid, because of her queer transgression of the separate spheres as a woman doctor—an accusation she appears to accept. The narrator refers to the laws of nature when Yorke makes his impassioned appeal, reminding the reader that Yorke is a lawyer—even if he is not practicing—with access to a competing regime of truth equal to Zay's: "'I love you,' he repeated,—'I love you!' as if the fact itself must be an appeal inexorable as the laws of light, or gravitation, or any natural code which she could not infringe without penalty."[118] Although he promises that she would not have to give up the practice of medicine if she married him, he attacks her career as the cause of her frigidity: "I believe they are right," he says, affirming the warnings of Clarke and others about the queer dangers of being a New Woman. "A woman cannot follow a career without ruin to all that is noblest and sweetest and truest in her nature. Your heart is as hard as your lancet. Your instinct has become as cruel" (210). Zay coldly medicalizes his talk of love as mere "pathological sentiment" (211). As a consequence of her assessment of the best course of action for his well-being and her own, her defiant response reappropriates the queer, unfeeling adjectives he uses to accuse her of frigidity. "'Mr. Yorke,' she said, in a tone of infinite gentleness, 'the time will come when you will be bless me for what I am doing now,—for my "heartlessness," my "cruelty," my "unwomanliness." They are three words easy to remember. I shall not forget them—at once.'" She is unmoved in the manner he desires, but not entirely unaffected.

In the final chapters Zay surrenders herself in the race of love, retroactively appearing to validate Yorke's insistence on reading their relationship as the arc of the marriage plot. Now employed and healthy, when he first returns his strategy has changed: rather than expressing his love, he confidently states, "You fear me because *you* love *me*" (228). And then she reluctantly admits to returning his affection. Tracey argues that the two returns of the revivified Yorke to Zay demonstrates the plasticity of negotiations around the marriage plot that redefines conventions of the suitor's masculinity.[119] He proclaims his pride in her profession, confident enough to generously concede that he will allow her to keep what she already has.[120] By contrast she has become so unsettled that her personality changes. "'I have lost my self-possession,' she pleaded. 'I have lost—myself'" (231). This vulnerable version of Zay even cries in front of Yorke as she articulates a new position on the institution of marriage: "Oh, women of my sort are thought not to reverence marriage, to undervalue it, to substitute our little personal ambitions for all that blessedness!" (241). Nonetheless, she is aware of the limits to the shifts in gender roles in the late nineteenth century: "You have been so unfortunate as to become interested in a new kind of woman. The trouble is that a happy marriage with such a woman demands a new type of man. By and by you would chafe under this transition position" (244). She believes that Yorke will grow to resent her career once he experiences the reality of everyday life married to a professional woman who cannot tend to his emotional needs "like the kitten . . . always there to purr about" (244). She outlines the historical, even eugenic, elements of this patriarchal schema: for him, she believes, this desire for a domestic woman is "an inherited instinct. Generations of your fathers have bred it into you" (244). Although she continues to spurn his proposal, this visit ends with her yielding some ground to him as she speaks of her growing affection for him in the language of the medically trained management of feelings: "It is because I love you that I—hurt you so," she admits, but then she notes that as a professional in her personal life as well, "I am accustomed to making difficult choices and abiding by decisions. It is hard at first, but I am trained to it" (248).

This scene hints at Zay's queerness not as a general sexual anesthesia, but only as a lack of desire for men. When she voices her understanding of the appeal of having a wife, she observes, "It is very natural to me to accept the devotion of such women" (244). On the pragmatic level, she is well aware of the value of marriage as an institution that offers women some succor in a man's world. For example, in one medical case she treats a young woman who is pregnant out of wedlock and saves her drowning lover—and then Zay pressures the man into marrying the woman who will bear his child. But Zay's interest in having a wife goes beyond a dispassionate thought experiment about social roles. One hint of this comes from Mrs. Butterwell who, in an earlier attempt to dissuade Yorke from pursuing Zay, tells him, "There are women that love *women*, Mr. Yorke, care for 'em, grieve over 'em, worry about 'em, feel a fellow feeling and a kind of duty to 'em, and never forget they're one of 'em, misery and all" (88). This love for other women is more than feminist solidarity for Zay: she lets slip in her penultimate rejection of Yorke that not only would it be "very natural" for her to have a wife, but she has already entertained the possibility of a Boston marriage with an unnamed woman. "There was one who wanted to come down here and stay with me. I wouldn't let her; but I wanted her," she says, giving a glimpse of the queer desire she has buried with the same professional control over her emotions and personal life that she in turn applies with Yorke (244). To borrow the sexological terms of Ellis, perhaps the success of her use of sexual anesthesia as a pragmatic tactic of her professionalism has suppressed all desires, even the possibility of her inversion. Yorke does not react to these subtle indications of Zay's closeted queerness: this aspect of his beloved is so unthinkable that he does not appear to register it at all.

Yorke's second return to Sherman concludes with Zay's acceptance of his proposal by surrendering into his arms. What is striking is that his romantic success is correlated to the arc of his relationship to the legal profession. In the opening of the novel, his impetus for traveling to Sherman involves the need to settle legal matters related to his uncle's property, but his mother remarks of her unemployed son, "Your having a profession so seldom occurs to one, Waldo" (6). During his initial courtship of Zay—or, from another angle, her treatment of him as her patient—Yorke contrasts her excellence in her profession to his own failure to have become an "eminent jurist" by this point in his career (165). After his first return, he reveals that he has resolved to take himself seriously as a professional. "I have been at work myself, this winter," he says, informing her of his commitment to building his legal practice (234). Notably, her confession of love during this visit moves away from her dedication to rationality and speaks of natural law in a way that mirrors its use as a rhetorical device in Yorke's previous arguments: "Love should be like a mighty sea. It should overflow everything. Nothing should be able to stand before it. Love is a miracle. All laws yield to it" (242). The ostensible reason for Yorke's final return is professional: Another letter from Mrs. Butterwell informs him that Zay is overworked and in ill health. However, he decides to travel back to Maine only because of a subsequent letter that contains no mention of Zay but that relates Mrs. Butterwell's concerns that the lawyer dealing with his uncle's estate was "drunk," so "if Mr. Yorke felt any uneasiness about his uncle's estate—Mr. Yorke did experience great uneasiness about his uncle's estate" (250). When Zay asks Yorke what brings him back to her town, his answer is the estate. Now he, too, is a professional.

Their final scene can be read simultaneously as the romantic resolution of the marriage plot and the troubling depiction of questionable circumstances that compel a woman's consent. In the final lines of the novel, Yorke asks Zay to give a sign of her love and to make a decision: "I don't want to feel as if I were taking a sort of—advantage. If you put me off one minute longer, I—shall. I shall take all I can get. I shall like to remember, all my life, that came to me first, of your own accord; that you loved me so much, you would grant me this—little proof." He gestures to encourage her embrace, spreading his arms wide, and, in the last sentence, "she glided across the little distance that lay between" (258). The wording of his proposal builds in the request for her response that appears to respect her agency, but it is accompanied by the threat of his prerogative as a man who loves a woman: he wants her to perform her consent so that he can fulfill his romantic fantasy. To find this romantic, the reader must hope that a New Man can emerge as the partner of the New Woman and to trust in the words about the overpowering force of love as a law of nature first uttered by Zay after Yorke's first return that he quotes back to her after the second.

A close reading of the circumstances unfolding just moments before, however, raises concerns about the coercive, reactionary powers of love as discussed by Ahmed.[121] To recall, Yorke uses the myth of Atalanta and Hippomenes to frame his triumph during their ride from her work to her home: his allusion during his proposal to "a leaden apple" as her downfall refers to the ball of a revolver that had been fired moments before, when she had to struggle with an armed, delirious patient (254). She is still shaken from dealing with masculine violence, but she does not respond to this questionable comparison. Yorke notices that "she was worn out" but still savors what will be his victory, "the first fumes from the incense of her surrender" (254). When she hesitates before responding, he does have an inkling of her queerness that could detach her from his love: "He dimly felt that only another woman could understand her at that moment, and had a vague jealousy of the strong withdrawal which nature had set between her strength and his tenderness, as if he found a rival in it" (256). As they shift from the buggy to her quarters, only a few passages before the novel's end, we are told that she notices how he enters her space "and vaguely resented his manner, which was that of a man who belonged there, and who intended to be where he belonged" (257). Nonetheless, he makes his proposal and they embrace. What initially appeared as the novel's mockery of Yorke's bad readings that projected his desires onto Zay's professional edifice turn out to have performative force, melting away the frigidity of her inchoate, queer, and ambiguous affects into the foreclosure of love and affirming the inevitability of the marriage plot.

In Bed with the Law / The Terms of Inclusion

"'There are new questions constantly arising' she went on, 'for a woman in my position. One ceases to be an individual. One acts for the whole,—for the sex, for the cause, for a future,'" says Zay (122). From one perspective, her choice to follow her heart is a rebellion against the overdetermination of her life due to her profession; from another, the lure of acting as an individual by returning Yorke's love is a false choice in a system that pressures even white middle-class women into legibility through heteronormative conventions. Unlike the definitive resolutions of the other woman doctor novels about the role of the New Woman in society and the kinds of legal recognition she may court or deny, by following Yorke's perspective Phelps's *Doctor Zay* allows us to interrogate the uncomfortable terrain of what makes the New Woman desirable to hegemony and the maintenance of white patriarchal power through adaptive co-optation and mutual investment in the biopolitical project. This successful resolution of the marriage plot—in spite of and because of giving space to the relative nonconformity of white middle-class professional women—signifies the union between the institutions of medical science and law that reconsolidates white racial reproductive futurity through the incorporation of deviance.

The affective conflicts of the woman doctor character skeptical about marriage and the conditional desires of the male lawyer mirror the compromises of fighting for women's rights to participate in the sentimental biopolitics of the state. If opposition to women's rights is purely sentimental, as Jacobi suggested, then what unfeeling approaches might act as forms of resistance or dissatisfaction? For women physicians, both fictional and real, the reclamation of professional frigidity acted as a kind of affective protest against these coercions, denying—or at least deferring—the satisfaction of acceding to patriarchal, heteronormative desires. Perhaps sexual anesthesia, applied to the body politic with surgical precision, could prepare it for the pains of feminist transformation. However, one must question the homonormativity of a queerness tied to professional identity. Indeed, as Schuller concludes, there was "space for women's queer sexual agency—as both celibacy and partnership—within the frame of biopower."[122] The critic Michelle Ann Abate, for instance, traces Jewett's belief in racial hierarchy and concludes that even the "seemingly progressive" Prince might have a homonationalist role to play in ensuring the health of white reproductive futurity.[123] Perhaps it was not the golden apples that distracted the New Woman from the race toward a more radical politics, but the race itself.

Through their examinations of conference proceedings and the *History of Woman Suffrage*, in which white feminist luminaries Stanton and Anthony praise phrenology, the scholars Nell Painter and Rosalyn Terborg-Penn bring to light the conspicuous absence or downplaying of the contributions and voices of Black activists like Watkins Harper who challenged white elitism, refused to divorce race and gender, and did not conform to the standards of white suffragists.[124] The Nineteenth Amendment, which granted women the right to vote, became law during the Jim Crow era—in effect, the amendment was a constitutional victory for white women alone. To further the cause of women's rights, Stanton returns to *Uncle Tom's Cabin* as a sentimental activist ur-text: "I have long waited and watched for some woman to arise to do for her sex what Mrs. Stowe did for the black race in 'Uncle Tom's Cabin,' a book that did more to rouse the national conscience than all the glowing appeals and constitutional arguments that agitated our people during half a century. If, from an objective point of view, a writer could thus eloquently portray the sorrows of a subject race, how much more graphically should some woman describe the degradation of sex."[125] Stanton calls for the logical weaponization of white women's tears for white women's ends. In this subgenre of New Woman novels, however, the catalyst of change is not white women's tears. Instead, the reproduction of hegemony lies in white women's hearts yielding to the desires of white men.

4

OBJECTIVE PASSIONLESSNESS /

Black Women Doctors and Dispassionate
Strategies of Uplifting Love

IN HER SPEECH "Enlightened Motherhood" (1892), Frances Ellen Watkins Harper addressed the Brooklyn Literary Society on the subject of a "science of the true life": "Would it not be well for us women to introduce into all of our literary circles, for the purpose of gaining knowledge, topics on this subject of heredity and the influence of good and bad conditions upon the home life of the race, and study this subject in the light of science for our own and the benefit of others?"[1] This model empowers Black women, centered as the vanguard of racial uplift, to bring literature and science together in the activism of everyday life. Watkins Harper wrests Black motherhood from the white sentimental stereotype of the mammy (exemplified by Harriet Beecher Stowe's Chloe and the unnamed Black woman with her child objectified by Herman Melville's Captain Delano; see chapter 1). Where Martin Delany viewed Black women as necessary but secondary in his project (see chapter 2), Watkins Harper foregrounds their importance. *Partus sequitur ventrum* ("that which is brought forth follows the belly"), the biologized inheritance of chattel slavery that Saidiya Hartman refers to as the mother's mark, becomes the basis for a Black politics of liberation that foregrounds Black women's agency.[2] As Brigitte Fielder argues about this irony, "We might regard hypodescent as a queer genealogy of race that oddly aligns with Black feminism in its resistance to patriarchal and even heterosexual notions of race's biological transfer. This understanding of hypodescent resists the antiBlackness inherent in the assumption that inherited Blackness is only or necessarily oppressive."[3] By asserting Black women as practitioners of science in tandem with motherhood, Watkins Harper pushes back against the unspoken specter of J. Marion Sims, the enslaver who became known as the founding father of American gynecology after carving his way into medical history through experiments on unanesthetized enslaved Black women. In *Iola Leroy; or, Shadows Uplifted* (1892), Watkins Harper's fourth novel but the first to be published as a single volume, the eponymous heroine presents her paper titled "Education of Mothers" to a circle of Black intellectuals and activist feminists who want to reclaim Black reproductive futurity for political ends. *Iola Leroy* follows the pious mixed-race Black heroine, who discovers she is not white after her wealthy father's death and is sold into slavery along with the surviving Black members of the family. Iola endures the sexual predations of white men until she is freed by the Union Army and becomes a nurse. After the Civil War, Iola is reunited with loved ones and connects with Black activists and professionals in Philadelphia. She turns down a proposal of marriage from the white liberal Dr. Gresham, who requires that she pass as white. Instead, now proudly identifying herself as Black, she chooses to marry the mixed-race Black Dr. Frank Latimer as someone equally dedicated to the cause of racial uplift.

This chapter pivots away from the compromised hearts of the white New Woman doctor to center Black women as formal and informal practitioners of science. Indebted to Carla Peterson's method of "speculation as feminist activity" to attend to Black women's lives in the nineteenth century, I read Watkins Harper's *Iola Leroy* as a suppressed woman doctor novel, a tacit counterpoint to the white bourgeois subgenre.[4] Watkins Harper was once wrongly dismissed as a mere advocate for Black respectability. However, important work by critics like Hazel Carby, Carla Peterson, and Pier Gabrielle Foreman has recovered the aesthetic, historical, and political complexities of her writings and activism as a significant early Black intellectual.[5] These scholars underline the fact that her engagements with sentimentalism do not reinscribe its values but critique its dependence upon white feelings and white women's tears in particular.[6] "I do not believe white women are dewdrops just exhaled from the skies," Watkins Harper declared at the Eleventh National Woman's Rights Convention in 1866, a wry comment that indicts the centrality of white women to sentimental discourse.[7] "When it

Objective Passionlessness · 139

was a question of race [I] let the lesser question of sex go. But the white women all go for sex, letting race occupy a minor position," she is reported to have said at the 1869 meeting of the American Equal Rights Association.[8] After Emancipation, Black women faced new challenges on the political stage as they were either sidelined as women (with the Fifteenth Amendment to the Constitution granting suffrage only to Black men) or as Black (with the racism of white women suffragists like Susan B. Anthony and Elizabeth Cady Stanton becoming increasingly blatant). Inveighing against the racism of white women, Watkins Harper is skeptical about whether the deceptively universal cause of woman suffrage "was broad enough to take colored women," leading to a difficult choice: "If the nation could only handle one question, she would not have the black women put a single straw in the way, if only the men of the race could obtain what they wanted."[9] In this famous moment the writer, orator, and activist chooses to side with Frederick Douglass on the question of Black suffrage versus women's suffrage that exposed the fault lines between former abolitionists and women's rights organizers. Committed to the project of racial uplift, Watkins Harper was deeply aware of the limits and compromises of political and national belonging, and she was not afraid to be divisive in using tactics that could hurt the feelings of white female allies.[10]

I suggest this deliberate alienation from whiteness is an integral element of Watkins Harper's scientific recalibration of sympathy and sentimentality for Black liberation akin to Delany's project.[11] To explore Black feminist scientific praxis, I juxtapose two phenomena that arose during the nineteenth century: the dispassionate objectivity of professional science and passionlessness, which Ann duCille argues is a subversive practice by Black women.[12] I emphasize the conceptual homology of affective detachment that is manifested in both scientific dispassion and Black women's passionlessness, despite the differences between their usual categorization as professional ideology and theory in the flesh, respectively. Furthermore, their coeval development is constitutive: the former was produced by the disavowed colonial violences wrought upon the bodies of Black women and other vulnerable populations, and the latter was both an effect of and a shield against those violences.

Scientific objectivity, according to Donna Haraway, is the "god trick": an enduring fantasy of omniscience and omnipotence, its purported virtues intermingle the epistemic and the ethical.[13] This epistemological technology developed its modern form during the nineteenth century as the meeting of image making, procedure, and trained judgment. Objectivity's foremost aspect is, according to Lorraine Daston and Peter Galison's landmark historical study, "the suppression of some aspect of the self, the countering of subjectivity" in the processes of knowledge production that seeks to access absolute reality.[14] These suppressions vary, but they often rely on emotional distance to attempt a bodiless vision that is free from individual perspective: in this sense, objectivity can mean "an attitude or ethical stance, which is grounds for praise as calm neutrality or blame as icy impersonality."[15] This scientific dispassionate objectivity emerged alongside what Jessica Riskin, Dana Nelson, Schuller, and others have identified as the discipline's dependence upon situated sentimentality as theory and practice: these developments are not so much self-defeating contradictions as they are further evidence of the effective ruses of the adaptable hegemonic emotional and political regime.[16] "'Objectivity' is itself an example of the reification of white-male thought," state Gloria T. Hull and Barbara Smith in *All the Women Are White, All the Blacks Are Men, but Some of Us Are Brave*, the important anthology of Black women's studies they edited with Patricia Bell-Scott.[17]

By contrast passionlessness involved nineteenth-century Black women's critique of the racist and sexist dimensions of that hegemony. In an appendix to his discussion of sexual frigidity or anesthesia that I discussed in chapter 3, the sexologist Havelock Ellis addresses the racial dimensions of this pathological condition. Contrary to stereotypes about Black sexual excess correlated to primitivism, Ellis claims that the "negress" is "rather cold, and indifferent to the refinements of love, in which respects she is very unlike the mulatto"—the mixed-race Black woman whose relative proximity to civilization signifies promiscuity.[18] Thus for Black women across the diaspora who were subjected to this bind that pathologized the entire spectrum of sexual desire, passionlessness was not reducible to an imitation of the respectability of white middle-class values that undergirded the cult of so-called true womanhood. Not so much an absence of passion, this somatic and affective unfeeling enacted a strategic withholding of the self to permit the possibility of personal and communal flourishing. Adapting the historian Nancy Cott's terminology, duCille examines the prevalence of the marriage plot in Black women's novels of the 1890s, in which passionlessness acts as a challenge to the racialized stereotypes of affective, sexual, and physical excesses used to justify sexual violence toward, and subjugation of, Black women. In her analysis of *Iola Leroy* and William Wells Brown's *Clotel*,[19] duCille argues that Black women's literary passionlessness is a kind of political work that reappropriates moral authority and Christian virtue as well as reclaiming their capacity for desire.[20] The historical specificity of passionlessness as an ideological stance bears a resemblance to what the groundbreaking historian of Black American women's history Darlene Clark Hine identifies more broadly as the culture of dissemblance among Black women from those who lived under the threat of rape resulting from chattel slavery to those in the present. "By dissemblance," Hine clarifies, "I mean the behavior and attitudes of Black women that created the appearance of openness and disclosure but actually shielded the truth of their inner lives and selves from their oppressors."[21] This dissemblance is not dishonesty or lack but a form of resistance that granted autonomy, dignity, and opportunity to generations of Black women, allowing them to survive as individuals and thrive as communities despite anti-Black hostilities.[22] Only under the guise of dissemblance, argues Hine, "could ordinary Black women accrue the psychic space and harness the resources needed to hold their own in the often one-sided and mismatched resistance struggle" and, in spite of these conditions of negativity, "collectively create alternative self-images and shield from scrutiny these private, empowering definitions of self."[23] This psychic space can be seen as congruent to Kevin Quashie's lyrical discussion of the importance of quiet informed by Black feminism, since Black culture is too often overdetermined as loud and resistant: "Quiet is the syntax of possibility, the capacity of the inner life. It is the unappreciated grace of every person who is black."[24]

Dispassionate objectivity and passionlessness: both are ideologies of virtue; ways to impose discipline over affects, mind, and body; strategic prioritizations of care and attention; and stances of unaffected distance as the catalyst for knowledge creation and action. One is the elevated episteme of the professional sciences dominated by white men, while the other is the pathologized practice of everyday life for Black women. Despite these asymmetries, the ideal of the objective scientific observer is akin to the framing by iconic Black women thinkers of Black women's structural positioning as a basis for epistemology. It is what Patricia Hill Collins calls the "outsider-within" and Sylvia Wynter terms "a frame of reference which parallels the 'demonic models' posited by physicists who seek to conceive of a vantage point outside the space-time orientation of the homuncular observer."[25] And, perhaps tellingly, Hine is responsible for both theorizing Black women's culture of dissemblance and bringing to light the lives of early Black women doctors.

In this chapter I examine the writings of the first two accredited Black American women doctors, Rebecca Lee Davis Crumpler and Rebecca J. Cole, alongside Watkins Harper's *Iola Leroy* to trace the doctors' Black feminist praxis of science that brings these two technologies of the self together—an objective passionlessness, to play off the sense of "objective" as in "purpose" or perhaps a subjective dispassion, with the "subjective" as a situated production of an agentic subject. Although Crumpler and Cole are held up as exemplary trailblazers, following Brittney Cooper's work in rectifying the lack of respect given to the intellectual thought of historical Black women, I contend that these women are still underacknowledged as knowledge producers and theorists.[26] In comparison to the first generation of white women doctors discussed in chapter 3, the first generation of Black women doctors received a fraction of the attention, accolades, and opportunities during their lives and continue to be sidelined today. I read Crumpler's *Book of Medical Discourses* (1883), and in particular Cole's medical school thesis, "The Eye and Its Appendages" (1867), as contributions from an earlier wave of Black women intellectuals; I believe that their writings address the lack of analyses from the "pure, or hard sciences" regretted by Hull and Smith in their foundational collection. "What impact do the basic concepts of science such as objectivity and scientific method have on researching Black women? Are there certain proscribed areas of the science profession that Black women are allowed to operate in? What are research priorities as Black women would establish and pursue them?" Hull and Smith ask.[27]

By foregrounding Black women as practitioners of and participants in medical science, I seek to contribute to countergenealogies of the history of Black women in science, making them more than the passive suffering subjects of medical experimentation and presenting them instead as participants in what Moya Bailey and Whitney Peoples might recognize as Black feminist health science studies.[28] The paradigmatic example of that infamous history is the research conducted by the abovementioned Sims. The future president of the American Medical Association developed surgical techniques still used today by repeatedly operating on the enslaved women Anarcha, Betsy, Lucy, and others whose names he does not document in his medical writings or his memoir. In that memoir he portrays himself as sympathetic to these women with vesico-vaginal fistulas, a hideously painful and humiliating condition considered to be incurable.[29] Nonetheless, these women did not receive anesthesia for the experimental surgeries that would make his career. For the scholar Rebecca Wanzo among many others, this is the quintessential case of how Black women's pain is overlooked by the medical establishment.[30] Sims went on to receive international acclaim and founded the first hospital for women and then the first hospital dedicated to the treatment of cancer. His unethical methods were criticized even by his professional contemporaries. In her history of women in medicine, Mary Putnam Jacobi of the inaugural generation of white women physicians writes bitingly, "Suffering womanhood undoubtedly owes much to Marion Sims's inventive genius. But, on the other hand, Sim's [sic] fame and fortune may be said to have been all made by women, from the poor slaves in Alabama who, unnarcotized, surrendered their patient bodies to his experiments, and to the New York ladies whose alert sympathies and open purses had enabled him to realize his dream, and establish his personal fortune."[31] Shifting this narrative, the historian Deirdre Cooper Owens urges a reappraisal of Anarcha, Betsy, Lucy, and their unnamed sisters as not simply victims of Sims's quest for glory, but also as nurses with their own considerable knowledge of the repair of obstetrical fistulas. Owens thus declares them to be the "rightful 'mothers' of this branch of medicine."[32] The turn to reassessing Black women's role in nineteenth-century American scientific history deepens our understanding of the nuances of Black feminist scientific praxis, as with Schuller's emphasis on Watkins Harper as a significant example of Black women's popular engagement with science and Britt Rusert's insights into the activism of Sarah Mapps Douglass, whose work on physiology and hygiene took place in the same city (Philadelphia) where the race scientist Samuel George Morton lived when writing *Crania Americana*.[33]

While acknowledging that alternative ways of healing have always been essential to Black women's control over their health, I specifically turn to Crumpler and Cole as formal medical practitioners in the same professional discipline as Sims to understand their confrontation with the tensions and congruences between the dispassionate objectivity of their medical training and their lived experiences of passionlessness. C. Riley Snorton powerfully argues that Sims's brutal work on Black women's ungendered flesh produced the grounds for modern medical understandings of sex and processes of gendering writ large for cis and trans people.[34] In this sense, the work of Black women doctors like Crumpler and Cole, as well as the mobilization of science by activists like Watkins Harper for Black feminist ends, present a countergenealogy that rearticulates the terms of sex and gender as practices. While their careers were bound up both directly and indirectly with those of the white woman doctors discussed in chapter 3, their struggles are not a racialized variation on the white professional women's navigation of frigidity and sentimentality. The naturalized claims to the art of healing through feminine sympathy that the historian Regina Morantz-Sanchez argues were pivotal to the acceptance of white women as doctors (see chapter 3) cannot be simply reproduced for Black women.[35] After all, Black women's emotional and physical labor is expected to be given freely to all, including white women. The Black women physicians theorized the embodied epistemology and political stakes of a Black feminist scientific praxis, adapting scientific objectivity and passionlessness as tactical disaffections for the cultivation of affective and political priorities.

In this light I advance a reevaluation of Watkins Harper's protagonist Iola Leroy as a practitioner of medical science in her own right, with the novel foreshadowing the possibility of her future career as a doctor in the footsteps of Crumpler and Cole. In contrast to earlier assessments of the novel as shallow sentimentalism and obsessed with whitened respectability, later critics have drawn attention to how the sophisticated text represents a rich plurality of Black experiences before and after emancipation in the North and the South by manipulating stereotypes, genre conventions, historical references, and medical biases.[36] *Iola Leroy* must be understood through Watkins Harper's extensive career as an activist who leveraged her privileges as an educated, free-born Black woman to advocate for uplift, while protesting the engrained structures of white womanhood as inextricable from white supremacy. Scholars point to her clashes with racist white women over the issue of suffrage and the erosions of the rights granted by Fourteenth and Fifteenth Amendments to the Constitution as key to framing how her politics inform questions of inclusion and citizenship in her fiction.[37] According to Carby, the narrative arc in the novel builds to "a complete separation of the black community from the white world and thus implicitly accepted the failure of Reconstruction."[38] In this respect, Iola's choice between the two doctors has been held up as pivotal to Watkins Harper's adaptation of the traditional white sentimental marriage plot into what Claudia Tate has called a domestic allegory of political desire in Black women's writing.[39] By taking Iola seriously as a medical professional specializing in women's health, we can further reconsider how her romantic decisions draw attention to the structural considerations that underlie the exercise of her affective and sexual agency. As Hartman has shown, chattel slavery subjected Black women to sexual violence, foreclosing capacities for consent afforded to the volitional liberal subject.[40] Thus, set on the cusp of Emancipation and the transition into the hopes and disappointments of Reconstruction, *Iola Leroy* shows how Black women wrested their agency from the grasp of those tenacious anti-Black systems of power that were mutating into new structures. The novel juxtaposes the circumstances of the eventually emancipated Iola with the experiences of her mother, Marie, under chattel slavery: mother and daughter are mixed-race Black women whose talents for healing bring them into contact with powerful white men who seek to collapse proximity into intimacy by blurring the lines between the women's care work and emotional—implicitly sexual—labor. While resisting the romantic coercions that echo her enslaved mother's lack of choice, Iola does not confuse the injustices of *patrus sequitur ventrum* with a subsequent disavowal of Black motherhood but instead sees the generative capacities of Black matrilineal kinship as articulated by Fielder in her reading of the novel.[41] Iola's love of her mother drives her work and informs her refusal of the white doctor's proposal. By joyfully choosing Latimer, Iola fully cures herself of the pathology of the "tragic mulatta" trope through a Black feminist scientific praxis. Through being objective in her passionlessness, she brings together her intermingled political and sexual desires to diagnose and treat members of the U.S. Black community through strategic detachment from white liberal sentimentalism. Thus, the novel imagines the promise of a holistic healing of the Black body politic that foregrounds Black women who are dispassionate enough in their passion for justice to question the terms of inclusion related to the struggles for meaningful Black citizenship and suffrage for Black women that Watkins Harper knew so well.

The "Colored" "Doctresses"

In 1890, two years before *Iola Leroy*'s publication, the Census Bureau reported that out of 104,805 practicing physicians in the United States, only 115 were Black women, compared to 909 Black men. Although Howard University had opened its medical school—the first institution dedicated to training Black physicians—in 1869, the first female graduate was white. The majority of the early wave of Black women doctors graduated from Meharry Medical College, founded in 1876, which did not graduate a Black woman until 1893. By the time that Crumpler graduated from the New England Female College in Boston on March 1, 1864, as the first accredited Black woman physician in the United States, it had been seventeen years and fifteen years since David John Peck and Elizabeth Blackwell became the first Black man and first white woman in the country to become doctors, respectively. When Crumpler achieved her milestone, the census in 1860 indicated that only 300 of 54,543 U.S. doctors were women. In 1867 Cole earned her degree from the Women's Medical College of Pennsylvania in Philadelphia. In her work unearthing this fragmentary archive, Hine emphasizes that these women and the rest of the first generation of Black women doctors made considerable contributions to their profession and society that were all the more remarkable given their small numbers and the many barriers they faced. They founded and ran hospitals, nurse training schools, social service agencies, and civic organizations for their communities, often paying particular attention to the needs of women, children, and underprivileged populations.[42]

Crumpler and Cole would have witnessed the negotiations of their white women peers and mentors with the pathologization of professional frigidity while undergoing their own navigations between the dispassionate objectivity of the formal structures of medical science and the passionless composure they needed to succeed in hostile institutional environments during the unfolding failure of Reconstruction. The only extant documentation of Crumpler's time in medical school are the minutes of the faculty meeting discussing her eligibility for graduation alongside two white colleagues. The minutes indicate the obstacles she faced: the faculty called her "colored" and voted to confer her the degree of "doctress of medicine."[43] Although she passed her final oral examination, the faculty awarded her degree with the following reservation: "Owing to the deficiencies in the academic education of Mrs. Lee and the slow progress she has made in her professional studies [we] have hesitated very seriously in recommending her."[44] In 1866 the new doctor worked for the Freedman's Bureau in Richmond, Virginia. Afterward she returned to Boston, where she married and took the surname Crumpler. Although on the 1880 census her occupation is listed as keeping house, she published *A Book of Medical Discourses* in 1883, which may be the only book published by a Black American woman doctor in the nineteenth century.[45]

As for Cole, Ann Preston—the first woman to be dean of a U.S. medical school—oversaw her medical thesis. And Cole worked with Elizabeth Blackwell, the first U.S. white woman doctor, and her sister Emily at the New York Infirmary for Women and Children, which was dedicated to medical social services for the poor. Cole earned Elizabeth Blackwell's praise as "an intelligent young coloured physician" who would be "a valuable addition to every hospital."[46] Like Crumpler, Cole practiced in the South during Reconstruction. When she returned to Philadelphia, she cofounded the Women's Directory, a medical and legal aid center for women and children. The rest of her long career involved balancing her private practice with work for a range of medical and social agencies. This fueled her public advocacy as a critic of racism, with a focus on the social and economic conditions that impacted health. Notably, her awareness of the gendering of Black women as contingent to white womanhood comes through in some of the letters she wrote to newspapers. For example, she attacked the segregation of Black women in a committee separate from the general one for white women established for the U.S. centennial.[47] Crumpler's and Cole's surviving writings demonstrate their commitment to structural critiques of Black health in the wake of enslavement. As Patrick Allen argues, their work in medical print should be seen as part of the tradition of Black women's critical writing in the late nineteenth and early twentieth centuries.[48] From what little we know of their lives, both Crumpler and Cole were acutely conscious of their status not only as "doctresses" but as "colored doctresses," and they transformed that marginality into positions of leadership in defiance of the emergence of the Jim Crow era.[49]

THE INTELLECTUAL THOUGHT OF DR. REBECCA LEE DAVIS CRUMPLER / REWRITING THE OBJECTIVITY OF MEDICAL DISCOURSES

In a handbill advertising "Doctress R. Crumpler's Book of Discourses," none other than "Mrs. F. W. Harper, Philadelphia, Pa" writes: "Dr. Rebecca Crumpler's manuscript contains very valuable information for women, and if published in book form I hope it will have a wide circulation." Her endorsement precedes two glowing reviews from medical doctors—one of whom was Isaac J. Wetherbee, cofounder of the Massachusetts Dental Society.[50] More than a decade before Watkins Harper's speech on enlightened motherhood, Crumpler's *A Book of Medical Discourses* anticipates and addresses the same needs. The book's dedication reads, "To mothers, nurses, and all who may desire to mitigate the afflictions of the human race, this book is prayerfully offered."[51] She claims that the impetus for publishing the work came from her Boston community: "I have, with no small degree of diffidence, consented to submit my long-kept journal to the public in the form of a book."[52] Susan Wells claims that "race was, and was not, central to Crumpler's medical practice," noting the absence of the topic until the end of the text.[53] According to Wells, Black physicians writing in the nineteenth century would briefly identify their race or gender, while "the rest of the text presented a relentlessly normalized surface" in a bid for "professional credibility."[54] This reading overlooks the physician's skillful engagement with the medical discourses of her title. With the plural "discourses," Crumpler draws attention to the heterogenous, polyphonic dynamics within the formal constraints of her ever-professionalizing discipline that represented itself as the only medical discourse capable of true knowledge production and legitimate practice. Moreover, as other critics argue, her book demonstrates a sustained engagement with her position as a Black woman dedicated to racial uplift.[55] Opening with her dedication to the universal "all who may desire to mitigate the afflictions of the human race" and building to a later reference to "that noble race with which we are identified," Crumpler demonstrates her capacity to shift between medical science's dispassionate objectivity—which gives her the authoritative title of "M.D." displayed next to her name as author—and the disciplined passionlessness as a Black woman that enables her to direct her sympathies toward the project of racial uplift.[56] In this manual on the health of women and children, she reformulates professional objectivity, exposing its politics and having her own situatedness emerge as the foundation for her medical praxis. Amid her medical advice, she continually refers to the struggle for women's suffrage, Jim Crow violences, and the wake of enslavement, underscoring that health must be considered in its social and historical context.

According to Nazera Sadiq Wright, attention to the needs and development of Black girls was key to the project of racial uplift during the period and a perennial concern for Watkins Harper, who had endorsed Crumpler's manuscript.[57] Before launching into her extensive practical advice on motherhood, Crumpler begins with a chapter titled "How to Marry." She implicitly speaks as a Black woman addressing Black girls, framing the chapter as a response to the ubiquitous "question frequently asked by young girls of some confiding friend."[58] Crumpler addresses the social dimensions of matrimony as well as issues of reproduction, emphasizing the necessity of healthy, egalitarian unions. The statement that "matrimony is a divine institution," requiring the guidance of medical science, reflects duCille's claim that passionlessness was an exercise of moral and spiritual authority for Black women.[59] Near the end of the manual, Crumpler addresses the condition that would eventually be termed John Henryism by the epidemiologist Sherman James in the 1970s: the connection between racial discrimination and overwork that together increase the erosion of Black health under structural stresses.[60] "Our women work hard, seemingly, and many of them against a heavy tide; nor does there ever seem to be an end to their toils," Crumpler laments, referring to Black women's sacrifices for others at the expense of their own well-being, "Especially do some of the laboring women of my race appear to work under heavy disadvantages."[61]

Her remedy for some of these ills, however, intensifies her sometimes moralizing tone, providing a thread of judgment that runs through the text and comes from her position of educated authority. "It is authoritatively stated that the colored population decreases in Boston, but it is not all the fault of the climate; for there have been native Africans who lived to a great age here. It is the neglect, in a great measure, to guard against the changes of the weather," she chides the reader in addressing the disproportionate Black mortality rate (116). This remonstrating is troubling in ways made clear when we consider how the theorist Christina Sharpe invokes the figure of the weather to discuss the wake of Black enslavement. Sharpe writes, "In what I am calling the weather, antiblackness is pervasive *as* climate. The weather necessitates changeability and improvisation; it is the atmospheric condition of time and place; it produces new ecologies."[62] To chide Black people for their high rate of early mortality due to the weather downplays anti-Blackness, which is as pervasive as the weather. Crumpler's own hard-won exceptionalism informs her emphasis on the individual will and her frustrations with what she perceives as the failings of others: "at the present, women appear to shrink from any responsibilities demanding patience and sacrifice."[63] By trying to affirm the fullness of Black agency in the midst of anti-Blackness, Crumpler sometimes confuses the symptom with the pathology, contradicting her awareness of the influence of structural oppressions.

Blackness is directly named in the manual's concluding paragraphs. Crumpler inveighs against popular entertainment on the Boston Common as indicative of the state of children's education. She demands of her readers: "Does anyone believe that the majority of the little children who witness the farce of 'Punch and Judy' on the Boston Common every summer, gain a moral, or feel that it is wrong to imitate beating a wife, killing a baby, or hanging a black man? The popular adage, 'No n[——], no fun,' is why such schools are tolerated on our Public Parks. Are they not a curse to our land?" (117–18).[64] The anti-Black violences of the Jim Crow era are clear, a reminder that Black childhood is denied the sentimental fantasies available to white innocence.[65] Her prescription is medical texts like her own: "Books on the laws of the health from the proper source . . . prove a blessing more lasting than gold," as opposed to "fictitious, and, in many cases, corrupt library books."[66] She hopes that with proper care there will be women graduating in "Pharmacy, Surgery, Dentistry and Medicine" as part of the objective to pursue "womanly usefulness in this field of labor" (119). Crumpler reshapes the objectivity of medical discourses and foils its universalizing erasures, attempting to center Black women's power over the sphere of their lives that had been wrested from them by chattel slavery and its legacies. Wells observes that Crumpler's text is remarkable for her attention to conversations with her patients and the material objects of ordinary life.[67] I view this sensitivity to detail as part of the Black feminist scientific counterdiscourse that the physician offers as a challenge to the work of Sims. By attending to the holistic dimensions of Black women's health, Crumpler places the focus on their lives and experiences beyond the operating table as opposed to surgeries that reduce them to what Hortense Spillers terms ungendered "flesh."[68]

THE INTELLECTUAL THOUGHT OF DR. REBECCA J. COLE / SITUATING THE DETACHED EYE

After a July 1896 presentation by W. E. B. Du Bois on the research that would become his landmark sociological study *The Philadelphia Negro*, Cole took the noted intellectual to task in the next meeting report for the *Woman's Era*, a publication of the National Federation of Afro-American Women.[69] Cole singles out Du Bois's statistics about the disproportionate mortality rate of Black people and his claim that Black people are overrepresented as perpetrators in the criminal justice system. Allen suggests that in her rebuttal to Du Bois, Cole challenges the intellectual erasure of Black women's expertise and labor.[70] On the matter of health, she addresses institutional racism in the medical field: Black patients are subjected to the biases of "inexperienced white physicians" who "have inherited the traditions of their elders," who in turn view Black people as "one more source of contagion."[71] As for the supposed predominance of Black criminality, she draws attention to the corruption and racism of the criminal justice system. She closes with prescriptions for change that would empower the Black people of Philadelphia with knowledge of healthy living and that would reform policy. Cole asserts that Black health—including its pathologization and criminalization—is a biopolitical phenomenon, a symptom of structural inequalities rather than essential racial difference.

At this established stage of her career, it is clear how Cole deftly uses her medical authority to further her social causes, for which she was an outspoken advocate. However, her theorizing of an objective passionlessness for a Black feminist scientific praxis can be seen as early as in her thesis for medical school, "The Eye and Its Appendages." This document, submitted in February 1867, has received passing historical acknowledgment but has yet to attract substantive scholarly attention, possibly because it is an unpublished handwritten manuscript. With no direct reference to race or politics, Cole's thesis may seem abstracted from her later dedication to outreach and activism. One might presume that its value lies in her successful completion of this requirement for graduation and thus her gaining the professional credibility she would then leverage for racial uplift. Yet I argue that her thesis on the eye is groundbreaking in this period, when scientific objectivity developed as a stance, a mode of image making, and a training of vision. Cole's emphasis on the embodiment of the observer rebuts the professional hardening of what the Black feminist astrophysicist Chanda Prescod-Weinstein terms "white empiricism"—which continues to undergird scientific objectivity and disproportionately impact Black women scientists marginalized by that epistemic norm.[72] Moreover, Cole's discussion of sight precedes Du Bois's famous formulation of double consciousness as second sight.[73] Cole was the first person at the Women's Medical College of Philadelphia to write about sight.[74] The extremely technical thesis details the physiology of the eye, the conditions and diseases that can affect it, possible treatments for them, and the latest ophthalmologic technology. Cole begins with an explanation of the eye's complexity: "Within the small compare of the organ of vision there is greater variety of structure than in any other part of the body. In it there are blood vessels and specimens of every animal tissue; osseous, areolar, mucous, fibrous, nervous membranes—all sharing in its formation; hence its sympathetic of functions in diseases of every variety [i.e., the eye is affected by all illnesses]."[75] Her language echoes the use of medical discourse as political. Moreover, her use of "sympathetic" here and below to describe susceptibility and correspondence draws upon the infiltration of sentimentalism into the sanitizing scientific paradigm (1 and 8). Written in the professional register, her descriptions of the mechanics of vision are clinical, and she demonstrates her mastery of medical terminology. Although ostensibly writing about a universal eye, Cole draws attention to the vulnerable materiality of vision, the inescapable situatedness of the embodied observer that includes herself, her faculty examiners, and any other reader. The title alone indicates how the eye—and, implicitly, the *I* as subject—is inseparable from the organic context of those "appendages" vital to its functioning, flourishing, and fragility. To recall chapter 1 of *Disaffected*, in a visual culture obsessed with Black and other peoples of color—and particularly Black women—as spectacles, the soon-to-be Dr. Cole affirms her identity as an agentic viewer and demonstrates her own trained vision and disciplined composure.

Her dispassionate detachment as author of the thesis does not erase but instead suggestively suspends race and gender in that strategic mode of passionlessness. "In albinos this margin is nearly white," she writes in her overview of the cornea, divorcing melanin from racial types while framing whiteness as a medical phenomenon (6). The delicacy of Cole's balancing act can be seen in her discussion of the primary diseases of the eye, which include the sexually transmitted infections gonorrhea and syphilis. She details three ways that gonorrhea leads to ophthalmia (15): "It can be produced by contact of the pestilent matter; it may occur by metastasis of the inflammation from the urethra to the eye; or it may accompany that disease as sometimes accompanies syphilis" (16–17). Syphilis in turn is a common cause of iritis, a form of inflammation focused on the iris. Cole concludes her thesis by listing the diagnostic symptoms that require attention to the shifts in the placement of iris, lymph, and pupil. The remedies she lists include astringents and the careful application of mercury. In her foundational work on Black female sexuality, Evelyn Hammonds notes that sexually transmitted infections and diseases, "especially syphilis," were historically assumed to proliferate among Black women at higher rates than in the rest of the population, leading to associations "between the black female and the prostitute."[76] One response has been "silence, secrecy, and a partially self-chosen invisibility," which, observes Hammonds, have led to the obscuration of Black women's sexuality.[77] However, Cole does not shy away from directly addressing gonorrhea and syphilis: she approaches them as a coolly objective medical professional who is rewriting how Black women can engage with issues of sexual health. As we recall, duCille shows that Black women's passionlessness is a practice of resistance through self-definition in reaction to the pathologization of their sexuality.[78] To the soon-to-be Dr. Cole, sexually transmitted infections are merely conditions that she has the power to treat.

Cole finishes her thesis with this flourish in the final sentence: "The virtue of mercury has been treated in this disease also—but in the words of Lawrence 'It's [sic] influence is not confined to the syphilitic—but extends equally to the idiopathic form of the disease.'"[79] In her only use of a direct quotation, she cites *A Treatise on the Venereal Diseases of the Eye* (1830) by Sir William Lawrence, a noted British surgeon who specialized in ophthalmology and counted Queen Victoria among his patients.[80] Lawrence may be better known by historians of science for his work as a pre-Darwinian proponent of monogenetic evolution who argued that all races were the same human race. Nonetheless, he believed the usual racist hierarchy that was part of the persistent colonial discourse of (white) universal sympathy. In his *Lectures on Physiology, Zoology, and the Natural History of Man* (1823), Lawrence claims that "the superiority of the whites is universally felt and readily acknowledged by the other races."[81] He shares Thomas Jefferson's claims about the usual racialized unfeeling attributed to Blacks, asserting that African-descended people can be found "generally submitting quietly to their state of slavery" and claiming that "their natural apathy and unvarying countenance are favourable to concealment."[82] Although Lawrence rejects as inhumane the claim that Black people are the most akin to simians, he still states, "That the Negro is more like a monkey than the European cannot be denied as a general observation."[83] In Cole's citation of his work, I suggest, she does not submit quietly to Lawrence's authority but demonstrates her own command of medical discourses in the document that would give her legitimacy as a physician. If anything, she highlights the fact that her knowledge of syphilis comes from a powerful white man in the field, part of the white racist "traditions of their elders" that she later inveighs against in her *Woman's Era* piece. With an objective passionlessness she ultimately refuses attachment to Lawrence and the colonial institutional histories he represents, using their professional proximity as a stepping-stone toward her personal success and the broader objective of Black uplift. Although theses were not widely distributed, Cole's deliberate presentation of her thesis stands out from those of the eight white students in her cohort. Unlike the plain cover sheets used by her peers, Cole's presents the thesis title in elaborate calligraphy, a self-referential nod to the organ of sight as her subject. And unlike the other students' generally perfunctory conclusions that pleaded the limits of time and space, she ends with flare by demonstrating her dedication to her studies with a direct quotation from a text that was not required reading for the anatomy or physiology courses. Prior to Du Bois's famous formulation of second sight and double consciousness, via her analysis of the embodied mechanics of sight Cole presents her negotiations of the tensions involved in the doubleness of her lived experience as a Black woman and her chosen career in a profession structured by patriarchal whiteness. Through her thesis on the eye, Cole uses the optics of her position to theorize a form of situated knowledge, a radical epistemology for a Black feminist scientific praxis.

Iola Leroy, M.D.? Black Women as Practitioners of Medical Science

No explicit literary equivalent to the late nineteenth-century fashion of American novels about white women doctors exists for Black women during the same period. Given the innovative practice, activism, and thought of doctors like Crumpler and Cole in the late nineteenth century, I discuss Iola Leroy's potential as a future physician and *Iola Leroy* the novel as a way to critique the absence of literature about Black women medical professionals. To discuss medical science in Watkins Harper's novel is to trace the narrative's subversions of medical discourses that pathologize and erase Black women as subjects even as the discipline violently extracts knowledge from their bodies. The literary depiction of Black women's health was fraught: on the one hand, illness could be seen as evidence of Black inferiority and biological unfitness for freedom; on the other hand, Black physical resilience justified enslavement and the perception of dulled humanity going back to Benjamin Rush's research. In particular, writing about a mixed-race Black character like Iola had to take into consideration the medicalization of the most morbid iteration of the sentimental tragic mulatta figure as a chronic and fatal condition. Diane Price Herndl reads the representation of Black female characters like Iola as adapting white sentimentalism's valorization of invalidism as a beautiful signifier of moral authority, both to resist viewing disability as ontology and to make space for the validity of Black suffering and the salutary effects of freedom.[84] Tracking the Leroy family's health, Michele Birnbaum suggests that the portrayals of both Leroy women and men exchange racial pathologization for the gendered condition of hysteria as a psychological manifestation of anxieties about racism that can be cured. While the white doctors Gresham and Latrobe misdiagnose racial identifications and offer racist remedies, Birnbaum views Latimer's proposal as offering Iola "a matrimonial tonic for the stress of racial uplift."[85] Treating Iola only as a receptive patient, however, ignores her dynamic engagement with medical expertise and her affective choices. Understanding Iola as a potential doctor reframes her choice between the white and Black doctors as one of objective passionlessness for an egalitarian life partner and possible colleague, an expression of Black feminist scientific praxis.

Iola's biography resembles both Crumpler's and Cole's. In her brilliant analysis of Watkins Harper's writing, Foreman argues that the dialogic complexity of the novel uses what she terms histotextuality—that is, the strategic use of allusions to historical events, debates, and understandings to deepen the novel's semantic layers in ways accessible to readers.[86] For instance, Iola's story would not be read by a contemporary audience as that of an apolitical sentimental heroine: her name is a reference to Ida B. Wells's pen name, and details of the character's life resonate with the biographies of Wells and Watkins Harper as renowned activists. In her excavations of the novel's histotextuality, Foreman highlights Watkins Harper's integration of Black participants in science and medicine. The name of Iola's eventual husband, Dr. Frank Latimer, recalls the historical figure Lewis Howard Latimer, a multitalented abolitionist who fought for the Union and became an inventor who worked with Alexander Graham Bell and Thomas Edison.[87] And the name of Lucille Delany refers to Martin Delany, discussed in chapter 2 of this book, who made uneven attempts to uplift Black women and had his own fraught relationship to science following the disruption of his medical studies at Harvard.[88] It is not unreasonable, then, to consider Crumpler and Cole as contributors to the novel's intricate amalgam of historical referents for Iola. Given the prominence achieved by these two women in their Boston and Philadelphia communities, respectively, and the fact that Watkins Harper shared their interests in advocacy, it is not surprising that she would know these two doctors. The historical record for Crumpler is sparser than that for Cole, but her association with Watkins Harper may have come from their mutual interest in suffrage and other forms of activism, for Crumpler likely had connections with what would become the Women's Era Club in Boston. Iola delivers a paper on the "Education of Mothers," and Crumpler's *Book of Medical Discourses*, endorsed by Watkins Harper, is the ur-text for scientifically informed understandings of Black motherhood that contributed to the project of uplift.[89] Although the reader is not given access to Iola's paper, there are glimpses of its content when she states in the ensuing discussion, "if we would have the prisons empty we must make the homes more attractive"—an echo of Crumpler's sentiments on the links between physical and social health.[90] Indeed, when Iola confesses to Latimer that she wishes to "do something of lasting service for the race," he suggests writing a book.[91] Crumpler's text provides a model for such a book, and Iola's desire to write "a successful book" that would have a moral impact speaks to Crumpler's frustration with frivolous novels.[92]

Like Iola, Cole was mixed-race Black: in the 1880 census, her family is listed as "mu" for "mulatto."[93] We know that Cole was a vocal member of the National Federation of Afro-American Women; that her critique of Du Bois appeared in the *Woman's Era* and drew its title from Watkins Harper's 1893 speech on "Women's Political Future"; and that Watkins Harper wrote and published *Iola Leroy* in Cole's city of Philadelphia—which boasted a lively community featuring Black women engaged in advocacy and intellectual societies that included an appreciation of science, thanks to the work of educators like Sarah Mapps Douglass.[94] These organizations are among the many that would join forces to form the National Association of Colored Women's Clubs in 1896, at a meeting where Harriet Tubman was a featured speaker—a meeting attended by Watkins Harper, who was a founding officer of the new organization, and Cole, who was a member of the younger generation of Black women activists.[95] Like Crumpler, Iola gains her initial medical experience working as a nurse with established doctors; and like both physicians, the heroine expresses dedication to women and children.

Even if neither Cole nor Crumpler directly informed Watkins Harper's writing of her protagonist, there is substantial evidence of Iola's potential to be a doctor combined with her early navigations of the confluences between passionlessness as survival and dispassionate medical objectivity. Before tragedy strikes, Iola's mother, Marie, praises the resourcefulness of the enslaved to her white enslaver husband Eugene Leroy: "Lying is said to be the vice of slaves. The more intelligent of them have so learned to veil their feelings that you do not see the undercurrent of discontent beneath their apparent good humor and jollity."[96] Rather than accepting the vilification of lying, she understands how dissembling operates as an unfeeling tactic of disaffection—given chattel slavery's demand for emotional, not simply physical, labor. Marie experiences another dimension of unfeeling when she and her children are remanded back into slavery after Eugene dies and his unscrupulous cousin finds the Leroy marriage invalid. Marie is "petrified," her heart broken "as if all the blood in her veins had receded to her heart," and she falls "senseless to the floor"—a response that can be seen as a physical and affective protest against the racialized condition of affectability formalized through chattel slavery (127). Her daughter Iola, duCille's paradigmatic example of Black women's literary passionlessness, develops her own strategies of disaffection when she is sold into slavery and uses them to maintain a sense of self despite the continual threat of sexual violence by white men. When Iola is lured to the South to be enslaved, she senses something venal about the flunky sent to bring her back: "During the rest of her journey, Iola preserved a most freezing reserve towards Bastine" (133). She refines this stance of alienating withholding to fend off the predations of white male enslavers who, frustrated, sell her seven times in six weeks before she is rescued (90). Although Iola's defiance exposes her to the risk of retaliation for her perceived frigidity, Watkins Harper adapts sentimental tropes to affirm that Iola's unfeeling is a shield that ensures her psychic survival.

When she becomes a nurse, Iola is finally able to direct her loving care in ways congruent with her chosen professional and personal objectives.[97] While she is said to be "strangely sympathetic" to her patients, in the same passage the formerly enslaved Tom Anderson, who rescued her with the Union army, speaks of how she fended off the advances of her latest enslaver, being averse to him as if he was "fire" or a "snake."[98] After her liberation, we are told that "the field hospital was needing gentle, womanly ministrations, and Iola Leroy, released from the hands of her tormentors, was given a place as a nurse; a position to which she adapted herself with a deep sense of relief" (88). Nursing is emphasized as a job that requires emotional labor just as much as it does physical labor, with the ugly consequences of war "constantly draining . . . her sympathies" (101). In the Union Army, the recorded 420 Black nurses account for only 6 percent of all nurses, a reflection of the segregation in the organization that typically relegated Black women to the less prestigious roles of doing laundry or cooking. However, 36 percent of the "contract" nurses (that is, hired on an ad hoc basis) were Black, which the historian Jane Schultz suggests was evidence that Black people even without formal connections to the medical profession could find work in hospital settings in some circumstances.[99] This situation gives Iola access to medical experience at a time when nursing began to be professionalized. (The first nursing school would not be opened until 1873, and the first Black nurse to graduate from such a school was Mary E. Mahoney in 1879.[100]) The professional context of Iola's work as a nurse is an important contrast to her mother's nursing of the enslaver who became her husband. Marie's forced care work makes her desirable to her patient, Eugene, who collapses the distinction between compulsory labor and romantic love and declares to his brother, "That is why I am about to marry my faithful and devoted nurse."[101] Years after the Civil War ended, Marie hints at this coercive situation during a broader discussion about the legacies of slavery and interracial entanglements: "the colored nurse could not nestle her master's child in her arms, hold up his baby steps on their floors, and walk with him through the impressible and formative period of his young life without leaving upon him the impress of her hand" (206). Marie evokes this scene both as metaphor and as her own bittersweet experience as a "colored nurse" who literally nurses—breast-feeds—"her master's child." Unlike her mother, Iola is able to choose her occupation as a nurse, in which the cultivation of her affective agency includes the suppression of those emotions to maintain her professional composure. When Anderson dies in the hospital, Iola has "tearful eyes and aching heart" for her friend's passing—but as a professional, she manages her emotions so that she can immediately return to her "daily round of duties" and help others in this war to end enslavement without becoming overwhelmed by personal grief (98).

RECLAIMING BLACK MATERNITY /
IOLA REFUSES A WHITE LIBERAL PROPOSAL

Iola's experience with this more formalized emotional distancing required of medical professionals informs her passionlessness toward her colleague Dr. Gresham who, in stark contrast, fails to maintain these boundaries in his workplace as a privileged white man. In the chapter following Tom's death, Gresham talks to Colonel Robinson about Iola, whom he perceives as white and a "born nurse": he is "mystified" that she "cried as if her heart was breaking" and kissed her Black patient (99). When the colonel says that Gresham talks "like a lover" about Iola, the doctor disavows any personal interest, stating: "I am not thinking of love or courtship. That is the business of the drawing-room, and not of the camp" (99). Nonetheless, he shares his extensive observations of his nurse, including her accent, manner, voice, and the shifts of emotion on her face. In response, the colonel reveals that Iola is Black and was recently emancipated, after which Gresham admits his true intentions: "Why, I was just beginning to think seriously of her" (100). Despite his stated racial prejudices—"I can eat with colored people, walk, talk, and fight with them, but kissing them is something I don't hanker after"—his romantic interest continues to develop through his proximity to Iola as they work together in the Union outpost (100). "As nurse and physician, Iola and Gresham were constantly thrown together," but the narrator stresses that the one-sided love is not met with consent, much less awareness, on Iola's part: "Without any effort of consciousness on her part, his friendship ripened into love" (101). The allure of Iola for Gresham lies not only in her beauty and virtue, but also in their structural dynamic as doctor and nurse: as the colonel comments, she is "faithful to her duties and obedient to [the doctor's] directions" (99). The novel draws the contrast between Iola's skillful management of her emotions in different areas of her life and her white male workplace superior's inability to control his desires despite his formal training in professional dispassion.

Gresham's love for Iola reveals the limits of white liberal sentimentalism that will not abolish the apparatuses that constrain Black liberation. He is drawn to the idea of playing savior to a woman he views as a tragic mulatta figure after learning the "deep pathos of her story" (100). Once "perfectly mystified by Miss Leroy"—the relevant chapter is titled "The Mystified Doctor"—Gresham incorrectly diagnosed her racial phenotype, but now the genre stereotype of the tragic mulatta renders Iola legible to him (99). His attention to her expressions of sadness is heightened: he sees her as "old in sorrow," with a "sad destiny," and he hopes to distract her from "her mournful past" (101). He is now confident that she is a transparent subject who can be affected by his gaze: "As he observed her, he detected an undertone of sorrow in her most cheerful words, and observed a quick flushing and sudden paling of her cheek, as if she were living over scenes that were thrilling her soul with indignation or chilling her heart with horror" (101). To Gresham, everything can be explained by projecting onto Iola the tragic mulatta trope as a pathologizing framework that reduces her to a generic type. For him, there is an erotic element to her vulnerability, arousing his "desire to defend and protect her" (100). The novel critiques the fantasy that love might be enough to lead to activism and a breaching of the color line, for "her loneliness drew deeply upon his sympathy" (101). However, Watkins Harper uses this moment to criticize the anti-Black racism embedded within white sympathies: "All the manhood and chivalry of his nature rose in her behalf, and, after carefully revolving the matter, he resolved to win her for his bride, bury her secret in his Northern home, and hide from his aristocratic relations all knowledge of her mournful past" (101). The phallic innuendo suggests that in his entitled white masculinity, Gresham of the Union Army shares more than he might realize with those Confederate enslavers who tried to rape Iola. His love demands the erasure of her Blackness, echoing the errors of her father, who attempted to hide his children's mixed-race Black heritage from them. Gresham draws attention to Iola's body under the auspices of concern for her health in the same roundabout way that he inquired about her of the colonel: "although you possess a wonderful amount of physical endurance, you must not forget that saints have bodies and dwell in tabernacles of clay, just the same as we common mortals"—in response to which she deftly cuts through his verbiage: "'Compliments aside,' she said, smiling; 'what are you driving at, Doctor?'" (101). He prescribes a furlough in the North, but she responds by foregrounding her hospital duties with what he reads as the manifestation of her inborn tragedy, striking him as "so sad, almost despairing" that she inadvertently "stirred Dr. Gresham's heart with sudden pity" (101-2). At this point he makes his first proposal, exposing his collapse between the personal and the professional: "Iola, I have loved you ever since I have seen your devotion to our poor, sick boys. How faithfully you, a young and gracious girl, have stood at your post and performed your duties. And now I ask, will you not permit me to clasp hands with you for life?" (102).

Passionless Iola rejects his proposal, maintaining her composure and refusing the possibility of greater intimacy. Before she responds to his offer, however, the novel sharply transitions from his marital offer to a flashback that lasts for several chapters and covers the history of the Leroy family, whose sorrows stem from their enslaver patriarch's folly. When the narrative resumes in the present with Iola's refusal of Gresham's proposal, the reader now knows the tragedy of Iola's mother, Marie, was an earlier iteration of a Black mixed-race nurse who married a privileged white man. Iola refuses to inherit this path, as a free woman operating in a more formal work environment with greater opportunities available to her than her enslaved mother had. It is important to note that despite Iola's dutifulness in her employment, she should not be viewed as simply subordinate to Gresham because she is a nurse. According to Schultz, during the Civil War nurses often fought with doctors to advocate for their patients, disrupting presumed gender dynamics.[102] The narrator emphasizes that while Iola appreciates Gresham's companionship, "he had never been associated in her mind with either love or marriage."[103] She politely rejects his proposal. With the arrival of an ambulance Iola leaves the scene, professional duty acting as one of the "barriers" she alludes to as being between her and Gresham. Although their professional intimacy grows as colleagues working in the terrible context of the Civil War, "she fought with her own heart and repressed its rising love" (138). Now sadly experienced with the nuances of Northern racism, Iola is skeptical about Gresham's suitability as a marriage partner: "She had learned enough of the racial feeling to influence her decision in reference to Dr. Gresham's offer" (137). What is significant is that Iola turns him down through a resolute claiming of her mother in spite of the flashback's reminder of the woes of *partus sequitur ventrum* that is then narrated in brief by Iola to the doctor. When he offers her "my mother to be your mother," her reply makes clear where her affections lie: "Oh, you do not know how hungry my heart is for my mother! . . . I have resolved never to marry until I have found my mother" (136). She will not accept his offer of his white mother to replace Marie: Iola affirms her love of her mother as part of her pride in her Blackness, rejecting his proposal of marriage that is bound to the acceptance of the pathologization of Black motherhood.

Underlying the dynamic between Iola and Gresham are Watkins Harper's own encounters with white sentimental liberalism that resulted from her activism. The doctor is generally represented as a noble character, "a fine specimen of the best brain and heart of New England," who goes on to be a friend to the novel's Black community after Emancipation (137). Nonetheless, he cannot fully extricate himself from the complicities of white sentimentalism: "He had lived in a part of the country where he had scarcely ever seen a colored person, around the race their misfortunes had thrown a halo of romance. To him the negro was a picturesque being, over whose woes he had wept when a child, and whose wrongs he was ready to redress when a man" (136). His perspective does shift when he falls in love with Iola, but the novel suggests that the "halo of romance" is linked to sentimental heterosexual masculinity with this "first grand and overmastering love," in which phallically once again "all the manhood and chivalry in his nature arose in her behalf" (137). A troubling undercurrent runs throughout his infatuated rhetoric. "Love, like faith, laughs at impossibilities," he pleads on another occasion. "I can conceive of no barrier too high for my love to surmount. Consent to be mine, as nothing else on earth is mine" (138). His possessive language echoes the logic of chattel slavery—which, to recall Hartman, renders null the possibility of consent for enslaved Black women.[104] This connection builds in the same chapter, as Iola describes the degradations she faced when white men viewed her "as an article of merchandise," but Gresham responds by deflecting responsibility for slavery to just a "few" men.[105] "'Did not the whole nation consent to our abasement,' asked Iola, bitterly," reframing the doctor's earlier use of "consent" in relation to structural complicity—while he then misses her point and claims as a white man that "we did not all consent to it," holding up the North in the Civil War (140). Gresham is a paradigmatic product of Northern white liberalism: "His father was a devoted Abolitionist. His mother was kindhearted, but somewhat exclusive and aristocratic" (137). Mrs. Gresham's racism, we are told, is the reason why her son seeks to bury Iola's Blackness through marriage, drawing attention to why the proposal scene is framed in terms of their mothers. (Here, we can hear Watkins Harper's famous clashes with Anthony and Stanton over their racism.) For Gresham, Iola's race both is and is not an issue: on the one hand, he insists that his love transcends racial barriers, while on the other hand, his love requires that she pass as white. The cost of inclusion in the Gresham family and the nation is the erasure of Blackness through the ideal of color blindness that universalizes whiteness.

Iola's exchanges with Gresham display her ability to hold her ground as his intellectual equal. At one point the physician draws upon race science for his arguments, referring to the strengths of the "Anglo-Saxon race" as a "conquering and achieving people" versus an allegedly "weaker race." Iola parodies this rhetoric in her critique: "I believe the time will come when the civilization of the negro will assume a better phase than you Anglo-Saxons possess. You will prove unworthy of your high vantage ground if you only use your superior ability to victimize feebler races and minister to a selfish greed of gold and a love of domination" (141). She skillfully adapts race science to gain the upper hand in their dispute, demonstrating her capability to engage in these debates. Iola does not need to be saved or to sacrifice her sense of self. She states: "I have too much self-respect to enter your home under a veil of concealment. . . . I would never enter a family where I would be an unwelcome member" (141). She presents herself as emotionally unaffected to stay true to her political resolve, as she once again turns down the doctor's marriage proposal and its promise of a comfortable life: "No quivering of her lip or paling of her cheek betrayed any struggle of her heart" (142). In her passionless response to his offer, she makes clear that her true passions lie beyond white conditional acceptance.

After the war Gresham reenters the narrative and Iola's life, consolidating his role as embodiment of the disparities between the necessities and failings of white liberal allyship. The Leroy family has been reunited, and most of its members now live in Philadelphia. Gresham happens to visit the city for a medical convention. Iola and he reconnect outside of a professional context, and she cares enough to introduce him to her undeniably Black family. Although Gresham speaks of the nation's need for reform after the war, hoping that the "best members of both races will unite for the maintenance of law and order and the progress and prosperity of the country," his old prejudices still linger (207). In this conversation, he expresses shock that Harry Leroy, like his sister, chooses not to pass as white. Gresham is a white moderate, which is best shown through the range of his professional acquaintances at the conference: while he is friends with Latimer, the passionate Black reformer whom Iola will eventually marry, he also associates with Dr. Latrobe, an outright racist Southern doctor who proclaims that "we will never abandon our Caucasian civilization to an inferior race" (209). Crucially, Watkins Harper chooses to introduce the reader to Latimer through Gresham, who helps his friend conceal his Blackness to play Latrobe for a fool over his specious scientific racism. Yet there are other tensions at play: Gresham orchestrates the debate about racial difference in America between his fellow doctors, along with Iola's uncle, Robert, and Reverend Carmicle. Here again Gresham espouses liberal values to refute the virulently bigoted Latrobe but also makes statements about his "faith in the inherent power of the white race" (211). Latimer, Robert, and the reverend play the role Iola once did to critique both blatant and more subtle forms of racism. Much as he did in his marriage proposals to Iola, Gresham is fixated upon the assimilation of Black people into whiteness to heal the nation: "I sometimes think that the final solution of this question will be the absorption of the negro into our race," he muses (214).

Gresham has changed, but not enough. During this period in Philadelphia Black women were reworking sentimentality to enact their own senses of Black womanhood. In their analyses of these middle-class women's friendship albums, Jasmine Cobb and Elise Kammerer note the influence of educator Sarah Mapps Douglass on the informal integration of science into these revisions of sentimentalism through flower images combined with poetry and botanical information, which often subtly commented upon Black women's modesty as control over their bodies and sexuality.[106] Iola's final refusal of Gresham must be seen as framed by the preceding series of arguments about America's racial future as well as the practices of these social circles of Black women in which she would be a likely member. Her previous refusal involved her mission to find her mother, and Iola returns to her mother as her foremost reason against marrying into Gresham's posh New England family, citing her mother's experiences with anti-Black racism in the church and her philanthropy. Similar to his politics of color-blind universalism, Gresham sees his proposal as a matter of individuals and their choices, not an issue of communities and structural forces: "No one has a right to interfere with our marriage if we do not infringe on the rights of others," he argues.[107] "'Doctor,' she replied gently, 'I feel that our paths must diverge. My life-work is planned. I intend spending my future among the colored people of the South'" (219). They part on amiable terms, but the failed proposal allegorizes the incommensurabilities between a Black project of liberation and a white liberal vision of national inclusion, even though the two may superficially overlap. There is the epistemic clash between Gresham's professed universalist objectivity that attempts to selectively discard context to further his personal desires and Iola's situated objectivity that takes into account her racialized and gendered positioning and uses passionlessness as an affective tool to achieve her ultimate objectives.

QUICKENING THE PASSIONLESS /
UNFEELING AS LATENT POTENTIAL

Iola's marriage to Latimer comes, as Koritha Mitchell quips, as "more of a bonus than the main prize" attached to her commitment to her mother and work for racial uplift.[108] Indeed, Marie's unstable health is one of the factors that brings together Iola and Latimer—the physician brought by Robert to the Leroy household after their verbal sparring with the white doctors. A gathering of Black activists and intellectuals serves as the field of courtship, where Iola presents her paper on the "Education of Mothers" and impresses the talented young doctor with her passion and intellect. He is a mirror image of Iola, having turned down the chance to be adopted by his rich white grandmother at the cost of disavowing his Blackness. He delivers a critique of white sentimentalism as a literary genre dependent upon true universal feeling as the key to political identification. And he remarks to Iola that while white writers "have written good racial books," he believes that "it seems to be almost impossible for a white man to put himself completely in our place."[109] Critics like duCille comment upon the sublimated erotic nature of their political desire: their shared passion manifests itself in ways that allow Iola greater affective range as a complex subject.[110] Unlike Iola's exchanges with Gresham, who reads her sentimentally as tragic and her in need of rescue, her relationship with Latimer is full of light wit along with the gravitas of their mission. Although Latimer, like Gresham, segues into his proposal by remarking upon Iola's health and well-being, the former delivers his offer of marriage with "a merry twinkle in his eye": she needs a "change of air, change of scene, and change of name," he prescribes.[111] She responds by mocking his playful parody of his medical authority:

> "Well, Doctor," said Iola, laughing, "that is the newest nostrum out. Had you not better apply for a patent?"
>
> "Oh," replied Dr. Latimer, with affected gravity, "you know you must have unlimited faith in your physician."
>
> "So you wish me to try the faith cure?" asked Iola, laughing.
>
> "Yes, faith in me," responded Dr. Latimer, seriously. (244)

In one of her few lighthearted scenes, Iola gently criticizes the cultural power of the doctor as expert, poking fun at his prescription as a specious "nostrum" and trusting her own knowledge. Her objectives and passions aligned, she happily enters marriage and partnership with Latimer, who would eventually be called the "Good Doctor" for his leadership in reform movements for Black people in the South (250). Their flirtations reveal a playful erotics of mutual respect for each other's intellect that is unlike the affective invasiveness of Gresham's sentimental sincerity.

Latimer is moved to propose to Iola because he intends to relocate to North Carolina, since "physicians were greatly needed there"—and there are implications that the call for doctors might become one that Iola will heed in more than a supporting role (242). Her potential as a medical professional does not end with the war. As she says in an earlier exchange with Gresham, she believes that "there is a large amount of latent and undeveloped ability in the race. . . . This my hospital experience has taught me" (140). When she is reunited with her family in the North, she insists on being financially independent, telling her uncle, "I have a theory that every woman ought to know how to earn her own living" (198). After her first job ends due to the racism of her employers, her next opportunity comes through a return to nursing akin to that in the early career of Crumpler, taking care of the sick daughter of a white northerner who uses his position to hire and protect Black people. She proudly tells her mother about her professional skill set: "Nursing. I was very young when I went into the hospital, but I succeeded so well that the doctor said I must have been a born nurse" (202). Marie is skeptical, perhaps due to her own complicated past as an enslaved nurse, but Iola is hired for her talents as a medical professional in Philadelphia—the American center of medical science that played host to Cole in the same period. While Iola is later employed by her patient's father, Mr. Cloten, as an accountant for his business, she says to Latimer, "But to be an expert accountant is not the best use to which I can put my life" (243). Even though teaching is ostensibly the occupation she chooses by the end of the novel, her interest in science remains. While upholding Christian moral development as pivotal to the strength of a nation, she also highlights "excelling in literature, art, and science" (208). The same phrase emerges when Harry prepares Iola to meet Lucille Delany. After hearing about her accomplishments, including graduating from college, Iola praises her brother's love interest: "Every person of unmixed blood who succeeds in any department of literature, art, or science, is a living argument for the capability which is in the race" (194–95). Although Latimer claims that Iola's "devotion to study and work is too intense," during their preparations to become life partners it is apparent that she will be his intellectual partner as well (243). Harry and Lucille discuss how the two educate one another, with Harry noting that his sister can speak about a rich range of topics, including "the latest discovery in science" (248). Iola is her own best example of the "latent and undeveloped ability in the race": she has extensive medical experience and a solid network of professional references, and her husband mentors her about the formal dimensions of medicine. The conditions are in place for Iola to successfully pursue a medical degree. Moreover, this option is more than plausible given her location in the South at a time when Meharry Medical College in Nashville, Tennessee, graduated the majority of Black women doctors, and her family's residence in Philadelphia, where the Woman's Medical College of Philadelphia, Cole's alma mater, would graduate the greatest number of Black women doctors later in the century.[112]

If Iola were to become a doctor and focus on women and children, thereby enacting the ideals of her paper on the "Education of Mothers" and Watkins Harper's "Enlightened Motherhood" speech, she would challenge the legacy of Sims through the realm of literature akin to the lived rebuttals of early Black women doctors like Crumpler and Cole. Through a holistic approach to pregnancy, birth, parenting, and social development counterposed to Sims's surgical gynecology, Iola could pay attention to the literal and metaphoric health of Black reproductive and political futurity. Watkins Harper's novel anticipates creative work over a century later like the Anarcha Project, which Wanzo views as exercising Black women's affective agency to offer an explicit counternarrative to Sims's violent erasures by reworking sentimentalism.[113] According to Zakiyyah Jackson, the "Black mater(nal)" threatens to rupture the representative order of Western science, with its potential to radically transform the terms of reality.[114] As this novel demonstrates, the Black maternal has long offered a rebuttal to how whiteness tries to define science and control the conditions of reality. Reading *Iola Leroy* in the twenty-first century vis-à-vis the disproportionate Black maternal mortality rates in the United States, it is significant to note that Watkins Harper concludes her narrative at a point full of possibilities for Iola to become a mother as well as a doctor who tends to mothers.[115]

ANTI-BLACKNESS IS CANCER / THE METASTASIS OF CHATTEL SLAVERY

Iola the medical professional also offers a provocation to the contemporary understanding of cancer, a lesser-known aspect of Sims's contributions to medical science. In the nineteenth century the principal clinical schools of oncology were the English, Scottish, and Irish schools; the French school; and the German, Austrian, and Swiss schools. American involvement was largely limited to individual Americans who worked in the laboratories of European scientists.[116] In contrast to the dominant opinion among his peers, who feared that the poorly understood disease was contagious, Sims supported the admission of patients with cancer to hospitals and helped found the New York Cancer Hospital, the first American institution dedicated to the disease.[117] In Watkins Harper's novel, the white Captain Sybil says to Robert Leroy, his fellow soldier, "Slavery was a deadly cancer eating into the life of the nation; but somehow, it had cast such a glamour over us that we have acted somewhat as if our national safety were better preserved by sparing the cancer than by cutting it out."[118] Following his oracular namesake, Sybil uses a prophetic metaphor that is later voiced by Iola in a conversation with Gresham after the war has ended: "'Slavery,' said Iola, 'was a fearful cancer eating into the nation's heart, sapping its vitality, and undermining its life" (205). Although her phrasing appears almost identical to Sybil's, Iola's experience in the health profession means that cancer is more than a metaphor to her. A significant deviation is her change from "the life of the nation" to "the nation's heart," suggesting the impact of the disease on the sentimental American way of feeling. The doctor chimes in with his modification of the second half of Sybil's statement, but Iola undercuts his pronouncement:

> "And war," said Dr. Gresham, "was the dreadful surgery by which the disease was eradicated. The cancer has been removed, but for years to come I fear we will have to deal with the effects of the disease. But I believe we have vitality enough to outgrow these effects."
>
> "I think, Doctor," said Iola, "that there is but one remedy by which our nation can recover from the evil entailed upon her by slavery." (205-6)

The answer is a reformed antiracist Christianity with an "application to our national life" (206). For Gresham, slavery can be successfully excised from the body politic—which will certainly recover through convalescence with no fear of remission. For Iola, however, slavery is part of the cancer of anti-Blackness in the heart of the nation that has metastasized into new forms. It is worth noting that oncologists of the period did observe how external factors like environment and geography impacted tumor induction, supporting the understanding that many factors affected cancer.[119] To recall Sharpe's use of the weather and climate in relation to anti-Blackness, Iola has a fuller sense of how comprehensive healing requires more than the excision of surgery, and she prescribes a holistic treatment of moral and social reform to counteract the carcinogenic environment of American nationhood.[120] Her diagnosis is supported by her mother: "'Slavery, said Mrs. Leroy, 'is dead, but the spirit which animated it still lives.'"[121] The Leroy women understand the epidemiological aspects of both cancer and chattel slavery, recalling how Crumpler and Cole emphasize poor health as a symptom of structural inequalities. Cancer as anti-Blackness also means anti-Blackness as cancer. According to a report from the American Cancer Society using data for 2016–18, Black Americans have the highest mortality rate and the shortest survival of any racial or ethnic U.S. population in regard to most cancers because of what Iola and Marie Leroy might view as the latest manifestation of the endemic American anti-Black blight that was chattel slavery.[122]

Reading *Iola Leroy* as the Challenge of Speculative Black Feminist Poesis

Whether medical school is a path that Iola will choose or be able to pursue after the novel's end is a serious question that Watkins Harper addresses only obliquely. In the much-cited scene in which Iola and Latimer discuss the possibility of her writing a book, it is curious that she is reluctant to entertain the possibility of authorship and even more shy about imagining herself as the protagonist. Latimer has to be the one to suggest writing as an outlet for her desire, saying to her, "I think there is an amount of dormant talent among us, and a large field from which to gather materials for such a book."[123] "Write, out of the fullness of your heart, a book to inspire men and women with a deeper sense of justice and humanity," he urges her. "Miss Leroy, out of the race must come its own thinkers and writers" (238). Throughout their exchange he has to work to persuade her of her "dormant talent" in the face of her objections that include her self-doubts about her ability and the material support needed to write. She warms to the idea, saying, "Well, Doctor, when I write a book, I shall take you for the hero of my story" (238). When he questions her rationale, she brings up his praiseworthy commitment not to pass as white, but Latimer turns the scenario around to focus on her by framing the same dynamics in the third person as a means of defamiliarization. The twist, though, concerns his hints about his knowledge of her rejection of Gresham, his friend: despite her "stricken heart," this "young lady" turned down "a brilliant offer of love, home, and social position. But she bound her heart to the mast of duty, closed her ears to the siren song, and could not be lured from her purpose" (239). Latimer makes it clear that he recognizes and lauds Iola's objective passionlessness, her purposeful control over her affects. "I know her and admire her," he teases, "and she ought to be made the subject of a soul-inspiring story. Do you know of whom I speak?" Iola has so decentered herself in her objectives that she must learn to value her own worth. Embarrassed, she takes her leave, but the narrator makes clear the conversation's significance as a turning point: "After this conversation, Dr. Latimer became a frequent visitor at Iola's home." In this chapter, titled "Dawning Affections," Latimer's faith in Iola's capacity to do great works is what finally catalyzes her belief in herself that grows along with their feelings for each other. Thus, her prior unfeeling passionlessness—shown in both her disregard of Gresham and her icy rejection of her enslavers—created the conditions of possibility for the flourishing of her love in her ideal egalitarian partnership.

Before Beneatha with her medical aspirations in Lorraine Hansberry's classic play *A Raisin in the Sun* (1959), there was Iola Leroy.[124] One of the goals of this chapter was to take Iola seriously as a medical professional with the potential to join the first generation of Black women doctors. The metacritical discussion about the writing of possible books and their potential power draws attention to the crucial literariness of Watkins Harper's project, which invites us to read beyond the ending for the flowering of dormant possibilities. Following the activist's feminist poesis, we might ask what else might Iola be positioned to achieve for herself and others that she might not yet consciously realize for herself.

If this narrative does not seem plausible to Iola or to readers either then or now, our attention should shift to why that might be the case and what fundamental changes would need to occur to make it plausible. Watkins Harper's novel illustrates that the strength of Black women does not mean they should be overburdened to the point of sacrificing their personal lives and the scope of their ambitions: their objective passionlessness as a survival and political tactic enables passion to thrive. While Black women are leaders, they cannot—and, should not—stand alone in the many labors of uplift: they need the loving support of Black men and the rest of their community. After all, while Watkins Harper took white women suffrage activists to task, she also decried the Black masculinist erasure of Black women's issues. "In the new conditions of things, the colored man vaulted into power, the colored woman was left behind to serve," she declaims, referring to the Fifteenth Amendment that gave Black men suffrage in her popular and much reprinted 1877 speech to the African American Woman's Congress titled "The Colored Women of America."[125] And a decade earlier her fellow activist Mary Ann Shadd Cary named Cole as the exemplar of physicians in her litany of accomplished Black women who "illustrate an ability among colored women which, if encouraged by Colored men, would be the signing of an era of thought and effort among colored women."[126]

After Watkins Harper's death, the 1920 census saw the number of Black men physicians grow to 3,495, but the ranks of Black women doctors shrank to 65 out of the national total of 144,977 doctors.[127] Although Hine notes there was also a decline in white women doctors because of a cultural backlash against women in medicine, 1920 saw the passage of the Nineteenth Amendment that enshrined women's suffrage—a constitutional right that Black women could not truly exercise in the Jim Crow era, despite their major contributions to the struggle for the vote. Nonetheless, in the realm of fiction, where one can "inspire men and women with a deeper sense of justice and humanity," Iola represents the hope for a Black feminist scientific praxis that can uplift her people to reimagine possibilities of nationhood and citizenship.[128]

ORIENTAL INSCRUTABILITY /

Sui Sin Far, Chinese Faces, and the
Modern Apparatuses of U.S. Immigration

"I HAVE COME FROM A RACE on my mother's side which is said to be the most stolid and insensible to feeling of all races, yet I look back over the years and see myself so keenly alive to every shade of sorrow and suffering that it is almost a pain to live," writes Edith Maude Eaton under the Chinese pen name Sui Sin Far in her memoir "Leaves from the Mental Portfolio of an Eurasian" (1909).[1] Oriental inscrutability is perhaps the most coherent racialized mode of unfeeling, the fact that it has a particular name indicating a structurally pervasive and lingering phenomenon in the Western cultural imagination.[2] "True to life, they give an insight into the thought and feeling of the Chinese who are with us, but not of us," praised the *American Antiquarian and Oriental Journal* in its assessment of Far's only published book, *Mrs. Spring Fragrance* (1912)—a collection of her short stories.[3] The anthropological journal's positive evaluation underscores the sentimental understanding of the short stories by this mixed-race daughter of a Chinese mother and white English father that runs throughout contemporary reviews. The value of her portrayal of the Chinese diaspora is based upon the conflation of the intimacies of ethnographic access and sympathetic identification to dispel that inscrutability and soften the barrier of obdurate impassivity into a more compliant mystique. The *American Antiquarian and Oriental Journal* concludes that the book "should do much to arouse sympathy through a better understanding."[4] The allusion is to ongoing anti-Chinese sentiments that escalated from regional to state to federal legal discrimination impacting geopolitics with the Page Act of 1875, excluding Chinese women from the United States as they were suspected of seeking to engage in sex work, and then the Chinese Exclusion Act of 1882. Far's sentimentalism, then, humanized the Chinese where the cultural phenomenon of the Yellow Peril dehumanized it through the counterpoised genres of realism, sensationalism, and naturalism.

The *New York Times*, however, dissented from the general acclaim for *Mrs. Spring Fragrance*: "Miss Eaton has struck a new note in American fiction. She has not struck it very surely or with surpassing skill."[5] The *Times* critic scrutinized the collection through the lens of sentimentality, commenting, "The thing she [Far] has tried to do is to portray for readers of the white race the lives, feelings, and sentiments of the Americanized Chinese of the Pacific Coast, of those who have intermarried with them and of the children who have sprung from such unions." Transparency is lauded: the review commends "the glimpses she gives into the lives, thoughts and emotions of the Chinese women who refuse to be anything but intensely Chinese." Obfuscation is not: "In some of the stories she seems not even to have tried to see inside the souls of her people, but has contented herself with the merest sketching of externals." Thus the author who would eventually be considered the point of origin for Asian North American literature is alleged to disappoint those "readers of the white race" seeking access into the "souls of her [Far's] people." The Exclusion Era (1882–1943) shapes expectations for Chinese literary representations that bear resemblance to the invasive scrutiny of the evolving apparatuses of U.S. immigration. Insofar as the Chinese were legally defined as aliens ineligible for citizenship, implicitly at stake in the domain of literature was their eligibility for sympathy in the hearts of American citizens. Nevertheless, according to the *New York Times*, Far's Chinese characters sometimes remain inscrutable Orientals who are, in multiple senses, hard to read.

In this final chapter, I linger over this perception of Far's failure as an opening for reading against the grain of her presumed sentimentalism through the lens of biopolitical affectability. Eaton, whose pen name was the Chinese name for the narcissus flower, was born in England, grew up in Canada, and then lived in San Francisco, Los Angeles, and Boston, spending notable periods of time in Jamaica and New York City.[6] She was a prolific journalist and short story writer who was active in the late nineteenth and early twentieth centuries. *Mrs. Spring Fragrance* was published in 1912 in a single edition of 2,500 copies.[7] Like Frances Ellen Watkins Harper, Far was once dismissed as a sentimental woman writer of color possessing limited skill. However, thanks to the efforts of scholars like Amy Ling and Annette White-Parks, critical attention to Sui Sin Far has grown from calls for a recovery project to rich examinations of the subversive complexity of her work that centers portrayals of queer, female, and disabled Chinese characters in the diaspora who live in the restrictive conditions of the Exclusion Era.[8]

The distinctiveness of Oriental inscrutability allows us to track how other racialized forms of unfeeling associated with immigrant populations manifested themselves through the evolving American culture of sentiment that was predicated upon structural violences against Black and Indigenous peoples. Oriental inscrutability as a quintessential nonreactive Asiatic quality bears a resemblance to what the theorist Mel Chen called the inanimacy of the element lead, which was linked to feared associations with Chineseness, disability, and queerness that threatened the figure of the white child and its associated body politic.[9] Indeed, this racialized insensibility operates as the affective effect produced by the peculiarities of the figure of the Asiatic subject that Chen and Anne Cheng use as a way to disrupt new materialist and posthumanist conversations about agency and subjectivity. The legibility of this Asiatic opacity may signal a begrudging recognition of this particular racialized mode as opposed to the gendered iterations of unsympathetic Blackness discussed in previous chapters—which may be considered in relation to Cheng's insistence on these contrasted processes of Asiatic racialization as synthetic objecthood that augment existing models of racialization focused on epidermalization and flesh that are based on Blackness.[10] Such unaffectedness is alternatively demonized as adversarial alien unassimilability or neutralized as a model of compliant passivity, indexing the uneasy positioning of Asian subjects subject to geopolitical developments and situated, as needed, as disciplinary mediator complicit in the ongoing subordination of Black and Indigenous populations. In the late nineteenth and early twentieth centuries, Chinese exclusion joined anti-Black legislation (such as the array of Jim Crow laws that legalized segregation and extrajudicial killings) and settler colonial laws (like the Dawes Act of 1887, which was designed to remove Indigenous people from their land and eliminate them) as interlocking logics of governmentality on local, national, and transnational scales whose assimilative and exclusionary violences produced the modern state and its ideal of American citizenship. These legal entanglements present a complicated system of comparative racialization involving both reductive equivalence and polarizing difference. For instance, anti-Chinese legislative discrimination in California included the 1854 *People v. Hall* decision by the California Supreme Court that categorized the Chinese alongside Black people and Native Americans as people ineligible to testify in cases involving a white person.[11] The Chinese were also excluded from naturalization despite petitioning in 1878 on the basis of the 1870 amendment that allowed African Americans to naturalize.[12] Significantly, the Exclusion Era begat the policies, procedures, and organizational structures that became the modern institution of what is now known as U.S. Citizenship and Immigration Services, which adapted existing taxonomies of human difference into the formal and cultural framework according to which the bodies and lives of immigrants, migrants, and refugees would all be scrutinized. The supplication required of minoritized individuals and populations to be deemed sympathetic took on a new valence in this system, producing coercive expectations about behavior; transparency; and, most of all, affective performances like gratitude.[13] Missionaries in the United States and abroad tried to shape the Chinese into respectable Christian subjects, projects of charitable benevolence informed by the white domesticity of post-Emancipation sentimentalism. As the critics Hsuan Hsu, Min Hyoung Song, and Yu-Fang Cho variously argue, for Far the crafting of a literary tradition through the embrace of her Chineseness required reckoning with the regulatory missionary sentimentalism that was the dominant lens used to produce knowledge about the Chinese.[14] Oriental inscrutability, a queerly dangerous epistemological instability, has been understood as bound up with the anthropological imperative that informs Far's play with these sentimental tools of colonialism.[15]

I do not disagree that Far leverages sentimentalism for the purposes of advocacy. In a December 1909 letter to her editors that was published in *Westerner*, she responds to a presumably white American reader's compliments in a previous issue by sharing the "object of [her] life": "not so much to put a Chinese name into American literature, as to break down prejudice, and to cause the American heart to soften and the American mind to broaden towards the Chinese people now living in America."[16] Nevertheless, doubt, ambivalence, and even disregard of this sentimental mission recurs throughout her work. A growing body of Asian Americanist scholarship teases out, rather than refutes, the racial associations with antisocial negativity and the potential for alternative forms of the social and care work. Examples include Summer Kim Lee's exploration of Asian American asociality and Vivian Huang's discussion of inscrutability's resistance to expectations of Asian American femme labor.[17] By suspending this expectation about Far's investment in true feeling, I put pressure upon a particularly contrarian aspect of what White-Parks has termed her "trickster" sensibility and Bo Wang her Orientalist "masquerade," which variously questions, defers, defies the need for the demystification of that inscrutability in a bid for the legibility of Chinese humanity through the schema of universal sympathy.[18] Counterintuitive and possibly dangerously counteractive, the queer, racialized mode of unfeeling derided as Oriental inscrutability obscures these politics of recognition, casting into doubt the desirability of fantasies of inclusion as the solution to Chinese exclusion.

Oriental inscrutability stands out as the primary expression (or lack of it) of the treacherous inhumanity of the Yellow Peril that threatens the good white American family and its health, its labor, and the foundation of its way of life.[19] In its 1877 report, the Joint Special Committee to Investigate Chinese Immigration recommended further restrictions on treaties and immigration policies related to the Chinese to manage "a race alien in all its tendencies," concluding that "public opinion is that Chinese immigration is exceedingly pernicious; that the presence of that element, perpetually alien in feeling and ideas, is a great disadvantage to the community."[20] "There is a race so different from our own that we do not permit those belonging to it to become citizens of the United States," wrote Associate Justice John Marshall Harlan decades later as the lone dissenter in the infamous *Plessy v. Ferguson* case (1896): "I allude to the Chinese Race."[21] Harlan denounced segregation as part of the trajectory of anti-Black legal injustices going back to *Dred Scott v. Sanford* (1857) by citing "the equality before the law of all citizens of the United States without regard to race." However, his minority opinion supported the extension of the Chinese Exclusion Act—thereby exposing the racial exceptions that undergird color-blind universal citizenship.

This Oriental alienness that is impervious to all senses of affect was central to the rhetoric used in the passage of the law. Senator John F. Miller's speech introducing the bill that would become the act presents the anti-immigration debate in terms of eugenic warfare. "It may seem strange that the apparently insignificant, dwarfed, leathery little man of the Orient should, in the peaceful contest for survival, drive the Anglo-Saxon from the field," Miller admits in his exegesis of race science.[22] The unimpressible Chinese pose a profound threat in this era, which Kyla Schuller characterizes by its obsession with the political and scientific implications of sentimental impressibility.[23] "The Chinese are alone perfectly unimpressible, and even their offspring born on American soil and who have grown up surrounded by American influences are Chinese in every characteristic of mind, feature, form, habit, and method, precisely the same as their fathers and their ancestors in China,"

Miller warns, while in comparison "the American people are far more impressible than the stoical Chinese."[24] Whiteness could be affected by Chineseness, which would be an affront to the colonial dynamics of affectability. The Chinese are impenetrable: unlike all other peoples, "they remain Chinese always and everywhere; changeless, fixed, and unalterable."[25] These unassimilable people are what the theorist Sara Ahmed would call affect aliens, to the extent that they are literalized as extraterrestrial.[26] According to Miller, "they have remained the same through all the changes of the world, and they are now a people as different from all other peoples in their characteristics, habits, methods, and physical appearance as if they were the inhabitants of another planet."[27] His rhetoric casts the Celestials, as they were sometimes called, as truly celestial in the alien sense to explain their racial inertia "as if they had all this time lived in the Mountains of the Moon."[28] The impervious Chinese are unaffected by evolutionary forces, and thus they threaten to pervert, if not incapacitate, the white body politic. An early instance of techno-Orientalism, the appearance of inscrutability reflects the essential difference of an unfeeling and inhuman race.[29] Miller insists on viewing the Yellow Peril as insensibly robotic, contributing to the cultural discourse traced by Colleen Lye that both rendered the coolie the ideal exploitable worker after the abolition of slavery and scapegoated a people for the evils of global capitalism.[30] In sharp contrast to the hapless but wholesome white American worker whose job is endangered, members of this strange group of people "have become machine-like in every physical characteristic . . . automatic engines of flesh and blood" with no affective interiority, for "they are patient, stolid, unemotional, and persistent."[31] In short, inscrutability might constitute not just an impassive mask indecipherable to Western eyes, but also the signifier of Oriental ontological hollowness.

Miller's speech engages in a clash of genres: he pits the Yellow Peril as a perverse science fictional nightmare against the wholesome sentimental ideals of white America. Along with the aliens and automatons of early science fiction, Miller draws upon the conventions of naturalism, as when he invokes Herbert Spencer's slogan that popularized Darwinian evolution: "In this persistent dreary struggle for existence the law of the 'survival of the fittest' has had full play, and from the process of induration which has been so long at work a race of men has resulted whose vital organism is adapted to the smallest needs of human life, with a capacity or physical endurance equal to that of the most stalwart races."[32] While the Chinese are unnatural, white American settlers are natural. At his speech's climax, Miller proclaims: "The land which is being overrun by the oriental invader is the fairest portion of our heritage. It is the land of the vine and the fig tree; the home of the orange, and the pomegranate. Its winter is a perpetual spring, and its summer is a golden harvest."[33] In this seeming digression, Miller waxes poetic about the pastoral landscape before populating it with "American homes—the homes of a free, happy people, resonant with the sweet voices of flaxen-haired children, and ringing with the joyous laughter of maidens fair."[34] California, too, is a site for the erasures of the sentimental American settler project, and Miller quotes Tennyson's *Idylls of the King*: "The flower of men / To serve as model for the mighty world, / And be the fair beginning of a time."[35] Much as Tennyson's poem used medieval Arthurian legends to justify the British empire, Miller uses Tennyson to naturalize and even indigenize American settler colonialism by connecting it to its long, transnational history.[36] The bucolic imagery of Miller's conclusion includes poetry from Lord Byron and Sir Walter Scott about nature, using the Western literary canon to support Miller's argument that naturalizes the dichotomy between the foreign dissonance of the Chinese and the organic harmony of American whiteness. To exclude the Chinese from the United States, then, would only reflect the reality that the alien Chinese inherently exclude themselves from the human race.[37]

I suggest that there is an overlooked factor to Oriental inscrutability that compounds this trope of racialized unfeeling bound to American economic anxieties: the challenge posed by the Chinese "face." By "face," I refer to the Chinese concept that brings together individual composure and social relations, an alternative taxonomy of affective expression that troubles the colonial ruse of universal true feeling. The slippage between the Chinese face as concept and embodiment brings us back to chapter 1 on the optical logics of American race science that was obsessed with faces, heads, and skulls and its confluence with sentimentalism as an ideology that lingers in white Anglo-American philosophical, scientific, and cultural considerations of feelings. Chinese faces and Oriental inscrutability, as I will show in this chapter, are intertwined in the genealogy of American-Chinese encounters and constitute a stubborn incommensurability that goes beyond intercultural frustrations to mark geopolitical and epistemic frictions.

Far's journalism and fiction explore the lived experiences on the fault lines between these emotional regimes for diasporic and mixed-race Chinese. In echoes of the literary strategies we have seen in Martin Delany's and Frances Ellen Watkins Harper's work, Far draws upon the conventions of white sentimentalism to critique its obscuring of other modes of feeling that vex in ways captured by the *New York Times*'s review. Although Far works through the clash between Chinese "face" and white American sympathies, her writings theorize how the phenomenon of Oriental inscrutability should not be vilified, given its function as an everyday means of psychic survival. This Chinese alienness, therefore, is an effect of structural alienation. Far traces the different gendered manifestations of the inscrutable face as a form of endurance, withholding, and even outright defiance through performances of composure that cannot be explained away as mere cultural misunderstanding. For Chinese men as sojourners in the West, their inscrutable uses of face emerge from the constitutive relationship between their physical and affective labor on behalf of their prioritization of Chinese kinships in Chinatown enclaves and overseas. Chinese women, in contrast, use the ornamentalist artifices deemed to be Oriental as a form of withholding from the gaze that fetishizes their inscrutability as a challenge to be overcome. Given that scholars like Nayan Shah have shown that even the ostensible Chinese gender binary was viewed as nonconforming according to white American norms, Far gestures toward how Oriental inscrutability queerly disrupts the racialized heteronormative equations of sex, gender, and sexuality.

Throughout this analysis I pay attention to how Far reuses phrases, passages, and scenes across her fiction and nonfiction to address perennial anti-Chinese issues. Mary Chapman, the editor of Far's rediscovered and reprinted writings, suggests that this signature "self-plagiarism" results from the pragmatic considerations of a writer who, to make her living from her craft, must produce material across different genres, meet deadlines, and fulfill word counts.[38] I speculate that in the context of the indistinguishably and interchangeably inscrutable Chinese, this writerly strategy of recycling and sameness ironizes that aspect of racialization, drawing attention to the exhaustive sameness of structural violences and everyday aggressions faced by the marginalized peoples. This formal technique reflects the strategic conservation of resources necessary for survival—serving, in Far's case, as a coping mechanism of detachment from the overwhelming sensitivity that characterizes her unnamed chronic disability. Among the forms of refusal through Oriental inscrutability, I map out how the mode of distancing she associates with Chinese women influences her self-representation in "Leaves from the Mental Portfolio of an Eurasian." By reworking scenes and phrases focused on dissatisfaction and dissent that already appeared elsewhere in her work, her memoir complicates a desire to expose the truth of her life using clear, unequivocal representations that can be marshalled for a project of political advocacy.

While Oriental inscrutability can map onto the practices of "face" as a suspension or escape from the pressures of that scopic culture of sentiment, Far is wary of endorsing an uncomplicated move to Chinese cultural nationalism. Her sense of belonging, as scholars have highlighted, is not nationally bounded, as she leans on her mixed-race heritage as metaphor for her feelings of liminality.[39] As she concludes at the end of her memoir, "After all I have no nationality and am not anxious to claim any."[40] Along with her ambivalence toward conventional attachments, in her writings her sense of community is often tenuous: although she celebrates Chinese communities as protective enclaves, there are disruptive antisocial threads running throughout her work. Her portrayals of loneliness and death echo sentimental tropes of tragedy without a sense of moral triumph. These losses that cannot be recuperated suggest her skepticism about the political instrumentality of the mode of unfeeling that she sees as necessary but, perhaps, not as generative of the flourishing of new structures of feeling for either successful inclusion into hegemony or emancipatory potential for a remaking of the world. Chinese faces have the right to turn away, but Far is uncertain about what they are facing toward instead.[41]

Inexpressive Asians / Encounters with the Chinese Face as Concept and Physiognomy

"I have not found them to be slow of intellect and alien to all other races in that 'they are placed and unfeeling, and so custom-bound that even their tears are mere waters of ceremony and flow forth at stated times and periods,'" Far writes, citing Orientalist ethnographies of the Chinese in the first installment of her "The Chinese in America" essay series for the *Westerner* (1909). "Thus a European traveler some centuries ago described the Chinese people, and travelers ever since, both men and women, have echoed his words and sentiments, while fiction writers seem to be so imbued with the same ideas that you scarcely ever read about a Chinese person who is not a wooden peg."[42] In her view, this unfeeling inscrutability is the origin of the cultural repertoire of Chinese stereotypes, in which Asian Americanist critics might include such figures as the expressionless mask, the double agent, and the alien sojourner.[43] "While the Chinese are inscrutable, I remain lucid; their objectlike obscurity constitutes my subjectivity, my humanity," observes Rey Chow about the logic underlying Jacques Derrida's construction of global theory by characterizing the Chinese language as inscrutable.[44] Inscrutability collapses Chinese faces, culture, and language into a surface that "stigmatizes another culture as at once corporeally and linguistically intractable" and may be "the cross-ethnic stereotype par excellence."[45] The image of the Chinese as inscrutable, Chow argues, renders "an entire people as (mere) face."⁴⁶ In other words, the inscrutability of Chinese characters as a language is intertwined with the racial and cultural essence of Chinese character and, I suggest, in turn molds the writing of Chinese characters in literature. In what follows, I look to the proto-anthropological tradition of travel and missionary writing cited by Far to explore how the unfeeling trope of Oriental inscrutability coheres a messy racialized genealogy of misreadings, practices, and resistances that focus on the corporeal, cultural, and symbolic Chinese face as the signifying zone of contact.

After his first encounter with the Chinese in Singapore in 1852, the influential American travel writer Bayard Taylor observed that they had "dull faces, without expression," filling him "with an unconquerable aversion."⁴⁷ The centrality of faces was more than chance in his description: according to the historian John Haddad, in his study of early American images of China, Taylor was a lifelong devotee of physiognomy.⁴⁸ According to James Redfield's physiognomic guide, for instance, the faculty of secretiveness is signaled by the degree that one's nostrils resembles those of a Chinese, for they are "the most remarkable people in the world for secretiveness"—a point illustrated with an engraving of a generic East Asian face.⁴⁹ Taylor presents us with a direct historical thread from embodied encounters with Chinese faces to the U.S. exclusion of the Chinese diaspora: his journey through Canton and Shanghai confirmed his physiognomic conviction of Chinese degradation, and his disgust later led to his political stance as an early authoritative voice against their immigration. The face of the Yellow Peril was terrifyingly inscrutable, being both deceitful and inhuman. "Child-like and bland" is how Bret Harte repeatedly describes the facial expression of the dissembling Chinese cardsharp Ah Sin in his popular 1870 poem with its refrain of racialized inscrutability: "That for ways that are dark / and tricks that are vain, / the heathen Chinee is peculiar."⁵⁰ Harte's poem, originally titled "Plain Language from Truthful James," was rebranded as "The Heathen Chinee" and would be quoted by members of the U.S. Senate and House of Representatives from 1871 through to the early 1960s in debates about Chinese immigration and as a generalized shorthand for deceptiveness in discussions unrelated to China or Chinese people.⁵¹

However, distrust of Chinese faces as illegible and nonhuman goes beyond the scapegoating of the racialized face as the embodied and symbolic site of emotional expressiveness. "Face" in Chinese culture articulates a complex cluster of social behaviors. In brief, there are two main types of face, *mien* and *lien*, both of which have rich taxonomies of concrete and figurative meanings contextualized by social dynamics.⁵² For Americans the encounter with this Chinese meaning of face, an alternative cultural taxonomy of feeling, disrupts a presumed universalist paradigm of affective and social expression that goes back to Adam Smith's "fellow-feeling."[53] With this other sense of face in play, the Chinese could be seen, as it were, as dangerously two-faced. The most-read American text on the Chinese through the early twentieth century—the missionary Arthur Smith's *Chinese Characteristics* (1890)—gives us this sense of face as a comprehensive metaphor for Oriental inscrutability and its attendant evils. Smith expands upon the physical "usual expressionless visage" of the Chinese, making the Chinese concept of face the defining Chinese concept, a legacy of cultural translation that the critic Lydia Liu argues continues to haunt both Chinese and American contexts today.[54] The first chapter of Smith's book begins, "At first sight nothing can be more irrational than to call that which is shared with the whole human race a 'characteristic' of the Chinese. But the word 'face' does not in China signify simply the front of the head, but is literally a compound noun of multitude, with more meanings than we shall be able to describe, or perhaps to comprehend."[55] In this shift from the corporeal to sociocultural codes and an inscrutable racial essence, we can see the reduction of an entire people to mere face, as articulated by Chow's critique of Derrida. Smith's unclear ethnographic exegesis of "face," which he views as consisting of insincerely "theatrical" Chinese customs and behaviors, mimics his paradoxical sense of Chinese inscrutability: on the one hand, he proclaims that "rightly apprehended, 'face' will be found to be in itself a key to the combination lock of many of the important characteristics of the Chinese"; and on the other hand, he argues that "the principles which regulate 'face' and its attainment are often wholly beyond the intellectual apprehension of the Occidental."[56] In the course of twenty-six chapters, Smith unpacks twenty-six implications of the inscrutable face for the Chinese as a people and a society. The chapters include "The Talent for Misunderstanding," "The Talent for Indirection," "The Absence of Nerves," "The Absence of Sympathy," and "The Absence of Sincerity." Sharing the popular eugenic rhetoric used by Miller, Smith worries about the threat posed by this unaffectable and unfeeling people: "Which is the best adapted to survive in the struggles of the twentieth century, the 'nervous' European, or the tireless, all-pervading, and phlegmatic Chinese?"[57]

This fear of the Yellow Peril gestures toward the situatedness of the Chinese configured between whiteness and Black and Indigenous peoples in geopolitical hierarchies of race, which makes face a paradoxically legible form of alien difference. This intermediary position entangles anti-Chinese violences with Chinese structural and active complicity in this transnational hegemony.[58] To unpack the hierarchy of comparative racialization, let us return to Samuel Morton's foundational race science treatise *Crania Americana*, in which the craniologist gives an overview of racial classificatory schemas by such famed scientists as Linnaeus, Georges Cuvier, and the Comte de Buffon. Morton eventually settles on the latest categories of race developed by Johann Blumenbach—Caucasian, Mongolian, Malay, American, and Ethiopian, roughly corresponding to white, East Asian, Southeast Asian, Indigenous (Turtle Island), and Black—ordered as a hierarchy with further subdivisions by language and ethnicity. Anticipating the modern concept of the model minority myth that contrasts Asians with other marginalized peoples, Morton describes the Mongolian race as "ingenious, imitative, and highly susceptible of civilization," comparatively privileged in their place just one tier down from Caucasians.[59] The Chinese pose a conundrum for Morton and his peers, following their criteria for civilization that rationalize Western dominance. Morton confesses that "the intellectual character of the Chinese is deserving of especial attention," and "their mechanical ingenuity is universally known" (46). In one instance he claims the Chinese lack originality since "their faculty of imitation is proverb," but he soon contradicts himself when he concedes that it is the West that imitates China: "European civilisation has borrowed largely from China, the Chinese nothing from Europe" (45 and 46). What offsets the advanced nature of Chinese civilization is the essential Chinese inertness that so distresses Smith (and Miller): "Hence it has been observed that unmovableness is the characteristic of the nation" (46). Despite Chinese advances across the arts and sciences, the scientist manages the threat of techno-Orientalism by reassuring the reader repeatedly of the static nature of the Chinese: "They are the same now what they were many centuries ago" and "remained stationary for thirty centuries" (46). Unable to dismiss Chinese civilization according to the colonial rubric of Western superiority that invalidates African and Indigenous cultures, Morton turns to the consequences of that unaffectability in the realm of feeling and morality to question the humanity of the Chinese, justifying his action by Oriental inscrutability. He quotes other scholars to affirm that "the Chinese are generally selfish, cold-blooded and inhumane," and their religion is "heartless" (45 and 46). He cites an expert who claims the Chinese are "barbarously cruel; that human suffering, or human life, are but rarely regarded by those in authority, when the infliction of the one or the destruction of the other, can be made subservient to the acquisition of wealth and power" (45). The enigma of the Chinese face cast as a negative judgment of a people and its culture offsets Morton's grudging admission of Chinese civilization and influence in world history.

Maintaining Face / An Alternative Taxonomy of Feeling

In a contrasting coeval history of encounters between the West and the East, there is perennial frustration among Chinese intellectuals about Western misunderstandings of "face." Indirectly commenting on the influence of Smith's *Chinese Characteristics*, Lu Xun, the leading Chinese writer of the early twentieth century, remarks that "face" is a "word on the lips of foreigners too, who seem to be studying it. They find it extremely hard to understand, but believe that 'face' is the key to the Chinese spirit."[60] Liu notes that Lu took issue with Smith's simplistic understanding that elided the complexity of social and power relations and implicated the American missionaries in cultural imperialism.[61] In comparison, the writer Lin Yutang was skeptical of the legibility of "face" to a Western audience, stating that "face cannot be translated or defined."[62] He remarks that "indeed, the Chinese mind is akin to the feminine mind in many respects," a statement suggestive of a racialized queerness.[63] Through the twentieth century, Chinese anthropologists and sociologists like Hsien Hu, David Ho, and others approach the demystification of "face" as a way of decentering Western ideas about the universality of social relations and affects.[64] As Xiaoying Qi argues, understanding the nuances surrounding "face" reveals the specificities behind somatic expressions of emotion: "Face arises in social interactions or relationships which are in turn responsible for emotional experiences, and it is these latter that underlie the processes of face."[65] In the field of Asian American studies, David Palumbo-Liu responds to an American sociologist's explication of the slippage between meanings of "face" by noting that the sociologist's mistranslation loses "the intensely collective phenomenon of 'face.'"[66] What is most germane to my discussion, however, is not so much a striving for accuracy in conveying the meaning of "face" to a Western audience but that—following the call of the decolonial thinker Sneja Gunew to provincialize Western affect theory—the entire Chinese concept of "face" challenges the presumed universality of how affects are generated and feelings are expressed.[67] In fact, as Qi points out, the modern sociological framework for the understanding of universal self-presentation and ritual in social interactions originated from Erving Goffman's foundational concept of "face-work," which was inspired in part by the Chinese concept.[68] Among the items cited in the first footnote to Goffman's now-classic article, the sociologist includes Smith's *Chinese Characteristics*.[69] Goffman's "face" as a generalizable social phenomenon inspired by the Chinese "face" reflects the extractive logics of Western knowledge production that preyed upon other epistemes and then discarded cultural and historical specificities to promote a mobile and engulfing universality. In this regard, Oriental inscrutability signifies the difficulties of cultural translation when the West refuses to decenter itself, both blaming and fetishizing the Orient for its illegibility.

Trapped between these incompatibilities and misunderstandings, the relationship of the Chinese diaspora in the settler colonies of North America to Oriental inscrutability was more complicated than one of acquiescing to the obligation to refute stereotypes to prove their humanity according to American standards of true feeling. The figures of the coolie and the sex worker—identified by Shah as the two pathologized and sexually deviant counterparts integral to the Yellow Peril—manifest different gendered dimensions of unfeeling Oriental inscrutability that reflect the American anxieties that coalesced around them.[70] The popular image of the insensate coolie, as Lye and Eric Hayot have argued, justified the exploitation of the coolies' labor and their disposability as the replacement for Black enslavement—which in turn was used to undercut white labor unions.[71] Whereas the unfeeling Chinese coolie was numbly machine-like in his inscrutability, the unfeeling female Chinese sex worker was insincerely artificial in hers, a heartlessness that I suggest is related to what Cheng calls the inorganic ornamentalism of the figure of the "yellow woman."[72] By not taking these unfeeling figures at face value, so to speak, we can follow the gendered tactics of how playing with and into the trope of Oriental inscrutability produces the capacity to shift between vocabularies of affective expression counter to expectations of a transparently legible subject as a condition of sympathetic identification, scientific and legal compliance, and potential inclusion in the nation. Such flexibility may be a necessity for survival particularly in hostile conditions following Lin's insight into what he calls the notorious "indifference" of his people: "a social attitude made necessary by the absence of legal protection. It is a form of self-protection, developed in the same manner as the tortoise develops its shell. The famous Chinese apathetic gaze is only a self-protective gaze, acquired by a lot of culture and self-discipline."[73] In critiquing the inadequacies of Western ethnographies and fiction about the Chinese, Far writes: "In this country they are slow to push their individual claims, and when with strangers, hide the passions of their hearts under quiet and peaceful demeanors; but because a man is indisposed to show his feelings is no proof that he has none. Under a quiet surface the Chinaman conceals a rapid comprehension and an almost morbid sensitiveness; he also possesses considerable inventive power and is more of an initiative spirit than an imitative one, whatever may be said to the contrary by those who know him but superficially."[74] While the Exclusion Act attempted to keep the specters of the coolie and the sex worker at bay, it is important to note that the Chinese ignored pressures to counter Orientalist stereotypes about deceitful practices: as Estelle Lau's work uncovers, the Chinese deliberately manipulated American misunderstandings about Chinese identities and customs to outwit the apparatuses of immigration.[75] In this regard, maintaining the inexpressive Oriental face along with retaining the practices around the Chinese concept of face offered a means of coping or defense, and possibly even of registering dissatisfaction if not outright defiance. For Far, as the literary face of the Chinese diaspora, creating characters and narratives that could be read as inscrutably Oriental obstructs the expressive demands of sentimentalism shaped by the Chinese Exclusion Era.

"The Chinaman Does Not Carry His Heart on His Sleeve" / Sui Sin Far on the Gendered Strategies of Inscrutability

"The Chinese people may have no souls, no expression on their faces, be altogether beyond the pale of civilization, but whatever they are, I want you to understand that I am—I am a Chinese," declares Far in "Leaves from the Mental Portfolio of an Eurasian," a kind of racialized coming out in her Chineseness that shatters how she as a mixed-race person is read as phenotypically white.[76] This gesture of defiance comes from her recollection of an event involving anti-Chinese comments sparked by the transcontinental railroad's running through a racist small Midwestern town. "Somehow or other," her employer had mused at the opening of the conversation, "I cannot reconcile myself to the thought that the Chinese are humans like ourselves. They may have immortal souls, but their faces seem to be so utterly devoid of expression that I cannot help but doubt."[77] Far was employed by him as a stenographer, a common occupation for single women, and we may note that her duty to faithfully translate his words into type dovetails into the trope of Chinese imitativeness.[78] In her response, Far reworks his phrases concerning the dubious nature of Chinese souls and expressionless Oriental faces—but she does not directly disprove the actual allegations of Oriental inscrutability.[79] Instead, she says that these tropes may be true, obstinately reaffirming the threatening instability of that epistemic, affective indeterminancy. The humanity of the Chinese may indeed be uncertain—"whatever they are"—but nonetheless Far is certain about her political choice to identify as Chinese despite the Yellow Peril connotations and the immediate implications for her welfare in this dinner discussion, in which both her boss and her landlady have voiced anti-Chinese sentiments. Although in her memoir Far draws attention to the disparity between the expectation of Oriental inscrutability and her own hypersensitivity as a disabled, possibly queer, and mixed-race woman, she does not seek to fully abolish the many-faceted trope of Chinese unfeeling. Her retort is not a refutation but rather a refiguration of that racialized unfeeling.

This embrace adds an element of perversity to Far's engagement with Oriental inscrutability across her writings. "These mysterious, inscrutable, incomprehensible Americans! Had I the divine right of learning I would put them into an immortal book!" declares the eponymous protagonist of the *Mrs. Spring Fragrance* short story collection.[80] This scene is widely read by critics as Far's subversion of the Orientalist ethnographic tradition through her positioning of Mrs. Spring Fragrance as amateur anthropologist.[81] But this lighthearted moment of reversal does not dismiss "inscrutability" as mere misunderstanding in a cultural relativist agenda. Later, Mrs. Carman, a progressive New Woman, views her Chinese friend as oddly inert: "Hitherto she had found the little Chinese woman sympathetic and consoling. Chinese ideas of filial duty chimed in with her own. But today Mrs. Spring Fragrance seemed strangely uninterested and unresponsive."[82] Significantly, this perception of her unfeeling occurs because Mrs. Spring Fragrance dissents from her friend's interpretation of how the sentimental love plot of the story should be resolved.

I choose to set aside Mrs. Spring Fragrance and the optimism of her stories' happy endings: what interests me are the perverse and negative elements of Far's writing that slip through the opening that Mrs. Spring Fragrance—the rare Chinese woman respectable enough to pass through the sieve of Exclusion-Era immigration as the wife of a successful merchant—makes possible as the eponymous character of Far's only book and its first short story. Throughout Far's journalistic and literary writings, she explores the racial and sexual politics of Oriental inscrutability as a maligned effect of structural alienation that refracts continually renegotiated relationships between the Chinese face as a cultural phenomenon and individual embodied performance. This mode of unfeeling operates as a condition of survival for the diasporic Chinese, a defensive calculus of affective and epistemological disclosures and withholdings that defies the heightened scrutiny of new forms of governmentality related to immigration and transnational migrations. It insists on the right to unassimilable alterity that stubbornly refuses to dissolve into the sameness of universal feeling.

Faces are a constant in Far's writings. In her earliest known published work, Edith Eaton delivers a sketch of social relations for Montreal's *Domin-*

ion Illustrated that was inspired by "contemplating the faces of my fellow passengers" on the horse-drawn mass transit of the time.[83] She observes the faces of these white passengers and how others respond to them as signifiers of morality and class. Her physiognomic evaluations take a more somber turn when she muses about the limits of emotional expression and sympathy, casting into doubt her playful speculations: "We pity all those whose lot in life is hard, and we pity them because they require pity; but there is a deeper feeling than pity in our breasts for the unknown ones who hide their sorrow from the world's curious gaze, to whom pity gives positive pain when coming from those who do not understand what they are pitying; for we know that they who sorrow the most give no sign; that the saddest hearts are oft the bravest." Raising the possibility of misrecognition, through her attention to faces Eaton reworks Adam Smith's conception of sympathy in this meditation on what develops into a principle of feeling and unfeeling in her thinking: apparent inexpression can be inversely correlated with affective intensity and vulnerability precisely because of the universalizing pressures of the sentimental gaze.

Far spends the rest of her career shifting away from unmarked universals to attend to the nuanced experiences of Chinese faces. The short story "The Gamblers" (1896), one of her first pieces of fiction involving Chinese subjects, appears a cliché of practices associated with Chinese depravity.[84] Ah Lin goes to an opium den to gamble and, after losing the last of his money, instigates a fight that results in his death. Parallels to Bret Harte's famous poem, however, suggest that Far's portrayal of Ah Lin offers an alternative reading of why someone like him might have a "bland" face to pair with "ways that are dark"; indeed, her brother-in-law Walter Blackburn Harte (no relation to Bret Harte) introduces "Sui Seen Far" to the readers of the *Lotus* that year by comparing the famous writer whose Chinatown sketches "were too colored by caricature to hold the touch of psychological reality" to this newcomer who "excels" in comparison.[85] In the opening description of Ah Lin, we are told that he "shambled on indifferently, slowly and heavily, apparently totally unconscious of physical discomfort. Looking into that bald face one could not penetrate its placidity, and even the eyes seemed expressionless."[86] The "apparently" hints that Ah Lin's conventional coolie insensibility is only what appears to the casual observer. Whereas in later writings, like the border-crossing cross-dressing love story "Tian Shan's Kindred Spirit," Far directly quotes Bret Harte's "ways that are dark and tricks that are vain" and gives insights into her Chinese characters' motives that capitalize upon the inscrutable stereotype, here the narrative is as withholding as its main character.[87] The narrator indicates that Ah Lin is not the coolie he appears, for his "ordinary blue blouse and pantaloon of a working Chinaman" clashes with his hands that "did not look as if they were accustomed to manual labor"—but the reader is never given access to his true identity.[88] What drives this man to gamble with such desperation that he risks his life? As in Far's earlier writing, often the most expressionless faces conceal the greatest woes. What we do know is that Ah Lin's unknown drive has him ignore "the scenes and faces about him" and that after his catastrophic loss "Ah Lin's face turned grey."[89] Rather than exploring characters in depth, the brief story is dominated by descriptions of the intricate mechanics of the gambling system that has the Chinese in its thrall, a cruel economic system with the illusion of agency and slim promise of fortune that is akin to the exploitative coolie trade. Ah Lin's insensible face functions as a defense and a gambling tactic until, with his failure, he loses first his face and then his life. Far's own gamble with clichés met with commercial success: this story was reprinted in the *Traveler* and *Westerner*.[90]

Far's nonfiction about the social, economic, and cultural contours of institutional anti-Chinese racism contextualizes the alienation of people like Ah Lin. These themes run throughout her advocacy writings to the point where she recycles key lines almost verbatim. For example, the following passages justifying the alleged unassimilable Chinese sojourner in "The Chinese Question" (1895) reappear in "A Plea for the Chinaman" (1896), both published in the *Montreal Daily Star*. Under the pseudonym "E. E.," Far makes the following comparison about transnational economic opportunism in two different articles: "It is well known that the Chinamen [sic] comes here alone to make money, and with the intention of returning sooner or later. See how he follows the example which we westerners set him. There are many foreigners in China, and with the exception of the missionaries, they are all there for the avowed purpose of making money. The ports of China are full of foreign private adventurers. After they've made their pile they'll return to their homes in Europe or America."[91] What is only business as usual for entrepreneurial white Westerners under the aegis of colonialism is vilified when done by Chinese men as part of what Aihwa Ong has illuminated as the Chinese diaspora's tactics of flexible citizenship, which follow transnational flows of capital and kin.[92] If the Chinese merchants appear overrepresented, it is because they constituted one of the few classes of Chinese who were exempt from the restrictions of the Exclusion Act in the United States and the head tax of the Canadian Chinese Immigration Act of 1885.

The alleged antisocial mysteriousness of the Chinese can be traced to resilient behaviors and attitudes developed in response to racist alienation: "The Chinaman does not come here to settle down. If such a notion as settling here ever entered his head our treatment of him would soon knock it out. He does not associate with our race at all—we don't and we won't associate with him."[93] "E. E." characterizes the Chinese as unassimilable sojourners in terms of a racialized manifestation of antisociality that is a defense against American and Canadian hostility, an argument so important that she reuses her wording to compound its importance.

Her journalism follows the uses of that composure of face by these allegedly inscrutable Chinese men, communities of so-called bachelors typically working to send money to family members back in China—which mediates the interplay between their wage labor and the affective labor of everyday survival. The following passage is repeated in two articles for the *Montreal Daily Star*: "The Chinaman does not carry his heart on his sleeve; he has affections, but he betrays them in actions, not words. Emigrants from other lands talk liberally and weep copiously about those they have left behind, but the Chinaman unbosoms not himself" (78 and 95). She reverses the colloquial saying about wearing one's heart on one's sleeve to demonstrate how such a common idiom about expressiveness is not universal. Instead, by drawing attention to the role of clothing in performances of self, she addresses the paradox that Chinese clothing expresses the self through concealment. In this passage she also refers to Bret Harte's influential poem: while his stereotyped cardsharp Ah Sin has tricks up his sleeve, Chinese laborers have reason to keep things hidden in theirs. This passage takes on different nuances in its two iterations. "The Chinese at Christmas" (1895) elaborates on alternative cultural modes of expression as part of a portrait of the Chinese at Christmas that emphasizes differing transnational familial structures against the unspoken backdrop of white heteronormativity—which in turn figured Chinese men as queerly emasculated but also dangerously lascivious. "The Chinese Defended" (1896) gives evidence of Chinese integrity in a blistering editorial against a missionary who called the Chinese "an unmitigated evil" (92). What is parsed as Chinese sexual and moral deviance results from the ignorance of white middle-class sentimental norms of kinship, behavior, and expression that are upheld as a universal standard.

Another oft-repeated assertion in Far's journalism is the significance of the Chinese signature silent composure that contributes to their appearance of insensibility. For example, she uses the phrase a "sturdy silence" in both of the articles mentioned above to characterize the composure of the overseas sojourner who sends money and letters home to family members in China: if he appears unfeeling to the white American and Canadian gaze, it is because his heart is elsewhere (78 and 95). In "A Chinese Party" (1890), a piece that discusses Chinese men traveling from Boston back to China by way of Vancouver, she notes that "the philosophy of the Chinese is—silence, but," she adds wryly, "no doubt when they get home they will have a few rather vigorous remarks to make about the beautiful laws of this great country" (43). The inscrutable silence of the Chinese is a deliberate stance toward outsiders: after all, they are hardly silent with each other. Defending the Chinese against the aspersions of a politician who views them as "docile and easily managed," she states, "The quiet dignity of the Chinese is worthy of admiration" (87). There is also another side to the Chinese face that belies perceptions of their passivity: "Perhaps he does not know that the Chinese are taught to treat the rude with silent contempt."

THE INSCRUTABLE ARTIFICE OF THE CHINESE FEMME

Far's attention to the specific Oriental inscrutability of Chinese women is inflected by their embodiment of a sexualized form of unknowability codified by the Page Act of 1875 that only amplified that fetishized mystery, because so few of them were allowed to enter the nation. Throughout her work, Far presents the Chinese woman as a foil to the New Woman and the presumed universality of white womanhood in general. As critics have noted, in one essay Far even applies the label "New Woman" to the supposedly unchanging Chinese who developed signifiers of white feminist modernity like the divided skirt long before the West—and, as she points out, "New Woman" is the direct translation of the Chinese term for new brides.[94] I seek to read the article "The Chinese Woman in America" (1897) as an articulation of woman of color feminism. In this piece, written for the *Land of Sunshine*, a magazine used to promote California that trafficked in the local color genre, Far explores how the Chinese woman's survival calculus of refusals plays into and against the Oriental ornamentalist erotics of concealment and hyperfeminization—which her writing mirrors by pairing each reveal with a reminder of the validity of withholding. Although there exists "the popular idea that the Chinese are a phlegmatic people," writes Far, the Chinese woman is "brimful of feelings and impressions."[95] Despite this tantalizing glimpse beneath the inexpressive Oriental face, she repeatedly affirms the right of Chinese women to indissoluble difference even if it confirms that they are unassimilable:

> The Chinese woman in America differs from all others who come to live their lives here, in that she seeks not our companionship, makes no attempt to know us, adopts not our ways and heeds not our customs. She lives among us, but is as isolated as if she and the few Chinese relations who may happen to live near were the only human beings in the world.
>
> So if you wish to become acquainted with her, if you wish to glean some knowledge of a type of which very little is known, you must seek her out. She will be pleased with your advances and welcome you with demure politeness, but you might wait to all eternity and she would not come to you. (59)

Foregrounding the importance of consent, white readers, for all their well-meaning liberal curiosity tied to the cultural politics of recognition, should tolerate the Chinese woman's refusal that would maintain the distancing barrier of inscrutability. In this piece that gives insights into the lives of Chinese women and their customs, Far emphasizes the Chinese woman's agency to turn away literally and symbolically: "Do not imagine for an instant that she is dull of comprehension and unable to distinguish friendly visitors from those who merely call to amuse themselves at her expense. I have seen a little Chinese woman deliberately turn her back on persons so ignorant as to whisper about her and exchange knowing smiles in her presence" (64). Although seemingly overdetermined by an ancient patriarchal culture, the invocation of traditional ways gives the Chinese woman a reprieve from the demands of American belonging: "she has a certain admiration for the ways of the foreigner; but nothing can change her reverence for the manners and customs of her own country" or prevent her from using the phrase "that not Chinese way" as a tactic of rejection (64). "More constant than sentimental is the Chinese woman" is how Far sums up the appearance of the Chinese woman's antisociality given the deliberate prioritization of the sphere of Chinese social life, implicitly contrasted with the sentimentalism of white womanhood (64).

Insofar as Chinese men do not wear their hearts on their sleeves, Far elaborates how the femme artificiality of the Chinese woman's dress and other signature ornamentation can be an exercise of personal sovereignty over disclosure and withholding. After all, the practices of face are gendered: "If it is necessary to pass a room occupied by men, they do so very demurely, holding open fans before that side of the face—not because they are so shy, but because it is the custom of their country" (62). Far describes the Chinese woman's love of material culture—which is inextricable from the construction of the Oriental artifice of her racialized gender that limits outsiders' access to her inner life—this way: "She will show you all her pretty ornaments, her jewelry and fine clothing, but never invite you near her private chapel."[96] Chinese women's vanity has a different relationship to spectatorship than white American women's vanity does: "A Chinese woman paints and powders, dresses and bejewels herself for her own pleasure; puts rings on her fingers and bracelets on her arms—and carefully hides herself from the gaze of strangers."[97] According to her cultural paradigm, she is not deceitful or false: again, her inscrutability is figured as a matter of consent and control over access to her body. To recall Cheng, the ornamentalism of the yellow woman centers on the inorganic.[98] Far's Chinese woman delights in her femme Orientalist artifice: expressing herself through "beautiful fancy-work, representations of insects, flowers and birds most dexterously wrought from silk and beads," this aesthetic practice is "not useless" because of its social value for family and herself.[99] In contrast to Western sentimental conflations of the categories of the natural and the good, for the Chinese woman the realm of the false and inorganic is no less valid: "She loves flowers, natural or artificial; and if not supplied with the former, makes herself great quantities of the latter and wears them on hair and breast."

In this exploration of Chinese femininity, Far touches upon one of the most contentious of these practices tied to the inscrutability of Chinese women: foot binding. Foot binding attracted fascination and condemnation from missionaries, anthropologists, and white New Woman activists, among others.[100] According to Dorothy Ko, what has been neglected by the fixation on the victimization of Chinese women is the significance of that concealment: "In refusing the [sic] submit to the foreign gaze, the footbound woman could have served as the very site of resistance against foreign encroachment."[101] Far's depiction acknowledges the resistance of that Oriental inscrutability and makes no judgment: "If she has Golden Lily feet (Chinese small feet) she is proudly conscious of it; but should she become aware that a stranger is trying to obtain a glimpse of them, they quickly disappear under her skirt."[102] Eschewing the privileging of exposure as truth and goodness, the Chinese woman has reason to take refuge in the feminized artifices regarded as emblematic of Oriental inscrutability.

"TRICKS THAT ARE STRANGE" / THOSE QUEER CHINESE

Although Far's fiction investigates how this structural queerness of inscrutable Chinese bodies, practices, and relations under the regime of sentimental biopolitics leads to conflict, she does not call for the dissolution of their racialized deviance by having the Chinese conform to white heteronormativity. Didactic moments that would clarify Chinese "ways that are dark / and tricks that are strange" for white characters and a white readership are inconsistent and often deny the reader the satisfaction of a revelation. For instance, at the end of "The Smuggling of Tie Co," considered the most overtly queer of the stories in her published collection, the white smuggler Jack Fabian is left with "the mystery of Tie Co's life—and death" because the person he understood to be a Chinese man professes his love to Jack and sacrifices himself for him and, posthumously, is revealed to have a body considered phenotypically female.[103] The tragedy of Tie Co is not the failure of redemptive demystification. Tie Co presents what Min Song calls the epistemological inscrutability of Oriental sexuality: the body is not presented as biological fact but unstable evidence that disrupts the distinction between sex and gender as well as the gender binary.[104] The entanglement between queer Chinese gender and desire does not need to be untangled.

The inscrutability of Chinese gender means that Miss Mason, the new Chinatown Mission teacher, mistakenly sees Ku Yum as a girl in "The Chinese Boy-Girl." Ku Yum's mother is dead and his father is ill, so Mason sympathetically takes it upon herself to become responsible for her student. She turns to the Superior Court and the Society for the Prevention of Cruelty to Children to separate Ku Yum from his family, replacing Chinese kinship structures with American state interference. In response, Ku Yum evades the authorities by hiding in Chinatown, his location as unknowable as his gender to Western eyes. The Chinese community turns to face as a means of carefully redrawing social boundaries to tactfully censure the white woman who can call upon invasive government apparatuses for aid: "All Chinatown [was] in sympathy with [Ku Yum] and arrayed against Miss Mason. Where formerly the teacher had met with smiles and pleased greetings, she now beheld averted faces and downcast eyes."[105] Although the story takes a positive turn, with Miss Mason finally learning from Ku Yum's father about Chinese norms of gender presentation, Ku Yum's final words still retain the possibility of gender nonconformity. "I never be a good girl, but perhaps I be good boy," he says, troubling a trajectory of assimilative development that might wish for Chinese masculinity in America to mature into the legibility of a version of white American masculinity.

HIDING ONE'S HEART IN ONE'S SLEEVES / THE IMPENETRABLE PERFORMANCE OF CHINESE FACE AND DRESS IN "ITS WAVERING IMAGE"

In this light, I read "Its Wavering Image" from Far's magnum opus *Mrs. Spring Fragrance* as the rendition of the recurring story of a mixed-race Chinese young woman's refusal of a white man's love that combines several aspects of Oriental inscrutability into a queerly feminized mode of unfeeling. In this iteration, the romantic refusal plot is the template for a critique of the voyeuristic Chinatown tour subgenre of journalism exemplified by Jacob Riis's influential photojournalist project *How the Other Half Lives* (1890): the mixed-race Pan's affections are manipulated by the enterprising Mark Carson for his work as a reporter who is trying to dispel the mysteries of San Francisco's Chinese community.[106] The general scholarly interpretation of this narrative of mixed-race or "wavering" liminality is perhaps best expressed by Guy Beauregard: "the exposure of the Chinese community parallels exposure of a woman's body; race and gender intersect in the exploitative practices of the white male character."[107] What I believe is overlooked in the scholarly discussion is that Pan's closing resistance involves her reclaiming of Oriental inscrutability—according to which she, like Far, identifies herself as Chinese rather than white (in Pan's case, in opposition to Mark's desires). "It was only after the coming of Mark Carson that the mystery of her nature began to trouble her," the narrator observes, recalling the indecipherable contradictions of naturalized essence versus outsider perception of the Chinese face in "Half-Chinese Children."[108] Initially Pan is disinterested and defensive, and she ignores Carson's presence: "As to Pan, she always turned from whites. With her father's people she was natural and at home; but in the presence of her mother's she felt strange and constrained, shrinking from their curious scrutiny as she would from the sharp edge of a sword" (85–86). Among white people she feels her estrangement, and her feelings themselves become strange. As for Carson, this reticent woman embodies the fetishized Oriental inscrutability as an epistemological and sexual challenge: this mystery girl "puzzled him. What was she? Chinese or white?" (86). Through his relationship with Pan, he gains access to intimate knowledge of the Chinese enclave whose members have accepted her, penetrating "the simple mystery and history of many things" (89).

Although Carson uses Pan for her Chineseness, he insists on her whiteness: the demystification of Oriental inscrutability translates that unknowable alterity into legibility as whiteness. He becomes more intimate by persuading her of her alienation from her Chinatown community, imposing the dichotomy of exclusionary racial categories so that she will have to formally choose a side. Rather than seeing her as an enigma to him, he reframes her as an enigma to her social sphere: "'But they do not understand you,' he went on. 'Your real self is alien to them'" (89). The winning move in his argument comes when he invokes the white American poetic tradition: he sings "The Bridge" by Henry Wadsworth Longfellow, the love poem that provides the phrase that is the short story's title, allowing him to bridge the remaining distance between them. As the critic June Howard notes about other stories by Far, the citation of American and Chinese poems serves as a sentimental education across different cultural vocabularies of feeling that Chinese characters deftly adapt and shift between.[109] Here, however, Pan is overwhelmed: under the onslaught of Mark "singing her heart away, the girl broke down and wept."[110] This moment signals her transition between these racialized cultural taxonomies of affect, from Chinese to white:

> "Look up at me," bade Mark Carson. "Oh, Pan! Pan! Those tears prove that you are white."
> Pan lifted her wet face. (91)

In this moment, which leads to their first kiss, he hails her tears as the characteristic sentimental tears of a white woman, while also commanding her to raise her face so that her evasive Chinese face can be seen by him as white. The equivalent of his aubade the next morning, appropriately enough, is his composition of his special feature on Chinatown triumphantly titled "Its Wavering Image." Pan's agony over the betrayal returns to the sword as a metaphor for the violence of the colonial epistemological imperative combined with the phallic symbol of sexual violence: "the sword which pierced her through others" had "stabbed her" in the vulnerability of that kiss (92). "None knew better than he that she would rather that her own naked body and soul had been exposed than that things, sacred and secret to those who loved her, should be cruelly unveiled and ruthlessly spread before the ridiculing and uncomprehending foreigner." The violation of the protective Oriental inscrutability of Chinatown's secretive ways paralleled the violation of her sovereignty over her body's inscrutability.

Their final encounter is an affirmation of Oriental inscrutability as a method used by the marginalized to defend their vulnerability. The masculinist colonial implications are part of the actual geography of the scene, as Carson prepares to meet Pan after his two-month absence beside the statue of Robert Louis Stevenson in Chinatown's Portsmouth Square. Mark's mental comparison between himself and Stevenson is a reminder of the violences erased when colonial events are cast as escapist boyish adventures. He justifies himself to Pan by arguing that Oriental inscrutability should be dispelled: "These things have got to be exposed and done away with" (94). In retaliation Pan draws upon the arsenal of practices that Far has attributed to Oriental inscrutability. When Carson attempts to rationalize his betrayal, she answers his excuses with "Silence" and again "Still silence." Her body is now armored by the sartorial ornamentation traditional to Chinese women, a performance of her deliberate affective and racial alienation from his whiteness: "Pan was not herself tonight. She did not even look herself. He had been accustomed to seeing her in American dress. Tonight she wore the Chinese costume. But for her clear-cut features she might have been a Chinese girl." Her face once clearly read by him as white is defamiliarized through the symbolic adoption of Chinese face through her behavior and dress. Oriental inscrutability meets the queer refusal of female frigidity, and he is "strangely chilled" and "shivered" at the sight. The inscrutable concealment of her dress is the focus of what unnerves the man who was once confident of his knowledge about Pan:

> "Pan," he asked, "why do you wear that dress?"
>
> Within her sleeves Pan's small hands struggled together; but her face and voice were calm.
>
> "Because I am a Chinese woman," she answered. (94)

She pairs her declaration of racial self-identification with the signature expressionless visage and unaffected composure of the Chinese. Pan hides her vulnerability "within her sleeves" of that alienating Chinese dress, recalling the phrase that recurred earlier in Far's journalism career about the Chinese not wearing their hearts on their sleeves (94). Where Carson attempted to read affection, she responds with disaffection. Rather than affirming universal sympathy that bridges racial difference, the disquieting conclusion legitimizes racialized unfeeling, suggesting the futility of submitting to the politics of recognition. Pan rejects Carson's love by embracing Oriental inscrutability that renders her unreadable to the knowing prerogative of his gaze as a white man. She takes refuge in her father's house, and when a little Chinese girl visits, "the feel of that little head brought tears"—prompting the child's mother to suggest that Pan will be healed by having a child of her own. The story concludes with her yellow woman's tears and the promise of Chinese reproductive futurity as the redemptive replacement for white sentimentalism: "And Pan, being a Chinese woman, was comforted" (95). She saves face by turning hers away. Perhaps this is one of the stories focused on unassimilable Chinese women that the *New York Times* had in mind both for its praise of the elucidation of stereotype—"the Chinese women who refuse to be anything but intensely Chinese"—and for its frustration that Far did "not even [seem] to have tried to see inside the souls of her people."[111]

Facing Away / Sui Sin Far's Queer Autobiographical Ambivalence

In "Half-Chinese Children" (1895), an early piece of journalism, Eaton remarks upon those mixed Chinese and white children who can pass as white, although "a person who has been informed of the child's parentage notices at once a peculiar cast about the face."[112] "This cast is over the face of every child who has a drop of Chinese blood in its veins. It is indescribable—but it is there," she states, echoing the one-drop rule of Black racial classification (54). Then Far shifts from physiognomy to composure: "They [these children] are by nature proud and reserved (some say, sullen and hardened)" (54). Regardless of their different configurations of features, which are considered phenotypically white or Chinese, these children have inherited the Oriental inscrutability of the Chinese face, paradoxically distinctive and indefinable. In this passage alone, this inscrutability is contradictory and unstable, both a projection of the observer and racial essence, and the phrase "by nature" puts into question what is nature and what is nurture. In any case, although these children may be viewed as symbols of cross-racial intimacies, they experience alienation from both communities as they are considered "neither Chinese nor white" (53). Curiously, even Eaton does not claim them: the essay was published anonymously, obscuring her own identification. While a reader may infer that the author draws from her own life, she is reluctant to expose herself. Her sense of authorship as performative identity, or perhaps the writerly manifestation of face, comes through her proliferation of pseudonyms like "Canadian Fire Fly" for her Jamaican writing, the variations on her Chinese name before settling on "Sui Sin Far," and even the persona of a male Chinese merchant named "Wing Sing."[113] There is something queerly and Orientally inscrutable about Eaton as a writer whose greatest fame came from sharing, producing, and controlling knowledge about the Chinese. It is worth noting the importance of gender indeterminancy in the introduction to her work by her brother-in-law: "Who Sui Seen Far may be in real life no one can guess. But whether or a man or a woman, the writer has a real and intimate knowledge of the inner and social life of the Chinese at home and in their exile in this country which has never been shown before in American fiction."[114]

Although Eaton does not write directly about her personal experiences until near the end of her career, themes, scenes, and passages scattered across her oeuvre of journalistic and fictional writings connected to mixed-race Chinese women eventually reemerge in her memoir "Leaves from the Mental Portfolio of an Eurasian." I am reluctant to promote a reading of her work as an arc bending toward a triumph of public self-identification. Instead, I propose that these repetitions reflect her understanding of the Chinese face as her own means of surviving the chronic condition of her affectable vulnerability that was produced by sentimental biopolitics. As scholars like Jennifer Sibara and Todd Vogel have argued, her unnamed disability is bound up in sentimentalism and the effects of empire: "I have no organic disease," she writes in her autobiography, "but the strength of my feelings seems to take from me the strength of my body. I am prostrated at times with attacks of nervous sickness. The doctor says that my heart is unusually large; but in the light of the present I know that the cross of the Eurasian bore too heavily upon my childish shoulders."[115] Unfeeling becomes a protective coping mechanism. Sensitive, as it were, to the intrusions of ethnography as a tool of colonialism, Far employs a strategy of depersonalization and distancing—a practiced insensitivity—concurrent with her carefully chosen disclosures that render ambiguous the boundaries between her fiction and nonfiction, destabilizing certainty as to whether she finally exposes her truth or weaves the same old story. Ambivalences in her writing are what led Ling to speculate about Far's "lesbian sensibility," a claim that sparked the widely accepted understanding of Far's queerness.[116] Much like the artificial silk flowers adored by the ornamental Chinese woman, Far the narcissus flower is an inorganic Oriental artifice in ways that complicate desires for the transparency, authenticity, and scrutability of a sentimental woman writer and, specifically, a Chinese woman writer during the Exclusion Era.

The ethnographic "Half-Chinese Children" for the *Montreal Daily Star* contains a key scene of refusal of the sympathetic scrutiny that seeks to figure out Oriental inscrutability. These children contend with overt discrimination: a mixed Chinese boy is bullied by white children yelling "'Chinese' 'Chinese,'" to which he inexplicably responds by shouting "Chinese" back at them.[117] However, many other white people are willing to accept them into respectable white middle-class American society. Although there are mixed children who enjoy the attention they receive for that "indescribable" element that marks their Chinese heritage, not all share this willingness to accept the white gaze in exchange for privilege. The anonymous Eaton tells her readers,

> But others who are not susceptible to such petting, feel like a little girl who is recorded to have said to her mother, "Mamma, I'm not going to see Mrs. G.— to-day." "Why not?" said the mother, "she is always so kind to you and gives you more toys than you know what to do with." "Yes!" said the child[,] "but I don't care for the toys. It is just because I'm Chinese that she likes to have me there. When I'm in her parlor she whispers to some people about me, and then they try to make me talk and pick up all that I say and I hear them whisper 'her father's a Chinese' 'Did you know' 'Isn't it curious'—and they examine me from head to toe as if I was a wild animal—and just because father is a Chinese. I'd rather be dead than be a 'show.'" (55)

In this anecdote, one can infer that "Mrs. G." is friends with the white mother, who is surprised that her mixed-race daughter would not welcome the material signifiers of acceptance by her peers. Instead, the unnamed girl rejects the kindnesses extended to her as a bribe for her presence as an Oriental curiosity in a white woman's parlor, a domestic version of popular spectacles like P. T. Barnum's that featured exotic animals alongside equally exoticized peoples of color like the "Chinese lady" Afong Moy or the "Hottentot Venus" Sarah Baartman.[118] The hyperbole in the assertion "I'd rather be dead than be a 'show'" expresses the intensity of the girl's antisocial response to the tacit dynamics of the family's social life. The scene ends there, with the remaining article dedicated to Chinese marriage customs because of a recent traditional Chinese wedding of a prominent mixed-race Chinese woman in New York. While there are outliers, the piece suggests, many of these "half-Chinese children" are not so obstinate and successfully integrate into American and diasporic Chinese society.

However, the outburst of a childish tantrum dissenting from the project of cross-racial understanding cannot be so easily dismissed, because this scene stubbornly resurfaces in Far's work. "Sweet Sin: A Chinese-American Story" (1898), published in the *Land of Sunshine*, revisits many elements of the earlier piece of journalism, with the eponymous character again having a white mother and Chinese merchant father. "Chinese! Chinese!" once again are the calls of bullies that opens the short story, provoking Sweet Sin to fight with all her might despite the remonstrations of a fearful friend.[119] The scene transitions to a near-duplicate of the earlier conversation between mother and daughter: Sweet Sin's aggression saves her from attending Mrs. Goodwin's party because she is "not fit to be seen" (167). Repeating the unnamed girl's lines about the scopic fascination with evaluating her "from head to toe as if I were a wild animal" because her father is Chinese, she presents a more violent version of that protest: "I'd rather be killed than be a show" (167). The scenario extends the anecdote, with the mother admonishing the girl not to alienate her friend. "'I don't care!' defiantly asserted Sweet Sin," demonstrating her unfeeling stance toward those coercive social intimacies (167). She adds another element to the parlor scenario that will reappear in Far's writing: the old bespectacled white man fascinated by the little mixed-race Chinese girl. The party host asks the staring man, "Do you not notice the peculiar cast of features?" And he agrees that she is a "very peculiar little girl," an exchange recalling the traces of inscrutability in the faces of half-Chinese children and the use of "peculiar" nodding to the refrain of Harte's poem: "The Heathen Chinee is peculiar."[120] Sweet Sin retaliates by accusing the old man of being the peculiar one and flees. Such behavior may confirm that she is "a little Chinese savage," as her mother says, but she continues to refuse to care about affirming racist stereotypes: "They can think what they like!"[121] Sweet Sin feels split into her "Chinese half" and "American half": the first is "good and patient," but the second is the one who wants to aggressively defend the other. Her alienation makes her inscrutable even to herself: "I feel all torn to pieces. I don't know what I am, and I don't seem to have any place in the world" (168).

Elsewhere Far emphasizes how Chinese communities offer a refuge from American society for her alienated Chinese characters, but Sweet Sin cannot conceive of an alternative sociality that would accept her. Although in school she counters the Christian creation story with Chinese cosmology, she does not find comfort in that other system or in her father's pragmatic acceptance of cultural relativism. Unlike the happy interracial marriages reported in "Half-Chinese Children," Sweet Sin turns down a proposal from her white lover, Dick Farrell, but she kills herself rather than return to China with her father to marry an unknown Chinese man. She reminds Dick that she has not forgotten his racist slight against her father, saying "I told you I did not care for you," and pairing her verbal claim of not caring with the embodied performance of Oriental inscrutability to hide her feelings from him: "Sweet Sin turned her face aside. She would not let him know" (169). With her death, Sweet Sin fulfills the childhood promise that she would rather be killed than be a show, and her father buries her at sea so she can "rest where no curious eyes may gaze" (170). She is committed to the self-destructive consequences of her refusal.

A Portfolio of Disaffection and Disconnection

Comparing Far's autobiographical "Leaves from the Mental Portfolio of an Eurasian" and these earlier writings, we notice an assemblage of scenes and lines associated with these recalcitrant mixed Chinese characters. From the beginning Far plants the seeds of doubt about her commitment to verisimilitude: the placement of her photograph at the beginning of her memoir anticipates the curiosity of people who would want to evaluate her physiognomy for the undefinable cast of the Chinese face, the photographic medium teasingly offering access to truth even as her face signifies inscrutability.[122] The first memory Far recounts shares some of the structure and phrasing of the parlor scene and ensuing conversation between mother and daughter. Although Far is only a few years old, she is aware that white nurses are gossiping about her Chineseness as they look her over "from head to foot" because her mother is Chinese, but when she tries to seek some form of justice from her mother she admits that "I fail to make myself intelligible," and the nurse states, "Little Miss Sui is a story-teller"—leading to her punishment.[123] This initial association between herself and fiction is presented as her failure to present herself as an advocate speaking out against anti-Chinese sentiment that backfires because her Chinese mother chooses to believe a white woman over her own daughter. While in this first scene Far learns that truth can be viewed as pernicious fiction, the second presents her storytelling as a contrarian obscuration of truth. When she plays with a white childhood friend, another white girl tells the friend to avoid "Sui" because she is part Chinese. The friend defends Far and tells her she prefers her over the other girl, "even if your mamma is Chinese." Far responds in a manner that appears self-defeating: "'But I don't like you,' I answer, turning my back on her. It is my first conscious lie'" (126). After all, lying, one of the traits of the treacherous Oriental, is an ugly word for fiction. What I make of this gesture of turning away is that in Far's representation of this originary moment of fiction-making, she chooses to misrepresent her feelings so as to avoid compromising her Chineseness—even if she alienates the sympathies of a white friend who could learn to become more supportive. The counterproductive and counterintuitive are inseparable from Far's project to speak for and as Chinese.

Despite growing up with the same anti-Chinese experiences, Far's siblings appear to be healthy, successful, and eager to integrate themselves into American and Canadian society. In one example, her sister overlooks the racist sentiments of classmates and befriends them, while the rest of the Eaton children are untroubled by the ontological questions that bother Far.

Furthermore, Far also believes that neither of her parents understands her: "What are we?" I ask my brother. "It doesn't matter, sissy," he responds (128). At one point she longs for "when the whole world becomes as one family" and asks if then, "will human beings be able to see clearly and hear distinctly?" However, the example of her own "Eurasian" family contradicts that fantasy of multiracialism as panacea (130).

Far remains the disaffected dissenter from this fantasy of assimilative prosperity for mixed Chinese people, which she conveys by incorporating and adapting those repeated scenes of discontent in her other writings. The scene of childhood bullying featuring an unnamed boy and then Sweet Sin is replayed with Far and her brother fighting against the taunts of "Chinky, Chinky, Chinaman, yellow-face, pig-tail, rat-eater," to which she retorts, "I'd rather be Chinese than anything else in the world" (126). When the family moves to Canada, all the children experience the stares of white Canadians "very much in the same way that I have seen people gaze upon strange animals in a menagerie" (127). These incidents linger for her in ways that do not appear to impact her siblings, and she concludes, "They are not sensitive in the sense that I am" (128). They are resiliently adaptive to the changes of the North American environment, whereas her sense of alienation cannot be dissolved in the solution of integration. Her loneliness becomes a position of antisocial critique.

These repeated scenes of dissatisfaction and small resistances baffle distinctions one may try to draw between Far's creative self-insertion into previously written scenarios repurposed for the memoir and the depersonalization of her experiences as ethnographic material for her prior reporting and storytelling in the third person. Another aspect of the parlor scene is revisited with Far as child protagonist, with a revised context that emphasizes colonial history: the hostess is the "wife of an Indian officer," and in the school Far attends with their children, they "learned that China is a heathen country, being civilized by England" (126). At this children's party the hostess brings Far over to an old bespectacled man for "the purpose of inspection": "'Ah, indeed!' he exclaims, 'Who would have thought it at first glance. Yet now I see the difference between her and other children. What a peculiar coloring! Her mother's eyes and hair and her father's features, I presume. Very interesting little creature!'" (126). The undefinable cast of that "peculiar" Chinese face marks her much as it does the other little mixed-race Chinese girls she has written about. In this variation she does not return to playing with the other children but withdraws from the social scene so she can obscure herself from the ethnographic gaze: "I hide myself behind a hall door and refuse to show myself" (126). Absent in this version of the scene is the repeated polemical declaration of death as rebellion. As a child, Far dreams only of "mysteriously disappearing" the way so many of her characters do (129). The most similar radical utterance is her childhood idea of justice that fixates on dramatic martyrdom ("I glory in the idea of dying at the stake"), but the older version of herself confronted by the anti-Chinese racism of her employer has a more mature understanding of what is actually at stake: "The prospect before me is not an enviable one—if I speak. I have no longer any ambition to die at the stake for the sake of demonstrating the greatness and nobleness of the Chinese people" (129 and 130). Nonetheless, she chooses to speak, making a small sacrifice that might have disappointed her younger, more idealistic self, who yearned for the grand tragic gesture. This latest assemblage of fragmented scenes, ideas, and phrases is less a self-identificatory claiming than a suggestive aligning of Far with the more perverse and contradictory elements of her oeuvre that indicate ambivalences about the project of diasporic Chinese representation that has become inseparable from her own life.

Near the end of "Leaves," Far shares another version of the story of a mixed-race Chinese young woman rejecting the advances of a white suitor, who fails the overburdened litmus test of interracial romance as an allegory for cross-racial sympathies. Despite incorporating other elements of Sweet Sin's story into her memoir, Far distances herself from her character's love plot. In this thematic predecessor to "Its Wavering Image," the unnamed woman has already refused her suitor nine times even as he professed his color-blind love by citing anti-Chinese and anti-Black racisms: "But the resolute and undaunted lover swore it was a matter of inference to him whether she was a Chinese or a Hottentot, that it would be his pleasure and privilege to allow her relations double what was in her power to bestow, and so as to not loving him—that did not matter at all. He loved her" (132). This young woman whose "independent manner of living" baffles her married mother and sisters eventually gives in to his pleas, writing in her diary "I have promised to become the wife of —— on ——, 189, because the world is so cruel and sneering to a single woman—and for no other reason" (132). The blank spaces for names and the exact year in the 1890s invite speculation about connections to the rest of the memoir, which is ostensibly focused upon the resolutely unmarried Far. The woman finally alienates her fiancé who claimed race does not matter by pressing the issue of her Chineseness, which require his acceptance of Chinese "laundrymen and vegetable farmers" as well as respectable merchants—for, as she says with great irony, "I don't believe in being exclusive in democratic America, do you?" (133). The fiancé admits that he wishes she would pretend to be Japanese, so she returns the ring, telling him to go find a Japanese woman. The baubles of his acceptance are not enough to sway her, and unlike the character Pan, a Chinese reproductive futurity is not what she turns to as an alternative. "Joy, oh joy! I'm free once more. Never again shall I be untrue to my own heart. Never again will I allow any one to 'hound' or 'sneer' me into matrimony," this unnamed "'ungrateful' Chinese Eurasian" female character writes, affirming her detachment from the institutions of heteronormativity. Perhaps it is only appropriate that Far has an orthogonal, distanced relationship to heterosexual romance and its promise of inclusion into whiteness, making it a story that happens to someone else in her memoir. If anything, her allusions to her past writings and the suggestion of ciphers that would reveal some epiphany indicate how she identifies *with*, as opposed to identifying herself *as*, her journalistic subjects and fictional characters.

Whether or not Far's writings, or even what she presents as her autobiography, maps onto her life is of less concern to me than how she commits to the crafting of artifice to both disclose and withhold. "Portfolio" in the memoir's title indicates how the work gathers a collection of highlights from her oeuvre, constituting a richly networked assemblage of stories, passages, and references. Her life, as she represents it, is an amalgam of the conventions that she as an author has developed through her career representing diasporic Chinese and mixed-race Chinese such as herself, and these conventions are at once familiar and distancing. In the conclusion of "Leaves," she tells about people who recommend that she seek literary success by Orientalizing herself: "I should dress in Chinese costume, carry a fan in my hand, wear a pair of scarlet beaded slippers, live in New York, and come of high birth," and she should quote Confucius (133). But what I believe should be emphasized is that she does not disavow the trappings of the intriguingly inscrutable Oriental, for her rebuttal actually quotes Confucius ("the way of sincerity is the way of heaven"), and she does visit New York for a time. The artifice of Oriental cliché is fundamental to her in ways that are true even as they are false. There is both irony and no irony when she asserts that "individuality is more than nationality," and she goes on to fulfill the stereotype by writing, "'You are you and I am I,' says Confucius." Hope countered by skepticism flickers in and out of her memoir: she claims to reject the restrictions of national belonging and to situate herself in her alienation, for she is "not anxious to claim any." She ends with a line now famous in Far scholarship: "I give my right hand to the Occidentals and my left to the

Orientals, hoping that between them they will not utterly destroy the insignificant 'connecting link.' And that's all." Although her memoir is replete with fantasies of cross-racial understanding and liberal inclusion, I stress the hesitations and ambivalences about connection that validate the necessity of disconnection. The disobedient streak running through Far's work implies her unresolved suspicion that, as in "Its Wavering Image," some bridges are not worth building and should be burned down.

A Yellow Woman's Tears / Deferral or Despair?

The dissonant moments in Far's sentimentalism allow space for her explorations of transgression that cannot easily be included in projects of political utility: such recalcitrance speaks to how the requirements for sympathetic literary representation intertwine with the evolving apparatus of immigration as a modern manifestation of sentimental biopolitics. The "'ungrateful' Chinese Eurasian" that Far identifies with pulls away from the overdetermination of her embodied sexual agency as a proxy for the compromises of interracial harmony under the guise of universal love and, symbolically, inclusion in citizenship. Cultural misunderstandings of the Chinese face reflect the radical alterity of an alternative paradigm of feeling that challenges the hegemonic episteme. For Far, Oriental inscrutability names the structural dimensions of alienation that intersect with alien affects. And those affects are inextricable from the nuances of individual performance and social engagement that exploit the potential of these misreadings, regardless of the consequences of demonization as queer, racialized unfeeling.

Nonetheless, while Far stresses Oriental inscrutability as a reprieve or what Lauren Berlant might regard as lateral agency, her habitual return to the negative and antisocial suggests that her skepticism extends to the possibility of another horizon for the social.[124] If optimism can be cruel, pessimism can be a way to protect one's self from the vulnerability of hope—even at the cost of flourishing. The diasporic Chinese recourse to Oriental inscrutability enables everyday survival and the semblance of personal sovereignty in the Exclusion Era, but like the hyperfeminized ornamentalism of the Chinese woman and her self-destructive inscrutable gestures, it does not appear to lend itself readily to political instrumentalism. If Oriental inscrutability is evasion, suspension, and distancing, does that suggest a deferral of action that dovetails with quiescence and perhaps complicity?

A year after Far's death, "The Chinese Spirit of Non-Resistance Will Disappear" (1915) appeared in the *Boston Daily Globe*—a collection of ideas and phrases scattered throughout her other work that was given an uncharacteristically foreboding title. "The Chinese feel keenly all the wrongs and indignities suffered by them, political and otherwise," the collection begins, echoing the language Far used to describe her own sensitivity in "Leaves."[125] Contrasting the treatment of the Chinese and Japanese in North America, she outlines the beleaguered situation of mainland and diasporic Chinese in conjunction with the promising rise of the Republic of China under the leadership of Sun Yat-sen. Their alleged nonresistance comes from the perception of their silence by outsiders. However, this absence of expression belies Far's reminder that "the Chinese narrate the stories of their many sufferings at the hands of the whites along the Pacific Coast." Again, a dimension of Oriental inscrutability is the management of face: "the Chinese are a self-controlled people, ruled by the head rather than by the heart." Quiet does not mean quiescence.[126] She insists, "I would like to exculpate them from the charge of lack of spirit; of bearing insult and wrong without resentment; of being obsequiously peaceful." Their unresponsiveness is explained as a matter of power, for, as she quotes a Chinese international student, "at present we are not powerful enough to assert our rights"—which she interprets as not referring to "lack of spirit or cowardice. On the contrary, it proves thoughtfulness, caution and wisdom." Inasmuch as Oriental inscrutability is in part an effect of power, a shift in the geopolitical situation could convert that disaffection into political potential: "When that time comes the Westerners may well watch the Chinese spirit with due anxiety." In contrast to her other statements in favor of liberal inclusion through the sentimental rhetoric of cross-racial sympathy, in this posthumous essay she insists on the need for global structural change as the condition for justice: "When China makes her vast power respected, and the Occident learns to deal justly with her, we may expect the barriers between the races to be broken down." The essay reads as much as a warning about retaliation for injustice as a self-reassurance that Chinese disaffection is not apathy.

At the end of her memoir, Far expresses the desire to visit China before she dies, but archival evidence indicates that she never did. Instead, the one place outside of the geographies of the "West" in which she lived was Jamaica, where in her memoir she identifies herself as one of the "'brown people' of the earth," a gesture that distances her from whiteness and seeks affiliation with other peoples of color.[127] Across her writings there are glimpses of Black, Indigenous, and other women of color characters. As I argue elsewhere, these representations are suggestive of a rethinking, however flawed, of racial global hegemony characterized by Lisa Lowe as the intimacies of four continents leading to the possibility of the counterintimacies of solidarity.[128] After all, in his novel Delany imagines "the Negroes, mulattoes and quadroons, Indians, and even Chinamen" drawn together in a Caribbean vibrant with the potential of decolonial revolution.[129] Reading Far's oeuvre, then, can one hope that Oriental inscrutability might be less furtive than fugitive, not just running away but running toward? In turning the Chinese face to look away, what can one look to instead?

CODA /

Notes toward a Disaffected
Manifesto beyond Survival

Those of us who stand outside the circle of this society's definition of acceptable women; those of us who have been forged in the crucibles of difference—those of us who are poor, who are lesbians, who are Black, who are older—know that *survival is not an academic skill*. It is learning how to stand alone, unpopular and sometimes reviled, and how to make common cause with those others identified as outside the structures in order to define and seek a world in which we can all flourish.—Audre Lorde, "The Master's Tools Will Never Dismantle the Master's House," in *Sister Outsider*

I HAVE BEEN CALLED A MACHINE and accused of being cold. I have chosen to remain expressionless when the racist and sexist microaggressions of everyday life have been directed at me. As a woman of color, I find that sometimes the performance of being unaffected is the form of resistance that enables the immediate safety of people like me and denies aggressors the satisfaction of seeing our affectability. Many people I care about have confided their suppressing of emotions to get through situations, numbing themselves to weather exhausting onslaughts of iterative traumas, and shutting down to defend against exposure. A moment of quotidian violence jabs at you in a professional setting: you, junior and precarious, weigh your vulnerability and might choose to be unresponsive. But sometimes we can turn to our chosen communities, where we can be vulnerable, to be seen, process, and organize.

I have suspended the expression of my affective investments until the end of this book. This project came out of my pondering the unfeeling alienation of those dear to me and my own disaffections as a non-Black non-Indigenous woman of color on the traditional lands of the Cayuga Nation, as well as later in the unceded, ancestral, occupied, and traditional lands of the Musqueam people, and now in the former heart of empire. I had to take seriously, for my sake and the sake of others, the ongoing act of reading queer and feminist of color critique as theory in the flesh. As I struggled with loss, chronic health problems, and precarity, I became increasingly aware of how my friendships—in particular with women and queers of color—are the ways in which the praxis of coalition unfolds. Scenes repeat themselves: a white activist centers their guilt at a Black Lives Matter candlelight vigil, settlers end up taking over a space meant for Indigenous students, and cisgender heterosexual allies complain about exclusion from LGBTQ2S+. White fragility shatters in front of us: we exchange side glances as we refuse to wipe away their tears, and then in our alternative social spaces in group text messages and hidden social media groups, we commiserate and strategize. In one instance, a friend recounted to me how she and another Black woman student activist ended up giving each other the same present: a mug with "white tears" printed on it—symbolically transforming a source of frustration into material and psychic nourishment that, sip by sip, may help sustain you through everyday encounters with the sentimental apparatuses of oppression.

We have had to become so strong, impervious, and seemingly invulnerable. If we expose our sensitivities we are soon scarred: we develop a thick skin to endure the abrasions of everyday life, a protective callousness. A friend calls attention to my impenetrable emotional armor that I wield in tandem with detached professionalism to keep others at a distance. As effective as that tactic might be, it means that I have shifted affective labor onto others, so I must learn how to be strategically vulnerable. Across geographies and time zones we help each other with the shifting calculus of disclosures and withholding to make sure that we can still be responsive and responsible to those we love. Together we guard our tendernesses beneath a shield of disaffection.

What critical demeanors and ways of being together emerge when we reclaim unfeeling from its demonization as moral and social annihilation and consider that its appearance of negation does not obviate or even conceal but rather enables generative and insurgent capacities? The antisocial declaration "I don't care" meets "we don't care": a mode of self-care grows into collective care. We can be disaffected together. It is no accident that during the later development of this book about unfeeling I found myself writing about solidarities among colonized, racialized, and otherwise minoritized peoples, because that is what has kept me alive.[1] Detaching from hegemonic feelings and decentering them are necessary for our flourishing. Disaffection converges with disidentification: yes, we are unfeeling, and perhaps that should be feared because it is the tool we can use to tear down dominant structures of feeling to build anew. Let us embrace disaffection as an important tool in what Sara Ahmed calls a killjoy survival kit instead of hastening to reassure ourselves that majoritarian feelings still matter to us.[2]

Empathy tends to be the word that circulates today instead of sympathy: the logic is that sympathy is a false feeling that masks and reinforces power differentials, while empathy is the truer form of feeling across difference. Empathy is good. Sympathy is bad. However, this nominal shift from Adam Smith's "fellow-feeling" disavows the episteme that produced universal sympathy by bestowing a fresh name on the unchanged concept that is bound to the same biopolitical hierarchies that in turn undergird the liberal politics of recognition.[3] The imbricated fantasy of right feeling, politics, and action endures as a foundational justification for the importance of reading, teaching, researching, and creating literature at a time when the humanities are under attack by the neoliberal university that demands instrumentalization. Instead of economic value, we offer moral worth. We need to reconsider how we approach antiracist social justice work in our institutions, pedagogy, activist spaces, and workshops. As we critique the liberal politics of recognition and inclusion, can we address the necessity of the antisocial and exclusionary moves by the marginalized? To notice how we are moved or not moved by others structured by the governmentality of aesthetics and representation?

Perhaps the field of politics itself must change in the face of the incompatible, inconsistent, and stubbornly uninstrumentalizable. Acknowledge, rather than disavow, your negative feelings about the unsympathetic refusals, but then train yourself to decenter your hurt feelings as a starting point for redressing the affective biopolitical hierarchy.

Universal feeling is a ruse when only some feelings are privileged as true. So let us push beyond the claim that all feelings matter.

NOTES

Introduction

1. Berlant, *The Female Complaint*; Lowe, *The Intimacies of Four Continents*; Schuller, *The Biopolitics of Feeling*.
2. Accapadi, "When White Women Cry"; DiAngelo, "White Fragility."
3. In one of many relevant memes, a Black woman delights over her collection of colorful fluid-filled bottles with the caption "Assorted White Tears." This gif, taken from a commercial, refashions Diane Amos aka the Pine-Sol® Lady from the spokeswoman for the cleaning product to a spokeswoman for subversive glee.
4. Son of Baldwin, "I Don't Give a Fuck about Justine Damond."
5. Son of Baldwin, "I Don't Give a Fuck about Justine Damond."
6. Son of Baldwin, "That essay really got a lot of folks way up in the Mount Everest of their feelings."
7. Baldwin, "Everybody's Protest Novel," 496.
8. Son of Baldwin, "That essay."
9. Sometime in the intervening years between the original post and the finalizing of my manuscript, Son of Baldwin deleted these notes. In reproducing his words, I hope I have not disrespected his intentions; the fleeting nature of the posts recalls for me the ephemerality of the queer of color archive that Muñoz expressed so well. Robert Jones Jr. references these posts in "Let It Burn," an essay for the *Paris Review* published June 8, 2020, during the global resurgence of the Black Lives Matter movement in response to the killing of George Floyd and Breonna Taylor.
10. Jacobs, *Incidents in the Life of a Slave Girl*, 5.
11. Stowe, *Uncle Tom's Cabin*, 385. For a discussion about views on Stowe's novel, see Halpern, "Beyond Contempt."
12. Stowe, *The Key to Uncle Tom's Cabin*. There is a considerable body of scholarship on Jacobs's trenchant critiques and adaptation of sentimentalism, but a good starting point is Jean Fagan Yellin's monumental recovery work that includes the letters in which Jacobs writes of her rage about the exchange with Stowe. See Yellin, "Written by Herself."

13 Wynter, "Unsettling the Coloniality of Being/Power/Truth/ Freedom"; McKittrick, *Sylvia Wynter*; da Silva, *Toward a Global Idea of Race*.
14 Da Silva, *Toward a Global Idea of Race*, xv.
15 Spinoza, *Ethics*, 128.
16 Palmer, "'What Feels More than Feeling?,'" 47.
17 Stowe, *The Key to Uncle Tom's Cabin*, 46.
18 Stowe, *The Key to Uncle Tom's Cabin*, 45.
19 M. Chen, *Animacies*.
20 Terada, *Feeling in Theory*, 11.
21 Hartman and Wilderson, "The Position of the Unthought," 189.
22 Even the most minor of divergent feelings has the potential to register disaffection. After all, according to J. L. Austin, right feelings are required for the "smooth or 'happy' functioning of a performative" (*How to Do Things with Words*, 14-15). Williams, *Marxism and Literature*, 128-35.
23 Compare to Fretwell's study during the period on psychophysics, aesthetics, and feeling that is organized by the five major senses (*Sensory Experiments*).
24 The Fourteenth Amendment in particular would become the basis for what George Lipsitz calls a "social warrant" for marginalized groups to procure justice in a society dependent upon their subjugation ("The Culture of War," 83).
25 Coulthard, *Red Skin, White Masks*.
26 M. Chen, *Animacies*. See also, for instance, Brinkema, *The Forms of the Affects*; Reddy, *The Navigation of Feeling*; Leys, "The Turn to Affect"; Connolly, "I. The Complexity of Intention."
27 Berlant, "Structures of Unfeeling," 197.
28 Hochschild, *The Managed Heart*.
29 Douglas, *The Feminization of American Culture*; Tompkins, *Sensational Designs*. This persistent obsession in Americanist intellectual history speaks to what Sean McCann calls "the desire for literature to be distinctive and uplifting that remains a foundational narrative of our profession" ("Structures of Feeling," 329).
30 Berlant, *Cruel Optimism*, *The Female Complaint*, and *The Queen of America Goes to Washington City*; Foreman, *Activist Sentiments*.
31 Sánchez-Eppler, *Touching Liberty*; Weinstein, *Family, Kinship, and Sympathy in Nineteenth-Century American Literature*.
32 Baym, "Melodramas of Beset Manhood"; Nelson, *National Manhood*; Romero, *Home Fronts*.
33 Merish, *Sentimental Materialism*.
34 For how Black and Indigenous women writers critiqued and adapted sentimentalism, see Foreman, *Activist Sentiments*; Piatote, *Domestic Subjects*; Carby, *Reconstructing Womanhood*.
35 Schuller, *The Biopolitics of Feeling*. See also Riskin, *Science in the Age of Sensibility*.
36 Samuels, "Introduction," 4.
37 I believe that it is worth noting the slippage between the studies of nineteenth-century sentimentalism and affect theory. In 2015, the Society for the Humanities, using the theme of sensation, brought back to Cornell

University graduate alumnae Lauren Berlant, Ann Cvetkovich, and Dana Luciano. During her talk, Berlant jokingly referred to the "Cornell School of Sentimentality," a term that Cvetkovich and Luciano would also use in subsequent events. This quip points to a shared connection: all three critics trained at Cornell (as well as the late Eve Sedgwick) began their research on sentimentality in nineteenth-century American and British literature, examining aspects of politics, citizenship, and culture, but they are now more widely known for their work as critics at the intersection of queer, feminist, and affect theory and as having made contributions not just to the nineteenth-century literary and cultural archive but also to studies of the twentieth and twenty-first centuries.

38 Wexler, *Tender Violence*.
39 Lowe, *The Intimacies of Four Continents*. See also Stoler, *Haunted by Empire*.
40 Du Bois, *The Souls of Black Folk*, 3.
41 Muñoz, *The Sense of Brown*, 37.
42 For a few illustrative examples of the perennial fascination with Bartleby as the locus of critique, see Edelman, "Occupy Wall Street"; W. Lee, "The Scandal of Insensibility"; Ngai, *Ugly Feelings*.
43 Hemmings, "Invoking Affect," 562. Apropos of Hemmings's view that the affective turn is the ontological turn, the feminist philosopher Zoe Todd argues that ontology is another name for colonialism ("An Indigenous Feminist's Take on the Ontological Turn").
44 Hemmings's indictment has been followed by analyses like those of Claudia Garcia-Rojas ("(Un)Disciplined Futures") and Tyrone Palmer ("'What Feels More than Feeling?'") from the standpoints of queer feminist of color critique and Black studies, respectively.
45 Ahmed, *The Cultural Politics of Emotion* and *The Promise of Happiness*; Ngai, *Ugly Feelings*. Ahmed's and Ngai's thoughtful reevaluations of the regulatory powers of so-called positive and negative emotions, along with their foregrounding of villainized figures and abject categories of feeling, inspired my project.
46 Eng, *The Feeling of Kinship*; Puar, *The Right to Maim*.
47 Hemmings highlights Fanon and Lorde; Garcia-Rojas discusses Lorde along with Anzaldúa and Moraga for a queer feminist of color tradition, while for Palmer, Rankine's poetry is a site for addressing Black affect and its erasures.
48 As Greyser writes, "Cherokee uwedolisdi/sympathy/ᎤᏪᏙᎵᏍᏗ unfolded across indigenous–settler contact, particularly after white people discovered gold in Cherokee homelands. In the Northern Paiute language Numu or Paviotso, sidaminimakiti/sympathy connoted compassion/pity, a mixed emotion with desirable and presumptuously intimate facets" (*On Sympathetic Grounds*, 17). For more on Indigenous engagements with sympathy and sentimentality, see Carpenter, *Seeing Red*; Piatote, *Domestic Subjects*.
49 "What if one of the reasons there is so little scholarship on affect and racialization," asks Schuller, "is because we have such scanty language to account for the ways violence registers in the body, the ways resilience, hope, and love take material form?" (*The Biopolitics of Feeling*, 212).

50 Gunew, "Subaltern Empathy"; Berg and Ramos-Zayas, "Racializing Affect."
51 Through Wynter scholar Rinaldo Walcott points out that the Caribbean's position in the project of Enlightenment modernity is uniquely situated to "assess and reformulate what might be at stake in the radical incompletion of the project of modernity and what might be necessary to reanimate the promises of modernity in order to differently imagine, and live, the human as an alterable species-subject" ("Genres of Human," 186).
52 Ahmed, *The Cultural Politics of Emotion* and *The Promise of Happiness*.
53 Manalansan, "Servicing the World," 217.
54 Manalansan, "Servicing the World," 217-18.
55 This paradox informs Wendy Lee's figuration of the unfeeling character, exemplified by Bartleby ("The Scandal of Insensibility"). By leading with the colonizing dynamics of race, I seek to contextualize her observations about how the insensible character drives the plot by becoming the target of frustration with his unmoving, antisocial stance. For Berlant, structures of unfeeling are the corollary to Williams's structures of feeling as the blurring between thought and feeling in the lived experience of ideology. I build upon what Berlant variously refers to as "inexpressive style" or "underperformativity" or "flattened affect," which temporarily suspends the social as a refusal of the presumed dynamics of affectability (Berlant, "Structures of Unfeeling," 193).
56 I owe my use of the phrase "politics of recognition" to Glen Coulthard's adaptation (in *Red Skin, White Masks*) of the philosopher Charles Taylor's concept (see C. Taylor et al., *Multiculturalism*) and Frantz Fanon's anticolonial analyses in *The Wretched of the Earth* that lead toward a framework for Indigenous decolonization outside the terms of the settler colonial state. For Taylor, the discourse of recognition functions on two interrelated levels: the intimate and the public sphere. See also Povinelli, *The Cunning of Recognition*.
57 Muñoz, "Ephemera as Evidence."
58 See Lee Edelman's polarizing use of the death drive to defy the sentimental heteronormative sociality signified by the figure of the universal child (*No Future*).
59 Edelman, *No Future*; Muñoz, *Disidentifications*, "Thinking beyond Antirelationality and Antiutopianism in Queer Critique," *Cruising Utopia*, and "Feeling Brown, Feeling Down"; Halberstam, "The Politics of Negativity in Recent Queer Theory."
60 I am influenced in particular by Cathy Cohen's insights into how queerness is more than desire and identification; it is also structural marginalization according to race, class, and ability that produces normative and deviant types of gender and sexuality ("Punks, Bulldaggers, and Welfare Queens").
61 Adam Smith, *The Theory of Moral Sentiments*, 9. Subsequent repeated references to this source will be given parenthetically in the text after the initial citation.
62 W. Lee, "The Scandal of Insensibility," 1410 and 1411.
63 Adam Smith, *The Theory of Moral Sentiments*, 204-5.
64 A few decades later *The Wealth of Nations* would follow Smith's work on the national and transnational circulations of sympathy and the differentials between the values of racialized affects. Perhaps we can see that the entangled

development of sympathy and economics recalls what Ahmed calls affective economies, the flows between objects and signs that accrue value and shape individual and collective bodies ("Affective Economies").

65 Darwin, *The Expression of the Emotions in Man and Animals*, 21.
66 Moraga, "La Jornada," xl–xli.
67 Anzaldúa, "La Prieta," 204; Lorde, *Sister Outsider*, 158. As Ahmed observes, "Harshness for Lorde is thus not the elimination of fragility; it is how we live with fragility" (*Living a Feminist Life*, 186).
68 Anzaldúa, "La Prieta," 204.
69 Lorde, *Sister Outsider*, 158.
70 Lorde, *Sister Outsider*, 70–71.
71 Lorde, *Sister Outsider*, 65.
72 Anzaldúa, *Borderlands/La Frontera*, 45.
73 Anzaldúa, *Borderlands/La Frontera*, 92.
74 Jefferson, *Notes on the State of Virginia*, 137.
75 Jefferson, *Notes on the State of Virginia*, 150. See also da Silva, *Toward a Global Idea of Race*; Ngai, *Ugly Feelings*.
76 Jefferson, *Notes on the State of Virginia*, 145. Subsequent repeated references to this source will be given parenthetically in the text after the initial citation.
77 S. Smith, *An Essay on the Causes of the Variety of Complexion and Figure in the Human Species*, 11 and 157.
78 S. Smith, *An Essay*, 195.
79 Jefferson, *Notes on the State of Virginia*, 147.
80 S. Smith, *An Essay*, 268. Subsequent repeated references to this source will be given parenthetically in the text after the initial citation.
81 Million, "Felt Theory," 54.
82 Rush, "Observations Intended to Favour a Supposition That the Black Color (As It Is Called) of the Negroes Is Derived from Leprosy," 292. Subsequent repeated references to this source will be given parenthetically in the text after the initial citation.
83 Byrd, *The Transit of Empire*; Lowe, *The Intimacies of Four Continents*.
84 Hartman and Wilderson, "The Position of the Unthought," 185.
85 McKittrick, *Sylvia Wynter*; da Silva, *Toward a Global Idea of Race* and "1 (Life) ÷ 0 (Blackness) = $\infty - \infty$ or ∞ / ∞"; Spillers, "Mama's Baby, Papa's Maybe."
86 Zakiyyah Jackson highlights the transformative potential of the black mater(nal) (*Becoming Human*), and Calvin Warren demonstrates, through Spillers, the paradox of Black queerness under erasure, undermining (with the goal of destroying) the grammar of anti-Blackness and developing a new semantic field ("Onticide").
87 Moten, *In the Break*, 1.
88 For a preliminary discussion of Afropessimism, see Wilderson, *Red, White and Black*.
89 McKittrick, *Dear Science*, 51.
90 Delany, "Mrs. Stowe's Position," 3.
91 Rusert, *Fugitive Science*.

92 Byrd, "Weather with You"; King, *The Black Shoals*; Leroy, "Black History in Occupied Territory"; R. Kelley, "The Rest of Us."
93 Fanon, *The Wretched of the Earth*; Coulthard, *Red Skin, White Masks*.
94 Muñoz, *The Sense of Brown*, 138.
95 Ellis, *Studies in the Psychology of Sex*, 3:203.
96 DuCille, *The Coupling Convention*.
97 Bailey and Peoples, "Toward a Black Feminist Health Science Studies."
98 Foreman, "Who's Your Mama?," 507.
99 Palumbo-Liu, *Asian/American*; Chuh, *Imagine Otherwise*. I am also thinking of the work of Aihwa Ong on flexible citizenship (*Flexible Citizenship*), Tina Chen on double agents or agency (*Double Agency*), and the reconsiderations of the alien construction of Asianness led by Rachel C. Lee (*The Exquisite Corpse of Asian America*) and broadened by Anne Anlin Cheng (*Ornamentalism*).
100 Shah, *Contagious Divides*, 87.
101 S. Lee, "Staying In"; Huang, "Inscrutably, Actually."
102 Bloom, *Against Empathy*; Frazer, *The Enlightenment of Sympathy*.
103 Glissant, *Poetics of Relation*, 194.

One. The Babo Problem

1 W. Lee, "The Scandal of Insensibility," 1411.
2 Melville, *Billy Budd, Bartleby, and Other Stories*, 17.
3 Adam Smith, *The Theory of Moral Sentiments*, 15.
4 Melville, *Billy Budd, Bartleby, and Other Stories*, 54.
5 Schuller, *The Biopolitics of Feeling*.
6 Du Bois, *The Souls of Black Folk*, 3.
7 Melville, *Billy Budd, Bartleby, and Other Stories*, 67.
8 Delano, *Narrative of Voyages and Travels*.
9 Melville, *Billy Budd, Bartleby, and Other Stories*, 55–56.
10 Stowe, *Uncle Tom's Cabin*, 452.
11 Hartman, *Scenes of Subjection*.
12 da Silva, *Toward a Global Idea of Race*.
13 Melville, *Billy Budd, Bartleby, and Other Stories*, 56.
14 See Rei Terada's expressive hypothesis that the expression of emotion creates the illusion (*Feeling in Theory*, 11). See also Martin Manalansan, "Servicing the World," on the disaffection of Filipinx professional caregivers in the global economies of emotion work. More generally, Lauren Berlant writes: "At the same time, biopolitical systems of supremacy often call on the problem populations—such as women, people of color, queers, and youth, but this too will vary—to have emotions for the privileged, to be vulnerable, expressive, and satisfying in the disturbance. If they withhold they are called inscrutable, which is a judgment against a form of composure that on other bodies would be honored as good manners, and is often deemed good manners in the servant class" ("Structures of Unfeeling," 197).

15 As Carolyn Karcher puts it, the narrative is "an exploration of the white racist mind and how it reacts in the face of a slave insurrection" (*Shadow over the Promised Land*, 128).
16 Samuels, "Introduction," 4.
17 Coviello, "The American in Charity," 163.
18 See Williams, *Marxism and Literature*; C. Taylor, "The Politics of Recognition."
19 See, for example, Berlant, *The Female Complaint*; Lowe, *The Intimacies of Four Continents*; Wexler, *Tender Violence*; Hendler, *Public Sentiments*, among others.
20 Melville, *Billy Budd, Bartleby, and Other Stories*, 56.
21 Fanon, *The Wretched of the Earth*; Coulthard, *Red Skin, White Masks*.
22 Da Silva, *Toward a Global Idea of Race* and "1 (Life)+0 (Blackness)=$\infty-\infty$ or ∞ / ∞"; McKittrick, *Sylvia Wynter*. See also Terada, *Looking Away*.
23 Ngai, *Ugly Feelings*.
24 This bringing together of Melville and science with the visualization of sentimentalism's violences owes much to Otter, *Melville's Anatomies*, and Wexler, *Tender Violence*.
25 For a reading of the novella via the politics of humanitarian intervention, see Downes, "Melville's *Benito Cereno* and the Politics of Humanitarian Intervention."
26 See Otter, *Melville's Anatomies*.
27 Melville, *Billy Budd, Bartleby, and Other Stories*, 55.
28 Fowler, "Analysis, Adaptation, Location, and the Cultivation of Individuality," 331.
29 Crary, *Techniques of the Observer*.
30 The late eighteenth-century field of physiognomy, based on the work of the Swiss writer Johann Kaspar Lavater, promoted the observation of faces and other outward physical traits as an objective means for judging the inner self and revealing the soul. For Lavater, this also meant the visible differences between peoples, for "that there is national physiognomy, as well as national character, is undeniable." However, he admits that "it will, sometimes, be very difficult to describe scientifically" (*Essays on Physiognomy*, 85). Phrenology gave physiognomy the more rigorous and scientific description that it had lacked: stemming from the work of the German physician Franz Josef Gall and his disciple Johann Gasper Spurzheim, phrenology adapted the principles of physiognomy into a more materialist critique of the head, whose external bumps reflected and quantified the inherent faculties of the brain—presumed to be the seat of human ability. The physicians' analyses combined physiognomy's privileging of the critical eye with the authenticating tangibility of haptic evidence. The widespread acceptance of phrenology in nineteenth-century America stemmed from the work of phrenology's proselytizers. They included the Scottish lawyer George Combe, whose *The Constitution of Man* (1828) was one of the best sellers of the era, with 200,000 copies sold before the Civil War; and the Fowler family, whose members printed numerous pamphlets on practical phrenology and gave many lecture tours and public demonstrations (Colbert, *A Measure of Perfection*, 23). The

promise of access to scientific knowledge that would train the individual to interpret everyday life and enable self-knowledge—and, therefore, self-improvement—was crucial to the successful dissemination of phrenology's precepts. Simultaneously with phrenology's life as a popular science, the study of skulls was practiced by esteemed craniologists like the Ivy League scientist Samuel George Morton, expanding it from the visual analysis of individual heads and faces to the mass collection of data about comparative anatomy in relation to the differences between civilizations and peoples. Such research provided the phenotypical evidence for the ethnological theory of polygenesis, also known as the American school, whose most prestigious advocate was the Harvard University scientist Louis Agassiz. In one of the most notorious examples of scientific racism, this theory's central claim was the separate origins of each race.

31 Many thanks to the Center for Historic American Visual Culture's 2014 summer seminar for giving me the opportunity to research this section at the American Antiquarian Society.
32 Lavater, *Essays on Physiognomy*.
33 Morton, *Crania Americana*.
34 Nott and Gliddon, *Types of Mankind*, 412.
35 Nott and Gliddon, *Types of Mankind*, title page.
36 Colbert, *A Measure of Perfection*, 41.
37 Colbert, *A Measure of Perfection*, 41 and 152.
38 Levinas, *Ethics and Infinity*, 86.
39 Deleuze and Guattari, *A Thousand Plateaus*, 178.
40 Nott and Gliddon, *Types of Mankind*, 458.
41 Da Silva, *Toward a Global Idea of Race*.
42 Significant histories of scientific racism include Gould, *The Mismeasure of Man*; Dain, *A Hideous Monster of the Mind*; Fredrickson, *The Black Image in the White Mind*; W. Stanton, *The Leopard's Spots*.
43 For instance, Fredrickson identifies what he calls "romantic racialism," which informed both pro- and antislavery positions through the white sentimental benevolence that associated Blackness with childlike good nature. Thus, Fredrickson comments that for scientific advocates of slavery, the "stereotype of the happy and contented bondsman" was propaganda that justified chattel slavery for the sake of the enslaved based on their nature and even allowed for conditional sympathies toward them (*The Black Image in the White Mind*, 52). Despite its authoritative posturing as objective, American science was a gendered and racialized practice that, as shown by Dana Nelson in *National Manhood*, grew out of the affective affiliations among white male scientists framed through national sentiment.
44 Riskin, *Science in the Age of Sensibility*, 2 and 5.
45 Riskin, *Science in the Age of Sensibility*, 72.
46 Schuller, *The Biopolitics of Feeling*, 2.
47 Lavater, *Essays on Physiognomy*, 85 and 127.
48 Lavater, *Essays on Physiognomy*, title page.

49 Combe, *The Constitution of Man Considered in Relation to External Objects*, 35; Fowler, *Fowler's Practical Phrenology*, 45; Combe, *Constitution*, 39.
50 Combe, "Phrenological Remarks," 290.
51 Fowler, *Hereditary Descent*, 33 and 34.
52 Nott and Gliddon, *Types of Mankind*, xxxiii.
53 Morton, *Crania Americana*, xxi.
54 Sealts, *Melville's Readings*, 89, 102, 55, 54.
55 Robillard, *Melville and the Visual Arts*, x.
56 Melville, *Journals*, 24, and *Correspondence*, 260.
57 Melville, *Correspondence*, 167–68.
58 Melville, *Correspondence*, 169.
59 Anonymous, "Is Man One or Many?," 9.
60 Anonymous, "Are All Men Descended from Adam?," 88.
61 Fowler, "Analysis, Adaptation, Location, and the Cultivation of Individuality," 331.
62 Melville, *Billy Budd, Bartleby, and Other Stories*, 59. Subsequent repeated references to this source will be given parenthetically in the text after the initial citation.
63 Fitzhugh, *Sociology for the South*, 96.
64 Coviello, "The American in Charity," 164.
65 Melville, *Billy Budd, Bartleby, and Other Stories*, 86.
66 Melville, *Billy Budd, Bartleby, and Other Stories*, 86. See also Hartman, *Scenes of Subjection*.
67 Melville, *Billy Budd, Bartleby, and Other Stories*, 66.
68 Fitzhugh, *Sociology for the South*, 46, 81.
69 In the original publication in *Putnam's*, the reference is to the Scottish Mungo Park. In Melville's revisions for *The Piazza Tales*, however, he refers instead to the American explorer John Ledyard, which brings the colonial dimension closer to the U.S. context.
70 Douglas, *The Feminization of American Culture*, 12.
71 Hutcheon, "Irony, Nostalgia, and the Postmodern"; Jameson, *Postmodernism*.
72 Kammen, *Mystic Cords of Memory*, 688.
73 Melville, *Billy Budd, Bartleby, and Other Stories*, 60 and 79.
74 Fitzhugh, *Sociology for the South*, 46.
75 Melville, *Billy Budd, Bartleby, and Other Stories*, 105 and 107.
76 Nostalgia, the word coined from the Greek *nosos* ("return to the native land") and *algos* ("suffering or grief"), originated in 1688 with Johannes Hofer's medical dissertation about the phenomenon as a wasting disease that was endemic to young people, particularly in the military, who wished to return home. Hofer writes that the phenomenon is "sympathetic of an afflicted imagination," connecting the brain to the body, and that it "originated by arousing especially the uncommon and everpresent idea of the recalled native land in the mind" ("Medical Dissertation on Nostalgia," 380). Nostalgia shifted from a physical medical condition in the seventeenth and eighteenth centuries to a psychological one in the twentieth. Hutcheon comments that nostalgia's

power "comes in part from its structural doubling-up of two different times, an inadequate present and an idealized past" and notes that this distance "sanitizes as it selects, making the past feel complete, stable, coherent" ("Irony, Nostalgia, and the Postmodern," 198).

77 Melville, *Billy Budd, Bartleby, and Other Stories*, 60.
78 Luciano, *Arranging Grief*, 206.
79 Adam Smith, *The Theory of Moral Sentiments*, 208.
80 Melville, *Billy Budd, Bartleby, and Other Stories*, 59.
81 Melville, *Billy Budd, Bartleby, and Other Stories*, 161.
82 Melville, *Billy Budd, Bartleby, and Other Stories*, 120 and 121.
83 Yellin, *The Intricate Knot*; Karcher, *Shadow over the Promised Land*. Legal scholar Robert Cover claims that Melville sets the ideal narrative conditions for testing abstract ideas about revolution and isolating the evils of slavery: "Finally the high seas themselves had something of the law of nature about them" (*Justice Accused*, 108–9). In her reading of Delano as exemplar of American legal reasoning, Susan Weiner unpacks a central paradox: "Melville explores how the law fails to find legal solutions to critical crises and instead subverts justice in the name of order" (*Law in Art*, 117).
84 Yellin, *The Intricate Knot*, 216.
85 Brophy, "Harriet Beecher Stowe's Critique of Slave Law in *Uncle Tom's Cabin*," 458–59.
86 Horwitz, *Transformation*, 254.
87 Horwitz, *Transformation*, 257.
88 Brophy, "Harriet Beecher Stowe's Critique of Slave Law," 457 and 480.
89 Cover, *Justice Accused*, 234.
90 Weiner, *Law in Art*, 117.
91 Sealts, *Melville's Readings*, 103–4.
92 S. Warren, *The Moral, Social, and Professional Duties of Attorneys and Solicitors*, 17. Subsequent repeated references to this source will be given parenthetically in the text after the initial citation.
93 Fitzhugh, *Sociology for the South*, 248.
94 T. Cobb, *An Inquiry into the Law of Negro Slavery in the United States of America*, 51.
95 Sawyer, *Southern Institutes*, 16. Subsequent repeated references to this source will be given parenthetically in the text after the initial citation.
96 Melville, *Billy Budd, Bartleby, and Other Stories*, 213.
97 N. Adams, *A South-Side View of Slavery*, 8 and 9. Subsequent repeated references to this source will be given parenthetically in the text after the initial citation.
98 Melville, *Billy Budd, Bartleby, and Other Stories*, 57.
99 N. Adams, *A South-Side View of Slavery*, 72 and 73.
100 Sawyer, *Southern Institutes*, 312.
101 Sawyer, *Southern Institutes*, 313.
102 Moten and Harney, *The Undercommons*, 30.
103 Melville, *Billy Budd, Bartleby, and Other Stories*, 117 and 118.
104 Campbell, *The Slave Catchers*, 23.
105 Campbell, *The Slave Catchers*, 5 and 8.

106 Campbell, *The Slave Catchers*, 24.
107 Middleton, *The Black Laws*, 202.
108 Fugitive Slave Act of 1850, Section 5.
109 Fugitive Slave Act of 1850, Section 5.
110 Melville, *Billy Budd, Bartleby, and Other Stories*, 118.
111 Thomas, "The Legal Fictions of Herman Melville and Lemuel Shaw," 117.
112 Weiner, *Law in Art*, 12.
113 Winter, "Melville, Slavery, and the Failure of the Judicial Process," 2474.
114 Cover, *Justice Accused*, 5.
115 Levy, *The Law of the Commonwealth and Chief Justice Shaw*, 91.
116 Melville, *Typee*, title page.
117 Thanks to American Studies at Cornell University for the research grant that allowed me to read the Lemuel Shaw papers at the Massachusetts Historical Society.
118 Shaw, *A Discourse Delivered before the Officers and Members of the Humane Society of Massachusetts*, 5. Subsequent repeated references to this source will be given parenthetically in the text after the initial citation.
119 Shaw, "Slavery and the Missouri Question," 138. Subsequent repeated references to this source will be given parenthetically in the text after the initial citation.
120 Thomas, "The Legal Fictions of Herman Melville and Lemuel Shaw," 123.
121 Melville, *Billy Budd, Bartleby, and Other Stories*, 120 and 135.
122 Pahl, "The Gaze of History in *Benito Cereno*," 180.
123 Weiner, *Law in Art*, 22.
124 Melville, *Billy Budd, Bartleby, and Other Stories*, 121 and 134.
125 Sundquist, *To Wake the Nations*, 170.
126 Melville, *Billy Budd, Bartleby, and Other Stories*, 126.
127 Here the Spanish enslavers engage in the misreading critiqued by Dana Luciano: "To read the skeleton as simply allegorizing the human condition, then, risks producing an ethical interpretation of the narrative at the expense of a historical one, sacrificing materiality for universality" (*Arranging Grief*, 206).
128 Melville, *Billy Budd, Bartleby, and Other Stories*, 119.
129 Melville, *Billy Budd, Bartleby, and Other Stories*, 135.
130 Delano, *Narrative of Voyages and Travels*, 352. Subsequent repeated references to this source will be given parenthetically in the text after the initial citation.
131 Fabian, *The Skull Collectors*, 4.
132 Morton, *Crania Americana*, 166.
133 C. James, *Mariners, Renegades and Castaways*, 112.
134 Melville, *Billy Budd, Bartleby, and Other Stories*, 137.
135 Du Bois, *The Souls of Black Folk*, 3.
136 Melville, *Billy Budd, Bartleby, and Other Stories*, 137.
137 Melville, *Billy Budd, Bartleby, and Other Stories*, 137.
138 Melville, *Billy Budd, Bartleby, and Other Stories*, 137.
139 Moten, *In the Break*, 1.
140 Mitchell, "No More Shame!," 143.

141 Many thanks to Emily Floyd for this research. See Jouve Martín, *The Black Doctors of Colonial Lima*, 22; Kole de Peralta, "Mal Olor and Colonial Latin American History."
142 Hartman and Wilderson, "The Position of the Unthought," 184–85.
143 Delano, *Narrative of Voyages and Travels*, 341.
144 Landers, "Founding Mothers," 7. See also McKittrick, *Demonic Grounds*.
145 Melville, *Billy Budd, Bartleby, and Other Stories*, 132.

Two. Feeling Otherwise

1 Sundquist, *To Wake the Nations*, 189.
2 Delany, *Blake*.
3 Douglass, "A Day and a Night in *Uncle Tom's Cabin*"; Stowe, *Uncle Tom's Cabin*.
4 Douglass, "A Day and a Night in *Uncle Tom's Cabin*."
5 Yarborough, "Strategies of Black Characterization in *Uncle Tom's Cabin* and the Early Afro-American Novel"; Levine, *Martin Delany, Frederick Douglass, and the Politics of Representative Identity*.
6 Delany, "Letter from M. R. Delany."
7 Delany, *The Condition, Elevation, Emigration, and Destiny of the Colored People of the United States*.
8 Douglass, "Remarks."
9 Delany, "Uncle Tom"; Stowe, *The Key to Uncle Tom's Cabin*.
10 Delany, "Mrs. Stowe's Position."
11 Delany, "Mrs. Stowe's Position."
12 Adam Smith, *The Theory of Moral Sentiments*, 208.
13 Adam Smith, *The Theory of Moral Sentiments*, 9.
14 Delany builds on the Black tradition of considering Blackness in relation to Indigeneity set by John Marrant in the late eighteenth century, with both writers presenting Indigenous peoples who practiced chattel slavery. Marrant's *A Narrative of the Lord's Wonderful Dealings with John Marrant, A Black* (1785) is a variation on the conventions of the conversion narrative: Marrant is adopted into the Cherokee nation, but he converts some Cherokees to Christianity. The appearance of both Marrant as the titular "Black" and Marrant as adopted Cherokee blurs exclusionary categories of racial classification: when he returns to Charleston he is read as Native, causing white people to flee and his family not to recognize him. He describes his appearance as an assemblage of Native signifiers: "My dress was purely in the Indian stile [sic]; the skins of wild beasts composed my garments, my head was set out in the savage manner, with a long pendant down my back, a sash round my middle without breeches, and a tomahawk by my side" (30). Marrant's intentions behind this comparative move, however, are decidedly different from Delany's: Tiya Miles comments that Marrant "trades on the idea of the idealized Indian to trade up his own position in the dominant racial hierarchy" by drawing upon the image of the noble savage so popular in early American democratic discourse ("'His Kingdom for a Kiss,'" 178).

Marrant's desire for inclusion is framed as a transformation through whiteness: he closes his narrative by asking for prayers "that the Indian tribes may stretch out their hands to God; that the black nations may be made white in the blood of the Lamb" (*Narrative*, 39). In writing about his encounter with the Creek, Catawar, and Housaw, he comments that the unity among the three nations is rooted in violent resistance to settler colonialism, but he confesses that "I had not much reason to believe any of these three nations were savingly wrought upon" (29). His portrayal of the Cherokee elides any expression of similar anti-colonial decolonial sentiments. In contrast, Delany uses his "Indian" character to express discontent as a rejection of whiteness, more aligned with the Creek, Catawar, and Housaw than the Cherokee of Marrant's *Narrative*.

15 Lowe, *The Intimacies of Four Continents*.
16 King, *The Black Shoals*, ix–xv.
17 Delany, "Mrs. Stowe's Position."
18 Delany, "Letter from M. R. Delany."
19 Levine, *Martin Delany, Frederick Douglass, and the Politics of Representative Identity*, 80.
20 Levine, *Martin Delany, Frederick Douglass, and the Politics of Representative Identity*, 18.
21 Delany, "Letter from M. R. Delany."
22 Gilroy, *The Black Atlantic*, 26.
23 Hendler, *Public Sentiments*, 61.
24 Rusert, *Fugitive Science*.
25 Rollin, *Life and Public Services of Martin R. Delany*, 69.
26 Levine, *Martin Delany, Frederick Douglass, and the Politics of Representative Identity*, 62.
27 Levine, *Martin Delany, Frederick Douglass, and the Politics of Representative Identity*, 60.
28 See Miles and Holland, *Crossing Waters, Crossing Worlds*, as a starting point.
29 Wilderson, *Red, White and Black*.
30 Powell, "Postcolonial Theory in an American Context," 358.
31 Levine, *Martin Delany, Frederick Douglass, and the Politics of Representative Identity*, 67.
32 Wolfe, "Settler Colonialism and the Elimination of the Native."
33 Byrd, *The Transit of Empire*, xxiii.
34 Delany, "Mrs. Stowe's Position."
35 Delany, *The Condition, Elevation, Emigration, and Destiny of the Colored People of the United States* (hereafter, *Condition*), 12.
36 Delany, *Condition*, 18.
37 Leroy, "Black History in Occupied Territory."
38 Delany, *Condition*, 20.
39 Delany, *Condition*, 20.
40 Delany, *Condition*, 22.
41 Forbes, *Africans and Native Americans*.
42 Delany, *Condition*, 172.

43 Katz, *Black Indians*, 3; Forbes, *Africans and Native Americans*, 189 (emphasis in original).
44 Delany, *Condition*, 172–73.
45 Delany, *Condition*, 172.
46 Zuck, "Martin R. Delany and Rhetorics of Divided Sovereignty," 46.
47 Delany, *Condition*, 57. Subsequent repeated references to this source will be given parenthetically in the text after the initial citation.
48 Delany, "Report on the Political Destiny of the Colored Race on the American Continent," 56.
49 Byrd, *The Transit of Empire*, xix.
50 Byrd, *The Transit of Empire*, xxvi.
51 Delany, "Report on the Political Destiny of the Colored Race on the American Continent," 57.
52 Delany, "Report on the Political Destiny of the Colored Race on the American Continent," 57.
53 Delany, "Report on the Political Destiny of the Colored Race on the American Continent," 58. Ron Welburn argues that the shifting complexity of Afro-Native identity is inadequately addressed—even by Katz's and Forbes's accounts of the changing taxonomies—given how location shaped identification and community associations (*Hartford's Ann Plato and the Native Borders of Identity*, 12).
54 Delany, *Principia of Ethnology*, 91.
55 Delany, *Principia of Ethnology*, 9.
56 Rollin, *Life and Public Services of Martin R. Delany*, 69.
57 Rusert, *Fugitive Science*, 88–89.
58 Lewis, *Light and Truth*.
59 Rusert, *Fugitive Science*, 80.
60 Delany, *Condition*, 129; Rusert, *Fugitive Science*, 89.
61 Eleanor Stanford writes, "Unfortunately, Delany's papers were destroyed in a fire at Wilberforce University in Ohio on April 14, 1865, leaving scholars forever to wonder which of his writings they haven't read and what other directions his mind might have taken him" ("Martin R. Delany (1812–1885)").
62 Rusert, *Fugitive Science*, 179.
63 Biggio, "The Specter of Conspiracy in Martin Delany's *Blake*," 452.
64 Delany, *Blake*, 245.
65 Du Bois, *Dark Princess*.
66 Schuller, *The Biopolitics of Feeling*.
67 Delany, *Condition*, 38.
68 Delany, *Blake*, 88.
69 Zuck, "Martin R. Delany and Rhetorics of Divided Sovereignty," 39.
70 Stowe, *Uncle Tom's Cabin*, 77.
71 Delany, *Blake*, 5.
72 Delany, *Blake*, 62.
73 Delany, *Blake*, 61; Crane, "The Lexicon of Rights, Power, and Community in *Blake*," 529; Clymer, "Martin Delany's *Blake* and the Transnational Politics of Property," 713.

74 Delany, *Blake*, 61. Subsequent repeated references to this source will be given parenthetically in the text after the initial citation.
75 Hartman, *Scenes of Subjection*, 3–4.
76 Delany, *Blake*, 68.
77 Ernest, *Liberation Historiography*, 18.
78 Yellin, *The Intricate Knot*, 199.
79 Zuck, "Martin R. Delany and Rhetorics of Divided Sovereignty," 46.
80 Delany, *Blake*, 85.
81 Katz, *Black Indians*, 135.
82 Jeltz, "The Relations of Negroes and Choctaw and Chickasaw Indians," 28.
83 Delany, *Blake*, 85.
84 King, *The Black Shoals*, 77.
85 Jeltz, "The Relations of Negroes and Choctaw and Chickasaw Indians," 28.
86 Delany, *Blake*, 86.
87 As a non-Black person of color, I have chosen to omit the anti-Black slur which appears in its entirety in the novel.
88 Simpson, "On Ethnographic Refusal."
89 Chipps, "Family First." See also TallBear, *Native American DNA*.
90 Delany, *Blake*, 86.
91 Jeltz, "The Relations of Negroes and Choctaw and Chickasaw Indians," 29.
92 Delany, *Blake*, 86.
93 Porter, *The Black Seminoles*, 6.
94 Delany, *Blake*, 87.
95 Holland, "'If You Know I Have a History, You Will Respect Me,'" 335.
96 Delany, *Blake*, 87.
97 Sexton, "The *Vel* of Slavery"; Wolfe, "Settler Colonialism and the Elimination of the Native." See also Leroy, "Black History in Occupied Territory"; Cheyfitz, "What Is a Just Society?"; Day, "Being or Nothingness."
98 Delany, *Blake*, 87.
99 Jeltz, "The Relations of Negroes and Choctaw and Chickasaw Indians," 31.
100 Delany, *Blake*, 87. See also Jeltz, "The Relations of Negroes and Choctaw and Chickasaw Indians," 31.
101 Chiles, "Within and without Raced Nations."
102 Jeltz, "The Relations of Negroes and Choctaw and Chickasaw Indians," 32.
103 Krauthamer, "In Their 'Native Country,'" 107, and *Black Slaves, Indian Masters*.
104 Krauthamer, "In Their 'Native Country,'" 115.
105 Naylor-Ojronge, "'Born and Raised among These People.'"
106 Delany, *Blake*, 87.
107 Doolan, "Be Cautious of the Word 'Rebel'"; Levine, *Martin Delany, Frederick Douglass, and the Politics of Representative Identity*.
108 Delany, *Blake*, 113.
109 Allewaert, *Ariel's Ecology*, 130.
110 Delany, *Blake*, 126.

111 Levine, *Martin Delany, Frederick Douglass, and the Politics of Representative Identity*, 198.
112 Sayers, *A Desolate Place for a Defiant People*, 85.
113 Sayers, *A Desolate Place for a Defiant People*, 88.
114 Delany, *Blake*, 113 and 115.
115 Delany, *Condition*, 67.
116 Delany, *Blake*, 87.
117 Delany, *Blake*, 87.
118 Wolfe, "Settler Colonialism and the Elimination of the Native," 397.
119 Delany, *Blake*, 112.
120 Parrish, *American Curiosity*, 270.
121 Parrish, *American Curiosity*, 295.
122 Delany, *Blake*, 112–13.
123 Delany, "Comets"; Delany, "The Attraction of Planets"; Rusert, *Fugitive Science*, 164.
124 Delany, "Comets," 60.
125 Bennett, *Vibrant Matter*; M. Chen, *Animacies*.
126 Delany, "The Attraction of Planets," 17.
127 Delany, "The Attraction of Planets," 20.
128 Delany, *Blake*, 124.
129 Delany, *Blake*, 124.
130 Rusert, *Fugitive Science*, 172.
131 Delany, *Blake*, 124.
132 Rusert, *Fugitive Science*, 168–69.
133 Delany, *Blake*, 132.
134 See my earlier rationale for omitting the n-word in quotation.
135 Wynter, "1492."
136 Rusert, *Fugitive Science*, 173.
137 Delany, *Blake*, 245.
138 Delany, *Blake*, 245.
139 López, *Chinese Cubans*; Yun, *The Coolie Speaks*.
140 Delany, *Blake*, 245.
141 Bennett, *Vibrant Matter*.
142 Delany, *Blake*, 251.
143 Delany, "The Attraction of Planets," 20.
144 Delany, *Blake*, 287.
145 Ogunleye, "Dr. Martin Robinson Delany, 19th-Century Africana Womanist."
146 A. Cooper, *A Voice from the South*, 30.
147 A. Cooper, *A Voice from the South*, 31.
148 Biggio, "The Specter of Conspiracy in Martin Delany's *Blake*," 446; Clymer, "Martin Delany's *Blake* and the Transnational Politics of Property," 727.
149 Delany, *Blake*, 239. For helping me think about African Indigeneity, I am grateful to T. J. Tallie.

150 TallBear, *Native American DNA*, 59.
151 Todd, "An Indigenous Feminist's Take on the Ontological Turn."
152 Coulthard, *Red Skin, White Masks*, 23.
153 Delany, *Blake*, 190–91.
154 Spillers, "Mama's Baby, Papa's Maybe," 68.
155 Delany, *Condition*, 199.
156 Delany, *Blake*, 180.
157 Indeed, the anti-Blackness and anti-Indigeneity fundamental to the American literary tradition may explain more broadly the anti-Indigenous and anti-Black complicities of Black and Native writers, respectively, who seek legitimacy as authoritative literary voices. For these observations I am indebted to Katie Walkiewicz, who also pointed out that Native American writers also attempted to envision a Black-Indigenous coalition.

Three. The Queer Frigidity of Professionalism

1 Jacobi, "Woman in Medicine," 148.
2 Nelson, *National Manhood*.
3 See Sánchez-Eppler, *Touching Liberty*; Foreman, *Activist Sentiments*.
4 Jacobi, "Woman in Medicine," 204.
5 Jacobi, "Woman in Medicine," 196.
6 On the embodied and textual practices of suffrage activists in relation to their race and other privileges, see Chapman, *Making Noise, Making News*.
7 Stanton et al., *History of Woman Suffrage*, 1:51.
8 Bittel, "Woman, Know Thyself"; Schuller, *The Biopolitics of Feeling*.
9 Schuller, *The Biopolitics of Feeling*, 100–133.
10 Petty, *Romancing the Vote*; Terborg-Penn, *African American Women in the Struggle for the Vote*; Dudden, *Fighting Chance*; Valelly, *The Two Reconstructions*.
11 Formative scholarly analyses of this history include Abram, *"Send Us a Lady Physician"*; Furst, *Women Healers and Physicians*; Morantz-Sanchez, *Sympathy and Science*.
12 Nina Baym reads writings by several prominent women in the first generation of female physicians for their senses of self and work in medical science (*American Women of Letters and the Nineteenth-Century Sciences*).
13 Stowe, *My Wife and I*; R. Davis, "A Day with Doctor Sarah"; H. James, *The Bostonians*. For broader discussions of literary depictions of doctor and medicine, see Browner, *Profound Science and Elegant Literature*; Rothfield, *Vital Signs*.
14 Howells, *Dr. Breen's Practice*; Phelps, *Doctor Zay*; Jewett, *A Country Doctor*; Meyer, *Helen Brent, M.D.*
15 Tocqueville, *Democracy in America*, 2:213.
16 DuPlessis, *Writing beyond the Ending*.
17 Tracey, *Plots and Proposals*.
18 Petty, *Romancing the Vote*.

19 Anonymous, "Would Women Vote?"
20 A possible factor contributing to the relatively sparse critical attention to Howells's and Phelps's novels could be present scholarly bias against their focus on homeopathic doctors as opposed to conventional practitioners. According to Harris Coulter, homeopathy represented the greatest threat of all medical schools of thought and trends to orthodox medicine because it had "an integrated and coherent doctrinal basis for its therapeutic practices" and "it recruited its practitioners to a large extent from among the ranks of orthodox physicians" (*Divided Legacy*, 6). This threat is what prompted the creation of the American Medical Association, with the goal of destroying public confidence in homeopathy. Nonetheless, homeopathy was fashionable among the upper classes in America through the end of the nineteenth century (Rothstein, *American Physicians in the Nineteenth Century*, 166).
21 One-tenth of all physicians belonged to sects like homeopathy in the nineteenth century (Squier, "Women in Nineteenth Century Homeopathic Medicine," 121).
22 Elder and Schwarzer, "Fictional Women Physicians in the Nineteenth Century."
23 Sarah Ensor explores the temporal logics of care for the queer spinster, particular in Jewett's work, in relation to ecofeminism ("Spinster Ecology").
24 Cott, "Passionlessness."
25 The medicalization of unruly female affects and behaviors as hysteria has been extensively studied. For a few important accounts, see Barker-Benfield, *The Horrors of the Half-Known Life*; Cott, "Passionlessness"; Haller and Haller, *The Physician and Sexuality in Victorian America*; Micklem, *The Nature of Hysteria*.
26 Elsewhere I focus on what is obscured and illuminated when we shift our attention to gender identification and gender expression in these texts. See Yao, "Femmes in Science."
27 Ahmed, *Living a Feminist Life*.
28 Petty, *Romancing the Vote*.
29 W. James, "What Is an Emotion?," 194.
30 Pernick, *A Calculus of Suffering*, 3.
31 Pernick, *A Calculus of Suffering*, 235.
32 Pernick, *A Calculus of Suffering*, 108. For more on the image of the masculine doctor in American culture, see Browner, *Profound Science and Elegant Literature*; Starr, *The Social Transformation of American Medicine*.
33 Melville, *White-Jacket*, 251.
34 For more on Cathell, see Furst, *Between Doctors and Patients*, 5.
35 Cathell, *Book on the Physician Himself and Things That Concern His Reputation and Success*, 45.
36 Bledstein, *The Culture of Professionalism*, 87; Larson, *The Rise of Professionalism*; Nelson, *National Manhood*; Barker-Benfield, *The Horrors of the Half-Known Life*; Nye, "The Legacy of Masculine Codes of Honor and the Admission of Women to the Medical Profession in the Nineteenth Century."

37 Cathell, *Book on the Physician Himself and Things That Concern His Reputation and Success*, 11.
38 Pernick, *A Calculus of Suffering*, 235. For more on how anesthesia disrupted established medical ideology and practices, see Boddice, *The Science of Sympathy*.
39 Morantz-Sanchez, *Sympathy and Science*; Pernick, *A Calculus of Suffering*.
40 More, *Restoring the Balance*.
41 Morantz-Sanchez, *Sympathy and Science*, 30.
42 Ellis, *Studies in the Psychology of Sex*, 3:203.
43 Krafft-Ebing, *Psychopathia Sexualis*, 42–48.
44 Ellis, *Studies in the Psychology of Sex*, 3:219.
45 On women doctors as a "third sex," see Jessee, "'The Third Sex.'"
46 Jacobi, *Mary Putnam Jacobi*, 372.
47 Clarke, *Sex in Education*, 14 and 18.
48 Morantz-Sanchez, *Sympathy and Science*, 50.
49 Coulter, *Divided Legacy*, 6; Rothestein, *American Physicians in the Nineteenth Century*.
50 Morantz-Sanchez, *Sympathy and Science*, 43.
51 Morantz-Sanchez, *Sympathy and Science*, 5.
52 Harding, *The Science Question in Feminism* and *Whose Science? Whose Knowledge?*; Jagger, "Love and Knowledge"; Schiebinger, *The Mind Has No Sex?*
53 Morantz-Sanchez, *Sympathy and Science*, 197.
54 Jacobi, *Mary Putnam Jacobi*, 346.
55 Da Silva, *Toward a Global Idea of Race*; Schuller, *The Biopolitics of Feeling*.
56 Jacobi, *Mary Putnam Jacobi*, 347 and 348. Subsequent repeated references to this source will be given parenthetically in the text after the initial citation.
57 This is a move Jacobi makes in her other writings on women's rights, such as "Common Sense" Applied to Woman Suffrage (1894), her reworking of Thomas Paine's famous pamphlet of the same title to advocate for the cause of suffrage.
58 Morgensen, "Settler Homonationalism"; Schuller, *The Biopolitics of Feeling*, 131.
59 Jacobi, *Mary Putnam Jacobi*, 356.
60 The essay was published as a book the following year; see Jacobi, *The Question of Rest for Women during Menstruation*.
61 Thanks to Fred Muratori, reference librarian at Olin Library, for research help.
62 For a different take on how the women doctor novels respond to Clarke's infamous tract through paradigms of open versus closed systems, see C. Davis, *Bodily and Narrative Forms*.
63 Blackwell, *Pioneer Work in Opening the Medical Profession to Women*, 28.
64 Baillie, "Should Professional Women Marry?," 293. Subsequent repeated references to this source will be given parenthetically in the text after the initial citation.
65 Morantz-Sanchez, *Sympathy and Science*, 135. Subsequent repeated references to this source will be given parenthetically in the text after the initial citation.
66 Schuller, *The Biopolitics of Feeling*, 131.

67. Sophia Jex-Blake was in a lifelong relationship with Dr. Margaret Todd, who later became her biographer. At the end of "Medical Women in Fiction," Jex-Blake praises *Mona Maclean, Medical Student*—a novel written by Todd under a pseudonym—for its accuracy.
68. Jex-Blake, "Medical Women in Fiction," 265.
69. Quoted in Masteller, "The Women Doctors of Howards, Phelps, and Jewett," 144.
70. Jex-Blake, "Medical Women in Fiction," 266.
71. Jex-Blake, "Medical Women in Fiction," 266.
72. Jex-Blake, "Medical Women in Fiction," 267 and 266.
73. On the contrast between Howells's realism and Phelps's sentimentalism, see C. Davis, *Bodily and Narrative Forms*.
74. Quoted in Masteller, "The Women Doctors of Howards, Phelps, and Jewett," 135.
75. Quoted in Masteller, "The Women Doctors of Howards, Phelps, and Jewett," 135.
76. Masteller, "The Women Doctors of Howards, Phelps, and Jewett," 141; Pryse, "'I Was Country When Country Wasn't Cool,'" 230.
77. Meyer, "Editor's Preface," iii.
78. Howells, *Dr. Breen's Practice*, 14, 76, and 248. Subsequent repeated references to this source will be given parenthetically in the text after the initial citation.
79. Bledstein, *The Culture of Professionalism*, 90.
80. Bledstein, *The Culture of Professionalism*, 120.
81. Morantz-Sanchez, *Sympathy and Science*, 62.
82. Ahmed, *The Cultural Politics of Emotion*, 124.
83. Jacobi, "Woman in Medicine," 196.
84. A variation of this woman doctor versus male lawyer dynamic can be seen with Dr. Mary Prance and Basil Ransom in H. James, *The Bostonians*.
85. Jewett, *A Country Doctor*, 161 and 166.
86. Storey, "A Geography of Medical Knowledge."
87. Jewett, *A Country Doctor*, 62.
88. Ann Shapiro argues of women and labor in Jewett's oeuvre that "in fact, women, like men, must follow their inner yearnings and perform life roles that are suitable for the individual, regardless of gender" (*Unlikely Heroines*, 75).
89. Jewett, *A Country Doctor*, 106.
90. Jewett, *A Country Doctor*, 107.
91. Jewett, *A Country Doctor*, 137.
92. Josephine Donovan, one of the first critics to note the queerness of Prince, claims that the character is Jewett's answer to the influential nineteenth-century sexologist Krafft-Ebing, "who saw women's choice of masculine vocations as unnatural, indeed pathological" ("Nan and the Golden Apples," 24). See also Roman, *Sarah Orne Jewett*.
93. Jewett, *A Country Doctor*, 137. Subsequent repeated references to this source will be given parenthetically in the text after the initial citation.

94 Meyer, *Helen Brent, M.D.*, 25–26. Subsequent repeated references to this source will be given parenthetically in the text after the initial citation.
95 Meyer, "Woman's Assumption of Sex Superiority."
96 Phelps, *Chapters from a Life*, 12.
97 Phelps, *Chapters from a Life*, 250.
98 See Stansell, "Elizabeth Stuart Phelps."
99 Clarke, *Sex in Education*, 24.
100 Howe, *Sex in Education*. I am indebted to previous research by Cynthia Davis on these archival links. See C. Davis, *Bodily and Narrative Forms*.
101 Phelps, untitled item in *Sex and Education*, 130.
102 Morris, "Professional Ethics and Professional Erotics in Elizabeth Stuart Phelps's *Doctor Zay*."
103 Kelly, *The Life and Works of Elizabeth Stuart Phelps*, 15; Kessler, *Elizabeth Stuart Phelps*, 74.
104 Swenson, "Doctor Zay and Dr. Mitchell."
105 Wegener, "'Should Female Physicians Treat Male Patients?'"
106 Phelps, *Doctor Zay*, 20. Subsequent repeated references to this source will be given parenthetically in the text after the initial citation.
107 Phelps, "Sympathy as a Remedy," 745.
108 Phelps, *Chapters from a Life*, 252.
109 For a discussion of how Phelps and Jewett represent different schools of medicine now considered alternative, see Storey, "A Geography of Medical Knowledge."
110 Fine, "Women Physicians and Medical Sects in Nineteenth-Century Chicago," 252; Wood, "'The Fashionable Diseases.'"
111 Pernick, *A Calculus of Suffering*, 114.
112 Starr, *The Social Transformation of American Medicine*, 97.
113 Squier, "Women in Nineteenth Century Homeopathic Medicine," 121 and 128.
114 Phelps, *Doctor Zay*, 39.
115 For a history of the shifting relationships between doctors and patients, see Furst, *Between Doctors and Patients*.
116 Phelps, *Doctor Zay*, 84.
117 For an analysis of the seeming reversal of gender roles for comedic effect during this era that includes a discussion of *Doctor Zay*, see Habegger, "Nineteenth-Century American Humor."
118 Phelps, *Doctor Zay*, 208.
119 Tracey, *Plots and Proposals*, 148–80.
120 Phelps, *Doctor Zay*, 238.
121 Ahmed, *The Cultural Politics of Emotion*, 122–43.
122 Schuller, *The Biopolitics of Feeling*, 131.
123 Abate, *Tomboys*, 67.
124 Painter, *Sojourner Truth*, 224–25; Terborg-Penn, *African American Women in the Struggle for the Vote*.
125 E. Stanton, preface, vi–vii.

Four. Objective Passionlessness

1. Harper, "Enlightened Motherhood," 8 and 6. I follow the practice developed and furthered by the scholars Carla Peterson, Meredith McGill, Andrea Williams, and Koritha Mitchell, who sometimes use "Watkins Harper," not just "Harper," to call attention to her substantial career before as well as after her marriage. However, works in the bibliography (and thus in the notes) are listed under the name Harper.
2. Hartman, *Lose Your Mother*, 80. See also Hartman, "The Belly of the World."
3. Fielder, *Relative Races*, 6.
4. Peterson, "Subject to Speculation," 114.
5. Carby, *Reconstructing Womanhood*; Peterson, *"Doers of the Word"*; Foreman, *Activist Sentiments*.
6. For an overview of the historical developments in Watkins Harper's posthumous reputation, critical reassessment, and reissues of her writings, see Mitchell, "Introduction."
7. Quoted in Parker, *Articulating Rights*, 117.
8. Quoted in Stanton et al., *History of Woman Suffrage*, 1:391.
9. Quoted in Stanton et al., *History of Woman Suffrage*, 1:392.
10. Dudden, *Fighting Chance*; Painter, "Voices of Suffrage"; Terborg-Penn, *African American Women in the Struggle for the Vote, 1850–1920*.
11. Schuller, *The Biopolitics of Feeling*.
12. DuCille, *The Coupling Convention*, 30–32, and 45.
13. Haraway, "Situated Knowledges," 581.
14. Daston and Galison, *Objectivity*, 36.
15. Daston and Galison, *Objectivity*, 52. For an overview of the work on the crafting of objectivity in feminist studies of science, see Collins, *Black Feminist Thought*, 205.
16. Riskin, *Science in the Age of Sensibility*; Nelson, *National Manhood*; Schuller, *The Biopolitics of Feeling*.
17. Hull and Smith, "Introduction," xxv.
18. Ellis, *Studies in the Psychology of Sex*, 3:271.
19. See Brown, *Clotel*.
20. Cott, "Passionlessness"; duCille, *The Coupling Convention*.
21. Hine, "Rape and the Inner Lives of Black Women in the Middle West," 912.
22. Similarly, Patricia Hill Collins cites the work of the writer Marita Bonner to explain that silence is not submission for Black women but the way "consciousness remained the one sphere of freedom available to her in the stifling confines of both her Black middle-class world and a racist white society" (*Black Feminist Thought*, 92). Collins uses the figure of the unaffected or disaffected woman to present the lived experience of Black women: "Like Marita Bonner, far too many Black women remain motionless on the outside . . . but inside?" (93).
23. Hine, "Rape and the Inner Lives of Black Women in the Middle West," 915 and 916.
24. Quashie, *The Sovereignty of Quiet*, 134.

25 Collins, *Black Feminist Thought*, 11; Wynter, "Beyond Miranda's Meanings," 479.
26 B. Cooper, *Beyond Respectability*.
27 Hull and Smith, "Introduction," xxxi.
28 Bailey and Peoples, "Towards a Black Feminist Health Science Studies." See also B. Smith, "Black Women's Health"; Washington, *Medical Apartheid*.
29 Sims, *The Story of My Life*.
30 Wanzo, *The Suffering Will Not Be Televised*.
31 Jacobi, "Woman in Medicine," 155.
32 Owens, *Medical Bondage*, 14.
33 Schuller, *The Biopolitics of Feeling*, 68–99; Rusert, *Fugitive Science*, 181–218.
34 Snorton, *Black on Both Sides*, 17–54.
35 Morantz-Sanchez, *Sympathy and Science*.
36 Carby, *Reconstructing Womanhood*; Ernest, *Resistance and Reformation in Nineteenth-Century African-American Literature*; Foreman, *Activist Sentiments* and "'Reading Aright'"; Birnbaum, "Racial Hysteria"; Griffin, "Frances Ellen Watkins Harper in the Reconstruction South"; Petty, *Romancing the Vote*.
37 For an excellent work on Watkins Harper and Delany with regard to conceptualizations of Black citizenship, see Spires, *The Practice of Citizenship*.
38 Carby, *Reconstructing Womanhood*, 93.
39 Tate, *Domestic Allegories of Political Desire*.
40 Hartman, *Scenes of Subjection*.
41 Harper, *Iola Leroy*, 130–42.
42 Hine, "Co-Laborers in the Work of the Lord" and "Physicians."
43 Quoted in Gates and Higginbotham, *African American Lives*, 199–200.
44 Quoted in Wells, *Out of the Dead House*, 51.
45 Wells, *Out of the Dead House*, 51. See also Crumpler, *A Book of Medical Discourses*.
46 Quoted in Hine, "Co-Laborers in the Work of the Lord," 113.
47 Hine, "Co-Laborers in the Work of the Lord" and "Physicians."
48 Allen, "'We Must Attack the System.'"
49 Vigil-Fowler, "'Two Strikes—a Lady and Colored.'"
50 "A Book for All Time!" [1882?], Rare Books, Gift of Charles E. Rosenberg 2018, Library Company of Philadelphia, Philadelphia. Thanks to Nazera Sadiq Wright for drawing this archival item to my attention.
51 Crumpler, *A Book of Medical Discourses*, iii.
52 Crumpler, *A Book of Medical Discourses*, 3.
53 Wells, *Out of the Dead House*, 54.
54 Wells, *Out of the Dead House*, 71.
55 Allen, "'We Must Attack the System.'"
56 Crumpler, *A Book of Medical Discourses*, 117.
57 Wright, *Black Girlhood in the Nineteenth Century*.
58 Crumpler, *A Book of Medical Discourses*, 5.
59 Crumpler, *A Book of Medical Discourses*, 3.
60 S. James, "John Henryism and the Health of African-Americans."
61 Crumpler, *A Book of Medical Discourses*, 115. Subsequent repeated references to this source will be given parenthetically in the text after the initial citation.

62 Sharpe, *In the Wake*, 106.
63 Crumpler, *A Book of Medical Discourses*, 119.
64 In Crumpler's text, the n-word appears in full. However, as a non-Black person, I chose not to render it that way. My practice is influenced by Koritha Mitchell's questioning of even the direct quotation of the n-word as the normalized replication of anti-Black violence in our teaching and scholarship. See Mitchell, "Teaching & the N-Word."
65 Bernstein, *Racial Innocence*.
66 Crumpler, *A Book of Medical Discourses*, 118–19, 117.
67 Wells, *Out of the Dead House*, 53.
68 Spillers, "Mama's Baby, Papa's Maybe," 68.
69 Du Bois, *The Philadelphia Negro*; Cole, "First Meeting of the Women's Missionary Society of Philadelphia."
70 Allen, "'We Must Attack the System,'" 105.
71 Cole, "First Meeting of the Women's Missionary Society of Philadelphia," 4–5.
72 Prescod-Weinstein, "Making Black Women Scientists under White Empiricism."
73 Du Bois, *The Souls of Black Folk*.
74 My research on Cole's work on the eye was conducted at the Legacy Center of the Drexel University College of Medicine, with the support of a fellowship from the Library Company of Philadelphia and the Historical Society of Pennsylvania.
75 Cole, "The Eye and Its Appendages," 1. Subsequent repeated references to this source will be given parenthetically in the text after the initial citation.
76 Hammonds, "Toward a Genealogy of Black Female Sexuality," 172.
77 Hammonds, "Toward a Genealogy of Black Female Sexuality," 171.
78 DuCille, *The Coupling Convention*, 30–32, and 45.
79 Cole, "The Eye and Its Appendages," 22.
80 Lawrence, *A Treatise on the Venereal Diseases of the Eye*, 193–94.
81 Lawrence, *Lectures on Physiology, Zoology, and the Natural History of Man*, 423.
82 Lawrence, *Lectures on Physiology, Zoology, and the Natural History of Man*, 420 and 423. See also Jefferson, *Notes on the State of Virginia*.
83 Lawrence, *Lectures on Physiology, Zoology, and the Natural History of Man*, 108.
84 Herndl, "The Invisible (Invalid) Women."
85 Birnbaum, "Racial Hysteria," 13.
86 Foreman, "'Reading Aright.'"
87 Foreman, "'Reading Aright,'" 345.
88 Foreman, *Activist Sentiments*, 99.
89 Harper, *Iola Leroy*, 232.
90 Harper, *Iola Leroy*, 233.
91 Harper, *Iola Leroy*, 238.
92 Harper, *Iola Leroy*, 238.
93 U.S. Census (1880), 36B. Many thanks to Eric Gardner for helping me verify this when I was unable to access these resources during the COVID-19 lockdown.
94 Armstrong, "A Mental and Moral Feast"; M. Kelley, "'Talents Committed to Your Care.'"

95 Sterling, *We Are Your Sisters*, 398.
96 Harper, *Iola Leroy*, 115. Subsequent repeated references to this source will be given parenthetically in the text after the initial citation.
97 Mitchell notes that Louisa May Alcott's 1863 short story "My Contraband" is an important intertext for Watkins Harper, who revises Alcott's racial dynamics. The story, set during the Civil War, follows a white nurse who cares for a mixed-race Black soldier. See Mitchell, "Introduction," 36.
98 Harper, *Iola Leroy*, 90.
99 Schultz, *Women at the Front*, 21–22.
100 Hine, "'They Shall Mount Up with Wings as Eagles,'" 479, and *Black Women in White*.
101 Harper, *Iola Leroy*, 110.
102 Schultz, *Women at the Front*, 6.
103 Harper, *Iola Leroy*, 136.
104 Hartman, *Scenes of Subjection*, 53.
105 Harper, *Iola Leroy*, 140.
106 Cobb, "'Forget Me Not'"; Kammerer, "Activism behind the Veil of Sentimentality."
107 Harper, *Iola Leroy*, 218.
108 Mitchell, "Introduction," 26.
109 Harper, *Iola Leroy*, 238.
110 DuCille, *The Coupling Convention*.
111 Harper, *Iola Leroy*, 243.
112 Hine, "Physicians."
113 Wanzo, *The Suffering Will Not Be Televised*, 146.
114 Jackson, *Becoming Human*, 39.
115 Martin and Montagne, "Black Mothers Keep Dying after Giving Birth"; "Racial and Ethnic Disparities Continue in Pregnancy Related Deaths."
116 Triolo, "Nineteenth Century Foundations of Cancer Research Advances in Tumor Pathology, Nomenclature, and Theories of Oncogenesis," 98, and "Nineteenth Century Foundations of Cancer Research. Origins of Experimental Research."
117 The institution moved from its original location and is now the Memorial Sloan Kettering Cancer Center, affiliated with Cornell University's Weill Medical Medicine. It is one of the leading hospitals for cancer treatment and research in the United States.
118 Harper, *Iola Leroy*, 150.
119 Triolo, "Nineteenth Century Foundations of Cancer Research Advances in Tumor Pathology, Nomenclature, and Theories of Oncogenesis," 97.
120 Sharpe, *In the Wake*, 104.
121 Harper, *Iola Leroy*, 206.
122 American Cancer Society, "Cancer Facts & Figures for African Americans 2016–2018," 1.
123 Harper, *Iola Leroy*, 238.
124 Hansberry, *A Raisin in the Sun*.

125 Quoted in Collier-Thomas, "Frances Ellen Watkins Harper," 54–55.
126 Quoted in Sterling, *We Are Your Sisters*, 413.
127 Hine, "Physicians."
128 Harper, *Iola Leroy*, 238.

Five. Oriental Inscrutability

1 Far, "Leaves from the Mental Portfolio of an Eurasian," 127.
2 For example, see Sunny Xiang's excellent work on the adaptation of Oriental inscrutability to the Cold War era (*Tonal Intelligence*).
3 Anonymous, "Mrs. Spring Fragrance," 181.
4 Anonymous, "Mrs. Spring Fragrance," 182.
5 Anonymous, "A New Note in Fiction."
6 In 1885 Canada passed an act that levied a prohibitive head tax on all Chinese immigrants. In 1923 Canada passed its equivalent of the Chinese Exclusion Act that banned most forms of immigration for the Chinese. It was repealed in 1947.
7 For comprehensive biographical information, see Far, *Becoming Sui Sin Far*; Ferens, *Edith and Winnifred Eaton*; White-Parks, *Sui Sin Far/Edith Maude Eaton*.
8 Ling, *Between Worlds*; White-Parks, *Sui Sin Far/Edith Maude Eaton*.
9 M. Chen, *Animacies*. In particular, see Chen's chapter on the queer racialization of the element lead in relation to children's toys manufactured in China.
10 Cheng, *Ornamentalism*.
11 Luibhéid, *Entry Denied*, 32; Salyer, *Laws Harsh as Tigers*, 8.
12 Salyer, *Laws Harsh as Tigers*, 13.
13 Mimi Thi Nguyen characterizes the expectation of gratitude from refugees as the updated colonialist structure of feeling that accompanied the gift of freedom bound to indebtedness later in the twentieth century (*The Gift of Freedom*).
14 Hsu, *Geography and the Production of Space in Nineteenth-Century American Literature*; Far, *Mrs. Spring Fragrance* (2011); Song, "Sentimentalism and Sui Sin Far"; Cho, "Domesticating the Aliens Within"; and Cho, "'Yellow Slavery,' Narratives of Rescue, and Sui Sin Far/Edith Maude Eaton's 'Lin John' (1899)."
15 Song, "The Unknowable and Sui Sin Far"; R. Lee, "Journalistic Representations of Asian Americans and Literary Responses."
16 Far and Eaton, "Word from Miss Eaton," 1.
17 S. Lee, "Staying In"; Huang, "Inscrutably, Actually."
18 White-Parks, "'We Wear the Mask'"; Wang, "Rereading Sui Sin Far," 251.
19 Luibhéid, *Entry Denied*; Shah, *Contagious Divides*.
20 U.S. Congress, "Report of the Joint Special Committee to Investigate Chinese Immigration," viii and vii.
21 Quoted in Thomas, *Plessy v. Ferguson*, 58.
22 J. Miller, "Chinese Immigration," 1484.
23 Schuller, *The Biopolitics of Feeling*.
24 Schuller, *The Biopolitics of Feeling*, 1483.

25 Schuller, *The Biopolitics of Feeling*.
26 Ahmed, *The Promise of Happiness*, 41-42.
27 J. Miller, "Chinese Immigration," 1484.
28 J. Miller, "Chinese Immigration," 1483.
29 See Roh, Huang, and Niu, *Techno-Orientalism*.
30 Lye, *America's Asia*.
31 J. Miller, "Chinese Immigration," 1484.
32 J. Miller, "Chinese Immigration," 1484.
33 J. Miller, "Chinese Immigration," 1488.
34 J. Miller, "Chinese Immigration," 1488.
35 J. Miller, "Chinese Immigration," 1488.
36 Jodi Byrd discusses how Asian alienness contributes to the self-Indigenizaton of white settlers (*The Transit of Empire*).
37 Asian American racial formation in general has been understood as the product of immigration laws and policies. Lisa Lowe brilliantly draws attention to the tensions between these disciplinary legal acts and the agentic acts of the immigrants themselves (*Immigrant Acts*). See also Salyer, *Laws Harsh as Tigers*.
38 Chapman, "Introduction," lvii.
39 See for instance, Diana, "Biracial/Bicultural Identity in the Writings of Sui Sin Far."
40 Far, "Leaves from the Mental Portfolio of an Eurasian," 133.
41 With this phrasing I am thinking of Rei Terada's figuration of the transgressive validity of looking away (*Looking Away*), as well as Judith Fetterley and Marjorie Pryse's articulation of the difference between regionalism like Far's writing and local color such as Bret Harte's as "the difference between 'looking with' and 'looking at'" (*Writing out of Place*, 36).
42 Far, *Mrs. Spring Fragrance and Other Writings*, 234.
43 See T. Chen, *Double Agency*; Palumbo-Liu, *Asian/American*; Lye, *America's Asia*.
44 Chow, "How (the) Inscrutable Chinese Led to Globalized Theory," 71.
45 Chow, "How (the) Inscrutable Chinese Led to Globalized Theory," 72 and 73.
46 Chow, "How (the) Inscrutable Chinese Led to Globalized Theory," 73.
47 B. Taylor, *A Visit to India, China, and Japan*, 285.
48 Haddad, *The Romance of China*, 228.
49 Redfield, *Outlines of a New System of Physiognomy*, 12.
50 B. Harte, *That Heathen Chinee, and Other Poems Mostly Humorous*.
51 See J. Miller, "Chinese Immigration." This fixation on Chinese faces—and eventually East Asian faces more generally—has evolved throughout the twentieth and twenty-first centuries. According to David Palumbo-Liu, early twentieth-century scientists reinvented physiognomy by drawing on Franz Boas's observations about the physical transformation of immigrants, focusing on the face as the phenotypical manifestation of cultural and racial differences. Palumbo-Liu notes that the "Oriental" face in these studies was seen as a "mask" that was "insincere, merely the blind repetition of traditional conventions," in contrast to American faces that were seen as "eminently 'real' in their unabashed individualistic freedom of expression" (*Asian/American*, 91).

The extent of transformation in the physical face of the so-called Oriental indexed the extent of the success or failure of the relevant group to assimilate into America, and using the face as a psychosomatic marker of assimilation contextualizes the politics behind the eventual development of plastic surgery to alter Asian features into more Western ones. Even in 1991, the psychologist Michael Bond claims that, for example, the Chinese "react less strongly to emotionally arousing events" (*Beyond the Chinese Face*, 7).

52 Qi, "Face"; Ho, "On the Concept of Face"; Hu, "The Chinese Concept of Face"; Liu, "The Ghost of Arthur H. Smith in the Mirror of Cultural Translation."
53 Adam Smith, *The Theory of Moral Sentiments*, 208
54 Arthur Smith, *Chinese Characteristics*, 66; Liu, "The Ghost of Arthur H. Smith in the Mirror of Cultural Translation," 414.
55 Arthur Smith, *Chinese Characteristics*, 16.
56 Arthur Smith, *Chinese Characteristics*, 17.
57 Arthur Smith, *Chinese Characteristics*, 96–97.
58 Such ugly collusions exposed by scholars include the casting of Chinese women in the Caribbean by British colonizers as the anti-Black "handmaidens of empire" (Lowe, *The Intimacies of Four Continents*), while in the context of American nationhood, the Yellow Peril enabled white American settlers to "play Indian" and project their genocidal settler colonialism onto the Chinese (Day, *Alien Capital*). From another angle, however, the possibility that the Chinese might leverage their privileges against whiteness and in possible solidarity with other subjugated peoples of color indicate another political aspect underlying fears about the treachery of the inscrutable Oriental.
59 Morton, *Crania Americana*, 5. Subsequent repeated references to this source will be given parenthetically in the text after the initial citation.
60 Lu, *Selected Works*, 4:131.
61 Liu, "The Ghost of Arthur H. Smith in the Mirror of Cultural Translation," 414.
62 Lin, *My Country and My People*, 200.
63 Lin, *My Country and My People*, 80. See also Song, "The Unknowable and Sui Sin Far."
64 Hu, "The Chinese Concept of Face"; Ho, "On the Concept of Face."
65 Qi, "Face," 288.
66 Palumbo-Liu, *Asian/American*, 425.
67 Gunew, "Subaltern Empathy."
68 Goffman, "On Face-Work."
69 Goffman, "On Face-Work," 213. Although this footnote focuses on the Chinese concept, listing four sources, Goffman ends it by referring to the "American Indian conception of face" in Marcel Mauss's *The Gift* (1954). In a future project I hope to explore the implications of this grouping in the wider context of Asian and Asian American comparative racialization with the Indigenous peoples of Turtle Island.
70 Shah writes: "The Chinese female prostitute became the economic counterpart of the Chinese male laborer—both characterized by 'excessively cheap

labor.' Like the 'coolie' who appealed to capitalists with his low wages, but whose employment could result in the degradation of American democracy, the Chinese prostitute offered sexual services for a bargain price that would later haunt the client, his spouse, and his progeny with venereal infection" (*Contagious Divides*, 87).

71. Lye, *America's Asia*; Hayot, "Chinese Bodies, Chinese Futures."
72. Cheng, *Ornamentalism*, ix. For more on Chinese women as sex workers, see Hirata, "Free, Indentured, Enslaved"; Wong, *Transpacific Attachments*.
73. Lin, *My Country and My People*, 49.
74. Far, *Becoming Sui Sin Far*, 234–35.
75. For a careful examination of the immigration practices by officials and Chinese during the Exclusion Era, see Lau, *Paper Families*.
76. Far, "Leaves from the Mental Portfolio of an Eurasian," 129.
77. Quoted in Far, "Leaves from the Mental Portfolio of an Eurasian," 129.
78. In "The Typewriter" (1891), Far comments on the emotional suppression required for the stenographer's professional composure when writing other people's words—specifically, love letters: "The typewriter has to exercise a great deal of control over her feelings" (215). This line is repeated in "The Girl of the Period: The Projectographe, Jamaica Lawyers" (1897), an article from her journalist work in Jamaica (*Becoming Sui Sin Far*, 115).
79. For the feminist depiction of the rebellious stenographer in Far, see Chapman, "A 'Revolution in Ink.'"
80. Far, *Mrs. Spring Fragrance* (1912), 30.
81. For instance, see Jirousek, "Spectacle Ethnography and Immigrant Resistance."
82. Far, *Mrs. Spring Fragrance* (1912), 41.
83. Far, *Becoming Sui Sin Far*, 3.
84. Far, *Becoming Sui Sin Far*, 141.
85. Far, *Becoming Sui Sin Far*, 141; B. Harte, *That Heathen Chinee*; W. Harte, "Bubble and Squeak," 217.
86. Far, *Becoming Sui Sin Far*, 141.
87. Far, *Mrs. Spring Fragrance* (1912), 224.
88. Far, *Becoming Sui Sin Far*, 141.
89. Far, *Becoming Sui Sin Far*, 141 and 143.
90. See Chapman's footnote in Far, *Becoming Sui Sin Far*, 141.
91. Far, *Becoming Sui Sin Far*, 76. See also 90.
92. Ong, *Flexible Citizenship* and "On the Edge of Empires."
93. Far, *Becoming Sui Sin Far*, 76; see also 89–90. Subsequent repeated references to this source will be given parenthetically in the text after the initial citation.
94. Chapman, "A 'Revolution in Ink'"; Patterson, *Beyond the Gibson Girl*.
95. Far, "The Chinese Woman in America," 59. Subsequent repeated references to this source will be given parenthetically in the text after the initial citation.
96. Far, "The Chinese Woman in America," 62. See also Chung, "Asian Object Lessons."
97. Far, "The Chinese Woman in America," 64.

98 Cheng, *Ornamentalism*.
99 Far, "The Chinese Woman in America," 62.
100 Ko, "Footbinding in the Museum" and *Cinderella's Sisters*.
101 Ko, "Bondage in Time," 13.
102 Far, "The Chinese Woman in America," 64.
103 Far, *Mrs. Spring Fragrance* (1912), 193.
104 Song, "The Unknowable and Sui Sin Far."
105 Far, *Mrs. Spring Fragrance* (1912), 330.
106 Riis, *How the Other Half Lives*.
107 Beauregard, "Reclaiming Sui Sin Far," 348.
108 Far, *Mrs. Spring Fragrance* (1912), 85. Subsequent repeated references to this source will be given parenthetically in the text after the initial citation.
109 Howard, "Sui Sin Far's American Words."
110 Far, *Mrs. Spring Fragrance* (1912), 89.
111 Anonymous, "A New Note in Fiction."
112 Far, *Becoming Sui Sin Far*, 54.
113 In the *Montreal Daily Star* articles discussed above, for example, Chapman reads how Eaton's racially ambiguous "E. E." and her personal identification shifts over the course of her letters to the editor. In her discussion of the methodology she used to unearth Eaton's expanded oeuvre, Chapman suggests that Eaton used other pseudonyms that have yet to be identified.
114 W. Harte, "Bubble and Squeak," 217.
115 Far, "Leaves from the Mental Portfolio of an Eurasian," 127. See also Sibara, "Disease, Disability, and the Alien Body in the Literature of Sui Sin Far"; Vogel, *Rewriting White*.
116 Ling, *Between Worlds*, 48.
117 Far, *Becoming Sui Sin Far*, 55.
118 For a starting point about the Chinese as spectacle during the period, see Moy, *Marginal Sights*.
119 Far, *Becoming Sui Sin Far*, 166.
120 Far, *Becoming Sui Sin Far*, 167. See also Harte, *That Heathen Chinee*.
121 Far, *Becoming Sui Sin Far*, 168.
122 Tonkovich, "Genealogy, Genre, Gender.'"
123 Far, "Leaves from the Mental Portfolio of an Eurasian," 125. Subsequent repeated references to this source will be given parenthetically in the text after the initial citation.
124 Berlant, *Cruel Optimism*, 100.
125 Far, "The Chinese Spirit of Non-Resistance Will Disappear."
126 Here I suggest a congruent, nonequivalent, but also nonexclusionary relationship between this Asiatic quiet, presumed to be apolitical, and Quashie's concept of Black quiet when Black culture is characterized predominantly as loud and political.
127 Far, "Leaves from the Mental Portfolio of an Eurasian," 130. For work on Afro-Asian links in the Caribbean, see, for example, Goffe, "Sugarwork"; Yun, *The Coolie Speaks*.

128 Lowe, *The Intimacies of Four Continents*; Yao, "Black-Asian Counterintimacies."
129 Delany, *Blake*, 245.

Coda

1 Phanuel Antwi writes: "One way for fugitive solidarity to deal with the promise of betrayal, politically, is to understand that imagination is more valuable than knowledge. Betrayal is born out of knowledge of legitimate fears, especially under conditions of racial and colonial violence. If we can imagine beyond fear, if we can imagine something more important than fear, we might imagine friendship. Fugitive solidarity in the academy is a way of cultivating friendships that exceed the political utility of colleague and ally relationships. After all, friendship is not only the principal way anything gets done in the academy, but also the only thing keeping so many of us alive" ("On Labor, Embodiment, and Debt in the Academy," 324).
2 Ahmed, *Living a Feminist Life*.
3 Adam Smith, *The Theory of Moral Sentiments*, 208.

BIBLIOGRAPHY

Abate, Michelle Ann. *Tomboys: A Literary and Cultural History*. Philadelphia: Temple University Press, 2008.

Abram, Ruth J., ed. *"Send Us a Lady Physician": Women Doctors in America, 1835–1920*. New York: W. W. Norton, 1985.

Accapadi, Mamta Motwani. "When White Women Cry: How White Women's Tears Oppress Women of Color." *College Student Affairs Journal* 26, no. 2 (Spring 2007): 208–16.

Adams, Nehemiah. *A South-Side View of Slavery: Three Months in the South*. Boston: T. R. Marvin and B. B. Mussey, 1854.

Ahmed, Sara. "Affective Economies." *Social Text* 22, no. 2 (2004): 117–39.

Ahmed, Sara. *The Cultural Politics of Emotion*. New York: Routledge, 2004.

Ahmed, Sara. *Living a Feminist Life*. Durham, NC: Duke University Press, 2017.

Ahmed, Sara. *The Promise of Happiness*. Durham, NC: Duke University Press, 2010.

Allen, Patrick S. "'We Must Attack the System': The Print Practice of Black 'Doctresses.'" *Arizona Quarterly* 74, no. 4 (2019): 87–113.

Allewaert, Monique. *Ariel's Ecology: Plantations, Personhood, and Colonialism in the American Tropics*. Minneapolis: University of Minnesota Press, 2013.

American Cancer Society. "Cancer Facts & Figures for African Americans 2016–2018." Atlanta, GA: American Cancer Society, 2016.

Antwi, Phanuel. "On Labor, Embodiment, and Debt in the Academy." *A/b* 33, no. 2 (2018): 301–26.

Anzaldúa, Gloria. *Borderlands/La Frontera: The New Mestiza*. San Francisco: Aunt Lute Books, 2007.

Anzaldúa, Gloria. "La Prieta." In *This Bridge Called My Back: Writings by Radical Women of Color*, edited by Cherríe Moraga and Gloria Anzaldúa, 198–209. 4th ed. Albany: State University of New York Press, 1981.

"Are All Men Descended from Adam?" *Putnam's Monthly Magazine of American Literature, Science, and Art* 5, no. 25 (January 1855): 79–88.

Armstrong, Erica R. "A Mental and Moral Feast: Reading, Writing, and Sentimentality in Black Philadelphia." *Journal of Women's History* 16, no. 1 (2004): 78–102.

Austin, J. L. *How to Do Things with Words*. New York: Oxford University Press, 1962.
Bailey, Moya, and Whitney Peoples. "Towards a Black Feminist Health Science Studies." *Catalyst* 3, no. 2 (2017): 1–27.
Baillie, Gertrude Stuart. "Should Professional Women Marry?" In *Public Women, Public Words*, edited by Dawn Keetley and John Pettegrew, 292–94. Madison, WI: Madison House, 1894.
Baldwin, James. "Everybody's Protest Novel." In *Uncle Tom's Cabin*, edited by Elizabeth Ammons, 495–501. New York: W. W. Norton, 1994.
Barker-Benfield, G. J. *The Horrors of the Half-Known Life: Male Attitudes toward Women and Sexuality in Nineteenth-Century America*. New York: Harper and Row, 1976.
Bascara, Vincent. *Model-Minority Imperialism*. Minneapolis: University of Minnesota Press, 2006.
Baym, Nina. *American Women of Letters and the Nineteenth-Century Sciences: Styles of Affiliation*. New Brunswick, NJ: Rutgers University Press, 2002.
Baym, Nina. "Melodramas of Beset Manhood: How Theories of American Fiction Exclude Women Authors." *American Quarterly* 33, no. 2 (1981): 123–39.
Beauregard, Guy. "Reclaiming Sui Sin Far." In *Re/Collecting Early Asian America*, edited by Josephine Lee, Imogene L. Lim, and Yuko Matsukawa, 304–54. Philadelphia: Temple University Press, 2002.
Bennett, Jane. *Vibrant Matter: A Political Ecology of Things*. Durham, NC: Duke University Press, 2009.
Berg, Ulla D., and Ana Y. Ramos-Zayas. "Racializing Affect." *Current Anthropology* 56, no. 5 (2015): 654–77.
Berlant, Lauren. *Cruel Optimism*. Durham, NC: Duke University Press, 2011.
Berlant, Lauren. *The Female Complaint: The Unfinished Business of Sentimentality in American Culture*. Durham, NC: Duke University Press, 2008.
Berlant, Lauren. *The Queen of America Goes to Washington City*. Durham, NC: Duke University Press, 1997.
Berlant, Lauren. "Structures of Unfeeling: *Mysterious Skin*." *International Journal of Politics, Culture and Society* 28, no. 3 (2015): 191–213.
Bernstein, Robin. *Racial Innocence: Performing American Childhood from Slavery to Civil Rights*. New York: New York University Press, 2011.
Biggio, Rebecca Skidmore. "The Specter of Conspiracy in Martin Delany's *Blake*." *African American Review* 42, nos. 3–4 (2008): 439–54.
Birnbaum, Michele. "Racial Hysteria: Female Pathology and Race Politics in Frances Harper's *Iola Leroy* and W. D. Howells's An Imperative Duty." *African American Review* 33, no. 1 (1999): 7–23.
Bittel, Carla. "Woman, Know Thyself: Producing and Using Phrenological Knowledge in 19th-Century America." *Centaurus* 55, no. 2 (2013): 104–30.
Blackwell, Elizabeth. *Pioneer Work in Opening the Medical Profession to Women*. New York: Longmans, Green, and Co., 1895.
Bledstein, Burton J. *The Culture of Professionalism: The Middle Class and the Development of Higher Education in America*. New York: W. W. Norton, 1976.
Bloom, Paul. *Against Empathy: The Case for Rational Compassion*. New York: HarperCollins, 2016.

Boddice, Rob. *The Science of Sympathy: Morality, Evolution, and Victorian Civilization*. Urbana: University of Illinois Press, 2016.
Bond, Michael Harris. *Beyond the Chinese Face: Insights from Psychology*. Hong Kong: Oxford University Press, 1991.
Brennan, Teresa. *The Transmission of Affect*. Ithaca, NY: Cornell University Press, 2004.
Brinkema, Eugenie. *The Forms of the Affects*. Durham, NC: Duke University Press, 2014.
Brophy, Alfred L. "Harriet Beecher Stowe's Critique of Slave Law in *Uncle Tom's Cabin*." *Journal of Law and Religion* 21, no. 2 (1995): 457–506.
Brown, William Wells. *Clotel; or, The President's Daughter*. London: Partridge and Oakey, 1853.
Browner, Stephanie P. *Profound Science and Elegant Literature: Imagining Doctors in Nineteenth-Century America*. Philadelphia: University of Pennsylvania Press, 2005.
Byrd, Jodi A. *The Transit of Empire: Indigenous Critiques of Colonialism*. Minneapolis: University of Minnesota Press, 2011.
Byrd, Jodi A. "Weather with You: Settler Colonialism, Antiblackness, and the Grounded Relationalities of Resistance." *Journal of the Critical Ethnic Studies Association* 5, nos. 1–2 (2019): 207–14.
Campbell, Stanley W. *The Slave Catchers: Enforcement of the Fugitive Slave Law, 1850–1860*. Chapel Hill: University of North Carolina Press, 1970.
Carby, Hazel V. *Reconstructing Womanhood: The Emergence of the Afro-American Woman Novelist*. New York: Oxford University Press, 1987.
Carpenter, Cari M. *Seeing Red: Anger, Sentimentality, and American Indians*. Columbus: Ohio University Press, 2008.
Cathell, Daniel Webster. *Book on the Physician Himself and Things That Concern His Reputation and Success*. Philadelphia: F. A. Davis, 1889.
Chapman, Mary. Introduction to *Becoming Sui Sin Far: Early Fiction, Journalism, and Travel Writing by Edith Maude Eaton*, edited by Mary Chapman, xiii–lxxvi. Montreal: McGill-Queen's University Press, 2016.
Chapman, Mary. *Making Noise, Making News*. New York: Oxford University Press, 2014.
Chapman, Mary. "A 'Revolution in Ink': Sui Sin Far and Chinese Reform Discourse." *American Quarterly* 60, no. 4 (2008): 975–1001.
Chen, Mel Y. *Animacies: Biopolitics, Racial Mattering, and Queer Affect*. Durham, NC: Duke University Press, 2012.
Chen, Tina. *Double Agency: Acts of Impersonation in Asian American Literature and Culture*. Stanford, CA: Stanford University Press, 2005.
Cheng, Anne Anlin. *Ornamentalism*. New York: Oxford University Press, 2018.
Cheng, Anne Anlin. "Ornamentalism: A Feminist Theory for the Yellow Woman." *Critical Inquiry* 44 (2018): 415–46.
Cheyfitz, Eric. "What Is a Just Society? Native American Philosophies and the Limits of Capitalism's Imagination: A Brief Manifesto." *South Atlantic Quarterly* 110, no. 2 (2011): 291–307.

Chiles, Katy. "Within and without Raced Nations: Intratextuality, Martin Delany, and *Blake*; or the Huts of America." *American Literature* 80, no. 2 (2008): 323–52.
Chipps, Pakki. "Family First." *Native Studies Review* 15, no. 2 (2004): 103–5.
Cho, Yu-Fang. "Domesticating the Aliens Within: Sentimental Benevolence in Late-Nineteenth-Century California Magazines." *American Quarterly* 61, no. 1 (2009): 113–36.
Cho, Yu-Fang. "'Yellow Slavery,' Narratives of Rescue, and Sui Sin Far/Edith Maude Eaton's 'Lin John' (1899)." *Journal of Asian American Studies* 12, no. 1 (2009): 35–63.
Chow, Rey. "How (the) Inscrutable Chinese Led to Globalized Theory." *PMLA* 116, no. 1 (2001): 69–74.
Christian, Barbara. *Black Feminist Criticism: Perspectives on Black Women Writers*. New York: Teachers College Press, 1997.
Christian, Barbara. *Black Women Novelists: The Development of a Tradition, 1892–1976*. Westport, CT: Greenwood Press, 1980.
Chu, Patricia P. *Assimilating Asians: Gendered Strategies of Authorship in Asian America*. Durham, NC: Duke University Press, 2000.
Chuh, Kandice. *Imagine Otherwise: On Asian Americanist Critique*. Durham, NC: Duke University Press, 2003.
Chung, June Hee. "Asian Object Lessons: Orientalist Decoration in Realist Aesthetics from William Dean Howells to Sui Sin Far." *Studies in American Fiction* 36, no. 1 (2017): 27–50.
Clarke, Edward H. *Sex in Education: Or, a Fair Chance for the Girls*. New York: Arno, 1873.
Clymer, Jeffory. "Martin Delany's *Blake* and the Transnational Politics of Property." *American Literary History* 15, no. 4 (2003): 709–31.
Cobb, Jasmine Nicole. "'Forget Me Not': Free Black Women and Sentimentality." *MELUS* 40, no. 3 (2015): 28–46.
Cobb, Thomas R. R. *An Inquiry into the Law of Negro Slavery in the United States of America*. Philadelphia: T. & J. W. Johnson, 1858.
Cohen, Cathy J. "Punks, Bulldaggers, and Welfare Queens: The Radical Potential of Queer Politics?" *GLQ* 3, no. 4 (1997): 437–65.
Colbert, Charles. *A Measure of Perfection: Phrenology and the Fine Arts in America*. Chapel Hill: University of North Carolina Press, 1997.
Cole, Rebecca J. "The Eye and Its Appendages." MD thesis, Women's Medical College of Pennsylvania, 1867.
Cole, Rebecca J. "First Meeting of the Women's Missionary Society of Philadelphia." *Woman's Era* 3, no. 4 (1896): 4–5.
Collier-Thomas, Bettye. "Frances Ellen Watkins Harper: Abolitionist and Feminist Reformer 1825–1911." In *African American Women and the Vote, 1837–1965*, edited by Ann Dexter Gordon, Bettye Collier-Thomas, John H. Bracey, Arlene Voski Avakian, and Joyce Avrech Berkman, 41–65. Amherst: University of Massachusetts Press, 1997.
Collins, Patricia Hill. *Black Feminist Thought: Knowledge, Consciousness, and the Politics of Empowerment*. New York: Routledge, 1991.

Combe, George. *The Constitution of Man Considered in Relation to External Objects*. Edinburgh: John Anderson, 1828.

Combe, George. "Phrenological Remarks on the Relation between the Natural Talents and Dispositions of Nations, and the Developments of Their Brains." In *Crania Americana*, edited by Samuel George Morton, 269–91. Philadelphia: Dobson, 1839.

Connolly, William E. "I. The Complexity of Intention." *Critical Inquiry* 37, no. 4 (2011): 791–98.

Coolidge, Mary. *Chinese Immigration*. New York: Henry Holt and Company, 1909.

Cooper, Anna Julia. *A Voice from the South*. New York: Oxford University Press, 1892.

Cooper, Brittney C. *Beyond Respectability: The Intellectual Thought of Race Women*. Urbana: University of Illinois Press, 2017.

Cott, Nancy F. "Passionlessness: An Interpretation of Victorian Sexual Ideology, 1790–1850." In *A Heritage of Her Own: Toward a New Social History of American Women*, edited by Nancy F. Cott and Elizabeth H. Pleck, 162–81. New York: Simon and Schuster, 1979.

Coulter, Harris L. *Divided Legacy: The Conflict between Homeopathy and the American Medical Association*. Richmond, CA: North Atlantic Books, 1982.

Coulthard, Glen Sean. *Red Skin, White Masks: Rejecting the Colonial Politics of Recognition*. Minneapolis: University of Minnesota Press, 2014.

Cover, Robert. *Justice Accused: Antislavery and the Judicial Process*. New Haven, CT: Yale University Press, 1984.

Coviello, Peter. "The American in Charity: *Benito Cereno* and Gothic Anti-Sentimentality." *Studies in American Fiction* 30, no. 2 (2002): 155–80.

Crane, Gregg D. "The Lexicon of Rights, Power, and Community in *Blake*: Martin R. Delany's Dissent from Dred Scott." *American Literature* 68, no. 3 (1996): 527–53.

Crary, Jonathan. *Techniques of the Observer: On Vision and Modernity in the Nineteenth Century*. Cambridge, MA: MIT Press, 1990.

Crumpler, Rebecca Lee. *A Book of Medical Discourses*. Boston: Cashman, Keating, and Co. Printers, 1883.

Dain, Bruce R. *A Hideous Monster of the Mind: American Race Theory in the Early Republic*. Cambridge, MA: Harvard University Press, 2002.

Darwin, Charles. *The Expression of the Emotions in Man and Animals*. Chicago: University of Chicago Press, 1965.

da Silva, Denise Ferreira. "1 (Life) ÷ 0 (Blackness) = $\infty - \infty$ or ∞ / ∞: On Matter beyond the Equation of Value." *E-Flux* 79 (2017). http://www.e-flux.com/journal/79/94686/1-life-0-blackness-or-on-matter-beyond-the-equation-of-value/.

da Silva, Denise Ferreira. *Toward a Global Idea of Race*. Minneapolis: University of Minnesota Press, 2007.

Daston, Lorraine, and Peter Galison. *Objectivity*. New York: Zone Books, 2007.

Davies, John D., and James H. Young. *Phrenology, Fad and Science: A 19th-Century American Crusade*. New Haven, CT: Yale University Press, 1955.

Davis, Cynthia J. *Bodily and Narrative Forms: The Influence of Medicine on American Literature, 1845–1915*. Stanford, CA: Stanford University Press, 2000.

Davis, Rebecca Harding. "A Day with Doctor Sarah." In *A Rebecca Harding Davis Reader: 'Life in the Iron Mills,' Selected Fiction, and Essays*, edited by Jean Pfaelzer, 317-28. Pittsburgh: University of Pittsburgh Press, 1995.

Day, Iyko. *Alien Capital: Asian Racialization and the Logic of Settler Colonial Capitalism*. Durham, NC: Duke University Press, 2016.

Day, Iyko. "Being or Nothingness: Indigeneity, Antiblackness, and Settler Colonial Critique." *Critical Ethnic Studies* 1, no. 2 (2015): 102-21.

Delano, Amasa. *Narrative of Voyages and Travels, in the Northern and Southern Hemispheres: Comprising Three Voyages Round the World; Together with a Voyage of Survey and Discovery, in the Pacific Ocean and Oriental Islands*. New York: Praeger Publishers, 1970.

Delany, Martin R. "The Attraction of Planets." *Anglo-African Magazine*, January 1859, 17-20.

Delany, Martin R. *Blake; or the Huts of America*. Edited by Floyd J. Miller. Boston: Beacon, 1970.

Delany, Martin R. "Comets." *Anglo-African Magazine*, February 1859, 59-60.

Delany, Martin R. *The Condition, Elevation, Emigration, and Destiny of the Colored People of the United States*. New York: Arno, 1855.

Delany, Martin R. "Letter from M. R. Delany." *Frederick Douglass' Paper*, April 1, 1853.

Delany, Martin R. "Mrs. Stowe's Position." *Frederick Douglass' Paper*, April 18, 1853.

Delany, Martin R. *Principia of Ethnology*. Philadelphia: Harper and Brother, 1879.

Delany, Martin R. "Report on the Political Destiny of the Colored Race on the American Continent." In *Proceedings of the National Emigration Convention of Colored People*, 33-70. Cleveland, OH: A. A. Anderson, 1854.

Delany, Martin R. "Uncle Tom." *Frederick Douglass' Paper*, April 29, 1853.

Deleuze, Gilles, and Félix Guattari. *A Thousand Plateaus: Capitalism and Schizophrenia*. Translated by Brian Massumi. Minneapolis: University of Minnesota Press, 1987.

DeLombard, Jeannine Marie. "Salvaging Legal Personhood: Melville's *Benito Cereno*." *American Literature* 81, no. 1 (2009): 35-64.

Diana, Vanessa Holford. "Biracial/Bicultural Identity in the Writings of Sui Sin Far." *MELUS* 26, no. 2 (2001): 159-86.

DiAngelo, Robin. "White Fragility." *International Journal of Critical Pedagogy* 3, no. 3 (2011): 54-70.

Dong, Lorraine, and Marlon K. Hom. "Defiance of Perpetuation: An Analysis of Characters in *Mrs. Spring Fragrance*." *Chinese America: History and Perspectives* 1 (1987): 139-69.

Donovan, Josephine. "Nan and the Golden Apples." *Colby Library Quarterly* 22, no. 1 (1986): 17-27.

Doolan, Andy. "Be Cautious of the Word 'Rebel': Race, Revolution, and Transnational History in Martin Delany's *Blake; or, The Huts of America*." *American Literature* 81, no. 1 (March 2009): 153-79.

Douglas, Ann. *The Feminization of American Culture*. New York: Doubleday, 1977.

Douglass, Frederick. "A Day and a Night in *Uncle Tom's Cabin*." *Frederick Douglass' Paper*, March 4, 1853.

Douglass, Frederick. "Remarks." *Frederick Douglass' Paper*, April 1, 1853.

Downes, Paul. "Melville's *Benito Cereno* and the Politics of Humanitarian Intervention." *South Atlantic Quarterly* 103, nos. 2-3 (2004): 465-88.

Du Bois, W. E. B. *Dark Princess: A Romance*. New York: Oxford University Press, 2007.

Du Bois, W. E. B. *The Philadelphia Negro*. Philadelphia: University of Pennsylvania, 1899.

Du Bois, W. E. B. *The Souls of Black Folk*. New Haven, CT: Yale University Press, 2015.

duCille, Ann. *The Coupling Convention: Sex, Text, and Tradition in Black Women's Fiction*. New York: Oxford University Press, 1993.

Dudden, Faye E. *Fighting Chance: The Struggle over Woman Suffrage and Black Suffrage in Reconstruction America*. New York: Oxford University Press, 2011.

DuPlessis, Rachel Blau. *Writing beyond the Ending: Narrative Strategies of Twentieth-Century Women Writers*. Bloomington: Indiana University Press, 1985.

Edelman, Lee. *No Future: Queer Theory and the Death Drive*. Durham, NC: Duke University Press, 2004.

Edelman, Lee. "Occupy Wall Street: Bartleby against the Humanities." *History of the Present* 3, no. 1 (2013): 99-118.

Elder, Nancy C., and Andrew Schwarzer. "Fictional Women Physicians in the Nineteenth Century: The Struggle for Self-Identity." *Journal of Medical Humanities* 17, no. 3 (1996): 165-77.

Ellis, Havelock. *Studies in the Psychology of Sex: Analysis of the Sexual Impulse, Love and Pain, the Sexual Impulse in Women*. Vol. 3. Philadelphia: F. A. Davis, 1913.

Eng, David L. *The Feeling of Kinship: Queer Liberalism and the Racialization of Intimacy*. Durham, NC: Duke University Press, 2010.

Eng, David L. *Racial Castration: Managing Masculinity in Asian America*. Durham, NC: Duke University Press, 2001.

Ensor, Sarah. "Spinster Ecology: Rachel Carson, Sarah Orne Jewett, and Nonreproductive Futurity." *American Literature* 84, no. 2 (2012): 409-35.

Ernest, John. *Liberation Historiography: African American Writers and the Challenge of History, 1794-1861*. Chapel Hill: University of North Carolina Press, 2004.

Ernest, John. *Resistance and Reformation in Nineteenth-Century African-American Literature: Brown, Wilson, Jacobs, Delany, Douglass, and Harper*. Jackson: University Press of Mississippi, 1995.

Fabian, Ann. *The Skull Collectors: Race, Science, and America's Unburied Dead*. Chicago: University of Chicago Press, 2010.

Fanon, Frantz. *The Wretched of the Earth*. Translated by Richard Philcox. New York: Grove Press, 2004.

Far, Sui Sin. *Becoming Sui Sin Far: Early Fiction, Journalism, and Travel Writing by Edith Maude Eaton*. Edited by Mary Chapman. Montreal: McGill-Queen's University Press, 2016.

Far, Sui Sin. "The Chinese Spirit of Non-Resistance Will Disappear." *Boston Daily Globe*, February 7, 1915.

Far, Sui Sin. "The Chinese Woman in America." *Land of Sunshine*, no. 6 (January 1897): 59-64.

Far, Sui Sin. "Leaves from the Mental Portfolio of an Eurasian." *Independent* 66 (January 1909): 125–33.
Far, Sui Sin. *Mrs. Spring Fragrance*. Chicago: A. C. McClurg and Co., 1912.
Far, Sui Sin. *Mrs. Spring Fragrance*. Edited by Hsuan L. Hsu. Peterborough, ON: Broadview Press, 2011.
Far, Sui Sin. *Mrs. Spring Fragrance and Other Writings*. Edited by Amy Ling and Annette White-Parks. Urbana: University of Illinois Press, 1995.
Far, Sui Sin. "The Typewriter." *National Stenographer* 2, no. 1 (1891): 215.
Far, Sui Sin, and Edith Eaton. "Word from Miss Eaton." *Westerner* 11, no. 5 (1909): 1.
Ferens, Dominika. *Edith and Winnifred Eaton: Chinatown Missions and Japanese Romances*. Urbana: University of Illinois Press, 2002.
Fetterley, Judith, and Marjorie Pryse. *Writing out of Place: Regionalism, Women, and American Literary Culture*. Urbana: University of Illinois Press, 2003.
Fielder, Brigitte. *Relative Races: Genealogies of Interracial Kinship in Nineteenth-Century America*. Durham, NC: Duke University Press, 2020.
Fine, Eve. "Women Physicians and Medical Sects in Nineteenth-Century Chicago." In *Women Physicians and the Cultures of Medicine*, edited by Ellen Singer More, Elizabeth Fee, and Manon Parry, 245–73. Baltimore, MD: Johns Hopkins University Press, 2009.
Fitzhugh, George. *Sociology for the South, or the Failure of Free Society*. Richmond, VA: A. Morris, 1854.
Fleissner, Jennifer. *Woman, Compulsion, Modernity: The Moment of American Naturalism*. Chicago: University of Chicago Press, 2004.
Forbes, Jack D. *Africans and Native Americans: The Language of Race and the Evolution of Red-Black Peoples*. 2nd ed. Urbana: University of Illinois Press, 1993.
Foreman, P. Gabrielle. *Activist Sentiments: Reading Black Women in the Nineteenth Century*. Urbana: University of Illinois Press, 2009.
Foreman, P. Gabrielle. "'Reading Aright': White Slavery, Black Referents, and the Strategy of Histotextuality in *Iola Leroy*." *Yale Journal of Criticism* 10, no. 2 (October 1, 1997): 327–54.
Foreman, P. Gabrielle. "Who's Your Mama? 'White' Mulatta Genealogies, Early Photography, and Anti-Passing Narratives of Slavery and Freedom." *American Literary History* 14, no. 3 (2002): 505–39.
Foster, Frances Smith. *Written by Herself: Literary Production by African American Women, 1746–1892*. Bloomington: Indiana University Press, 1993
Foucault, Michel. *The Birth of the Clinic: An Archaeology of Medical Perception*. Translated by A. M. Sheridan Smith. New York: Vintage Books, 1994.
Foucault, Michel. *Discipline and Punish: The Birth of the Prison*. Translated by Alan Sheridan. New York: Vintage Books, 1995.
Foucault, Michel. *The History of Sexuality: Volume 1*. Translated by Robert Hurley. New York: Vintage Books, 1990.
Fowler, Orson Squire. "Analysis, Adaptation, Location, and the Cultivation of Individuality." *American Phrenological Journal* 8, no. 11 (1846): 327–34.
Fowler, Orson Squire. *Fowler's Practical Phrenology; Giving a Concise Elementary View of Phrenology*. 2nd ed. New York: O. S. and L. N. Fowler, 1845.

Fowler, Orson Squire. *Hereditary Descent: Its Laws and Facts Applied to Human Improvement*. New York: Fowlers and Wells, 1847.
Frazer, Michael L. *The Enlightenment of Sympathy*. New York: Oxford University Press, 2010.
Fredrickson, George M. *The Black Image in the White Mind: The Debate on Afro-American Character and Destiny, 1817-1914*. New York: Harper and Row, 1971.
Freeburg, Christopher. *Melville and the Idea of Blackness: Race and Imperialism in Nineteenth-Century America*. New York: Cambridge University Press, 2012.
Fretwell, Erica. *Sensory Experiments: Psychophysics, Race, and the Aesthetics of Feeling*. Durham, NC: Duke University Press, 2020.
Fugitive Slave Act of 1850. 31st United States Congress, September 18, 1850. Yale Law School, Lillian Goldman Law Library. https://avalon.law.yale.edu/19th_century/fugitive.asp.
Furst, Lilian R. *Between Doctors and Patients: The Changing Balance of Power*. Charlottesville: University Press of Virginia, 1998.
Furst, Lilian R. *Women Healers and Physicians: Climbing a Long Hill*. Lexington: University Press of Kentucky, 1997.
Garcia-Rojas, Claudia. "(Un)Disciplined Futures: Women of Color Feminism as a Disruptive to White Affect Studies." *Journal of Lesbian Studies* 21, no. 3 (2017): 254-71.
Gardner, Jared. *Master Plots: Race and the Founding of an American Literature, 1787-1845*. Baltimore, MD: Johns Hopkins University Press, 1998.
Gates, Henry Louis, and Evelyn Brooks Higginbotham. *African American Lives*. New York: Oxford University Press, 2004.
Gilroy, Paul. *The Black Atlantic: Modernity and Double Consciousness*. Cambridge, MA: Harvard University Press, 1993.
Glissant, Édouard. *Poetics of Relation*. Translated by Betsy Wing. Ann Arbor: University of Michigan Press, 1997.
Goffe, Tao Leigh. "Sugarwork: The Gastropoetics of Afro-Asia after the Plantation." *Asian Diasporic Visual Cultures and the Americas* 5, nos. 1-2 (2019): 31-56.
Goffman, Erving. "On Face-Work: An Analysis of Ritual Elements in Social Interaction." *Psychiatry* 18, no. 3 (1955): 213-31.
Gould, Stephen Jay. *The Mismeasure of Man*. New York: W. W. Norton, 1981.
Greyser, Naomi. *On Sympathetic Grounds: Race, Gender, and Affective Geographies in Nineteenth-Century North America*. New York: Oxford University Press, 2017.
Griffin, Farah Jasmine. "Frances Ellen Watkins Harper in the Reconstruction South." Supplement, *Sage* 5 (1988): 45-47.
Gunew, Sneja. "Subaltern Empathy: Beyond European Categories in Affect Theory." *Concentric* 35, no. 1 (2009): 11-30.
Habegger, Alfred. "Nineteenth-Century American Humor: Easygoing Males, Anxious Ladies, and Penelope Lapham." *PMLA* 91, no. 5 (1976): 884-99.
Haddad, John. *The Romance of China: Excursions to China in U.S. Culture, 1776-1876*. New York: Columbia University Press, 2008.
Halberstam, J. "The Politics of Negativity in Recent Queer Theory." *PMLA* 121, no. 3 (2006): 823-25.

Haller, John S. *Outcasts from Evolution: Scientific Attitudes of Racial Inferiority, 1859–1900*. Urbana: University of Illinois Press, 1971.
Haller, John S., and Robin M. Haller. *The Physician and Sexuality in Victorian America*. Urbana: University of Illinois Press, 1974.
Halpern, Faye. "Beyond Contempt: Ways to Read *Uncle Tom's Cabin*." PMLA 133, no. 3 (2018): 633–39.
Hammonds, Evelyn M. "Toward a Genealogy of Black Female Sexuality: The Problematic of Silence." In *Feminist Genealogies, Colonial Legacies, Democratic Futures*, edited by M. Jacqui Alexander and Chandra Talpade Mohanty, 170–82. London: Routledge, 1997.
Hansberry, Lorraine. *A Raisin in the Sun*. New York: Vintage, 2004.
Haraway, Donna. "Situated Knowledges: The Science Question in Feminism and the Privilege of Partial Perspective." *Feminist Studies* 14, no. 3 (1988): 575–99.
Harding, Sandra. *The Science Question in Feminism*. Ithaca, NY: Cornell University Press, 1986.
Harding, Sandra. *Whose Science? Whose Knowledge? Thinking from Women's Lives*. Ithaca, NY: Cornell University Press, 1991.
Harper, Frances Ellen Watkins. "Enlightened Motherhood: An Address." *Brooklyn Literary Society*, November 15, 1892. https://lccn.loc.gov/91898488.
Harper, Frances Ellen Watkins. *Iola Leroy; or, Shadows Uplifted*. Edited by Koritha Mitchell. Peterborough, ON: Broadview Press, 2018.
Harte, Bret. *That Heathen Chinee, and Other Poems Mostly Humorous*. London: John Camden Hotten, 1871.
Harte, Walter Blackburn. "Bubble and Squeak." *Lotus*, October 1896, 216–17.
Hartley, Lucy. *Physiognomy and the Meaning of Expression in Nineteenth-Century Culture*. New York: Cambridge University Press, 2005.
Hartman, Saidiya V. "The Belly of the World: A Note on Black Women's Labors." *Souls* 18, no. 1 (2016): 166–73.
Hartman, Saidiya V. *Lose Your Mother: A Journey along the Atlantic Slave Route*. New York: Farrar, Straus and Giroux, 2007.
Hartman, Saidiya V. *Scenes of Subjection: Terror, Slavery, and Self-Making in Nineteenth-Century America*. New York: Oxford University Press, 1997.
Hartman, Saidiya V. "Venus in Two Acts." *Small Axe* 26, no. 26 (2008): 1–14.
Hartman, Saidiya V., and Frank B. Wilderson III. "The Position of the Unthought." *Qui parle* 13, no. 2 (2003): 183–201.
Hayot, Eric. "Chinese Bodies, Chinese Futures." *Representations* 99, no. 1 (2007): 99–129.
Hemmings, Clare. "Invoking Affect: Cultural Theory and the Ontological Turn." *Cultural Studies* 19, no. 5 (2005): 548–67.
Hendler, Glenn. *Public Sentiments: Structures of Feeling in Nineteenth-Century American Literature*. Chapel Hill: University of North Carolina Press, 2001.
Herndl, Diane Price. "The Invisible (Invalid) Women: African-American Women, Illness, and Nineteenth-Century Narrative." *Women's Studies* 24, no. 6 (1995): 553–72.
Hine, Darlene Clark. *Black Women in White: Racial Conflict and Cooperation in the Nursing Profession, 1890–1950*. Bloomington: Indiana University Press, 1989.

Hine, Darlene Clark. "Co-Laborers in the Work of the Lord: Nineteenth-Century Black Women Physicians." In Abram, *"Send Us a Lady Physician,"* 107–20.

Hine, Darlene Clark. "Physicians." In *Black Women in America*, edited by Darlene Clark Hine. New York: Oxford University Press, 2005.

Hine, Darlene Clark. "Rape and the Inner Lives of Black Women in the Middle West: Preliminary Thoughts on the Culture of Dissemblance." *Signs* 14, no. 4 (1989): 912–20.

Hine, Darlene Clark. "'They Shall Mount Up with Wings as Eagles': Historical Images of Black Nurses, 1890–1950." In *Women and Health in America*, edited by Judith Walzer Leavitt, 475–88. 2nd ed. Madison: University of Wisconsin Press, 1999.

Hirata, Lucie Cheng. "Free, Indentured, Enslaved: Chinese Prostitutes in Nineteenth-Century America." *Signs* 5, no. 11 (1979): 123–49.

Ho, David Yau-fai. "On the Concept of Face." *American Journal of Sociology* 81, no. 4 (1976): 867–84.

Hochschild, Arlie Russell. *The Managed Heart: Commercialization of Human Emotion.* Berkeley: University of California Press, 1979.

Hofer, Johannes. "Medical Dissertation on Nostalgia." Translated by Carolyn Kisre Anspach. *Bulletin of the Institute of the History of Medicine* 2 (January 1, 1934): 376–91.

Holland, Sharon P. "'If You Know I Have a History, You Will Respect Me': A Perspective on Afro-Native American Literature." *Callaloo* 17, no. 1 (1994): 334–50.

Horwitz, Morton J. *The Transformation of American Law, 1780–1860.* Cambridge, MA: Harvard University Press, 1977.

Howard, June. "Sui Sin Far's American Words." *Comparative American Studies* 6, no. 2 (2008): 144–60.

Howe, Julia Ward, ed. *Sex in Education: A Reply to Dr. E. H. Clarke's "Sex in Education."* Boston: Roberts Brothers, 1874.

Howells, William Dean. *Dr. Breen's Practice.* Boston: Houghton Mifflin, 1881.

Hsu, Hsuan L. *Geography and the Production of Space in Nineteenth-Century American Literature.* Cambridge: Cambridge University Press, 2010.

Hu, Hsien Chin. "The Chinese Concept of Face." *American Anthropologist* 46 (1944): 45–64.

Huang, Vivian L. "Inscrutably, Actually: Hospitality, Parasitism, and the Silent Work of Yoko Ono and Laurel Nakadate." *Women and Performance* 28, no. 3 (2018): 187–203.

Hull, Gloria T., and Barbara Smith. "Introduction: The Politics of Black Women's Studies." In *All the Women Are White, All the Blacks Are Men, but Some of Us Are Brave: Black Women's Studies*, edited by Gloria T. Hull, Patricia Bell Scott, and Barbara Smith, xvii–xxxii. Old Westbury, NY: Feminist Press, 1982.

Hutcheon, Linda. "Irony, Nostalgia, and the Postmodern." *Methods for the Study of Literature as Cultural Memory*, edited by Raymond Vervliet and Annemarie Estor, 189–207. Amsterdam: Rodopi, 2000.

"Is Man One or Many?" *Putnam's Monthly Magazine of American Literature, Science, and Art*, 4, no. 19 (July 1854): 9.

Jackson, Zakiyyah Iman. *Becoming Human: Matter and Meaning in an AntiBlack World*. New York: New York University Press, 2020.
Jacobi, Mary Putnam. *"Common Sense" Applied to Woman Suffrage*. New York: Putnam, 1894.
Jacobi, Mary Putnam. *Mary Putnam Jacobi: A Pathfinder in Medicine, with Selections from Her Writings and a Complete Bibliography*. Edited by the Women's Medical Association of New York. New York: Putnam, 1925.
Jacobi, Mary Putnam. *The Question of Rest for Women during Menstruation*. New York: G. P. Putnam's Sons, 1877.
Jacobi, Mary Putnam. "Woman in Medicine." In *Women's Work in America*, edited by Annie Nathan Meyer, 139–205. New York: H. Holt and Co., 1891.
Jacobs, Harriet. *Incidents in the Life of a Slave Girl*. Edited by Nellie Y. McKay and Frances Smith Foster. New York: W. W. Norton, 2001.
Jagger, Alison M. "Love and Knowledge: Emotion in Feminist Epistemology." *Inquiry* 32, no. 2 (1989): 151–76.
James, C. L. R. *Mariners, Renegades and Castaways: The Story of Herman Melville and the World We Live In*. Hanover, NH: Dartmouth College Press, 1953.
James, Henry. *The Bostonians*. New York: Oxford University Press, 2009.
James, Sherman A. "John Henryism and the Health of African Americans." *Culture, Medicine and Psychiatry* 18 (1994): 163–82.
James, William. "What Is an Emotion?" *Mind* 9, no. 34 (1884): 188–205.
Jameson, Fredric. *Postmodernism, or, The Cultural Logic of Late Capitalism*. Durham, NC: Duke University Press, 1991.
Jefferson, Thomas. *Notes on the State of Virginia*. Edited by Frank Shuffleton. New York: Penguin Books, 1999.
Jeltz, Wyatt F. "The Relations of Negroes and Choctaw and Chickasaw Indians." *Journal of Negro History* 33, no. 1 (1948): 24–37.
Jessee, Margaret Jay. "'The Third Sex': Nineteenth-Century Doctresses in Liminal Literary Spaces." In *Liminality, Hybridity, and American Women's Literature*, edited by Kristin J. Jacobson, 165–81. London: Palgrave Macmillan, 2018.
Jewett, Sarah Orne. *A Country Doctor*. Boston: Houghton Mifflin, 1884.
Jex-Blake, Sophia. "Medical Women in Fiction." *Nineteenth Century* 33 (February 1893): 261–72.
Jirousek, Lori. "Spectacle Ethnography and Immigrant Resistance: Sui Sin Far and Anzia Yezierska." *MELUS* 27, no. 1 (2002): 25–52.
Jordan, Winthrop D. *White over Black: American Attitudes toward the Negro, 1550–1812*. Chapel Hill: University of North Carolina Press, 1968.
Jouve Martín, José Ramón. *The Black Doctors of Colonial Lima: Science, Race, and Writing in Colonial and Early Republican Peru*. Montreal: McGill-Queen's University Press, 2014.
Kammen, Michael. *Mystic Chords of Memory: The Transformation of Tradition in American Culture*. New York: Vintage Books, 1991.
Kammerer, Elise. "Activism behind the Veil of Sentimentality: The Amy Matilda Cassey Friendship Album." *Critical Studies* 2 (2016): 112–21.

Karcher, Carolyn. *Shadow over the Promised Land: Slavery, Race, and Violence in Melville's America*. Baton Rouge: Louisiana State University Press, 1980.

Katz, William Loren. *Black Indians: A Hidden Heritage*. New York: Atheneum, 1986.

Kavanagh, James H. "'That Hive of Subtlety': *Benito Cereno* as Critique of Ideology." *Bucknell Review* 28, no. 1 (1984): 127-57.

Kelley, Mary. "'Talents Committed to Your Care': Reading and Writing Radical Abolitionism in Antebellum America." *New England Quarterly* 88, no. 1 (2015): 37-72.

Kelley, Robin D. G. "The Rest of Us: Rethinking Settler and Native." *American Quarterly* 69, no. 2 (2017): 267-76.

Kelly, Lori Duin. *The Life and Works of Elizabeth Stuart Phelps, Victorian Feminist Writer*. Troy, NY: Whitston, 1983.

Kessler, Carol Farley. *Elizabeth Stuart Phelps*. Boston: Twayne, 1982.

King, Tiffany Lethabo. *The Black Shoals: Offshore Formations of Black and Native Studies*. Durham, NC: Duke University Press, 2019.

Ko, Dorothy. "Bondage in Time: Footbinding and Fashion Theory." *Fashion Theory* 1, no. 1 (1997): 3-28.

Ko, Dorothy. *Cinderella's Sisters: A Revisionist History of Footbinding*. Berkeley: University of California Press, 2007.

Ko, Dorothy. "Footbinding in the Museum." *Interventions* 5, no. 3 (2003): 426-39.

Kole de Peralta, Kathleen. "Mal Olor and Colonial Latin American History: Smellscapes in Lima, Peru, 1535-1614." *Hispanic American Historical Review* 99, no. 1 (2019): 1-30.

Krafft-Ebing, Richard von. *Psychopathia Sexualis*. Translated by Charles Gilbert Chaddock. 7th ed. Philadelphia: The F.A. Davis Company, 1894.

Krauthamer, Barbara. *Black Slaves, Indian Masters: Slavery, Emancipation, and Citizenship in the Native American South*. Chapel Hill: University of North Carolina Press, 2015.

Krauthamer, Barbara. "In Their 'Native Country': Freedpeople's Understandings of Culture and Citizenship in the Choctaw and Chickasaw Nations." In *Crossing Waters, Crossing Worlds: The African Diaspora in Indian Country*, edited by Tiya Miles and Sharon P. Holland, 100-120. Durham, NC: Duke University Press, 2006.

Landers, Jane. "Founding Mothers: Female Rebels in Colonial New Granada and Spanish Florida." *Journal of African American History* 98, no. 1 (2013): 7-23.

Larson, Magali Sarfatti. *The Rise of Professionalism: A Sociological Analysis*. Berkeley: University of California Press, 1977.

Lau, Estelle T. *Paper Families: Identity, Immigration Administration, and Chinese Exclusion*. Durham, NC: Duke University Press, 2006.

Lavater, Johann Kasper. *Essays on Physiognomy*. Translated by Thomas Holcroft. London: G. G. J. and J. Robinson, 1789.

Lawrence, William. *Lectures on Physiology, Zoology, and the Natural History of Man, Delivered at the Royal College of Surgeons*. 3rd ed. London: Benbow, 1823. https://archive.org/details/lecturesonphysiooolawrrich.

Lawrence, William. *A Treatise on the Venereal Diseases of the Eye*. London: John Wilson, 1830.

Lee, Rachel C. *The Exquisite Corpse of Asian America: Biopolitics, Biosociality, and Posthuman Ecologies*. New York: New York University Press, 2014.

Lee, Rachel C. "Journalistic Representations of Asian Americans and Literary Responses." In *An Interethnic Companion to Asian American Literature*, edited by King-Kok Cheung, 249–73. New York: Cambridge University Press, 1997.

Lee, Summer Kim. "Staying In: Mitski, Ocean Vuong, and Asian American Asociality." *Social Text* 37, no. 1 (2019): 27–50.

Lee, Wendy Anne. "The Scandal of Insensibility; or, the Bartleby Problem." *PMLA* 130, no. 5 (2015): 1405–19.

Leroy, Justin. "Black History in Occupied Territory: On the Entanglements of Slavery and Settler Colonialism." *Theory and Event* 19, no. 4 (2016). https://muse.jhu.edu/article/633276.

Levinas, Emmanuel. *Ethics and Infinity: Conversations with Phillipe Nemo*. Translated by Richard A. Cohen. Pittsburgh: Duquesne University Press, 1985.

Levine, Robert. *Martin Delany, Frederick Douglass, and the Politics of Representative Identity*. Chapel Hill: University of North Carolina Press, 1997.

Levy, Leonard W. *The Law of the Commonwealth and Chief Justice Shaw*. Cambridge, MA: Harvard University Press, 1957.

Lewis, Robert Benjamin. *Light and Truth*. Boston: Benjamin F. Roberts, 1844.

Leys, Ruth. "The Turn to Affect: A Critique." *Critical Inquiry* 37, no. 3 (2011): 434–72.

Lin Yutang. *My Country and My People*. New York: John Day, 1935.

Ling, Amy. *Between Worlds: Women Writers of Chinese Ancestry*. New York: Pergamon, 1989.

Ling, Amy, and Annette White-Parks, eds. *Mrs. Spring Fragrance and Other Writings*. Urbana: University of Illinois Press, 1995.

Lipsitz, George. "The Culture of War." *Critical Survey* 18, no. 3 (2006): 83–91.

Liu, Lydia H. "The Ghost of Arthur H. Smith in the Mirror of Cultural Translation." *Journal of American-East Asian Relations* 20, no. 4 (2013): 406–14.

López, Kathleen. *Chinese Cubans: A Transnational History*. Chapel Hill: University of North Carolina Press, 2013.

Lorde, Audre. *Sister Outsider: Essays and Speeches*. Berkeley, CA: Crossing Press, 1984.

Lowe, Lisa. *Immigrant Acts: On Asian American Cultural Politics*. Durham, NC: Duke University Press, 1996.

Lowe, Lisa. *The Intimacies of Four Continents*. Durham, NC: Duke University Press, 2015.

Lu Xun. *Selected Works*. Translated by Yang Xianyi and Gladys Yang. Vol. 4. Beijing: Foreign Languages Press, 1956.

Luciano, Dana. *Arranging Grief: Sacred Time and the Body in Nineteenth-Century America*. New York: New York University Press, 2007.

Luibhéid, Eithne. *Entry Denied: Controlling Sexuality at the Border*. Minneapolis: University of Minnesota Press, 2002.

Lye, Colleen. *America's Asia: Racial Form and American Literature, 1893–1945*. Princeton, NJ: Princeton University Press, 2005.

Manalansan, Martin F., IV. "Servicing the World: Flexible Filipinos and the Unsecured Life." In *Political Emotions*, edited by Janet Staiger, Ann Cvetkovich, and Ann Morris Reynolds, 215–28. New York: Routledge, 2010.

Marrant, John. *A Narrative of the Lord's Wonderful Dealings with John Marrant, a Black*. London: Gilbert and Plummer, 1785.

Martin, Nina, and Renee Montagne. "Black Mothers Keep Dying after Giving Birth. Shalon Irving's Story Explains Why." *All Things Considered*, December 7, 2017. https://www.npr.org/2017/12/07/568948782/black-mothers-keep-dying-after-giving-birth-shalon-irvings-story-explains-why.

Massumi, Brian. *Parables for the Virtual: Movement, Affect, Sensation*. Durham, NC: Duke University Press, 2002.

Masteller, Jean Carwile. "The Women Doctors of Howards, Phelps, and Jewett: The Conflict of Marriage and Career." In *Critical Essays on Sarah Orne Jewett*, edited by Gwen L. Nagel, 135–47. Boston: G. K. Hall, 1984.

McCann, Sean. "Structures of Feeling." *American Literary History* 27, no. 2 (2015): 321–30.

McCullough, Kate. *Regions of Identity: The Construction of America in Women's Fiction, 1885–1914*. Stanford, CA: Stanford University Press, 1999.

McKittrick, Katherine. *Dear Science and Other Stories*. Durham, NC: Duke University Press, 2021.

McKittrick, Katherine. *Demonic Grounds: Black Women and Cartographies of Struggle*. Minneapolis: University of Minnesota Press, 2006.

McKittrick, Katherine, ed. *Sylvia Wynter: On Being Human as Praxis*. Durham, NC: Duke University Press, 2015.

Melville, Herman. *Billy Budd, Bartleby, and Other Stories*. Edited by Peter Coviello. New York: Penguin Books, 2016.

Melville, Herman. *Correspondence*. Edited by Lynn North. Evanston, IL: Northwestern University Press, 1993.

Melville, Herman. *Journals*. Edited by Howard C. Horsford and Lynn Horth. Evanston, IL: Northwestern University Press, 1989.

Melville, Herman. *Melville's Short Novels*. Edited by Dan McCall. New York: W. W. Norton, 2002.

Melville, Herman. *Typee: A Peep at Polynesian Life*. London: John Murray, 1847.

Melville, Herman. *White-Jacket*. Evanston, IL: Northwestern University Press, 1970.

Merish, Lori. *Sentimental Materialism: Gender, Commodity Culture, and Nineteenth-Century American Literature*. Durham, NC: Duke University Press, 2000.

Meyer, Annie Nathan. "Editor's Preface." In *Woman's Work in America*, edited by Annie Nathan Meyer, iii–vi. New York: Henry Holt, 1891.

Meyer, Annie Nathan. *Helen Brent, M.D.: A Social Study*. New York: Cassell, 1892.

Meyer, Annie Nathan. "Woman's Assumption of Sex Superiority." *North American Review* 178, no. 566 (1904): 103–9.

Micklem, Niel. *The Nature of Hysteria*. New York: Routledge, 1996.

Middleton, Stephen. *The Black Laws: Race and the Legal Process in Early Ohio.* Athens: Ohio University Press, 2006.

Miles, Tiya, "'His Kingdom for a Kiss': Indians and Intimacy in the *Narrative of John Marrant.*" In *Haunted by Empire: Geographies of Intimacy in North American History*, edited by Ann Laura Stoler, 163–88. Durham, NC: Duke University Press, 2006.

Miles, Tiya, and Sharon P. Holland, eds. *Crossing Waters, Crossing Worlds: The African Diaspora in Indian Country.* Durham, NC: Duke University Press, 2006.

Miller, John F. "Chinese Immigration." Cong. Rec. S1470–1504 (February 28, 1882).

Miller, Stuart C. *The Unwelcome Immigrant: The American Image of the Chinese, 1785–1882.* Berkeley, CA: University of California Press, 1969.

Million, Dian. "Felt Theory: An Indigenous Feminist Approach to Affect and History." *Wicazo Sa Review* 24, no. 2 (2009): 53–76.

Mitchell, Koritha. "Introduction." In *Iola Leroy; or, Shadows Uplifted*, edited by Koritha Mitchell, 13–50. Peterborough, ON: Broadview Press, 2018.

Mitchell, Koritha. "No More Shame! Defeating the New Jim Crow with Antilynching Activism's Best Tools." *American Quarterly* 66, no. 1 (2014): 143–52.

Mitchell, Koritha. "Teaching & the N-Word: Questions to Consider." March 23, 2018. http://www.korithamitchell.com/teaching-and-the-n-word/.

Moraga, Cherríe. "La Jornada." In *This Bridge Called My Back: Writings by Radical Women of Color*, edited by Cherríe Moraga and Gloria Anzaldúa, xxxv–xli. 4th ed. Albany: State University of New York Press, 1981.

Morantz-Sanchez, Regina Markell. "The 'Connecting Link': The Case for the Woman Doctor in 19th-Century America." In *Sickness and Health in America: Readings in the History of Medicine and Public Health*, edited by Judith Walzer Leavitt and Ronald L. Numbers, 117–28. Madison: University of Wisconsin Press, 1978.

Morantz-Sanchez, Regina Markell. "The Female Student Has Arrived: The Rise of the Women's Medical Movement." In Abram, *"Send Us a Lady Physician,"* 59–67.

Morantz-Sanchez, Regina Markell. *Sympathy and Science: Women Physicians in American Medicine.* New York: Oxford University Press, 1985.

More, Ellen Singer. *Restoring the Balance: Women Physicians and the Profession of Medicine, 1850–1995.* Cambridge, MA: Harvard University Press, 1999.

Morgensen, Scott Lauria. "Settler Homonationalism." *GLQ* 16, nos. 1–2 (2010): 105–31.

Morris, Timothy. "Professional Ethics and Professional Erotics in Elizabeth Stuart Phelps's *Doctor Zay.*" *Studies in American Fiction* 21, no. 2 (1993): 141–52.

Morton, Samuel George. *Crania Americana.* Philadelphia: Dobson, 1839.

Moten, Fred. *In the Break: The Aesthetics of the Black Radical Tradition.* Minneapolis: University of Minnesota Press, 2003.

Moten, Fred, and Stefano Harney. *The Undercommons: Fugitive Planning and Black Study.* Brooklyn: Autonomedia, 2013.

Moy, James S. *Marginal Sights: Staging the Chinese in America.* Iowa City: University of Iowa Press, 1994.

"Mrs. Spring Fragrance." *American Antiquarian and Oriental Journal* 35 (July–September 1913): 181–82.

Muñoz, José Esteban. *Cruising Utopia: The Then and There of Queer Futurity*. New York: New York University Press, 2009.

Muñoz, José Esteban. *Disidentifications: Queers of Color and the Performance of Politics*. Minneapolis: University of Minnesota Press, 1999.

Muñoz, José Esteban. "Ephemera as Evidence: Introductory Notes to Queer Acts." *Women and Performance* 8, no. 2 (1996): 5–16.

Muñoz, José Esteban. "Feeling Brown, Feeling Down: Latina Affect, the Performativity of Race, and the Depressive Position." *Signs* 31, no. 3 (2006): 675–88.

Muñoz, José Esteban. *The Sense of Brown*. Edited by Joshua Chambers-Letson and Tavia Nyong'o. Durham, NC: Duke University Press, 2020.

Muñoz, José Esteban. "Thinking beyond Antirelationality and Antiutopianism in Queer Critique." *PMLA* 121, no. 3 (2006): 825–26.

Naylor-Ojronge, Celia E. "'Born and Raised among These People, I Don't Want to Know Any Other': Slaves' Acculturation in Nineteenth-Century Indian Territory." In *Confounding the Color Line: The Indian-Black Experience in North America*, edited by James F. Brooks, 161–91. Lincoln: University of Nebraska Press, 2002.

Nelson, Dana D. *National Manhood: Capitalist Citizenship and the Imagined Fraternity of White Men*. Durham, NC: Duke University Press, 1998.

"A New Note in Fiction: Mrs. Spring Fragrance." *New York Times*, July 7, 1912.

Ngai, Sianne. *Ugly Feelings*. Cambridge, MA: Harvard University Press, 2005.

Nguyen, Mimi Thi. *The Gift of Freedom: War, Debt, and Other Refugee Passages*. Durham, NC: Duke University Press, 2012.

Nott, Josiah Clark, and George Robins Gliddon. *Types of Mankind*. Philadelphia: J.B. Lippincott, 1854.

Numbers, Ronald L. *Darwinism Comes to America*. Cambridge, MA: Harvard University Press, 1998.

Nye, Robert A. "The Legacy of Masculine Codes of Honor and the Admission of Women to the Medical Profession in the Nineteenth Century." In *Women Physicians and the Cultures of Medicine*, edited by Ellen Singer More, Elizabeth Fee, and Manon Parry, 141–59. Baltimore, MD: Johns Hopkins University Press, 2009.

Ogunleye, Toalagbe. "Dr. Martin Robinson Delany, 19th-Century Africana Womanist: Reflections on His Avant-Garde Politics Concerning Gender, Colorism, and Nation Building." *Journal of Black Studies* 28, no. 5 (1998): 628–49.

Ong, Aihwa. *Flexible Citizenship: The Cultural Logics of Transnationality*. Durham, NC: Duke University Press, 1998.

Ong, Aihwa. "On the Edge of Empires: Flexible Citizenship among Chinese in Diaspora." *Positions* 1, no. 3 (1993): 745–78.

Otter, Samuel. *Melville's Anatomies*. Berkeley: University of California Press, 1999.

Owens, Deirdre Cooper. *Medical Bondage: Race, Gender, and the Origins of American Gynecology*. Athens: University of Georgia Press, 2017.

Pahl, Dennis. "The Gaze of History in *Benito Cereno*." *Studies in Short Fiction* 32, no.2 (1995): 171–83.

Painter, Nell Irvin. *Sojourner Truth: A Life, A Symbol.* New York: W. W. Norton, 1996.
Painter, Nell Irvin. "Voices of Suffrage: Sojourner Truth, Frances Watkins Harper, and the Struggle for Woman Suffrage." In *Votes for Women: The Struggle for Suffrage Revisited*, edited by Jean H. Baker, 42–55. New York: Oxford University Press, 2002.
Palmer, Tyrone S. "'What Feels More than Feeling?'" *Critical Ethnic Studies* 3, no. 2 (2017): 31–56.
Palumbo-Liu, David. *Asian/American: Historical Crossings of a Racial Frontier.* Stanford, CA: Stanford University Press, 1999.
Parker, Alison Marie. *Articulating Rights: Nineteenth-Century American Women on Race, Reform, and the State.* DeKalb: Northern Illinois University Press, 2010.
Parrish, Susan Scott. *American Curiosity: Cultures of Natural History in the Colonial British Atlantic World.* Chapel Hill: University of North Carolina Press, 2006.
Patterson, Martha H. *Beyond the Gibson Girl: Reimagining the American New Woman, 1895–1915.* Urbana: University of Illinois Press, 2005.
Pernick, Martin S. *A Calculus of Suffering: Pain, Professionalism, and Anesthesia in Nineteenth-Century America.* New York: Columbia University Press, 1985.
Peterson, Carla L. *"Doers of the Word": African-American Women Speakers and Writers in the North (1830–1880).* New York: Oxford University Press, 1995.
Peterson, Carla L. "Subject to Speculation: Assessing the Lives of African-American Women in the Nineteenth Century." In *Women's Studies in Transition: The Pursuit of Interdisciplinarity*, edited by Kate Conway-Turner, Suzanne Cherrin, and Jessica Schiffman, 109–17. Newark: University of Delaware Press, 1998.
Petty, Leslie. *Romancing the Vote: Feminist Activism in American Fiction, 1870–1920.* Athens: University of Georgia Press, 2006.
Phelps, Elizabeth Stuart. *Chapters from a Life.* Boston: Houghton Mifflin, 1897.
Phelps, Elizabeth Stuart. *Doctor Zay.* New York: Feminist Press, 1987.
Phelps, Elizabeth Stuart. "Sympathy as a Remedy." *Harper's Bazaar*, August 1909, 743–49.
Phelps, Elizabeth Stuart. Untitled item in *Sex and Education: A Reply to Dr. E. H. Clarke's "Sex in Education,"* edited by Julia Ward Howe, 126–138. Boston: Roberts Brothers, 1874.
Piatote, Beth H. *Domestic Subjects: Gender, Citizenship, and Law in Native American Literature.* New Haven, CT: Yale University Press, 2013.
Porter, Kenneth W. *The Black Seminoles.* Gainesville: University of Florida Press, 1996.
Povinelli, Elizabeth. *The Cunning of Recognition: Indigenous Alterities and the Making of Australian Multiculturalism.* Durham, NC: Duke University Press, 2002.
Powell, Timothy. "Postcolonial Theory in an American Context: A Reading of Martin Delany's *Blake*." In *The Pre-Occupation of Postcolonial Studies*, edited by Fawzia Afzal-Khan and Kalpana Seshadri-Crooks, 347–65. Durham, NC: Duke University Press, 2000.
Pratt, Lloyd. *Archives of American Time: Literature and Modernity in the Nineteenth Century.* Philadelphia: University of Pennsylvania Press, 2010.

Prescod-Weinstein, Chanda. "Making Black Women Scientists under White Empiricism: The Racialization of Epistemology in Physics." *Signs* 45, no. 2 (2020): 421–47.

Pryse, Marjorie. "'I Was Country When Country Wasn't Cool': Regionalizing the Modern in Jewett's *A Country Doctor*." *American Literary Regionalism in a Global Age* 34, no. 3 (2002): 217–232.

Puar, Jasbir. *The Right to Maim: Debility, Capacity, Disability*. Durham, NC: Duke University Press, 2017.

Qi, Xiaoying. "Face: A Chinese Concept in a Global Sociology." *Journal of Sociology* 47, no. 3 (2011): 279–95.

Quashie, Kevin. *The Sovereignty of Quiet: Beyond Resistance in Black Culture*. New Brunswick, NJ: Rutgers University Press, 2012.

"Racial and Ethnic Disparities Continue in Pregnancy-Related Deaths." Centers for Disease Control and Prevention, September 5, 2019. https://www.cdc.gov/media/releases/2019/p0905-racial-ethnic-disparities-pregnancy-deaths.html

Rankine, Claudia. *Citizen: An American Lyric*. Minneapolis: GrayWolf Press, 2014.

Rebhorn, Matthew. "Minding the Body: *Benito Cereno* and Melville's Embodied Reading Practice." *Studies in the Novel* 41, no. 2 (2010): 157–77.

Reddy, William M. *The Navigation of Feeling: A Framework for the History of Emotions*. New York: Cambridge University Press, 2001.

Redfield, James W. *Outlines of a New System of Physiognomy*. New York: J. S. Redfield, 1849.

Riis, Jacob A. *How the Other Half Lives: Studies among the Tenements of New York*. New York: Dover, 1971.

Riskin, Jessica. *Science in the Age of Sensibility: The Sentimental Empiricists of the French Enlightenment*. Chicago: University of Chicago Press, 2002.

Robillard, Douglas. *Melville and the Visual Arts: Ionian Form, Venetian Tint*. Kent, OH: Kent State University Press, 1997.

Roh, David S., Betsy Huang, and Greta A. Niu, eds. *Techno-Orientalism: Imagining Asia in Speculative Fiction, History, and Media*. New Brunswick, NJ: Rutgers University Press, 2015.

Rollin, Frank. *Life and Public Services of Martin R. Delany*. New York: Arno, 1883.

Roman, Margaret. *Sarah Orne Jewett: Reconstructing Gender*. Tuscaloosa: University of Alabama Press, 1992.

Romero, Lora. *Home Fronts: Domesticity and Its Critics in the Antebellum United States*. Durham, NC: Duke University Press, 1997.

Rothfield, Lawrence. *Vital Signs: Medical Realism in Nineteenth-Century Fiction*. Princeton, NJ: Princeton University Press, 2013.

Rothstein, William G. *American Physicians in the Nineteenth Century: From Sects to Science*. Baltimore, MD: Johns Hopkins University Press, 1972.

Rusert, Britt. "Delany's Comet: Fugitive Science and the Speculative Imaginary of Emancipation." *American Quarterly* 65, no. 4 (2013): 799–829.

Rusert, Britt. *Fugitive Science: Empiricism and Freedom in Early African American Culture*. New York: New York University Press, 2017.

Rush, Benjamin. "Observations Intended to Favour a Supposition That the Black Color (As It Is Called) of the Negroes Is Derived from Leprosy." *Transactions of the American Philosophical Society* 4 (1799): 289–97.

Salyer, Lucy. *Laws Harsh as Tigers: Chinese Immigrants and the Shaping of Modern Immigration Law*. Chapel Hill: University of North Carolina Press, 1995.

Samuels, Shirley. "Introduction." In *The Culture of Sentiment: Race, Gender, and Sentimentality in Nineteenth-Century America*, edited by Shirley Samuels, 3–8. New York: Oxford University Press, 1992.

Sanborn, Geoffrey. *The Sign of the Cannibal: Melville and the Making of a Postcolonial Reader*. Durham, NC: Duke University Press, 1998.

Sánchez-Eppler, Karen. *Touching Liberty: Abolition, Feminism, and the Politics of the Body*. Berkeley: University of California Press, 1993.

Sawyer, George S. *Southern Institutes: or, an Inquiry into the Origin and Early Prevalence of Slavery and the Slave-Trade*. Philadelphia: J. B. Lippincott & Co., 1858.

Sayers, Daniel O. *A Desolate Place for a Defiant People: The Archaeology of Maroons, Indigenous Americans, and Enslaved Laborers in the Great Dismal Swamp*. Gainesville: University of Press of Florida, 2014.

Schiebinger, Londa L. *The Mind Has No Sex? Women in the Origins of Modern Science*. Cambridge, MA: Harvard University Press, 1989.

Schuller, Kyla. *The Biopolitics of Feeling: Race, Sex, and Science in the Nineteenth Century*. Durham, NC: Duke University Press, 2018.

Schultz, Jane E. *Women at the Front: Hospital Workers in Civil War America*. Chapel Hill: University of North Carolina Press, 2004.

Sealts, Merton M. *Melville's Readings: A Checklist of Books Owned and Borrowed*. Madison: University of Wisconsin Press, 1966.

Sedgwick, Eve. *Touching Feeling: Affect, Pedagogy, Performativity*. Durham, NC: Duke University Press, 2003.

Sexton, Jared. "The *Vel* of Slavery: Tracking the Figure of the Unsovereign." *Critical Sociology* 42, nos. 4–5 (2016): 583–97.

Shah, Nayan. *Contagious Divides: Epidemics and Race in San Francisco's Chinatown*. Berkeley: University of California Press, 2001.

Shapiro, Ann R. *Unlikely Heroines: Nineteenth-Century Women Writers and the Woman Question*. New York: Greenwood, 1987.

Sharpe, Christina Elizabeth. *In the Wake: On Blackness and Being*. Durham, NC: Duke University Press, 2016.

Shaw, Lemuel. *A Discourse Delivered before the Officers and Members of the Humane Society of Massachusetts*. Boston: John Eliot, 1811.

Shaw, Lemuel. "Slavery and the Missouri Question." *North-American Review* 10, no. 26 (1820): 137–68.

Sibara, Jennifer Barager. "Disease, Disability, and the Alien Body in the Literature of Sui Sin Far." *MELUS* 39, no. 1 (2014): 56–81.

Simpson, Audra. "On Ethnographic Refusal: Indigeneity, 'Voice' and Colonial Citizenship." *Junctures* 9, no. 4 (2007): 67–80.

Sims, J. Marion. *The Story of My Life*. New York: D. Appleton, 1884.

Smith, Adam. *The Theory of Moral Sentiments*. Edited by David Daiches Raphael and Alec Lawrence Macfie. New York: Oxford University Press, 1976.
Smith, Arthur Henderson. *Chinese Characteristics*. 2nd ed. London: K. Paul, Trench, Trübner, 1894.
Smith, Beverly. "Black Women's Health: Notes for a Course." In *All the Women Are White, All the Blacks Are Men, but Some of Us Are Brave: Black Women's Studies*, edited by Akasha (Gloria T.) Hull, Patricia Bell-Scott, and Barbara Smith, 103–14. Old Westbury, NY: Feminist Press, 1982.
Smith, Samuel Stanhope. *An Essay on the Causes of the Variety of Complexion and Figure in the Human Species*. 2nd ed. New Brunswick, NJ: J. Simpson and Co., 1810.
Snorton, C. Riley. *Black on Both Sides: A Racial History of Trans Identity*. Minneapolis, MN: University of Minnesota Press, 2017.
Song, Min Hyoung. "Sentimentalism and Sui Sin Far." *Legacy* 20, nos. 1–2 (2003): 134–52.
Song, Min Hyoung. "The Unknowable and Sui Sin Far: The Epistemological Limits of 'Oriental' Sexuality." In *Q&A: Queer in Asian America*, edited by David L. Eng and Alice Y. Hom, 304–22. Philadelphia: Temple University Press, 1988.
Son of Baldwin. "I Don't Give a Fuck about Justine Damond." *Medium*, 2017. https://medium.com/@SonofBaldwin/i-dont-give-a-fuck-about-justine-diamond-1e60003ee961. Accessed July 25, 2017.
Son of Baldwin. "That essay really got a lot of folks way up in the Mount Everest of their feelings." Facebook, July 22, 2017. https://www.facebook.com/sonofbaldwinfb/posts/10155074013407862.
Sorisio, Carolyn. *Fleshing Out America: Race, Gender, and the Politics of the Body in American Literature, 1833–1879*. Athens: University of Georgia Press, 2002.
Spillers, Hortense. "Mama's Baby, Papa's Maybe: An American Grammar Book." *Diacritics* 17, no. 2 (1987): 64–81.
Spinoza, Baruch. *Ethics*. Translated by James Gutmann. New York: Hafner, 1949.
Spires, Derrick R. *The Practice of Citizenship: Black Politics and Print Culture in the Early United States*. Philadelphia: University of Pennsylvania Press, 2019.
Squier, Harriet A. "Women in Nineteenth Century Homeopathic Medicine." *Journal of Medical Humanities* 16, no. 2 (1995): 121–31.
Stanford, Eleanor. "Martin R. Delany (1812–1885)." *Encyclopedia Virginia*. Virginia Foundation for the Humanities, 2014. https://encyclopediavirginia.org/entries/delany-martin-r-1812-1885/
Stansell, Christine. "Elizabeth Stuart Phelps: A Study in Female Rebellion." *Massachusetts Review* 13, nos. 1–2 (1972): 239–56.
Stanton, Elizabeth Cady. Preface to *Pray You, Sir. Whose Daughter?*, by Helen H. Gardener, v–x. New York: R. F. Fenno, 1892.
Stanton, Elizabeth Cady, Susan B. Anthony, Matilda Joslyn Gage, and Ida Husted Harper. *History of Woman Suffrage*. Vol. 1. Rochester, NY: Susan B. Anthony and Charles Mann Press, 1881.
Stanton, William. *The Leopard's Spots: Scientific Attitudes toward Race in America, 1815–59*. Chicago: University of Chicago Press, 1960.

Starr, Paul. *The Social Transformation of American Medicine*. New York: Basic Books, 1982.
Sterling, Dorothy. *We Are Your Sisters: Black Women in the Nineteenth Century*. New York: W. W. Norton, 1984.
Stoler, Ann Laura, ed. *Haunted by Empire: Geographies of Intimacy in North American History*. Durham, NC: Duke University Press, 2006.
Storey, Mark. "A Geography of Medical Knowledge: Country Doctors in Elizabeth Stuart Phelps and Sarah Orne Jewett." *Journal of American Studies* 44, no. 4 (2010): 691–708.
Stowe, Harriet Beecher. *The Key to Uncle Tom's Cabin*. London: Clarke, Beeton, 1853.
Stowe, Harriet Beecher. *My Wife and I: or, Harry Henderson's History*. New York: J. B. Ford and Company, 1871.
Stowe, Harriet Beecher. *Uncle Tom's Cabin*. Edited with an introduction and notes by Jean Fagan Yellin. Oxford: Oxford University Press, 2008.
Sundquist, Eric J. *To Wake the Nations: Race in the Making of American Literature*. Cambridge, MA: Belknap Press of Harvard University Press, 1993.
Swenson, Kristine. "Doctor Zay and Dr. Mitchell: Elizabeth Stuart Phelps's Feminist Response to Mainstream Neurology." In *Neurology and Literature, 1860–1920*, edited by Anne Stiles, 97–115. New York: Palgrave Macmillan, 2007.
TallBear, Kim. *Native American DNA: Tribal Belonging and the False Promise of Genetic Science*. Minneapolis: University of Minnesota Press, 2013.
Tallie, T. J. *Queering Colonial Natal: Indigeneity and the Violence of Belonging in Southern Africa*. Minneapolis: University of Minnesota Press, 2020.
Tate, Claudia. *Domestic Allegories of Political Desire: The Black Heroine's Text at the Turn of the Century*. New York: Oxford University Press, 1992.
Tawil, Ezra. "Captain Babo's Cabin: Stowe, Race, and Misreading in *Benito Cereno*." *Leviathan* 8 no. 2 (2006): 37–51.
Tawil, Ezra. *The Making of Racial Sentiment: Slavery and the Birth of the Frontier Romance*. New York: Columbia University Press, 2009.
Taylor, Bayard. *A Visit to India, China, and Japan: In the Year 1853*. New York: G. P. Putnam, 1855.
Taylor, Charles. "The Politics of Recognition." In *Multiculturalism*, edited and introduced by Amy Guttmann, 25–74. Princeton, NJ: Princeton University Press, 1994.
Taylor, Charles, K. Anthony Appiah, Jürgen Habermas, Steven C. Rockefeller, Michael Walzer, and Susan Wolf. *Multiculturalism*. Edited and introduced by Amy Guttmann. Princeton, NJ: Princeton University Press, 1994.
Terada, Rei. *Feeling in Theory: Emotion after the "Death of the Subject."* Cambridge, MA: Harvard University Press, 2001.
Terada, Rei. *Looking Away: Phenomenality and Dissatisfaction, Kant to Adorno*. Cambridge, MA: Harvard University Press, 2009.
Terborg-Penn, Rosalyn. *African American Women in the Struggle for the Vote, 1850–1920*. Bloomington: Indiana University Press, 1998.
Thomas, Brook. "The Legal Fictions of Herman Melville and Lemuel Shaw." *Critical Inquiry* 1, no. 1 (1984): 24–51.

Thomas, Brook. *Plessy v. Ferguson: A Brief History with Documents*. New York: Bedford, 1997.

Tocqueville, Alexis de. *Democracy in America*. Translated by Henry Reeve. Vol. 2. New Rochelle, NY: Arlington House, 1840.

Todd, Zoe. "An Indigenous Feminist's Take on the Ontological Turn: 'Ontology' Is Just Another Word for Colonialism." *Journal of Historical Sociology* 29, no. 1 (2016): 4–22.

Tompkins, Jane. *Sensational Designs: The Cultural Work of American Fiction, 1790–1860*. New York: Oxford University Press, 1986.

Tonkovich, Nicole. "Genealogy, Genre, Gender: Sui Sin Far's 'Leaves from the Mental Portfolio of an Eurasian.'" In *Beyond the Binary: Reconstructing Cultural Identity in a Multicultural Context*, edited by Timothy B. Powell, 236–60. New Brunswick, NJ: Rutgers University Press, 1999.

Tracey, Karen. *Plots and Proposals: American Women's Fiction, 1850–90*. Urbana: University of Illinois Press, 2000.

Triolo, Victor. "Nineteenth Century Foundations of Cancer Research. Origins of Experimental Research." *Cancer Research* 24, no. 1 (1964): 4–27.

Triolo, Victor A. "Nineteenth Century Foundations of Cancer Research Advances in Tumor Pathology, Nomenclature, and Theories of Oncogenesis." *Cancer Research* 25, no. 2 (1965): 75–106.

U.S. Census (1880), Philadelphia Enumeration District 116, 7th Ward, 3rd Precinct.

U.S. Congress, Joint Special Committee to Investigate Chinese Immigrants. "Report of the Joint Special Committee to Investigate Chinese Immigrants." Washington: Government Printing Office, 1877.

Valelly, Richard M. *The Two Reconstructions: The Struggle for Black Enfranchisement*. Chicago: University of Chicago Press, 2004.

Vigil-Fowler, Margaret. "'Two Strikes—a Lady and Colored': Gender, Race, and the Making of the Modern Medical Profession, 1864–1941." PhD diss, UC San Francisco, 2018.

Vogel, Todd. *Rewriting White: Race, Class, and Cultural Capital in Nineteenth-Century America*. New Brunswick, NJ: Rutgers University Press, 2004.

Walcott, Rinaldo. "Genres of Human: Multiculturalism, Cosmo-Politics, and the Caribbean Basin." In *Sylvia Wynter: On Being Human as Praxis*, edited by Katherine McKittrick, 183–202. Durham, NC: Duke University Press, 2015.

Wang, Bo. "Rereading Sui Sin Far: A Rhetoric of Defiance." In *Representations: Doing Asian American Rhetoric*, edited by LuMing Mao and Morris Young, 244–65. Logan: Utah State University Press, 2008.

Wanzo, Rebecca. *The Suffering Will Not Be Televised: African American Women and Sentimental Political Storytelling*. Albany: State University of New York Press, 2009.

Warren, Calvin. "Onticide: Afro-Pessimism, Gay Nigger #1, and Surplus Violence." *GLQ* 23, no. 3 (2017): 391–418.

Warren, Samuel. *Moral, Social, and Professional Duties of Attorneys and Solicitors*. New York: Harper and Brothers, 1849.

Washington, Harriet A. *Medical Apartheid: The Dark History of Medical Experimentation on Black Americans from Colonial Times to the Present*. New York: Doubleday, 2007.

Wegener, Frederick. "'Should Female Physicians Treat Male Patients?' Doctoring the Other Sex, 'Love Sickness,' and Representations of the American Woman Doctor, 1850-1900." *Arizona Quarterly* 74, no. 4 (2018): 145-71.

Weiner, Susan. *Law in Art: Melville's Major Fiction and Nineteenth-Century American Law*. New York: Peter Lang, 1992.

Weinstein, Cindy. *Family, Kinship, and Sympathy in Nineteenth-Century American Literature*. New York: Cambridge University Press, 2006.

Welburn, Ron. *Hartford's Ann Plato and the Native Borders of Identity*. Albany: State University of New York Press, 2015.

Wells, Susan. *Out of the Dead House: Nineteenth-Century Women Physicians and the Writing of Medicine*. Madison: University of Wisconsin Press, 2001.

Wexler, Laura. *Tender Violence: Domestic Visions in an Age of U.S. Imperialism*. Chapel Hill: University of North Carolina Press, 2000.

White-Parks, Annette. *Sui Sin Far/Edith Maude Eaton: A Literary Biography*. Urbana: University of Illinois Press, 1995.

White-Parks, Annette. "'We Wear the Mask': Sui Sin Far as One Example of Trickster Authorship." In *Tricksterism in Turn-of-the-Century American Literature*, edited by Elizabeth Ammons and Annette White-Parks, 1-20. Hanover, NH: University Press of New England, 1994.

Wilderson, Frank B., III. *Red, White and Black: Cinema and the Structure of U.S. Antagonisms*. Durham, NC: Duke University Press, 2010.

Williams, Raymond. *Marxism and Literature*. New York: Oxford University Press, 1977.

Winter, Steven L. "Melville, Slavery, and the Failure of the Judicial Process." *Cardozo Law Review* 26, no. 6 (2005): 2471-96.

Wolfe, Patrick. "Settler Colonialism and the Elimination of the Native." *Journal of Genocide Research* 8, no. 4 (2006): 387-409.

Wong, Lily. *Transpacific Attachments: Sex Work, Media Networks, and Affective Histories of Chineseness*. New York: Columbia University Press, 2018.

Wood, Ann Douglas. "'The Fashionable Diseases': Women's Complaints and Their Treatment in Nineteenth-Century America." *Journal of Interdisciplinary History* 4, no. 1 (1973): 25-52.

"Would Women Vote?" *Brandon Mail*, November 8, 1888.

Wright, Nazera Sadiq. *Black Girlhood in the Nineteenth Century*. Urbana: University of Illinois Press, 2016.

Wu, Ellen D. *The Color of Success: Asian Americans and the Origins of the Model Minority*. Princeton, NJ: Princeton University Press, 2013.

Wu, William F. *The Yellow Peril: Chinese Americans in American Fiction, 1850-1940*. Hamden, CT: Archon Books, 1982.

Wynter, Sylvia. "1492: A New World View." In *Race, Discourse, and the Origin of the Americas: A New World View*, edited by Vera Lawrence Hyatt and Rex Nettleford, 5-57. Washington: Smithsonian Institution Press, 1995.

Wynter, Sylvia. "Beyond Miranda's Meanings: Un/Silencing the 'Demonic Ground' of Caliban's 'Woman.'" In *The Routledge Reader in Caribbean Literature*, edited by Alison Donnell and Sarah Lawson Welsh, 476-82. New York: Routledge, 1996.

Wynter, Sylvia. "Unsettling the Coloniality of Being/Power/Truth/ Freedom." *CR* 3, no. 3 (Fall 2003): 257-337.

Xiang, Sunny. *Tonal Intelligence: The Aesthetics of Asian Inscrutability during the Long Cold War*. New York: Columbia University Press, 2020.

Yao, Christine "Xine." "Black-Asian Counterintimacies: Reading Sui Sin Far in Jamaica." *J19* 6, no. 1 (2018): 197-202.

Yao, Christine "Xine." "Femmes in Science: Queer Erasure and the Politics of Dress in Nineteenth Century America." In *Gender in American Literature and Culture*, edited by Jennifer Harris and Jean Lutes, 237-254. New York: Cambridge University Press, 2021.

Yarborough, Richard. "Strategies of Black Characterization in *Uncle Tom's Cabin* and the Early Afro-American Novel." In *New Essays on Uncle Tom's Cabin*, edited by Eric J. Sundquist, 45-84. New York: Cambridge University Press, 1986.

Yellin, Jean Fagan. *The Intricate Knot: Black Figures in American Literature, 1776-1863*. New York: New York University Press, 1972.

Yellin, Jean Fagan. "Written by Herself: Harriet Jacobs' Slave Narrative." *American Literature* 53, no. 3 (1981): 379-486.

Yun, Lisa. *The Coolie Speaks: Chinese Indentured Laborers and African Slaves in Cuba*. Philadelphia: Temple University Press, 2008.

Zuck, Rochelle Raineri. "Martin R. Delany and Rhetorics of Divided Sovereignty." In *African American Culture and Legal Discourse*, edited by Lovalerie King and Richard Schur, 39-56. New York: Palgrave Macmillan, 2009.

INDEX

Abate, Michelle Ann, 136
abjection, 19, 35, 39, 68, 73
abolition of slavery, 21, 74, 86, 176; abolitionists and, 8, 53–56, 61, 75, 86–87, 140, 155, 162
access, affective, 7, 114
activism and advocacy, 156, 164, 174, 188, 209
Adam and Eve, 20, 41
Adams, Nehemiah, 58; *A South Side View of Slavery*, 57
affect, affects, 10, 13, 24, 74, 77, 100, 135, 169, 187, 205, 213n43, 214n55, 215n64; alien, 176, 205; antisocial, 17–20; Black, 21, 33, 67, 77, 213n47; racialized, 33, 35, 75, 214n64; universality of, 15, 33; women's, 116, 228n25
affectable, affectability, 14, 27, 38, 39, 75, 83, 117, 172, 198, 214n55; affective vs. affectable and, 38, 44, 50, 60, 65; of Black people, 33, 66; colonialism and, 113, 176; disaffection and, 5, 7; racialized, 4, 34, 157
affection, 43, 55, 58, 91; between men and women, 123, 129, 132, 133, 196
affective labor and tools, 32, 87, 130, 157, 164, 209
affect theory and affect studies, 5, 9–15, 183, 212–13n37
Africa, Africans, 15, 65–66; in Melville's *Benito Cereno*, 30, 32–35, 41–50, 52, 57–58, 61, 63, 68, 103
African American Woman's Congress, 170

African Indigeneity, 24, 77, 103
Afro-Latinx peoples, 101
Afro-Natives, 79, 101, 224n53
Afropessimism, 23, 35, 67, 68
Agassiz, Louis, 36, 55, 218n30
agency, 110, 115, 173, 205, 216n99; affective, 25, 38, 158, 166; of Asian Americans, 191, 237n37; Black, 50, 62, 63, 150; of Black women, 138, 145, 158
Ahmed, Sara, 10, 11, 21, 123, 135, 176, 213n45, 215n64, 215n67; on feminist killjoy tool kit, 111, 210
Alcott, Louisa May, "My Contraband," 235n97
alienation, 11, 140, 196; of Far, 202, 204; of mixed-race Chinese women and children, 195, 197; structural, 186, 205
alienness, aliens, 172, 173, 175, 178, 237n36
allegory, 73, 83, 88, 109, 127, 164, 203, 221n127
Allen, Patrick, 147, 151
Allewaert, Monique, 94
American Antiquarian and Oriental Journal, 171, 172
American Cancer Society, 168
American Equal Rights Association, 140
American Institute of Homeopathy, 130
American Medical Association, 115, 143, 228n20
American Phrenological Journal, 36
American Revolution, 94, 95
Amistad case, 53
Anarcha, 143, 144

Anarcha Project, 166
anatomy, 36
anesthesia, 24, 112–14, 129; sexual, 114–18; Sims's nonuse of, 143, 144
Anglo-African Magazine, 97; Delany's *Blake* serialized in, 75
"Anglo-Saxon race," 5, 56, 162, 175
animacy hierarchy (Chen), 5, 7, 97
animatedness (Ngai), 10, 33, 96
Anna "Nan" Prince, in Jewett's *A Country Doctor*, 110, 121, 123–26, 136, 230n92
Anthony, Susan B., 140; *History of Woman Suffrage* (1881), 108, 136; racism of, 109, 162
anthropology, anthropologists, 174, 183
anti-Blackness, 23, 42, 61, 65, 80, 90, 215n86, 227n157, 238n58; as cancer, 167–68; pervasiveness of, 44, 150; structural centrality of, 33; violence of, 142, 150; of white nostalgia, 44–49. *See also* racism: anti-Black
anticolonialism, 32, 70, 73, 214n56, 223n14
antiracism, 1, 81–83, 99–102, 168
antislavery, 53, 60, 218n43
Antwi, Phanuel, 241n1
Anzaldúa, Gloria, 10, 15–18, 213n47
apathy, Black, 3, 20, 153
Aranda, in Melville's *Benito Cereno*, 46, 63; skeleton of, 33, 35, 49–51, 62–67, 221n127
Arkansas, 90; Choctaw in, 88, 89
art, 37, 40
Asian Americans, 9, 21, 27, 174, 236n6, 237n37
Asian American studies, 12, 26, 174
Asian diaspora, 26, 28
Asianness, 27, 216n99
Asians, 15, 32, 173; in Delany's *Blake*, 105–6; as inexpressive, 179–85. *See also* "Chinese" entries
assimilation, 9, 116, 163, 238n51; inability of, 173, 176, 188, 191, 197
astrophysics and physics, Delany and, 97–100
Atalanta and Hippomenes myth, 128, 135

Atlantic magazine, 109
attraction, 97–98, 100
Attucks, Crispus, 95
Austin, J. L., 212n22

Baartman, Sarah, 199
Babo in Melville's *Benito Cereno*, 9, 29–34, 46, 63, 66, 70, 87; Cereno and, 44–45; Delano and, 21, 32, 49–50, 56–57; execution of, 30, 49, 52, 53, 65, 68; as leader of slave revolt, 50, 62, 68; severed head of, 33, 35, 65–67; as unsympathetic, 64–66
Bailey, Moya, 25, 143
Baillie, Gertrude Stuart, "Should Professional Women Marry?," 119, 125
Baldwin, James, 2–3
Barbados, 48
Barnard College, 125
Barnum, P. T., 199
Bartleby, 9, 13, 214n55; as universal figure, 29, 30
Beauregard, Guy, 194
Bell, Alexander Graham, 155
Bell-Scott, Patricia, 141
Benito Cereno, 29, 30; Babo and, 44–45; Delano on, 42, 46–50; as sympathetic, 64–66, 87
Benito Cereno (Melville, 1855), 6, 21, 30, 66, 77; Africans in, 30, 32, 34–35, 41–42, 46–50, 52, 57–58, 63, 68; Black sociality in, 67–68; law in, 34–35, 52–66; publication of, 40, 41, 53, 57; racialized affects in, 23, 33, 54; unsympathetic Blackness in, 29–69
Bennett, Jane, 97, 100
Berlant, Lauren, 7, 8, 11, 205, 213n37, 214n55, 216n14
Betsy, 143, 144
Biggio, Rebecca, 84, 103
Billy Budd (Melville), 59–60
biopolitics and biopower, 4, 17, 21, 56, 70, 74, 76, 83, 151; hierarchies of oppression and, 7, 12, 15, 210; knowledge systems and, 37–38; sentimental, 62, 83, 102

biopolitics of feeling, 2, 8, 32, 34, 39, 51, 53, 60–61, 64, 73, 97; hegemonic, 109, 210; Schuller on, 38, 85; unfeeling and, 30, 52

Birnbaum, Michele, 155

Black affect, 21, 33, 67, 77, 213n47

Black and Indigenous peoples, 73, 76, 227n157; histories of, 75, 79. *See also* Black-Indigenous counterintimacies

Black apathy and passivity, 3, 20, 91, 153

Black community, 94, 99, 161

Black diaspora, 94, 95, 97; in Delany's *Blake*, 84, 101

Black emancipation, 23, 25, 70, 86, 91, 145, 161; Indigenous sovereignty and, 76, 88, 90, 92

Black feminine poesis, in *Iola Leroy* and, 168–70

Black feminists, 21, 25, 26, 139, 151; health science studies by, 143, 150; praxis of science of, 142, 144, 146, 151, 154–55, 170

Black fugitivity, fugitives, 91, 95. *See also* Fugitive Slave Act

Black Indigeneity, 77

Black-Indigenous counterintimacies, 23, 24, 75, 80; in Delany's *Blake*, 83–97, 106; disruption of structural apparatuses through, 76–77; fantasies of, 88–93; insurgent, 75–76

Black liberation, 24, 138, 140, 159, 164; Indigenous people and, 80, 103

Black Lives Matter movement, 1, 2, 28, 209, 211n9

Black men: citizenship and, 26; as doctors, 170; masculinity of, 103, 104. *See also* Black people

Black motherhood and Black maternal, 43, 138, 145, 156, 161, 166–67

Black nationalism, of Delany, 70, 76, 79

Blackness, 19–21, 26–27, 45, 58, 75–79, 83, 94, 96, 100, 102–3, 139, 150, 161, 173; abjection of, 21, 68; as benign childlikeness, 42, 218n43; colonialism and, 17, 77; criminalization and stigmatization of, 27, 67; erasure of, 160, 162; Indigeneity and, 24, 70, 72, 77, 97, 222n14; transnational, 75, 84; unsympathetic, 6, 21, 23, 29–69, 70, 75, 83, 102, 173

Black nurses, 157–58. *See also* Iola Leroy

Black patriarchal sentimentalism, 73–74, 84

Black people, 18, 67, 71, 72, 75, 76, 139, 174, 181, 215n86; affectability of, 33, 44; affective labor of, 32, 44; citizenship of, 6–7; health of, 20, 151, 168; inferiority of, 42, 45, 56, 80, 154; psychic survival strategies of, 17, 21; racial classification of, 34, 182, 197; structural oppression of, 150, 173. *See also* Black men; Black women and Black womanhood

Black rebellion and resistance, 34; in Delany's *Blake*, 105–6, 207; Indigeneity and, 94–95; in Melville's *Benito Cereno*, 52, 53

Black speculative fiction, 83

Black studies, 12, 24, 213n44

Blackwell, Elizabeth, 25, 116, 124, 147; as first American women doctor, 109, 146; *Pioneer Work in Opening the Medical Profession to Women* (1895), 118–19

Blackwell, Emily, 120, 147

Black women and Black womanhood, 16, 25, 43, 68, 74, 103, 139, 146 49, 153–56, 163, 170, 211n3, 232n22; agency of, 145, 166; in Delany's *Blake*, 77, 92, 105; erasure of, 102–6, 108, 154; organizations of, 151, 156; power of, 138, 150; in medicine and science, 25, 139, 143, 151–58; racial uplift and, 138, 155; violence against, 104, 140–41. *See also* Black people

Black women doctors, 138, 142, 146, 148, 154, 166, 169–70

Blake (Henry Holland), 70, 75, 96, 104; revolution of, 84, 88, 92, 96–99; as unsympathetic, 23, 75; visits Choctaw Nation, 88–92

Blake; or the Huts of America (Delany, 1861), 6, 23, 24, 68, 70, 78, 207; Black-Indigenous counterintimacies in, 83–97; erasure of women in, 102–6; Fugitive Slave Act and, 83, 85, 86; as rebuttal to *Uncle Tom's Cabin*, 72–73, 83; serial publication of, 75, 93, 97, 101
Bledstein, Burton, 123
Blumenbach, Johann, 182
Boas, Franz, 237n51
Bonner, Marita, 232n22
Book of Medical Discourses, A (Crumpler, 1883), 25, 143, 148–50, 156
Boston, 35, 59, 61, 146, 149, 150, 155, 156, 190; Crumpler in, 147, 148; Eaton in, 172
Boston marriage, 124, 133
Braithwaite, Kamau, 81
Breen, in Howells's *Dr. Breen's Practice*, 121–22
Brooklyn Literary Society, 138
Brophy, Alfred, 53, 54
Brown, William Wells, *Clotel*, 141
Brownness, 24
Buffon, Georges-Louis Leclerc, Comte de, 182
Byrd, Jodi, 24, 77, 81, 237n36
Byron, Lord, 177

California, 173–74, 177, 190
Canada, 7, 75, 84, 98–99; anti-Chinese immigration acts in, 188, 236n6; Eaton in, 172, 202
cancer, 167–68, 168, 235n117
capitalism, capitalists, 11, 19, 176, 239n70
Carby, Hazel, 139, 145
Caribbean, 15, 77, 99, 100, 172, 207, 214n51, 238n58
Cary, Mary Ann Shadd, 170
Cathell, Daniel Webster, 113
Caucasian, as racial category, 182
Cayuga Nation, 209
Celestials, Chinese as, 176
Chapman, Mary, 178, 240n113
Chapters from a Life (Phelps, 1897), 126
chattel slavery, 18–19, 35, 47, 61–62, 90, 102, 138, 150, 157, 161; Indigenous people practice, 93, 222–23n14; in Melville's *Benito Cereno*, 30, 57–58; defense of, 42, 218n43; metastasis of, 167–68; sexual violence under, 142, 145, 157; white women and, 86, 108. *See also* enslavement of Black people
Chen, Mel, 5, 7, 97, 173
Chen, Tina, 216n99
Cheng, Anne Anlin, 173, 184, 192, 216n99
Cherokees, 213n48, 222–23n14
Chesapeakes, 95
Chickasaws, 77, 89, 93
Child, Lydia Maria, 108
children: Black, 150; mixed-race Chinese, 197–200
Chiles, Katy, 93
China, 180, 190, 206
Chinatown enclaves in U.S. cities, 178, 187, 193–95
"Chinese at Christmas, The" (Far, 1895), 189
"Chinese Boy-Girl, The" (Far), 193
Chinese civilization, 182
"Chinese Defended, The" (Far, 1896), 189
Chinese diaspora, 184, 186, 188, 205, 206; Far and, 185, 203
Chinese exclusion, 173, 185
Chinese head tax, 236n6
Chinese Exclusion Act (United States, 1882), 7, 21, 26, 172, 175, 188
Chinese Exclusion Era (1882–1943), 172–74, 185
Chinese immigration, immigrants, 193; opposition to, 173, 175–76, 180
Chinese Immigration Act (Canada, 1885), 188
"Chinese in America, The" (Far, 1909), 179
Chinese language, 179–80
Chinese mixed-race children, 197–200
Chineseness, 173, 174, 176, 195; of Eaton, 185, 201
"Chinese Party, A" (Far, 1890), 190
Chinese people, 27, 172, 174, 177, 181, 189, 194; anxiety over, 26, 172, 184;

depravity of, 187, 189. *See also* Chinese women; coolie, coolies
"Chinese Question, The" (Far, 1895), 188
"Chinese Spirit of Non-Resistance Will Disappear, The" (Far, 1915), 205–6
"Chinese Woman in America, The" (Far, 1897), 190
Chinese women, 172, 191, 193, 196; artifice of, 178, 190–92; as sex workers, 184–85, 238–39n70
Chipps, Pakki, 90
Cho, Yu-Fang, 174
Choctaws, 23, 88, 93; in Delany's *Blake*, 73, 76, 88–96, 103; displacement of, 95–96
Chow, Rey, 179–80, 181
Christianity, 20, 129, 141, 166, 168, 174, 200, 222n14. *See also* missionaries
Chuh, Kandice, 26
cisgender heterosexuals, as LGBTQ2S+ allies, 209
citizenship, 8, 21, 73–74, 96, 173, 175; Black, 93, 146, 170; flexible, 188, 216n99
Civil War, 93, 160, 162, 167, 235n97; nurses in, 157–58, 160
Clarke, Edward H., 117, 120, 132; *Sex in Education: Or a Fair Chance for the Girls* (1873), 115, 118, 126
Clarkson, Thomas, 61
Clymer, Jeffory, 103
coalition, coalitions, 76, 209
Cobb, Jasmine, 163
Cobb, Thomas R. R., 56, 58; *An Inquiry into the Law of Negro Slavery*, 55
Cohen, Cathy, 214n60
Cole, Rebecca J., 142–44, 147, 155, 165–66, 168, 170; activism of, 147, 151; intellectual thought of, 151–54; "The Eye and Its Appendages" (1867), 25–26, 143, 151–54, 234n74; Watkins Harper and, 155–56
Collins, John, 36
Collins, Patricia Hill, 142, 232n22
colonial history and politics, 24, 63, 82

colonialism, 13, 19, 81, 83, 91, 103, 182, 213n43, 214n55, 219n69; anthropology and, 174, 198; intimacies of, 79–80; violence of, 8, 81; whites and, 77, 188. *See also* decolonization; settler colonialism
coloniality of sympathy, 4, 5, 7, 21, 23; universal feeling and, 12–15
color, as term in Delany's *Blake*, 77, 81, 102
color blindness, whiteness universalized by, 162, 164, 175
Columbus, Christopher, 63
Combe, George, 39, 108; *The Constitution of Man*, 40, 217n30
comets, 97, 99
community, 209; Black, 93, 146, 156; Chinese, 179, 194, 195; in Delany's *Blake*, 70, 78, 84, 98–100
Compromise of 1850, 58
concealment, Chinese and, 190, 192, 202–3
Condition, Elevation, Emigration, and Destiny of the Colored People of the United States, The (Delany, 1852), 71, 79–82, 85, 95, 104
Confucius, 204
Congolese, 103
consent, 191, 192
coolie, coolies, 26, 100, 176, 184–85, 238–39n70; in Far's writings, 187, 188
Cooper, Anna Julia, 103
Cooper, Brittney, 143
Cooper, James Fenimore, 104
Cornell School of Sentimentality, 213n37
Cornell University, 212–13n37; Weill Medicine, 235n117
cosmologies, 19, 94, 103
Cott, Nancy, 111, 141
Coulter, Harris, 228n20
Coulthard, Glen, 7, 24, 32, 103–4, 214n56
counterintimacies, 15, 73, 81, 207; cross-racial, 73, 82, 99–100. *See also* Black-Indigenous counterintimacies
Country Doctor, A (Jewett, 1884), 25, 109–10, 120–22
Cover, Robert, 54, 59–60, 220n83

Coviello, Peter, 32, 43
craniology, 21, 34, 37, 82, 218n30; race science and, 36, 182
Crary, Jonathan, 36
Creeks, 91
critical race studies, 21, 27
crossblood people, 92, 95, 101, 171. *See also* "mixed-race" *entries*
Crumpler, Rebecca Lee Davis, 142, 144, 146–47, 165–66, 168; *A Book of Medical Discourses* (1883), 25, 143, 147, 156, 234n64; intellectual thought of, 148–50; Watkins Harper and, 155–56
Cuba, 75, 89, 100; in Delany's *Blake*, 24, 84, 87, 99, 101–2, 104
cult of so-called true womanhood, 141
cultural differences, 195, 237n51
cultural imagination, 33, 171
culture, American, 8, 32, 40
culture, popular, 36
culture of sentiment, 1–28, 3, 20, 54, 66
Cushier, Elizabeth, 120
Cuvier, Georges, 182; *The Animal Kingdom*, 40
Cvetkovich, Ann, 213n37

Daly, Mary, 16
Damond, Justine, 2
Darwin, Charles, 40, 82, 176; *The Expression of Emotions in Man and Animals* (1872), 15; *On the Origin of the Species* (1859), 101
da Silva, Denise Ferreira, 4, 14, 21, 31, 32, 68; on affectability, 5, 18, 38, 117; on raciality, 37–38
Daston, Lorraine, 140
Davis, Cynthia, 231n100
Davis, Rebecca Harding, 109
Dawes Act (1887), 173
"Declaration of Sentiments, The" (1848), women's rights and, 108
decolonization, 70, 84, 183; Delany's vision of, 72, 105; Indigenous, 103, 214n56; by resistance and revolution, 94, 97–99, 207
deference, 7, 48, 66

Delano, Amasa (historical person), *Narrative of Voyages and Travels* (1817), 30, 33, 35–36, 43, 62, 64, 67–68
Delano in Melville's *Benito Cereno* (literary character), 31, 32, 40, 42, 62, 64, 138; Babo and, 21, 32; cultural imperialism of, 33–34; gaze of, 34, 66; on gender and race, 42–43; as good natured, 35, 49; nostalgia of, 44, 45, 48, 56–57; sentimentalism of, 33, 40–44, 54, 57; sympathy of, 29, 66, 87
Delany, Catherine Richards, 74
Delany, Martin Robinson, 9, 21, 72, 74, 103, 140, 155, 177, 222n14, 224n61; Black-Indigenous counterintimacies and, 70–106; Black women and, 103, 138; *Blake; or the Huts of America* (1861), 6, 23, 68, 207; "Comets," 97, 100; *The Condition, . . . and Destiny of the Colored People of the United States*, 71, 79, 81, 82, 85, 95, 104; Harvard Medical College and, 74–75, 107; law and, 85–86; nonfiction writings of, 75–76; "old American story" of, 72, 79, 83, 88; *Principia of Ethnology: The Origins of Races and Color*, 81–82; "Report on the Political Destiny of the Colored Race . . . ," 81; science and, 94, 99; Stowe vs., 70–72; "The Attraction of the Planets," 97, 99
Delany, Samuel, 83
Deleuze, Gilles, 10, 37, 74
democracy, 48, 204, 222n14, 239n70
deposition, in Melville's *Benito Cereno*, 62–63
Derrida, Jacques, 179, 181
desire, 91, 110, 124, 137, 141, 146, 159, 193; political, 145–46, 164
detachment, 17, 31, 77, 105, 178, 209; affective, 28, 140, 210; in Far's characters, 27, 204; scientific and medical objectivity and, 25, 98, 108, 112–13, 116, 126, 129. *See also* passionlessness
dialect, in Delany's *Blake*, 90, 91
diaspora: affect and, 10; Asian, 26, 27, 28; Black, 77, 84, 91, 95, 97; Chinese, 171, 173, 177, 180, 184–86, 188, 203, 205–6

disability and disabled sensibility, 27, 173, 186, 198
disaffection, 5, 15, 31, 39, 112, 157, 206, 209–10; Anzaldúa and, 16–17; of Babo, 33, 68; challenge of, 5–6; defiance as, 18, 27, 196; Fugitive Slave Law and, 58–63; Manalansan on, 11, 216n14; of peoples of color, 70, 73, 80, 83–87; racialized, 51, 77; unfeeling and, 6, 83; of women, 202, 232n22
Dismal Swamp, 76, 88, 94–97
dispossession. *See* Indigenous dispossession
dissatisfaction, 2, 7, 11, 27, 111, 136, 178, 185, 202; unfeeling and, 16, 32. *See also* dissent
dissembling, dissemblance, 142, 157, 180
dissent, 11, 202; unfeeling and, 6, 8, 32, 35
dissonance, 6, 177, 205
distancing, emotional, 11, 141, 209; of Chinese women, 27, 178, 191, 195; of Far, 198, 203, 205, 206; of medical professionals, 142, 158. *See also* alienation; disaffection; unfeeling
Doctor Zay, 132; queerness of, 25, 133–34
Doctor Zay (Phelps), 25, 121, 122, 128; fallacy of reverse sexism and, 126–35
dogs, sentimentality and, 45, 56
domesticity, 119, 174
domination: biopolitical, 32, 38; global systems of, 82
Dominion Illustrated (Montreal), Far's first publication in, 186–87
Donovan, Josephine, 230n92
double consciousness, 26, 152, 154
Douglas, Ann, 8, 44
Douglass, Frederick, 86; Delany vs., 23, 74, 82–83; on *Uncle Tom's Cabin*, 70–71, 78; women's suffrage and, 109, 140
Douglass, Sarah Mapps, 144, 156, 163
Dr. Breen's Practice (Howells, 1881), 25, 110; Jex-Blake on, 120–21
Dred Scott v. Sanford (1857), 86, 175
Du Bois, W. E. B., 30, 66, 151, 156; *Dark Princess* (1928), 84; on double consciousness, 25–26, 152, 153; *The Philadelphia Negro*, 151; *The Souls of Black Folk*, 9

duCille, Ann, 25, 140, 141, 149, 164; on passionlessness, 153, 157
DuPlessis, Rachel Blau, 110
Duyckinck, Evert A., 40

East Asian, as race, 182
Eaton, Edith Maude, 172–73, 178, 185–87, 237n41; gender indeterminacy and, 197–98; pseudonyms of, 6, 171, 197, 240n113; queerness and, 193, 197–200; sentimentalism of, 172, 173; siblings of, 201–2. *See also* Far, Sui Sin
ecologies, in Delany's *Blake*, 102–6
Edelman, Lee, 12, 214n58
Edison, Thomas, 155
Eliza Harris, in *Uncle Tom's Cabin*, 85–87, 104
Ellis, Havelock, 24, 124, 133, 141; *Studies in the Psychology of Sex* (1900), 114–15
emotion, emotions, 13–16, 39, 213n45, 216n14; disciplining of, 55, 113; Spinoza on, 4–5. *See also* affect, affects; emotional labor; expression; feeling, feelings
emotional labor (Hochschild), 7–8, 44–45, 49, 112
empathy, 2, 28, 86, 210
empire, 9, 177, 198. *See also* colonialism; imperialism
empiricism, 38, 66; white, 151–52
Eng, David, 10
England, 40, 172
"Enlightened Motherhood: An Address" (Watkins Harper, 1892), 138, 148, 166
Enlightenment, 4, 14, 17, 37, 214n51; sympathy and, 12, 73
enslaved Black women, 143, 161
enslavement of Black people, 3, 18–23, 30, 43, 53, 55, 57, 79, 83–84, 90, 95, 149–50, 167, 184; Indigenous dispossession and, 76, 84; by Indigenous people, 76, 88–89; justification for, 50, 154; legacies of, 2, 73, 158; sentimentalism and, 9, 42; slave sales and, 75, 87, 162. *See also* abolition of slavery, abolitionism; Black emancipation; chattel slavery; slavery

enslavers, 56–57, 65, 86, 90, 102–6, 156, 160
Ensor, Sarah, 228n23
environmentalism, 38, 96, 101, 122
erasure, 68, 108, 162, 166, 177, 215n86; Black women and, 102–6, 108, 151, 154, 170; Indigenous women and, 89, 102–6
Ernest, John, 88
erotics and homoerotics, 77, 90–91, 190
Essay on the Causes of the Variety of Complexion and Figure in the Human Species, An (Stanley Stanhope Smith, 1787), 18
Ethiopian, as racial category, 182
ethnicity, 88, 179, 182
ethnic studies, 21, 27
ethnography, ethnographies, 179, 184, 198. *See also* anthropology, anthropologists
etiology, frigidity as, 112–14
eugenics, 108, 113, 133, 175, 181
Eva, in *Uncle Tom's Cabin*, 44
evolution, 22, 26, 101, 153, 176. *See also* Darwin, Charles
exploitation, 83–84, 93, 108, 194; of Black people, 25, 52, 89, 93; of coolies, 176, 184, 188
expression, 18, 111, 189, 190, 216n14; affective, 177, 184, 209; of Black affect, 21, 33; in-, 18–19. *See also* emotion, emotions; feeling, feelings
Expression of Emotions in Man and Animals, The (Darwin, 1872), 15
expressive hypothesis (Terada), 5
eye, eyes, Cole's research on, 151–54. *See also* vision
"Eye and Its Appendages, The" (Cole, 1867), 151–54

Fabian, Ann, 65
face, Chinese concept of, 10, 26–27, 178–79, 182, 190–91, 238n69; as alternative taxonomy of affective expression, 177, 180–81, 183–85; as impenetrable performance, 194–97
faces, 35, 180; Chinese, 197, 237–38n51; in Far's writings, 186–87; in Melville's *Benito Cereno*, 41, 44–46, 48–52, 63; in pseudosciences, 36, 37, 177. *See also* physiognomy
Fanon, Frantz, 10, 24, 32, 213n47; *The Wretched of the Earth*, 103–4, 214n56
Far, Sui Sin, 9, 21, 26, 28, 173, 184, 205–6; "A Chinese Party" (1890), 190; "A Plea for the Chinaman" (1896), 188; on gendered strategies of inscrutability, 27, 185–97; "Half-Chinese Children," 194; "Its Wavering Image," 194, 203, 205; "Leaves from the Mental Portfolio of an Eurasian" (memoir), 171, 178, 198, 201–5; *Mrs. Spring Fragrance* (1912), 6, 26, 171–73, 186, 194; "Sweet Sin: A Chinese-American Story" (1898), 199–200; "The Chinese at Christmas" (1895), 189; "The Chinese Boy-Girl," 193–94; "The Chinese Defended" (1896), 189; "The Chinese in America" (1909), 179; "The Chinese Question" (1895), 188; "The Chinese Spirit of Non-Resistance Will Disappear" (1915), 205–6; "The Chinese Woman in America" (1897), 190–92; "The Gamblers" (1896), 187–88; "The Smuggling of Tie Co," 193; "The Typewriter" (1891), 239n78; "Tian Shan's Kindred Spirit," 187. *See also* Eaton, Edith Maude
feeling, feelings, 10, 20, 38–39, 44–55, 68, 78, 98, 112, 167, 174; alternative cultural taxonomies of, 177, 180, 183–85; hegemonic structures of, 17, 34; racial dynamics of, 73, 76; structures of, 6, 33, 45; universal, 12–15, 210; of whites, 1, 2, 70, 76, 86, 102, 115. *See also* affect, affects; biopolitics of feeling; emotion, emotions; empathy; fellow-feeling; sympathy; unfeeling
fellow-feeling, 13, 15; of Adam Smith, 30, 35, 98, 181; Delany retheorizes, 73, 83
femininity, 123; Chinese women's inscrutability and, 190–92
feminism, 108, 116, 228n23; Black, 22, 139, 142; woman of color, 190

feminists, 8, 10, 15–17, 25, 111, 116, 213n43; of color, 15–17, 21; Indigenous, 19, 73; white, 109, 136
feminist theory, theorists, 15–17, 21, 213n37
feminized unfeeling as queer, 194
femmes, 174, 190
Fetterley, Judith, 237n41
Fielder, Brigitte, 138–39, 146
Fifteenth Amendment, 6–7, 25–26, 109, 140, 145, 170
Filipinx, 11, 216n14
Fillmore, Millard, 58
Fitzhugh, George, *Sociology of the South*, 42–45, 55
Five Civilized Tribes, 89, 93
Florida, 90, 92
Floyd, George, 211n9
foot binding, 192
Forbes, Jack D., 80, 224n53
Foreman, Pier Gabrielle, 8, 26, 139, 155
Foucault, Michel, 36
Fourteenth Amendment, 6–7, 25–26, 145, 212n24
Fowler, Lorenzo, 40, 109, 217n30
Fowler, Lydia Folger (Mrs. Lorenzo Fowler), 108–9
Fowler, Orson Squire, 36, 39, 40
fragility of whites, 1, 152, 209, 215n67
Francesco, in Melville's *Benito Cereno*, 48, 49
Franklin, Benjamin, 38
Frank Rollin. *See* Rollin, Frances Anne
Fredrickson, George M., 218n43
free Black people, 66, 74, 78, 84, 145; Delany and, 71, 84; Shaw on, 61–62
Freedman's Bureau, 147
freedom, 74, 154–55, 232n22, 236n13; Delany and, 83, 86–87, 91
frigidity, 108, 157; of first white women doctors, 112–14; pathologization of, 116, 127; professionalized, 112, 129; queer unwomanliness as, 24, 111, 196; women and, 114–15
fugitive and runaway slaves, 58, 85–86, 91, 96. *See also* Fugitive Slave Act

fugitive science (Rusert), 23, 74; Delany and, 82, 99
Fugitive Slave Act (1850), 6, 21, 54, 62, 78; Delany and, 74–75; Delany's *Blake* and, 23, 83, 85, 86; disaffection and, 58–63; Melville and, 35, 53, 59–60, 62; requirements of, 58–59
fugitivity, 58, 91, 95, 97
Fuller, Margaret, 108

Gage, Matilda Joslyn, *History of Woman Suffrage* (1881), 108
Galison, Peter, 140
Gall, Josef, 217n30
"Gamblers, The" (Far, 1896), 187–88
gambling, Chinese people and, 187–89
Garcia-Rojas, Claudia, 213n44, 213n47
gaze, 187; Chinese apathetic, 184; ethnographic, 202; Foucault and, 36; male, 159, 196; in Melville's *Benito Cereno*, 34, 41, 66; white, 27, 67, 190, 196, 199
gender, 8, 25, 31, 104, 109, 124, 214n60, 218n43; Chinese people and, 184, 191, 193–94; equality of, 25, 105; homeopathy and, 129–30; identification and expression of, 111, 228n26; indeterminacy of, 197–98; inscrutability and, 185–97; nonconformity of, 115, 124; politics of, 104, 110; racialized, 178, 192; roles of, 108, 110–11, 126, 130–31
gender binary, Chinese, 178, 193
gendered feeling and unfeeling, 30, 112
Geneva Medical College, 109
genocide, 19, 89, 91, 238n58
genres and subgenres, 172, 178; Chinatown tour journalism, 194; local color, 190; New Woman novels, 137; science fiction, 176; sentimental fiction, 8, 65, 71, 145, 164, 176; slave narratives, 3; woman doctor novels, 118, 120–21, 139
Gilroy, Paul, 74
Gliddon, George R., 82; *Types of Mankind*, 36–37, 39–41, 55, 82
Glissant, Édouard, 28
global capitalism, 11, 176
Goffman, Erving, 183, 238n69

golden apples, in Atalanta and Hippomenes myth, 128, 136
governmentality, 31, 58, 173, 186, 210; sentimentalism and, 8, 39, 52–53
Grace Breen, in Howell's *Dr. Breen's Practice*, 110
gradualism, 60, 61
gratitude, as affective performance, 174, 236n13
Greenfield, Eliza, 74
Gresham, in *Iola Leroy*, 26, 155, 158–64, 167–69
Greyser, Naomi, 10, 213n48
Guattari, Félix, 37, 74
Gunew, Sneja, 183
gynecology, 7, 21, 24, 139, 166

Haddad, John, 180
Haitian Revolution, 53, 78
"Half-Chinese Children" [Eaton], 194
Hammonds, Evelyn, 153
Hanhemann, Samuel, 129
Hansberry, Lorraine, *A Raisin in the Sun* (1959 play), 169
Haraway, Donna, 140
Harding, Sandra, 116
Harlan, John Marshall, 175
Harney, Stefano, 58
Harper, Frances Ellen. *See* Watkins Harper, Frances Ellen
Harper, Ida Husted, *History of Woman Suffrage* (1881), 108
Harper's Bazaar, 129
Harris, Mary Briggs, 126
Harte, Bret, 180, 187, 189, 200, 237n41
Harte, Walter Blackburn, 187
Hartman, Saidiya, 5, 57, 67, 86–87, 138; on Black humanity, 31, 43; on enslaved people, 21, 43; on sexual violence, 145, 161
Harvard University, 118, 218n30; Medical College of, 74–75, 107–8, 155
Hayot, Eric, 184
Hayot, Lye, 184
heads: in Melville's *Benito Cereno*, 33, 35, 41, 64–66; in pseudosciences, 36, 217n30; race science and, 65–66. *See also* physiognomy; skulls
hegemony, 9, 12, 23, 84, 111, 136–37, 141, 179; biopolitics and, 73, 109; feeling and, 17, 73, 210; global, 181–82, 206
Helen Brent, M.D. (Meyer, 1892), 25, 109–11, 121, 125
Hemmings, Clare, 9, 10, 213n43, 213n47
Hendler, Glenn, 74
Henson, Josiah, 71–72
Herndl, Diane Price, 155
heteronormativity, 25, 124, 136, 204, 214n58; white, 189, 193
hierarchy, hierarchies, 15; of animacy, 5, 7, 97; of oppression, 7, 12, 15, 210; racial, 5, 39, 48–49, 76, 80, 82, 87, 136, 182
High Conjurors, in Delany's *Blake*, 94, 96–97
Hine, Darlene Clark, 141–42, 146, 170
historical dichotomies, between Black, Red, and White, 78–81
history, 44, 88
History of Woman Suffrage (Stanton et al., 1881), 108, 136
histotextuality, of *Iola Leroy*, 155
Ho, David, 183
Hoadley, John C., 40
Hochschild, Arlie, 7–8
Hofer, Johannes, 219n76
Holland, Sharon, 76, 92
Holmes, Oliver Wendell, Sr., 75, 107
homeopathy, homeopathic doctors, 115, 129–30, 228n20, 228n21
homonationalism, 118, 136
homosexuality, 124. *See also* lesbianism; queerness; *and "queer" entries*
homosociality, in Delany's *Blake*, 92
Hopkins, Sarah Winnemucca, 10
Horth, Lynn, 40
Horwitz, Morton J., 53–54
Howard, June, 195
Howard University, medical school of, 146
Howells, William Dean, *Dr. Breen's Practice* (1881), 25, 109–10, 112, 120–21, 228n20
Hu, Hsien Chin, 183

Hsu, Hsuan L., 174
Huang, Vivian L., 27, 174
Hull, Gloria T., 141, 143
Humane Society of Massachusetts, 60
humanism and humanities, 21, 210
humanity, 5, 13, 18–19, 31, 34, 37, 43;
  Chinese and, 175, 177, 182; of marginalized and minoritized people, 3, 4, 38; universality and, 33, 39, 71
Hunt, Harriot, 107
Hurston, Zora Neale, 125
Hutcheon, Linda, 44, 219–20n76
hypodescent, 139
hysteria, 111, 115, 127, 131, 155, 228n25

immigration: to Canada, 188, 236n6; Chinese, 27, 175–76, 180, 185–86, 188, 236n6, 237n37; immigrants and, 9, 28, 173, 174, 236n6, 237n37, 237n51; modern apparatuses of, 26, 27, 172, 185, 193, 205; sympathy and, 26, 27, 205. *See also* "*Chinese exclusion" entries*
imperialism, 9, 83; cultural, 33–34, 183; violence of, 12, 81. *See also* colonialism
impressibility, 8, 117, 175
inclusion, 6, 175, 210
Indianness, 81
Indian Removal Act (1830), 89, 95
Indigeneity, 27, 77, 95, 227n157, 237n36; Blackness and, 24, 70, 72, 97, 222n14; Black rebellion and, 94–95; colonialism and, 17, 19, 24, 77; Delany and, 75, 77, 105
Indigenous dispossession, 9, 73, 77, 80, 97, 173, 209; enslavement of Black people and, 76, 79, 84; as structural, 3, 23
Indigenous feminists, 19, 73
Indigenous people, peoples, 7, 15, 19, 34, 72, 73, 103, 173, 181, 182, 213n48, 238n69; chattel slavery practiced by, 76, 222–23n14; resistance of, 17, 19, 32, 52; situatedness of, 21, 95. *See also* Black and Indigenous peoples
Indigenous sovereignty, 80, 104; Black emancipation and, 76, 90, 92

Indigenous studies, 12, 24
Indigenous women, 10; in Delany's *Blake*, 77, 92, 105; erasure of, 89, 102–6
inexpression, inexpressiveness, 18–19, 26
Inman, Henry, 37
inscrutability, Oriental, 6, 10, 26, 171, 173, 176, 186, 193, 195, 197, 205, 216n14, 238n58; Chinese language and, 179–80; Chinese women and, 190–92; Far and, 27, 185–86, 194–97, 200; as gendered strategy, 184–97; queerness and, 174, 178
insensibility, 13–14, 173; of Black people, 18, 20; of Chinese people and coolies, 187, 189–90
insensitivity, 11, 16, 113, 125, 198
interiority: absence of, 11, 176; affective, 18, 27, 29, 33, 34, 46, 176; Chinese, 27, 176
intermarriage: Black-Indigenous, 90–91, 93; Chinese-white, 172, 194
intimacy, intimacies, 73, 197; colonial, 2, 78; transnational, 32, 84. *See also* Black-Indigenous counterintimacies; counterintimacies
Iola Leroy, 26, 145, 154
Iola Leroy; or Shadows Uplifted (Watkins Harper, 1892), 6, 25–26, 139, 141–42, 145, 154–70
"Its Wavering Image" (Far), 205; romantic refusal plot in, 194, 203

Jackson, Zakiyyah, 166, 215n86
Jacobi, Abraham, 120
Jacobi, Mary Putnam, 25, 107–8, 120, 136, 143–44, 229n57; "*Common Sense" Applied to Woman Suffrage* (1894), 229n57; "Shall Women Practice Medicine?" (1882), 115; "The Question of Rest for Women during Menstruation" (1876), 118; "Would Women Vote?" (1888), 110
Jacobs, Harriet, 4, 211n12; *Incidents in the Life of a Slave Girl* (1861), 3
Jagger, Alison, 116
Jamaica, 172, 197, 206
James, C. L. R., 66

James, Henry, *The Bostonians*, 109, 230n84
James, Sherman, 149
James, William, 112
Jameson, Fredric, 44
Japanese people, 206
Jefferson, Thomas, 19, 24, 153; *Notes on the State of Virginia* (1785), 17–18
Jeltz, Wyatt F., 89
Jewett, Sarah Orne, 123, 136, 228n23, 230n88; *A Country Doctor* (1884), 25, 109, 110, 120, 121, 122; "Would Women Vote?" (1888), 110
Jex-Blake, Sophia, 120–21, 230n67
Jim Crow, 67, 149, 150, 173; era of, 137, 148, 170. *See also* racial segregation
John Henryism, 149
Johnson, Samuel, 42
Jones, Robert, Jr. *See* Son of Baldwin
Judge Ballard, in Delany's *Blake*, 86, 87
justice, 5, 27–28, 35, 78, 151, 212n24; fantasies of, 6, 33, 52–58; in Melville's *Benito Cereno*, 64–66; natural, 81, 85; order and, 81, 220n83; racial, 83, 85. *See also* law and legal system

Kammen, Michael, 44
Kammerer, Elise, 163
Karcher, Carolyn, 53, 217n15
Katz, William L., 79–80, 224n53
Kelley, Robin D. G., 24
Kelly, Lori Duin, 127
Kessler, Carol Farley, 127
Key to Uncle Tom's Cabin, The (Stowe, 1853), 4, 5, 71
King, Tiffany, 24, 73, 89
kinship, 10, 110, 146, 178, 189; Afro-Native, 80, 82; in Delany's *Blake*, 98, 103; Indigenous, 19, 90
knowledge production, Western, 141–43, 148, 174, 183
Krafft-Ebing, Richard von, 124, 230n92; *Psychopathia Sexualis* (1886), 114

Laing, Daniel, Jr., 75
Landers, Jane, 68

Land of Sunshine, Far publishes in, 190, 199
language, 182, 213n49; Chinese, 179–80
Lathers, Richard, 40
Latimer, in *Iola Leroy*, 26, 139, 146, 155–56, 163–66, 168–69
Latimer, Lewis Howard, 155
Latin America, 34
Lau, Estelle, 185
Lavater, Johann Kaspar, 39, 217n30; *Essays on Physiognomy*, 36, 40
law and legal system, 35, 75, 78, 85, 123, 134; Asian Americans and, 173–74, 237n37; Delany and, 85–86; legal formalism and, 33, 53–55, 62; in Melville's *Benito Cereno*, 33, 34, 52; politics of recognition and, 52–58; science and, 55, 66. *See also* justice; lawyers
Lawrence, William, 154; *A Treatise on the Venereal Diseases of the Eye* (1830), 153
lawyers, 54–55, 60, 123, 217n30; male, in women doctor novels, 25, 110, 112, 122–28, 132, 134, 136, 230n84; in Melville's "Bartleby the Scrivener," 9, 29; proslavery, 35, 55–56
"Leaves from the Mental Portfolio of an Eurasian" (Far, 1909), 171, 185, 198, 201–6
Ledyard, John, 43–44, 219n69
Lee, Rachel C., 216n99
Lee, Summer Kim, 27, 174
Lee, Wendy, 11, 13, 29, 214n55
Leroy, Justin, 24, 79
lesbianism, 198. *See also* Boston marriage; homosexuality; queerness; *and* "queer" entries
Levinas, Emmanuel, 37
Levine, Robert, 71, 74–76, 94–95
Levy, Leonard, 59–60
Lewis, Robert Benjamin, *Light and Truth* (1836), 82
LGBTQ2S+ people, allies of, 209
liberalism, 14, 73, 159; inclusion and, 6, 205; politics of recognition and, 103, 210
liberation, 17, 88. *See also* Black liberation
Liberia, 66, 78

lien, in Chinese concept of face, 180
Light and Truth (Lewis, 1836), Delany on, 82
liminality, 179, 194
Ling, Amy, 173, 198
Linnaeus, Carl, 182
Lin Yutang, 183, 184
Lipsitz, George, 212n24
literature, 3, 6-7, 9, 21, 26, 84, 109, 154, 166, 212n29; Afro-Native, 92; Asian North American, 172, 174, 180, 212n29, 213n37; marginalized and minor, 28, 74, 210. *See also* genres and subgenres; and names of specific genres
lithographs, 36, 40
Liu, Lydia H., 181, 183
local color, 190, 237n41
Longfellow, Henry Wadsworth, "The Bridge," 195
Lorde, Audre, 10, 16, 18, 213n47, 215n67
Lotus, 187
love, 123, 135; in *Iola Leroy*, 159, 161, 169
Lowe, Lisa, 9, 73, 206, 237n37
Lu Xun, 183
Luciano, Dana, 213n37, 221n127
Lucille Delany, in *Iola Leroy*, 155, 166
Lucy, 143, 144
Lye, Colleen, 176
lynching, 67

Maggie, in Delany's *Blake*, 87, 104-5
Mahoney, Mary E., 158
Malay, as racial category, 182
male chauvinism, 123
male lawyers: in Meyer's *Helen Brent, M.D.*, 125; in Phelps's *Doctor Zay*, 128-35; white women doctors vs., 112, 122-23, 135-37
mammy trope, 2, 43, 138
Manalansan, Martin F., IV, 11, 216n14
manhood and masculinity, 8, 115, 124, 130-32, 135, 194-95; Black, 74, 170; chivalry and, 159, 161; Delany and, 23, 74, 77, 91-92, 103-4; in medicine, 112-14, 116-18, 122; outraged, 73-74; self-control and, 13, 113; white, 160, 194

marginalization, 178, 195, 214n60
maroons, in Delany's *Blake*, 76, 88, 94-97
Marrant, John, *A Narrative of the Lord's Wonderful Dealing with John Marrant, A Black* (1785), 222-23n14
marriage, 109, 112, 117, 126, 149; Chinese, 190, 199; Doctor Zay on, 132-33; in *Iola Leroy*, 155, 160-61, 163-65; Jewett's Anna Prince on, 124-25; white women doctors and, 110, 111
marriage plot, 135; in Black women's novels, 141, 145; medical careers and, 118-22; in Phelps's *Doctor Zay*, 132, 134-35; in woman doctor novels, 25-26, 107-37
Massachusetts: Delano and, 42, 45, 56-57; Supreme Judicial Court of, 21, 35, 60
Massachusetts Dental Society, 148
Massachusetts General Hospital, 112
mass incarceration, 67
Massumi, Brian, 10
Masteller, Jean Carwile, 121
Mauss, Marcel, *The Gift* (1954), 238n69
McCann, Sean, 212n29
McGill, Meredith, 232n1
McKittrick, Katherine, 23
medicine, medical science, 114, 126, 129, 152, 167; Black people and, 20, 82; Black women in, 24, 143, 154-58; professionalization of, 113, 161; race and racism in, 89-90, 151; women in, 21, 24, 108, 170. *See also* homeopathy, homeopathic doctors; science, scientists
Meharry Medical College, 146, 166
Melville, Allan, as friend of Shaw, 59
Melville, Elizabeth Shaw (Mrs. Herman Melville), 59
Melville, Herman, 9, 21, 23, 35, 54, 86, 138, 220n83; "Bartleby the Scrivener," 9, 29, 40; *Benito Cereno* (1855), 6, 9, 21, 29-69; *Billy Budd*, 59-60; *Israel Potter*, 40; *The Piazza Tales*, 219n69; *Timoleon*, 40; *Typee*, 60; *White-Jacket* (1850), 113

Memorial Sloan Kettering Cancer Center, 235n117
Meyer, Annie Nathan, *Helen Brent, M.D.* (1892), 25, 109–11, 121, 125
microaggressions, 208
middle class: Black, 232n22; Chinese mixed-race children and, 198–99; white, 108–9, 136, 141, 189, 199; women of, 108–9, 136, 141, 163
Middle Passage, 87
Middleton, Stephen, 59
mien, in Chinese concept of face, 180
Miles, Tiya, 76, 222n14
Miller, John F., 181–82; anti-Chinese Senate speech of, 175–77
Million, Dian, 19
minoritarian critique, unfeeling and, 20–28
minoritized people, 3, 32, 85, 174, 210
miscegenation, 48–49. *See also* intermarriage; *and "mixed-race" entries*
misogyny, 104, 110, 120, 122, 126
missionaries, 174, 180, 183, 188–89, 193
Missouri Compromise, 61
Mitchell, Koritha, 67, 164, 232n1, 234n64, 235n97
Mitchell, Silas Weir, 127
mixed-race Black men, 139, 235n97. *See also* mulattoes
mixed-race Black women, 141, 154, 156; Iola Leroy as, 26, 139, 145, 160; Marie as, 145, 160. *See also* tragic mulatta trope
mixed-race Chinese children, 197, 199–200, 202
mixed-race Chinese people, 177
mixed-race Chinese women, 194; Far as, 27, 179, 185–86, 198, 203–4
modernity, 14, 73, 76, 99, 108, 111, 115, 121, 214n51
Mohawks, 90
Mongolian, as racial category, 182
monogenesis, 7, 18, 20, 41, 81, 101, 153
Moraga, Cherríe, 10, 213n47; *This Bridge Called My Back*, 15
morality, moral law, 28, 83, 85, 168

Morantz-Sanchez, Regina, 114, 116, 119–20, 123, 144
Morris, Timothy, 126
mortality rates, of Black people, 149–51, 167
Morton, Samuel George, 55, 82, 218n30; *Crania Americana*, 36, 39, 65–66, 144, 182
Morton, William T. G., 112
Moseley, Benjamin, 20
Moten, Fred, 21, 58, 67
motherhood, mothers, Black, 43, 138, 145, 156, 161, 166–67
Moy, Afong, 199
Mr. Culver, in Delany's *Blake*, 88–92
Mrs. Spring Fragrance (Far, 1912), 6, 26, 186, 194; publication of, 172–73; reviews of, 171–72
mulattoes, 48–49, 141, 156, 235n97
multiculturalism, as fantasy, 202
Muñoz, José Esteban, 9, 12, 17, 24, 211n9
Musqueam people, 209

narcissus flower, 172, 198
Narrative of Voyages and Travels (Delano, 1817), as basis of *Benito Cereno*, 30
Natick Indians, 95
Nation, 121
National Association of Colored Women's Clubs, 156
national civic identity, white fraternity and, 108
National Emigration Convention of Colored People (1854), 81
National Federation of Afro-American Women, 151, 156
nationalism, Chinese cultural, 178–79
National Woman's Rights Convention, 139
nation building, 72
nationhood, 78, 168, 170
nation-state, 109
Native Americans, 89, 174, 227n157. *See also "Indigenous" entries*
Nat Turner's rebellion, 53, 65, 94
natural history, 17, 81
naturalism, 172, 176

282 · Index

natural law, 53, 55, 64, 85, 220n83; in Phelps's *Doctor Zay*, 132, 134; science and, 101, 122–26
natural order, 44, 85
natural rights, 85
negation, 5–6, 8, 16, 23, 31, 33, 67, 68, 209
negativity, antisocial, 174
Negro Convention movement, 74
Nelson, Dana, 108, 141, 218n43
neoliberalism, 210
neuroscience, 36
New England, 44–45, 86, 163
New England Female College, 146
newspapers: *Boston Daily Globe*, 205; *Frederick Douglass' Paper*, 70, 71; *Montreal Daily Star*, 188–89, 198, 240n113; *New York Times*, 172, 177, 197; *Weekly Anglo-African*, 75, 93
New Woman, 127–28, 135–37, 190; anxiety over, 112, 120, 123; ideal of, 121–22; marriage and, 125–26; movement of, 109–11, 130; as physician, 122–23; queer dangers of, 111, 132
New York Cancer Hospital, 167, 235n117. *See also* Memorial Sloan Kettering Cancer Center
New York City, 40, 59, 172, 199, 204
New York Infirmary for Women and Children, 147
Ngai, Sianne, 10, 18, 21, 33, 213n45
Nguyen, Mimi Thi, 236n13
Nineteenth Amendment, 7, 26, 109, 136–37, 170
North American Review, 61
North Carolina, 94, 165
Northern white liberalism, 162
North Star, 98–99
nostalgia, 56–57, 219–20n76; white, 44–49
Notes on the State of Virginia (Jefferson, 1785), 17–18
Nott, Josiah Clark, 82; *Types of Mankind*, 36–37, 39, 40–41, 55
nursing, nurses, 157–58; in *Iola Leroy*, 158–59, 165
N-word: in nineteenth-century texts, 90, 99; author's treatment of, 234n64

obduracy, 7, 11, 171
obfuscation, of Chinese women, 130, 172
objectification of Black people, 58, 138
objectivity, 149, 164; dispassionate, 142, 144, 147–48, 152, 156; distanced, 35, 62; scientific, 116, 140
Ogunley, Toalgabe, 103
"old American story," of Delany, 72, 79, 82–83, 88
Olmstead, Frederick Law, 53
oncology, oncologists, 167, 168
Ong, Aihwa, 188, 216n99
ontology, 176, 213n43
opium, 187
oppression, 150, 209; Delany on, 79, 80; racialized, 84, 90; shared, 100, 102
ophthalmology, 153. *See also* eye, eyes; vision
order, 35, 50, 58, 81, 220n83; law and, 53, 55–56; in Melville's *Benito Cereno*, 63–66
ornamentalism, 178, 184; of Chinese women, 192, 205
Owens, Deirdre Cooper, 144

Pacific Coast, 172, 206
Page Act (1875), 172, 190
Pahl, Dennis, 62
Paine, Thomas, *Common Sense*, 229n57
Painter, Nell, 136
Paiutes, 213n48
Palmer, Tyrone, 5, 213n44, 213n47
Palumbo-Liu, David, 26, 183, 237n51
paranoia, of white supremacy, 84
Park, Mungo, 43, 44, 219n69
Parrish, Susan Scott, 96
partus sequitur ventrum ("that which is brought forth follows the belly"), 26, 138, 145, 161
passing, racial, 26, 163, 169, 197
passionlessness, 25; of Black women, 6, 21, 140–41; of Cole, 144, 151–52, 154; of Crumpler, 144, 148; of Iola Leroy, 155, 158, 162, 164, 169; objective, 6, 21, 142, 146, 151, 155–56, 169

patriarchy, 74, 77, 104, 123, 128, 136, 191
Peck, John David, 146
people of color, peoples of color, 14, 52, 70, 77, 81, 99, 216n14; affect and, 10, 101; counterintimacies of, 23, 102
Peoples, Whitney, 25, 143
People v. Hall (California Supreme Court, 1854), 174
performance and performativity, 174, 208, 214n55; Chinese concept of face and, 194–97
Pernick, Martin, 113
pessimism, as protection from hope, 205. *See also* Afropessimism
Peterson, Carla, 139, 232n1
Petty, Leslie, 110, 112
Phelps, Elizabeth Stuart, 9, 21, 121, 127; *Chapters from a Life* (1897), 126; *Doctor Zay*, 25, 109, 110–11, 120, 122, 126–35, 228n20; *The Gates Ajar*, 126; "Sympathy as a Remedy" (1909), 129; "Would Women Vote?" (1888), 110
Philadelphia, 139, 144, 146–47, 152, 155, 165–66; Black people in, 151, 163; *Iola Leroy* and, 156, 163
phrenology, 21, 34–40, 65, 108–9, 136, 217n30
physiognomy, 21, 34, 40, 187, 237n51; Chinese faces and, 179–85, 197; Lavater and, 36, 39, 217n30; in Melville's *Benito Cereno*, 41, 46, 48–49, 63; race science and, 36, 40–41
Pierpont, John, "Slaveholder's Address to the North Star," 99
Pittsfield, Mass., Melville's Arrowhead farm in, 59
plantation slavery, 87, 89, 94, 95
plastic surgery, 238n51
"playing Indian," 238n58
"Plea for the Chinaman, A" (Far, 1896), 188
Plessy v. Ferguson (1896), 61–62, 175
Pocahontas, 80
police, 2
politics, 71; affect and, 6, 28; racial, 7, 24, 75, 186; sexual, 7, 24

politics of recognition, 8, 11, 21, 62, 175, 191, 196, 214n56; individual vs. state, 52–53; law and legal system and, 52–58; liberal, 103, 210; sentimentalism and, 21, 27, 33, 66–67; structuring of, 35–40; white sentimentalism and, 32, 78, 83–84
polygenesis, 7, 18, 21, 40, 81–82, 101, 218n30
postcolonialism, 10, 63, 76
posthumanism, 173
Powell, Timothy, 76
Powers, Hiram, 37
Powhatans, 80
precedent, legal, 56, 61, 62
Prescod-Weinstein, Chanda, 151–52
Preston, Ann, 147
primitivism, Black, 34, 141
Principia of Ethnology: The Origins of Races and Color (Delany), 81–82
professional frigidity: of Doctor Zay, 126, 131; of white women doctors, 136, 146–47
professionalism, 113, 119, 127, 209; Jacobi on, 116–17; queer frigidity of, 107–37
professionalization, 55, 112, 115–16, 123, 158
proslavery discourse, 53, 54
Prosser, Gabriel, 94
prostitution, prostitutes. *See* sex workers
Pryse, Marjorie, 121, 237n41
pseudonyms of Eaton, 197, 198
pseudoscience, 36. *See also* phrenology; physiognomy; race science
psychiatry and psychology, 36, 130
psychic survival, 17, 178
Puar, Jasbir, 10
Putnam's Monthly Magazine, Melville's *Benito Cereno* originally serialized in, 40, 41, 53, 219n69

Qi, Xiaoying, 183
Quashie, Kevin, 142, 232n22, 240n126
queer annihilation and queer negativity, 12
queer desire, 110

queer feminist of color critique, 209, 213n44, 213n47. *See also* queer of color critique

queer feminist sensibility, 27

queer frigidity: of professionalism, 107–37; of women, 6, 21, 24, 25

queer mode of unfeeling, 30, 132, 175

queerness, 27, 114, 173, 183, 193, 205, 214n60; of Anna Prince in Jewett's *A Country Doctor*, 124–25, 230n92; Black, 215n86; of Doctor Zay, 133–34; Far and, 186, 197–200; of inscrutable Chinese bodies, 178, 193

queer of color critique, 12, 15–17, 123, 211n9. *See also* queer feminist of color critique

queer relationships, of white women doctors, 120

queers, 209, 216n14

queer spinsterhood, 122, 126, 228n23

queer theory, 12, 21, 213n37

queer unwomanliness, 111

queer woman doctors, fear and anxiety over, 116, 118–22

queer women of color, 16

quiet, 240n113; Black, 142; Chinese, 206. *See also* silence

race, 31, 95, 148, 214n55, 218n43; affect studies and, 9–12; notions of inheritance and, 47, 139

race science, 7, 34–35, 45, 55, 82, 162, 175, 182, 218n30; antiracist, 81–83; Black people and, 45, 50; Delany and, 23, 81, 102; heads and, 35, 65–66, 177; Jefferson's, 17–18; Melville and, 21, 74; Melville's *Benito Cereno* and, 35–40, 48, 54; seeing mania (Fowler) of, 40–44; visual evidence of, 40–42, 63

racial classification and difference, 14, 20, 21, 72, 163, 182, 197, 237n51; in Jefferson's *Notes on the State of Virginia*, 17–18; physiognomy and, 40–41. *See also* race science

racial discrimination and prejudice, 36, 66, 149, 174, 198

racial equality, 82

racial hierarchy, 5, 39, 48–49, 76, 80, 82, 87, 136; Black inferiority in, 81, 102; in Melville's *Benito Cereno*, 42–43

raciality and racialization, 2, 14, 26, 77; affectability and, 4, 24; analytics of, 37–38; comparative, 82, 173; of feeling and unfeeling, 30, 68, 75

racial justice, 85, 86

racial politics, 7, 24, 75, 186

racial segregation, 100, 147, 173; Shaw on, 61–62. *See also* Jim Crow

racial stereotypes, 90, 138; of Black people, 2, 141, 145, 159, 218n43; of Chinese people, 26, 179–80, 184–85, 187, 189, 197, 200, 204

racism, 21, 32, 36, 38, 66, 147, 162; anti-Black, 45, 86, 109, 159–60, 163, 203; anti-Chinese, 173–74, 178, 185–86, 188, 201–3, 206; of Delano, 40, 48; institutional, 61, 151, 188; Northern hypocrisies and, 62, 161; of whites, 140, 155, 232n22. *See also* anti-Blackness; antiracism

Raisin in the Sun, A (Hansberry, 1959), 169

Rankine, Claudia, 10, 213n47

rationalism, 18, 38, 98, 120, 134. *See also* Enlightenment; science, scientists

realism, 120, 172

recognition, 32, 41; politics of, 3, 9, 35–40

Reconstruction, 145, 147

Redfield, James, 180

regionalism, 237n41

remittances, of Chinese workers, 189, 190

repulsion, attraction and, 97–98

resistance, 32, 142, 208; of Black people, 21, 50, 67; of Indigenous people, 88, 223n14; shared Black and Indigenous experience of, 76, 88. *See also* Black rebellion and resistance; revolution

reverse sexism, Phelps's *Doctor Zay* and, 126–35

revolution, 23, 76, 98; in Delany's *Blake*, 105–6, 207
right feeling, 7, 56, 60, 73, 77, 210, 212n22; in Melville's *Benito Cereno*, 53–54, 63–64; Stowe and, 3, 6, 31
Riis, Jacob, *How the Other Half Lives* (1890), 194
Riskin, Jessica, 38, 141
ritual, 94; hoodoo practices and, 96, 99
Roberts v. The City of Boston, 35; *Plessy v. Ferguson* and, 61–62
Rolfe, John, 80
Rollin, Frances Anne, 82
romantic racialism (Fredrickson), 218n43
Rusert, Britt, 23, 82, 97, 98, 144; on fugitive science, 74, 82, 99
Rush, Benjamin, 17, 20, 113, 116, 118, 154
Ruskin, John, 40

Saint-Gaudens, Augustus, 37
Samuels, Shirley, 8, 32
San Francisco, 172, 194, 196
savagery, 14, 19, 51, 73
Sawyer, George S., 58; *Southern Institutes*, 55–56
Schiebinger, Londa, 116
Schuller, Kyla, 109, 118, 120, 136, 141, 144, 213n49; on biopolitics of feeling, 8, 30, 38, 85; on impressibility, 117, 175
Schultz, Jane, 157–58, 160
science, scientists, 24, 37, 39, 40, 55, 74, 101, 140, 163, 166, 218n43; Black women and, 139, 143; Delany and, 74–76, 78, 82, 94, 97, 99; discourses of, 33, 34; feelings and emotions and, 39, 177; law and, 55, 66; of nature, 122–26; objectivity of, 25, 33, 54, 116, 140, 151; sentiment and, 35–40; of solidarity, 99–102; Western, 98, 101, 166. *See also* medicine, medical science
science fiction, 83, 176
scientific racism, 21, 33, 38, 41, 163
Scott, Sir Walter, 177
sculpture, 37

Sealts, Merton, 54
Second Seminole War, 66
secretiveness, Chinese, 180, 195
Sedgwick, Eve, 9, 213n37
seeing mania (Fowler), 36; of race science, 40–44
self-determination: of Black people, 46, 71; Enlightenment and, 37
self-discipline, 113, 184
self-hatred, 74
self-identification, racial, 196, 198
self-love and self-respect, 74, 78, 162
Seminoles, 66, 88, 91–93
Senator Bird, in *Uncle Tom's Cabin*, 85, 86
Seneca Falls, N.Y., women's rights convention, 108
Senegalese, 9, 46, 67
sentiment, 111, 113, 218n43; culture of, 1–28, 53, 173, 178; law and, 54–55; race science and, 34, 38; science and, 35–40
sentimental biopolitics, 33, 62, 83, 136, 193, 198, 205
sentimental discourse, 44, 74, 119, 139
sentimentalism, 8, 9, 27, 70, 116, 145, 166, 174, 177, 185, 191, 209, 211n12; affect theory and, 212–13n37; conventions of, 3, 7, 26; Delany and, 73–74, 83; Far and, 172, 198, 205; governmentality and, 52–53; in Melville's *Benito Cereno*, 40–44, 64–65; science and, 38, 39, 152; sympathy and, 6, 12; of *Uncle Tom's Cabin*, 71, 104; white, 1–2, 21, 29–69; white feminized, 74, 195; white liberal, 146, 159
sentimentality, 5, 8, 31–32, 42, 53–54, 127, 140, 163, 174; Baldwin on, 2–3; in opposition, 108, 136; *Uncle Tom's Cabin* and, 2–3, 74, 85; whites and, 1–2, 27
sentimental novels, by white women, 2–3, 71, 74, 85
separate spheres, 108, 125; in Phelps's *Doctor Zay*, 131
settler colonialism, 84, 89–90, 103, 118, 173, 177, 238n58; Delany and, 76–80,

286 · Index

105; in Delany's *Blake*, 95–96, 102; resistance to, 88, 223n14; thinking of, 102–6
settler colony, 10, 19, 184, 214n56; United States as, 9, 17
settler homonationalism (Morgensen), 118
Sex and Education . . . (Howe, ed.), Phelps's essay in, 126
sex and sexuality, 111, 178, 214n60; Black women and, 153, 163; Chinese women and, 153, 189, 193; politics of, 24, 186; STIs and, 153, 239n70; violence and, 141, 157
sexology, sexologists, 21, 24, 114, 141
Sexton, Jared, 92
sexual agency, 25, 136, 145, 205
sexual anesthesia, 24, 124, 133, 136, 141; cutting edge of medicine and, 114–18
sexual inversion and perversions, 114, 124, 131, 134
sex workers, 26, 153, 172, 184, 185, 238–39n70
Shah, Nayan, 26, 178, 184
Shapiro, Ann, 230n88
Sharpe, Christina, 149–50, 168
Shaw, Lemuel, 21, 60, 62, 66; Melville and, 35, 53, 59–60
Sherwood, Mary, 120
Sibara, Jennifer, 198
silence: of Black women, 232n22; of Chinese people, 190, 196, 206. *See also* quiet
Simpson, Audra, 90
Sims, J. Marion, 139, 143–44, 150, 166–67
Sims, Thomas, 35, 66
Singapore, 180
situatedness, 73, 95, 149; of Chinese, 181–82
skulls: collection of, 65–66; in phrenology, 36, 37
slave law, 53, 55. *See also* Fugitive Slave Act
slave narratives, 3, 71
slave revolts, 49–52, 53, 58, 62, 94, 217n15. *See also* Black rebellion and resistance

slavery: Delano on, 42, 46; evils of, 220n83; justifications of, 39, 45, 55–57; law and legal system and, 52–63; sentimentalization of, 43, 46. *See also* enslavement of Black people
slave ships, 87
slave trade, 36, 44, 48, 60, 61, 68, 75
Smith, Adam, 13–14, 17, 19; culture of sentiment and, 15, 20; fellow-feeling and, 73, 181, 210; sympathy and, 21, 23, 30, 35, 51, 73, 76, 78, 187; *Theory of Moral Sentiments* (1759), 12–13; *The Wealth of Nations*, 214–15n64
Smith, Arthur, 182; *Chinese Characteristics* (1890), 181, 183
Smith, Barbara, 141, 143
Smith, Stanley Stanhope, 17–19, 24
smuggling, Chinese immigrants and, 193
"Smuggling of Tie Co, The" (Far), 193
Snorton, C. Riley, 144
Snowden, Isaac H., 75
social contract, 33
social inequality, 54
sociality, sociability, 13, 67, 73, 77, 90–91, 174; anti-, 12, 27, 33, 189, 191, 199; insurgent, 17–20
social justice, 1, 210
social management, 54–55
social reform, 168
society, 55, 73, 85
Society for the Humanities, 212–13n37
sociology, sociologists, 183
solidarity, 76, 81, 106, 207, 210; between peoples of color, 77, 78; science of, 83–102
Song, Min Hyoung, 174, 193
Son of Baldwin (Robert Jones, Jr.), 2, 211n6, 211n9; on black apathy, 3, 20
Souls of Black Folk, The (Du Bois), 9
Southeast Asian, as race, 182
Spain, 34, 47
speculation, as feminist activity, 139
Spencer, Herbert, 176
Spillers, Hortense, 21, 104, 150, 215n86
Spinoza, Baruch, 4–5

spinsterism, 117; of white women doctors, 119, 122, 124
Spurzheim, Johann Gasper, 108, 217n30
Stanford, Eleanor, 224n61
Stanton, Elizabeth Cady, 120, 137, 140; *History of Woman Suffrage* (1881), 108, 136; racism of, 109, 162
Starr, Paul, 130
state of nature, 52, 55
state politics of recognition, 52–53
stenographers, in Far's "The Typewriter," 239n78
Stevenson, Robert Louis, 196
Stowe, Harriet Beecher, 4, 14, 21, 57, 71, 74, 138; Delany on, 71–72, 78; *The Key to Uncle Tom's Cabin* (1853), 4–5, 71, 211n12; *My Wife and I; or Harry Henderson's Story* (1871), 109; right feeling and, 3, 6, 31, 54; sentimentalism of, 20, 40, 53, 70, 85; sympathy and, 21, 75. See also *Uncle Tom's Cabin*
structures of feeling, 33, 34, 68, 83, 168, 178, 210, 214n55; of enslavers, 102–6
subjectivity, 5, 54, 173, 179
sui sin far, as term, 172
Sundquist, Eric, 63, 70
"Sweet Sin: A Chinese-American Story" (Far, 1898), 199–200
Swenson, Kristine, 127
sympathetic Blackness, 34
sympathetic identification, 21, 26, 31, 73, 184
sympathetic recognition, 7, 8, 32
sympathy, 3, 5, 7, 9, 10, 16, 19, 21, 27, 39, 54–55, 60, 111, 117, 129, 140, 175, 177, 214n64; Adam Smith on, 12–13, 23, 51; Delany and, 84, 98–100; empathy and, 28, 210; of enslavers, 56, 87; in *Iola Leroy*, 157, 159; in Melville's *Benito Cereno*, 41, 46, 64–66; provincializing, 12–15; racialized, 2, 21, 34; universalist humanity and, 4, 20, 76, 78, 175; white, 72, 159–60, 218n43
syphilis, 152–54

TallBear, Kim, 103
Taney, Roger B., 86
Tate, Claudia, 145
Taylor, Bayard, 180
Taylor, Breonna, 211n9
Taylor, Charles, 214n56
technology, 140; frigidity as, 112–14; techno-Orientalism and, 176, 182
Tennyson, Alfred, Lord, *Idylls of the King*, 177
Terada, Rei, 5, 216n14, 237n41
Terborg-Penn, Rosalyn, 136
Theory of Moral Sentiments, The (Adam Smith, 1759), 12–13
thick skins, as psychic survival strategy, 11, 16, 18, 209
Third World, 11, 15
Thomas, Brook, 59
"Tian Shan's Kindred Spirit" (Far), 187
Tocqueville, Alexis de, 119; *Democracy in America* (1835), 109
Todd, Margaret, *Mona Maclean, Medical Student*, 230n67
Todd, Zoe, 103, 213n43
Tomkins, Silvan, 9–10
Tompkins, Jane, 8
Tracey, Karen, 110
tragic mulatta trope, 26, 146, 155, 159
Trail of Tears, 96
transparency and transparent I (da Silva), 5, 117
Traveler, Far's stories reprinted in, 188
travel writing, 180
trickster, 175
Truth, Sojourner, 109
Tryal, 36, 64
Tubman, Harriet, 156
Turner, Nat, rebellion of, 53, 65, 94
Turtle Island (North America), 77, 104, 182, 238n69
Tuscaroras, 95
Typee (Melville), dedicated to Shaw, 60
types, racial, 36–37
Types of Mankind (Nott and Gliddon), 36–37, 39–41
"The Typewriter" (Far, 1891), 239n78

unaffectability, Chinese, 181, 182
Uncle Remus, 2
Uncle Tom, 71
Uncle Tom's Cabin (Stowe, 1852), 3, 8, 21, 31, 44, 56–57, 59, 137; Baldwin on, 2–3; Delany's *Blake* restages scene from, 85–87; Delany and, 72, 73–74, 82, 104; Delany v. Douglass about, 23, 82–83; Douglass on, 70–71; Fugitive Slave Act and, 75, 83
Underground Railroad, 56
unfeeling, 7, 8, 11–15, 20–21, 24–27, 56, 67, 112, 129, 169, 214n55; affective, 32, 141; of Black people, 18, 21, 73, 77, 153; of Chinese people, 176, 181, 184, 186; as constitutive outside, 5–6; definition of, 11; Delany and, 24, 75, 87; demonization and, 17, 209; disaffected, 6, 52, 157; feeling and, 10–11; inscrutability and, 179, 186; as latent potential, 164–67; minoritarian critique and, 20–28; politics and, 2–3, 7, 24; queerness and, 111, 194, 205; racialized modes of, 171, 173, 175, 177, 186, 196, 205; somatic, 112, 141; strategic uses of, 16–17, 198; theory and, 15–17
unimpressibility, of Chinese people, 175–76
United States, 9, 12, 75, 76, 84
universal and universality, 5, 11, 15, 31, 38, 183, 214n58, 221n127; of affect, 9, 33, 183; of Enlightenment, 4, 37; of feeling, 12–15; humanity and, 9, 33, 39, 71, 101; sympathy and, 20, 27, 60, 61
unmoveableness, 11, 66, 132, 182
unnaturalness, 127, 176
unsympathetic Blackness, 33, 34, 67, 68, 70; in Delany's *Blake*, 75, 83, 102; in Melville's *Benito Cereno*, 29–69
unsympathetic villain, 31–32, 65
uplift, racial, 105, 145, 154; Black girls and, 149; Black motherhood and, 156; of Black women, 138, 155, 170; Crumpler and, 148, 149; Iola Leroy's work for, 164, 170

U.S. Census: of 1890, 146; of 1920, 170
U.S. Citizenship and Immigration Services, 174; apparatus of, 172
U.S. Congress, 58, 175, 180
U.S. Constitution, 6, 56, 58, 109. *See also* names of Amendments to
U.S. marshals, in Fugitive Slave Act, 58, 59
U.S. Supreme Court: *Amistad* case in, 53; *Dred Scot* decision in, 86; *Plessy v. Ferguson* in, 61–62

vanishing Indian myth, 80, 91
Vasari, Giorgio, 40
Vesey, Denmark, 94
vibrant matter (Bennett), 100
Victoria, Queen of Great Britain, 153
violence, 8, 9, 19, 33, 53, 135, 140, 173, 178, 181, 208, 213n49; against Black people, 76, 95–96; against Black women, 104, 140, 145; of colonialism, 8, 12, 51, 78, 81; against enslaved people, 62, 86–87; against Indigenous people, 76, 91; of Jim Crow, 149, 150; racial, 8, 15; sexual, 15, 145; structural, 73, 173
Virginia, 94
vision, 36, 152. *See also* eye, eyes; ophthalmology
visual culture, 36, 40, 63, 152
Vogel, Todd, 198
vulnerability, 198, 209

Walcott, Rinaldo, 214n51
Walkiewicz, Katie, 227n57
Wang, Bo, 175
Wanzo, Rebecca, 143, 166
Warren, Calvin, 215n86
Warren, Samuel, *Moral, Social, and Professional Duties of Attorneys ad Solicitors*, 54–55
Watkins Harper, Frances Ellen, 9, 21, 23, 25, 109, 139, 144, 169, 170, 173, 177, 232n1, 235n97; as Black activist, 136, 155, 161; clashes with women's suffrage leaders, 162, 170; on Crumpler's book, 148, 156; "Enlightened Motherhood"

Index · 289

Watkins Harper (continued)
(1892), 138, 166; *Iola Leroy* (1892), 6, 25, 139, 154–70; "The Colored Women of America" (1877), 170; "Women's Political Future" (1893), 156
Wegener, Frederick, 127
Weiner, Susan, 54, 62, 220n83
Welburn, Ron, 224n53
Wells, Ida B., 109
Wells, Susan, 148
Welsh, Lillian, 120
West Africa, 75, 77, 84
Western civilization and culture, 4, 5, 73, 89, 182, 184; science and, 98, 101
Westerner, 174; Far's writings in, 179, 188
Wetherbee, Isaac J., 148
Wexler, Laura, 9
Wheatley, Phillis, 18, 19
white body politic, 176
white family, threats to, 173, 175, 177
"White Gap" (Delany), 86
white hegemony, 23
white liberals, 162, 164
whiteness, 4, 20, 23, 26, 34, 42, 46, 48, 51, 66, 77–78, 80, 105–6, 140, 152, 154, 166, 177, 185, 194, 223n14; affect and, 10, 50; Chineseness vs., 176, 181; decentered in Delany's *Blake*, 90–91, 102; unfeeling and, 26, 75, 83–84; universality and, 12, 20, 37, 162
White-Parks, Annette, 173, 175
white privilege, 4, 7, 14, 37, 41, 51, 63, 65, 102, 158, 160, 210
white racism, 21, 217n15
whites, 5, 14, 34, 70, 73, 100, 182, 184, 197; sentimentality of, 1–2, 21, 71–72, 78, 102, 138, 218n43
white sentimentalism, 32–33, 51, 72, 86, 161, 164, 177, 197; Black patriarchal sentimentalism and, 73–74; in Melville's *Benito Cereno*, 29–69
white sentimental politics of recognition, 32; Delany's *Blake* and, 83–85
white superiority and supremacy, 47, 64, 72, 78, 82, 84, 90, 145, 153

white sympathy, 78, 104, 159–60; disaffection from, 83, 85–87
white tears, 1, 3, 86–87, 209, 211n3; of women, 137, 139, 195
white women and white womanhood, 26, 108, 145, 190, 191; suffrage and, 7, 26, 109, 140
white women doctors, 25, 111, 114, 124; earliest, 107–9, 112–14, 116; history of, 112, 123, 170; Jacobi on, 117–18; male lawyers vs., 112, 230n84; queerness and, 120, 126; rights struggle of, 107–37
Wilberforce, William, 60–61
Wilberforce University, 224n61
Wilderson, Frank, III, 5, 67, 76
Williams, Andrea, 232n1
Williams, Raymond, 6, 214n55
Winter, Steven, 59
Wolfe, Patrick, 77, 92, 96
womanhood, 117, 122, 190–91. *See also* white women and white womanhood
Woman's Era, Cole's rebuttal to Du Bois in, 151, 154, 156
Woman's Medical Journal, 119
women, 21, 25, 110–11, 165, 216n14; Delany and, 103, 105; frigidity and, 114–15. *See also* Black women; Black women doctors; Chinese women; Indigenous women; white women and white womanhood; white women doctors; women of color; women's rights; women's suffrage
women doctors. *See* Black women doctors; white women doctors
women of color, 15, 90–91, 103, 108, 173, 190, 208–9
Women's Directory, Philadelphia, 147
Women's Era Club, 156
Women's Medical College of New York Infirmary, 116
Women's Medical College of Pennsylvania, 146, 152, 166
women's rights, 24, 44, 108–9, 112, 120, 136, 140, 229n57; public sphere and, 125–26

women's suffrage, 26, 110, 125–26, 146; Crumpler and, 149, 155–56; whiteness of, 108, 140, 170. *See also* Nineteenth Amendment
Wollstonecraft, Mary, 108
Wright, Nazera Sadiq, 149, 233n50
Wynter, Sylvia, 4, 21, 32, 68, 99, 142, 214n51

Yarborough, Richard, 71
Yellin, Jean Fagan, 53, 88, 211n12
Yellow Peril stereotype, 26, 172, 175–76, 180–81, 184, 238n58
Yorke, in Phelps's *Doctor Zay*, 110, 126–35
Yucatan Indians, 100

Zuck, Rochelle, 80, 88

www.ingramcontent.com/pod-product-compliance
Lightning Source LLC
Chambersburg PA
CBHW070937230426
43666CB00011B/2474